On the FREEDOM *of the* SEA

Published by
Talbot Publishing/The Lawbook Exchange, Ltd.

By William E. Butler

Editor

On the Freedom of the Sea by Gerard de Rayneval (2013)

Adventures in Internationalism: A Biography of James Brown Scott by George A. Finch (2012)

The Nakaz of Catherine the Great: Collected Texts (with Vladimir A. Tomsinov) (2010)

On the History of International Law and International Organization: Collected Papers of Sir Paul Vinogradoff (2009)

Introduction

The Illustrious Hugo Grotius Of the Law of Warre and Peace by Hugo Grotius, Clement Barksdale, transl. (2013)

The Most Excellent Hugo Grotius, His Books Treating of the Rights of War & Peace by Hugo Grotius, William Evats, transl. (2013)

De Jure Belli et Pacis by Hugo Grotius, William Whewell, transl. (2012)

A Treatise on the Laws of Commerce and Manufactures by Joseph Chitty (2012)

On the Origin, Nature, Progress and Influence of Consular Establishments by David B. Warden (2011)

The Syllabi: Genesis of the National Reporter System (2011)

The American Institute of International Law by James Brown Scott (2010)

A Manual of the Law of Maritime Warfare by William Hazlitt (2009)

The Catholic Conception of International Law by James Brown Scott (2008)

A Treatise on the Law of War by Cornelius van Bynkershoek (2008)

Pennsylvania Blackstone by John Reed (with Mark Podvia) (2006)

On the FREEDOM *of the* SEA

JOSEPH-MATHIAS GÉRARD DE RAYNEVAL

Sometime premier commis, Ministry of Foreign Affairs, France

Translated from the French by

PETER STEPHEN DU PONCEAU

Sometime President, American Philosophical Society
Corresponding Member. Institut de France

Edited with an Introduction by

WILLIAM E. BUTLER

John Edward Fowler Distinguished Professor of Law,
Pennsylvania State University
Foreign Member, National Academy of Sciences of Ukraine
and National Academy of Legal Sciences of Ukraine

TALBOT
PUBLISHING
Clark, New Jersey

ISBN 978-1-61619-404-8

TALBOT PUBLISHING
AN IMPRINT OF
THE LAWBOOK EXCHANGE, LTD.
33 Terminal Avenue
Clark, New Jersey 07066-1321

*Please see our website for a selection of our other publications
and fine facsimile reprints of classic works of legal history:*
www.lawbookexchange.com

Library of Congress Cataloging-in-Publication Data

Gérard de Rayneval, J.-M. (Joseph-Mathias), 1736-1812, author.
[De la liberté des mers English]
On the freedom of the sea / Joseph-Mathias Gérard de Rayneval, sometime premier commis, Ministry of Foreign Affairs, France ; translated from the French by Peter Stephen Du Ponceau, sometime president, American Philosophical Society, corresponding member. Institut de France ; edited with an Introduction by William E. Butler, John Edward Fowler Distinguished Professor of Law, Pennsylvania State University, Foreign Member, National Academy of Sciences of Ukraine and National Academy of Legal Sciences of Ukraine. -- Lawbook exchange edition 2013.
pages cm.
Includes bibliographical references and index.
ISBN 978-1-61619-404-8 (hardcover : alk. paper)
1. Freedom of the seas. 2. War, Maritime (International law) 3. Maritime law. I. Du Ponceau, Peter Stephen, 1760-1844, translator. II. Butler, William Elliott, 1939- editor. III. Title.
KZA1348.G4713 2013
341.4'5--dc23

2013035837

Printed in the United States of America on acid-free paper

CONTENTS

VOLUME TWO

ACKNOWLEDGMENTS

In the present volume there are four layers or strata of text/commentary on the freedom of the seas. First, there is Gérard de Rayneval's treatise itself; second, there are Gérard de Rayneval's critical comments on the materials reproduced in volume two of the treatise; third, there are Du Ponceau's observations on Gérard de Rayneval; and fourth, there are the present writer's emendations in the form of editorial practices and footnotes. On the whole, volume one consists of Gérard de Rayneval's treatise and occasional footnote observations on other writers; volume two comprises principally other documents or texts that are the subject of a running commentary by Gérard de Rayneval in the footnotes. Exceptionally, Du Ponceau will intervene, almost always in footnotes; these are set out in square brackets with the initials PSD. Finally, annotations provided by the present editor are in square brackets and designated by the initials WEB.

Du Ponceau generally followed the original text, a small octavo in two volumes, with care. From time to time, however, he introduced his own editorial practices, very occasionally pruned the text, and in the early parts of the work added his own headings or subheadings to the section numbers within chapters. He ceased this practice after Chapter 5. All of these changes were in the interests of clarity to assist the reader. The same perhaps is true of his emendations in Chapter VIII, §7, where he has rearranged the text.

The original text often runs on for pages without introducing paragraph indentations. Du Ponceau does the same, but not necessarily replicating Gérard de Rayneval. This version follows Du Ponceau.

The original published copy of the Gérard de Rayneval's work filmed for the Google project is held by the Harvard Law School Library and was presented to the University by Jared Sparks (1789-1866), sometime President of Harvard University. The gift is recorded by the bookplate affixed to both volumes.

I am grateful to the American Philosophical Society for permission to publish the Du Ponceau manuscript, most especially to Charles Greifenstein, Manuscripts Librarian, for assistance in obtaining an image of the text and numerous courtesies extended during the transcription stage.

W. E. Butler
Newville, Pennsylvania
September 2013

GERARD DE RAYNEVAL AND THE LAW OF NATIONS

W. E. Butler

On 17 July 1840, not long after celebrating his eightieth birthday, a distinguished American jurist of French origin, philologist, historian, educator, translator, legal practitioner, international and comparative lawyer, and civic patriot devoted to Pennsylvania stumbled out of his home in central Philadelphia to deliver a substantial bundle of bound papers to the American Philosophical Society just nearby. The bundle contained a manuscript translation of Joseph Mathias Gérard de Rayneval's two-volume work, *De la liberté des mers* (Paris, 1811).

When precisely the author of the translation, Peter Stephen Du Ponceau (1760-1844), had commenced his task remains unknown. In all likelihood, one may speculate, shortly after the United States had declared war in 1812 on the United Kingdom. Gérard de Rayneval's study had appeared in the preceding year and addressed topics directly germane to the Anglo-American conflict: claims to sea expanses, the scope of neutral and belligerent rights at sea, the meaning of the freedom of the seas, among others. The translator, moreover, acted professionally to represent interests of the French Government[1] in the courts of the United States and had an active practice in maritime and prize law. He had recently published a new translation of Cornelis van Bynkershoek's treatise on the law of war at sea to

[1] Du Ponceau came to the attention of the French Foreign Ministry in a letter from the Chevalier de la Luzerne to the Comte de Vergennes dated 1 November 1781 reporting that Livingston had appointed Du Ponceau to be one of his secretaries: "... a Frenchman of good family, he was aide-de-camp to an American General ... he has taken the Oath of an officer, and I hope that you will not disapprove that I have applauded the part that he has taken, and for which it was impossible to ask and to await the orders of the Court ...". See M. A. Giunta (ed.), *The Emerging Nation: A Documentary History of the Foreign Relations of the United States under the Articles of Confederation, 1780-1789* (1996), I, p. 260.

considerable acclaim among the American professional legal community.[2] Could anything be more consistent with American interests at the time than access to a leading and penetrating analysis by a continental diplomat and jurist, known to be well-disposed to America, of those principles of international law at the very center of the war with England?

This is all plausible, but fanciful, speculation. No record survives as to when Du Ponceau acquired his copy of Gérard de Rayneval's treatise, or when he commenced his translation, or when he completed it. Twenty-eight years elapsed between the earliest possible date of acquisition of the treatise and the ultimate deposit of the manuscript with the American Philosophical Society, of which Du Ponceau was the President. That Du Ponceau, despite his laconic observation on the manuscript that "this translation was not intended for publication",[3] undertook the task purely as a relaxing diversion is belied by marginal instructions on the manuscript intended for a typesetter.

More than two centuries have elapsed since the publication of Gérard de Rayneval's treatise. Few Anglo-American international lawyers were familiar with him or his works, although the founding fathers of the United States knew him personally or at least who he was. This volume makes his learning on the subject available to at least the historian of international legal doctrine for the first time in the English language.

---

[2] C. van Bynkershoek, *A Treatise on the Law of War*, transl. P. S. Du Ponceau (1810; reprint ed., 2008, intro. W. E. Butler).

[3] Du Ponceau said the same thing in his Introduction to his translation of Bynkershoek: "The following translation was made several years ago for my own private use, and without any intention of ever publishing it". Ibid., p. v.

The Author

Joseph-Mathias Gérard de Rayneval (25 February 1736-1731 December 1812) was born at Massevaux, Upper Alsace,[4] one of seven children. His parents were Claude Gérard, secretary to the Comte de Rothenbourg and procureur fiscal of the seigneuries of Rougemont and Massevaux, and Françoise Wetzel. Sometimes he has been, and continues to be, confused in the sources with his elder brother,[5] Conrad Alexandre Gérard (1729-1790); to minimize the possibilities of confusion, Joseph-Mathias added in about 1774 the suffix "de Rayneval", a practice which his descendants followed. Although Conrad Alexandre could have added "de Munster" as a suffix, he refrained from doing so and is, except where the confusion is perpetuated, known simply by the surname Gérard. We shall distinguish between the two brothers by following their usages (in French the elder brother is occasionally referred to as "le Grand Gérard").

---

[4] See F. D. Cogliano (ed.), *A Companion to Thomas Jefferson* (2012); E. S. Corwin (1878-1963), *French Policy and the American Alliance of 1778* (1916); [F.-M. Gérard de Rayvenal], "Notice Biographique", in J.-M. Gérard de Rayvenal, *Institutions du droit de la nature et des gens* (rev. ed.; 1832), pp. [v]-xvi; D. C. Gilman (1831-1909), H. T. Peck (1856-1914), and F.M. Colby (1865-1925) (eds.), *The New International Encyclopedia* (1905), VIII, p. 596: F. Masson (1847-1923), *Le Département des affaires étrangères pendant la revolution, 1787-1804* (1877); John J. Meng, *Despatches and Instructions of Conrad Alexandre Gérard 1778-1780: Correspondence of the First French Minister to the United States with the Comte de Vergennes* (1939); E. Regnard, "Rayneval, Joseph Matthias Gérard de", *Nouvelle Biographie Générale depuis les temps les plus regulés* (1862), LI, cols. 769-770.

[5] Among those contributing to the confusion were the French diplomatic historian, Henri Doniol (1818-1906), *Histoire de la participation de la France à l'établissement des Etats-Unis d'Amérique* (1886-1892). 5 vols.; and the American historians, Edward S. Corwin, note 4 above, p. 420; G. C. Wood, *Congressional Control of Foreign Relations During the American Revolution 1774-1789* (1919), p. 80; and the British historians, F. Piggott (1852-1925) and G. W. T. Omond (1846-1929), *Documentary History of the Armed Neutralities 1780 and 1800* (1919), p. 54.

Gérard de Rayneval initially matriculated at the University of Fribourg en Brisgau (founded in 1457 at Baden-Württemburg) and completed his higher education at the University of Strasbourg. He followed his brother Conrad by attending in Strasbourg the lectures of Johann-Daniel Schoepflin (1694-1771), responsible for training a remarkable school of Alsatian diplomats and possibly influential in securing diplomatic appointments for Conrad and Joseph-Mathias.

Joseph-Mathias entered French diplomatic service in 1757, He was initially appointed as interpreter and secretary of the French legation in Mannheim at the Court of the Elector Palatine. He moved on in 1763 to Dresden, where he was secretary of the legation, and then acted from 1767 as *chargé d'affaires* at Ratisbon, better known to English readers as Regensburg, in Bavaria, Germany. On 15 July 1768 he was assigned to Danzig (now Gdansk, Poland), where he spent five years as resident and consul.

On 7 January 1774 he returned to Paris to assume the office of *premier commis*, replacing Jean Ignace, l'Abbé de la Ville (1690-1774). He served there for nearly two decades, departing from the Foreign Ministry without pension in March 1792 when Charles-François de Périer Dumouriez (1739-1823) was appointed Minister of Foreign Affairs by the Revolution and replaced all senior levels of personnel.

Gérard de Rayneval was ennobled and made a secretary of the *Conseil d'Etat* in 1778 and *conseiller d'Etat* in 1783, the last elevation in recognition of the success of his mission to London. He served briefly as French Minister to the Court of St. James in 1783. Upon retirement he removed to his country estate and remained there throughout the Revolution.

Gérard de Rayneval's elder brother, Conrad, had apparently, while serving as Minister in the United States, invested in companies who speculated in land located in the Virginia, Mississippi, Ohio and Illinois regions. Whatever those interests may have been, they formed part of Conrad's estate. Gérard de Rayneval took it upon himself to pursue the claims arising out of these investments in various letters to influential Americans, including to Thomas Jefferson on 1 January 1801. In a lengthy reply dated 20 March 1801, Jefferson explained that the claim was hopeless, acknowledging "... all the attentions which you were so good as to render me while I resided in Paris ...".[6]

Having been retired without a pension in 1792, Gérard de Rayneval was on 25 November 1802 given a pension of 4,000 francs,[7] with an increase in 1806. The publication of his classic treatise on the law of nations led to his being awarded the Cross of the Legion of Honor on 29 June 1804 and his election in that same year as a corresponding member of the Institut de France in the category of history and ancient literature. In 1808 he was appointed to act as Vice President of a Protocol Commission.[8]

At the end of 1808 he was invited by the Margrave of Baden to advise on issues of constitutional law. Gérard de Rayneval delivered a draft document to Carlsruhe by safe hand which made provision for the introduction of a Senate, *Conseil d'Etat*, legislature, and right of plebiscite to extinguish the House of Baden. The hereditary heir of the Margrave demanded the arrest of the reformers, the seizure of papers, and the escort of Gérard de Rayneval to the frontier. Upon his return to Paris Gérard de Rayneval was arrested and confined in the Château de Vincennes as a prisoner of State without ever learning the reason. He was released upon the return of the Emperor to Paris.[9]

Gérard de Rayneval was a key figure in Franco-American relations. When the War of Independence commenced in the North American colonies of Great Britain, Gérard de Rayneval prepared, or participated in the preparation, of a memorandum entitled "Reflections on the Situation in America". This document embodied the French strategy for extending secret assistance to the Americans; it is believed to have been composed in April 1776.[10]

---

[6] The letter is reproduced in P. L. Ford (ed.), *The Writings of Thomas Jefferson* (1897), VIII, pp. 19-20.

[7] Masson, note 4 above, p. 456.

[8] Masson, note 4 above, p. 457.

[9] Regnard, note 4 above, col. 770; Masson, note 4 above, p. 457.

[10] Meng, note 4 above, p. 57, fn. 2. The draft of the Reflections "is in the handwriting of Gérard de Rayneval". Authorship may belong to his brother, Conrad Gérard, or there may be joint contributions. For a version held by The William Clements Library, see F. G. Watts (ed.), "The Rayneval Memorandum of 1782)", *Indiana Magazine of History*,

Although Conrad Gérard is peripheral to the matters here considered, it should be noted that his appointment as the first Minister to the United States was in pursuance of the French strategy articulated in the "Reflections" and, by all accounts, successful in facilitating the development of Franco-American relations. Gérard's presence personified the alliance with France. On the eve of his departure to return home, Congress resolved on 3 September 1779 to ask Gérard to sit for a portrait. The commission was given to Charles Willson Peale (1741-1827). The sittings were completed by 18 September 1779. Peale was paid the sum of $9333.30 by the Treasury (inflated currency). Gérard, acutely aware of the symbolic importance of his portrait,[11] chose for the background an image of what today is Independence Hall in Philadelphia and garlanded figures embracing, the United States and France.[12]

Diplomatist

Although Gérard de Rayneval appears to have no personal archive as such, his correspondence and related documents figure in the holdings of others, including prominent Americans with whom he dealt (John Adams, Benjamin Franklin, John Jay, Thomas Jefferson). In his capacity as under-secretary of foreign affairs to the Comte de Vergennes, he wrote to John Adams

---

XXXVIII (June 1942), pp. 167-207. Also see C. Luraschi, *Conrad-Alexandre Gérard (1729-1790): artisan de l'indépendance Américaine* ([2008]).

[11] Gérard wrote to the Comte de Vergennes on 8 September 1779 and mentioned the portrait commission as evidence of support for Franco-American friendship.

[12] For reasons unknown, Congress never took possession of the painting. Peale wrote to Conrad Gérard on 18 September 1779 requesting to make mezzotints of the portrait and that for this purpose Gérard should send from Paris a copper plate duly prepared for mezzotints and quires of paper. The mezzotints were never executed. The portrait reposes in the Independence National Historical Park Collection. See L. B. Miller (ed.), *The Selected Papers of Charles Willson Peale and His Family* (1983), I, pp. 330-331. The painting is reproduced in C. Coleman Sellers, *Portraits and Miniatures by Charles Willson Peale* (1952), pp. 86, 297, where it is wrongly identified as being of Joseph-Mathias Gérard de Rayneval.

(1735-1826), then in Paris, on 20 June 1780 to inquire whether Adams was acquainted with an Englishman named Montagu Fox.[13] His brief within the Ministry of Foreign Affairs in Paris included England, Holland, and the United States. So far as the United States was concerned, he was in effect the "American desk". When the Congress in America approved a draft Franco-American Consular Convention on 25 January 1782, the text was transferred to Anne-César Chevalier de la Luzerne (1741-1791), the second Minister Plenipotentiary of France and successor in that post to Conrad Gérard, in Philadelphia for referral on to the French Naval Minister, Charles Eugêne Gabriel de la Croix de Castries (1727-1801), who was responsible for consular arrangements. Robert R. Livingston (1746-1813), the Secretary of Foreign Affairs, in turn sent a copy to Benjamin Franklin (1705-1790) in Paris with discretion to make changes, as necessary. The French side considered the draft for nearly a year while Franklin worked closely with Gérard de Rayneval to reconcile the rival drafts. Gérard de Rayneval proved to be adept in handling the international legal issues arising out of consular relations and worked amicably and constructively to achieve a positive result. By December 1783 the negotiations were completed and the transcription of the authentic text undertaken. Differences between the Comte de Vergennes and the Marquis de Castries over minor details were resolved; the Convention was signed on 29 July 1784.

In the annals of American diplomatic history Gérard de Rayneval perhaps is best known for the so-called "Rayneval Memoranda of 1782".[14] Three issues preoccupied American diplomacy above all in the negotiations for a peace settlement with England: recognition of independence; defining the western

[13] See G. L. Lint and R. A. Ryerson (eds.), *The Adams Papers* (1996), IX, p. 452. Adams replied the following day to say he had never heard of nor met Fox. It was later suspected that Montagu Fox was probably a British spy attempting to persuade the French and the Americans to pursue ambitious projects that might discredit leading opposition figures in England. Fox's scheme eventually came to nothing.

[14] S. F. Bemis, "The Rayneval Memoranda of 1782 on Western Boundaries and Some Comments on the French Historian Doniol", *Proceedings of the American Antiquarian Society* (1937), pp. 15-92.

boundary of the United States; access to fishing grounds off the coast of Newfoundland. The French admiral, Comte François Joseph Paul de Grasse (1722-1788), captured by the British in a naval encounter, called on William Petty, 1st Marquess of Lansdowne, known herein as Lord Shelburne (1737-1805), in London on 10 August 1782 and reported upon his return to Paris that Shelburne was ready to acknowledge the complete independence of the United States, together with other attractive concessions. Discussions were proceeding simultaneously between the American commissioners in Paris and the Spanish ambassador to France, Don Pedro Pablo Abarca de Bolea y Jiménez de Urrea, 10th Conde d'Aranda (1718-1798) on the western boundary of the United States. Gérard de Rayneval, by all accounts fluent in English, acted as interpreter between the Spanish ambassador and John Jay (1745-1829),[15] one of the American representatives. It was believed that the Comte de Vergennes was tacitly supporting the Spanish position in the Spanish-American talks.[16]

On 5 September 1782 Gérard de Rayneval, informing Jay that he would be absent "for some days", set out for London to consult Shelburne, traveling incognito under the name "Castel".[17] Jay learned on 9 September that the absence involved a trip to London. By coincidence one of the British peace commissioners handed Jay a copy of an intercepted despatch which François Barbé de Barbois (1745-1837), secretary of the French legation in the United States, had written to the Comte de Vergennes on 13 March 1782; the despatch suggested that France should not support American claims to the Grand Bank Newfoundland fisheries. Jay read the intercepted communication and the Gérard de Rayneval trip abroad as linked and suspected French perfidy in delaying British recognition of American independence. Jay broke off talks with the Conde d'Aranda and

---

[15] W. Stahr, *John Jay: Founding Father* (2005), p. 147.

[16] See, generally, J. J. Meng, *The Comte de Vergennes: European Phases of His American Diplomacy (1774-1780)* (1932). Remarkably, there is no mention of Gérard de Rayneval in the monograph.

[17] Gérard de Rayneval made a second visit to London in December 1782. See G. C. Lewis, *Essays on the Administrations of Great Britain from 1783 to 1830* (1864), p. 42.

sent his own messenger, Benjamin Vaughan (1751-1835), one of the British peace commissioners, directly to Shelburne. The outcome led expeditiously to British agreement to recognize American independence and the conclusion of the peace settlement.

When Gérard de Rayneval informed Jay of his pending absence, he had delivered a memorandum that outlined a possible territorial compromise which, if implemented, would have "… cooped up the United States between the Appalachian Mountains and the Atlantic Seaboard".[18] The substance of the Rayneval Memorandum led Jay to circumvent the French ally and seek direct contact with Lord Shelburne. But Gérard de Rayneval continued to pursue this agenda. On 24 October 1782, when he dined with Benjamin Franklin and John Jay, he contested the rights of the United States to the Newfoundland fishing grounds. Similar considerations appeared in a document setting out the "Idea on the manner of determining and fixing the boundaries between Spain and the United States".[19]

Gérard de Rayneval's interest in and expert knowledge of boundary issues led to his appointment on 17 October 1784 to the commission established in France to define the boundaries between Senegal and Gambia.

When Thomas Jefferson was appointed to Paris as Minister in 1785, he found himself dealing with Gérard de Rayneval on, among other matters, a relaxation of the French tobacco monopoly. Jefferson sought to persuade the Comte de Vergennes that the monopoly and monopsony powers granted to a French company, Ferme générale, with regard to the purchase of tobacco damaged Franco-American commercial relations and

---

[18] See Bemis, note 14 above, p. 16.

[19] Luzerne wrote to Vergennes on 26 September 1782 that the principles established in the Gérard de Rayneval document "… are so consistent with equity and with natural and international law, therein prevails an impartiality so exact with regard to Spain and the United States, that it is inconceivable that Mr Jay could take umbrage at it". Giunta, note 1 above, I, p. 944. Gérard de Rayneval believed that the ultimate disposition of the Newfoundland fisheries issue "… appeared to him as a dream, and the English ministers in according it had had in view ultimately the defection of the Americans". See Corwin, note 4 above, p. 355.

were, in principle, unjust. Although Gérard de Rayneval, to whom he outlined his proposals, believed they had merit,[20] the French had given the exclusive right to import to Robert Morris (1734-1806) and were reluctant to renege on a contract freshly concluded. Jefferson wrote to James Madison on 30 January 1787 that Gérard de Rayneval possessed "... the most of the confidence of the Count [de Vergennes], he is rather cunning than wise, his views of things being neither great nor liberal. He governs himself by principle which he has learnt by rote ... and is fit only for the detail of execution, his heart is susceptible of little passions but not of good. He is brother in law [sic] to M. [Conrad] Gerard from whom he received disadvantageous impressions of us which cannot be effaced. He has much duplicity ... I think it a great misfortune that the U.S. are in the department of ... [Gérard de Rayneval]".[21] When, however, the United States and France decided to conclude a new Consular Convention, Jefferson was full of praise for Gérard de Rayneval: "Monsieur de Rayneval has had the principal charge of arranging this instrument with me; &, in justice to him, I must say I could not have desired more reasonable & friendly dispositions than he demonstrated through the whole of it".[22]

Gérard de Rayneval was greatly involved in negotiating the Anglo-French commercial treaty authorized by the 1783 Treaty (Article 18) concluding the peace with America. Although there was some delay, the so-called Eden Treaty, named for the signatory on behalf of England, was signed by Gérard de Rayneval on behalf of France on 26 September 1786.[23] His negotiations with the Netherlands are recounted with relevant documents and correspondence in Dutch sources.[24]

---

[20] Cogliano, note 4 above, p. 209. By spring 1786 the French company had agreed to no longer enter into contracts of the nature concluded with Morris and allowed a small number of tobacco imports above the quotas given to Morris.

[21] Giunta, note 1 above, III, p. 409.

[22] Ibid., III, pp. 862-868.

[23] See A. W. Ward and G. P. Gooch (eds.), *The Cambridge History of British Foreign Policy 1783-1919* (1922), I, p. 164.

[24] See sundry volumes in H. Tollius (ed.), *Staatkundige geschriften, betreffende eenige gewigtige gebueurtenissen in de Vereenigde*

Law and Literature

Gérard de Rayneval published extensively during and after his diplomatic career. A full and proper bibliography of his works, some of which are anonymous or under pseudonyms, remains to be compiled. During his declining years, he devoted himself to preparing a commentary on Niccoló Machiavelli (1469-1527), *Discorsi ... sopra la prima deca di Tito Livio* ([1531]), which was never completed.

How precisely he acquired his foreign language skills is unknown, but Gérard de Rayneval was fluent in French, German and English, among others. Doubtless those skills facilitated his early diplomatic assignments in Germany, including as interpreter of the legation, and assuredly accounted for some of his early publications.

Translator. The partition of Poland was addressed in a two-volume work associated with Theophilus Lindsey (1723-1808) critically evaluating the rights of the three allied powers who had divided Poland amongst themselves. Whether Lindsey and Gérard de Rayneval personally knew one another is unclear. The first volume appears to be in fact a work by the Polish historian and patriot, Feliks Franciszek Loyko (1717-1779).[25]

Lindsey is the acknowledged author, writing under the pseudonym Gotlieb Pansmouser, of literary dialogues set in the form of a drama, which Gérard de Rayneval translated from the English, he using the pseudonym "miladi". The book was

---

Nederlanden, gedurende de jaren MDCCLXXXVI, MDCCLXXXVII, en vervolgens (The Hague, 1814).

[25] [F. F. Loyko], *Les Droits des trois puissances alliâees sur plusieurs provinces de la râepublique de Pologne* (London, 1774). 2 v. The text is attributed to Loyko, the introductory preface to Lindsey, and the translation to Gérard de Rayneval. The imprint is most certainly false and continental. Volume 2 is entitled: *L'insuffisance et la nullité des trois puissances co-partageantes sur plusieurs provinces de la râepublique de Pologne*. On Loyko, see H. Madurowicz-Urbańska, *Prace Feliksa Łoyki nad historia gospodarcza i ekonomika Polski* (Wrocław, 1976); A. F. Grabski, *Myśl historyczna polskiego oświecenia* (Warsaw, 1976).

published at Berlin with a false London imprint.[26] Lindsey is best known to history as the founder of Unitarianism.

Gérard de Rayneval's diplomatic responsibilities included frequent negotiations over territorial boundaries in Europe, North America, and elsewhere. For some time from 1784 he headed the department within the Ministry of Foreign Affairs responsible for boundary questions. Anton Friedrich Büsching (1724-1793), among the first to approach geography as a science, published a monumental "universal geography", a French translation of the fifth edition of which was published at Strasbourg. Gérard de Rayneval was among the team of three who undertook the French translation.[27] He is regarded as a contributor to an Atlas of the German Empire[28] prepared by Jean-Baptiste Courtalon (1740-1797), known as Abbé Courtalon; the compiler drew upon Gérard de Rayneval's treatise on German law for the Atlas.

Legal Treatises. Reportedly at the request of the Minister of Foreign Affairs,[29] César Gabriel de Choiseul (1712-1785), he

---

[26] [Theophilus Lindsey], *Le Partage de la Pologne: en sept dialogues en forme de drame, ou conversation entre des personages distingues, Dans laquelle en fait parler les interlocuteurs conformement a leurs Principes & a leur Conduite* ([Berlin], [1775]). Why Lindsey was so interested in the Polish question remains something of a mystery, as do his links with Gérard de Rayneval. Lindsey's biographers omit entirely any reference to his Polish interests. See A. Nicholson, rev. G. M. Ditchfield, "Lindsey, Theophilus", *Oxford Dictionary of National Biography* (2004).

[27] French editions based on the fifth and seventh German editions appeared at Strasbourg. Some components of Büsching were issued as individual country volumes, among them Hans Thunman's description of the Crimea (Strasbourg, 1785), which designated Gérard de Rayneval as being among the translators. Also see *El Imperio de Osman, comunmente llamado Otomano, ó la Turquia européa* (Madrid, 1785), where Gérard de Rayneval is listed as translator.

[28] J.-B. Courtalon, *Atlas élémentaire où l'on voit sur des cartes et des tableaux relatifs à l'objet l'état actuel de la constitution: politique de l'empire d'Allemagne* (1774).

[29] Regnard, note 4 above, col. 770; F-M. Gérard de Rayneval, note 4 above, p. vi.

published a significant study of German public law that went through eight printings between 1766 and 1771.[30]

Pamphleteering was frequently indulged in on a quasi-official basis throughout the eighteenth century as an instrument of foreign policy. In 1779 the British Government charged the distinguished historian Edward Gibbon (1737-1794) to respond in pamphlet form to an anonymous French work setting out the conduct of France in assisting the American colonies in their struggle for independence.[31] Gibbon's contribution in turn prompted two replies, one by Pierre Augustin Caron de Beaumarchais (1732-1799),[32] and the other by Gérard de Rayneval.[33] The French version of the reply by Gérard de Rayneval was translated and published in the United States by Peter S. Du Ponceau.[34]

---

30 Gérard de Rayneval, *Institutions au droit public d'Allemagne* (1766).

31 E. Gibbon, *Memoire justificatif pour servir de réponse à l'Exposé, &c. de la cour de France* ([London], 1779). [2], 32 p. Printed by Thomas Harrison (1723-1791).

32 [P. Beaumarchais], *Observations sur le Mémoire justificatif de la Cour de Londres* ([Paris], 1779). 56 p. Showing London and Philadelphia as false imprints. The French version was suppressed by *arrêt* of the *Conseil d'Etat du roi*, 19 December 1779. A revised version issued in 1780 added letters concerning the controversy over Beaumarchais' allegation that the Treaty of Paris contained a secret clause imposing limits of the number of French naval vessels, a position that César Gabriel de Choiseul, Duke of Praslin (1712-1785) protested to the Minister of Foreign Affairs, Charles Gravier, Count of Vergennes (1717-1787), who supported the objections. Three other editions appeared in 1780.

33 [J.-M. Gérard de Rayneval], *Observations sur le Mémoire justificatif de la cour de Londres* (Paris, 1780). 84 p. A *Supplement aux Observations sur le Mémoire justificatif de la Cour de Londres* (Paris, 1780) by Gérard de Rayneval appeared the same year. 26 p.

34 The original anonymous French version was attributed to Gérard de Rayneval by M. Barbier, *Dictionaire des ouvrages anonymes et pseudonyms* (2d ed.; 1827), No. 23110. Evans attributed the work to Beaumarchais and named Du Ponceau as the translator. For the American imprint, see Gérard de Rayneval, *Observations on the Justificative Memorial of the Court of London* (Philadelphia, F. Bailey, 1781). 129, [3] p. One must assume that the American editions enjoyed French and American official support.

Perhaps Thomas Jefferson's arguments against the tobacco monopsony in France, to which Gérard de Rayneval was initially more sympathetic than his Minister, the Comte de Vergennes, took root more deeply over time. By 1790 Gérard de Rayneval had produced a French translation of Benjamin Vaughan's *New and Old Principles of Trade Compared* (1788), a vigorous advocacy of freer trade policies.[35]

The foregoing works were the contributions of an experienced diplomatic practitioner to the law of nations. Gérard de Rayneval's major contributions, however, some would say classic contributions, appeared after the French Revolution had run its course. The first was a general treatise entitled *Institutions du droit de la nature et des gens* (1803). A posthumous edition, revised by the author's son, appeared in two volumes in 1832 and was reissued again in 1851. There were Spanish translations, *Instituciones de derecho natural y de gentes* (Madrid, 1821), all posthumous. The Madrid edition contained an Appendix by Marcial Antonio Lopez (d. 1857).[36] The Spanish edition published at Paris in 1825 was prepared under the direction of José René Masson, the publisher, by the anonymous translator D.L.B. and was reissued in 1827.

The present treatise on the freedom of the seas was published only once, in 1811, although it found in due course its own place in the literature of maritime law.

Miscellany. In retirement Gérard de Rayneval produced a translation from the third Italian edition of Giambattista Mancini (1714-1800), *Réflexions pratiques sur le chant figuré* (Paris, [1796]) addressed to practical reflections on the figurative art of singing; and a translation from the German of August Lafontaine, *Hermann et Émile* (Paris, 1802) in four volumes. The musical and literary dimension of Gérard de Rayneval was

---

[35] B. Vaughan, *Principes de commerce entre les nations* (Paris, [1790]). Vaughan and Gérard de Rayneval met while Vaughan (1751-1835) served as a British commissioner in the peace negotiations at Paris between the American and British commissioners. Vaughan, born in Jamaica, wrote a number of works on political subjects and in 1797 settled permanently in Massachusetts.

[36] Benjamin Constant (1767-1830), *Curso politica constitutional*, transl. M. A. Lopez (Madrid, 1820; 2d ed.; Burdeos, 1823)

expressed in his collaboration with the journal *Le clef du cabinet des souverains* (1797-1805), founded by Charles-Joseph Panckoucke (1736-1798) and edited by Jacques Peuchet (1758-1830). The journal ranged widely over history, politics, economics, literature, and philosophy.

Joseph-Mathias Gérard de Rayneval married Sophie Marie Adélaïde Gaucherel (1736-1812) on 8 August 1776. One son and two daughters were born of the marriage.[37] His son, François-Maximilien Gérard de Rayneval (08.10.1778-16.08.1836) followed in his father's footsteps to become a distinguished French diplomat in his own right.[38]

The Treatise

Gérard de Rayneval brought to his works on international law experience as a senior French diplomat who was engaged on a daily basis with issues of the law of nations. His diplomatic background strongly informed his views on individual issues of international law.[39] As a European jurist and statesman, he was accustomed to thinking strategically about the course of foreign policy, as were his mentors and superiors. His treatise on the freedom of the seas was received in French circles as outlining an approach to maritime policy that would guide French diplomacy until the 1856 Declaration of Paris.[40]

---

[37] Masson, note 4 above, p. 23.

[38] François M. Gérard de Rayneval served as second secretary at St. Petersburg (1801), first secretary in Lisbon (1804); first secretary at St. Petersburg (1807-1812); French negotiator at the Congress of Prague and Chatillon (1814); Consul General in London, under-secretary of State (1820); Minister to Berlin (1821); Ambassador to Berne (1825), and Acting Minister of Foreign Affairs and ambassador (1829), among other postings.

[39] For a warm appreciation of the combination in Gérard de Rayneval's background of diplomacy and international law and their importance for young people, see Jean André Perreau (1749-1813), *Élémens de legislation naturlle, destines a l'usage des élèves de l'école central du Panthéon* (2d ed.; 1807), p. 114.

[40] Masson, note 4 above, p. 483.

For Peter Du Ponceau, a legal practitioner experienced in the law of prize, shipping, and neutrality issues generally, the appearance of Gérard de Rayneval's treatise just as the War of 1812 commenced was serendipity to be taken advantage of. Gérard de Rayneval's positions on most issues of neutrality were consistent with American views. For the United States at the time, Gérard de Rayneval was a kindred spirit whose vigorous arguments against long-standing British claims and policies complemented the considerable literature on the subject — legal and political — generated by the course of Anglo-American relations. As the course of events would demonstrate, during the Napoleonic wars American vessels likewise found themselves in French prize courts. Issues of maritime neutrality vexed Franco-American relations just as they did Anglo-American relations.[41]

Gérard de Rayneval was regarded by his successors in France and elsewhere as a diplomat and an international lawyer of the "old school".[42] His *Institutions du droit de la nature et des gens* (1803) (hereinafter: *Institutions*) did not purport to offer a new system for nor to exhaustively treat the law of nations. Its service to international law was, however, secure.[43]

---

[41] For how these incidents affected Franco-American consular relations, see W. E. Butler, "David Bailie Warden and the Development of Consular Law", in D. B. Warden, *On the Origin, Nature, Progress and Influence of Consular Establishments* (2011), pp. iii-xlviii.

[42] See F. de Holtzendorff and A. Rivier, *Introduction au droit des gens. Recherches philosophiques, historiques et bibliographiques* (Hamburg, 1889), p. 412 ("bon diplomate de l'ancienne école").

[43] Gérard de Rayneval, *Institutions du droit de la nature et des gens* (Paris, 1803). The Peace Palace Library in The Hague holds a copy designated on the title page as "second edition". The pagination collates identically with the original version; however, on the title page the French republican calendar date on the original edition is "XI" and on the "second edition" is "XII". The Gregorian date in both instances is 1803. The second edition is not recorded in the Worldcat. The Peace Palace copy is available on microfiche as ILM 185. See W. E. Butler (ed.), *International Law: Olivart Collection*, published by IDC, Leiden. See G. F. Martens, *Précis du droit des gens modern de l'Europe fondé sur les traités et l'usage; pour servir d'introduction a un cours politique et diplomatique* ed. M. S. Pinheiro-Ferreira (rev.ed.; Paris, 1831), p. 58; A. W. Heffter, *Das Europäische*

In his view, the "law of nations – code of nations" was the "common rule which natural reason prescribes to nations for their reciprocal preservation".[44] He was among those international lawyers who followed Grotius in recognizing natural law and positive law, but accorded to natural law an elevated position to which positive law must conform.[45] More

---

Völkerrecht der Gegenwart (Berlin, 1844), p. 20. Charles de Martens wrote of the treatise that it "set out the institutions of the law of nature and nations with great wisdom, and the developments and notes which the author included for each section made the volume more instructive", referring to the 1832 edition. See Charles de Martens, *Le guide diplomatique. Précis des droits et des fonctions des agents diplomatiques et consulaires*, ed. M. F. H. Geffcken (Leipzig, 1866), I, p. 8. Also see H. W. Halleck, *International Law; or, Rules Regulating the Intercourse of States in Peace and War* (San Francisco, 1861), p. 29. For the relevance of the work to the reception of Western concepts of international law in Japan and China, see D. R. Howland, *Translating the West: Language and Political Reason in Nineteenth-Century Japan* (2002), p. 66. Although Gérard de Rayneval was never translated into the Japanese or Chinese languages (nor into English but for the present work), the Japanese and Chinese reader became aware of his views through Henry Wheaton's references to him that also appeared in the Chinese and Japanese translations of Wheaton. Henry Wheaton quoted from Gérard de Rayneval in his *Elements of International Law* (3d rev. ed.; 1846), §11, pp. 42-43, but did not indicate which edition he used. Wheaton was generally familiar, indeed perhaps more than most Americans, with French doctrinal writings on international law. The references to Gérard de Rayneval were retained through the sixth and eighth posthumous editions. See Wheaton, *Elements of International Law*, ed. W. B. Lawrence (6th ed.; 1855), p. 17; Wheaton, *Elements of International Law*, ed. R. H. Dana, Jr. (8th ed.; 1866), §12, pp. 18-19. When counting editions of Wheaton, it should be borne in mind that apparently he and certainly his later editors counted foreign translations and printings as an "edition". Thus, for example, the fourth and fifth French language versions of the treatise are regarded as the fourth and fifth editions of the book. See Dana, "Editor's Preface", ibid., pp. x-xi.

[44] James Kent, *Kent's Commentary on International Law, Revised with Notes and Cases Brought Down to the Present Time*, ed. J. T. Abdy (Cambridge, 1866), p. 5. Also see A. Mérignhac, *Traité de droit public international* (Paris, 1905), p. 234.

[45] See H. Wheaton, *Commentaire sur les éléments de droit international et sur l'histoire des progrès du droit des gens*, ed. W. B. Lawrence (Leipzig, 1868), I, p. 111.

particularly, Gérard de Rayneval saw himself, and was seen, as a follower of Christian von Wolff (1679-1754), and through Wolff, Emer de Vattel (1714-1767), "who reproduced faithfully the ideas of Wolff".[46] Gérard de Rayneval, together with other French jurists, wrote in the "old style of natural law".[47] He emphasized the values of truth, honesty, and honor in the conduct of foreign affairs.[48]

The *Institutions* was celebrated and referred to especially for issues of diplomatic and consular law:[49] the immunity of ambassadors and other public ministers;[50] the jurisdiction and right of surveillance of the receiving State over the suite accompanying a minister;[51] exterritoriality;[52]

As for the present work on the freedom of the seas, Gérard de Rayneval's was the first work in two centuries, since Hugo Grotius' *Mare Liberum* (1609), to appear with this title.[53] It was

---

[46] G. Carnazza-Amari, *Traité de droit international public en temps de paix*, transl. From Italian by C. Montanari-Revest (Paris, 1880), I, p. 181. To be sure, this link was made not least because Gérard de Rayneval drew attention to it in the preface to note 4 above. See A. de Lapradelle, in E. de Vattel, *Le droit des gens ou principes de la loi naturelle. Appliqués à loi conduite et aux affaires des Nations et des Souverains* (Washington D. C., 1916), I, p. xl.

[47] Holtzendorff and Rivier, note 40 above, pp. 438, 484.

[48] E. Chevalley, *Droit des gens Napoléonien d'après la correspondance 1800-1807* ([1912]), p. 41. Napoleon, of course, knew Gérard de Rayneval and honored his achievements.

[49] P. Pradier-Fodéré, *Cours de droit diplomatique a l'usage des agents politiques du ministère des affairs étrangères des états européens et américains* (Paris, 1899). Gérard de Rayneval is cited twelve times in two volumes.

[50] P. G. Odier, *Des privileges et immunités des agents diplomatiques en pays de chrétiente* (Paris, 1890), p. 196.

[51] J.-L. Klüber, *Droit des gens moderne de l'Europe*, ed. M. A. Ott (rev. ed.; Paris, 1861), pp. 277-278.

[52] Em. Vercamer, *Des franchises diplomatiques et spécialement de l'exterritorialité* (1891), p. 123.

[53] See E. Cauchy, *Le droit maritime international considéré dans ses origines et dans ses rapports avec les progrès de la civilisation* (1862), II, pp. 355-356.

addressed as much to maritime policy as to maritime law.[54] Although it is based on treaties, customs, proclamations, and other evidence of State practice, Gérard de Rayneval affirmed the principles of natural law and the law of nations applicable to the sea. He saw the littoral sea as a rampart against surprise attack and interference with commerce; the dependence of coastal States upon fishing was a dependence of nature.[55] His resolute defense of neutral rights,[56] which he attributed to the convenience of belligerents, a century later was invoked as entirely just, but now protected by international law: "although written in 1811, this is once again correct save for one point: it is law, not convenience, which actually protects neutrality".[57]

Blockade, said he, must in order to be respected exist in fact, not merely in thought and words. The operation must be actual and real, not fictitious and nominal. It did not suffice merely to declare a blockade, for one cannot rule over or conquer a country unless the country is occupied.[58]

As for war itself, Gérard de Rayneval was among those who insisted that for war to be regulated by the law of nations, it must be declared. In this he was joined by many writers (Gentili, Grotius, Pufendorf, Vattel, Burlamaqui, Barbeyrac, and Emerigon, but he joined Pufendorf in believing that all acts preceding a declared war were piracy.[59] It would follow that, for

---

[54] E. Nys, *Le droit international. Les principes, les théories. Les faits* (rev. ed; 1912), I, p. 296.

[55] Ibid., I, p. 543. Gérard de Rayneval criticized the cannon shot rule and those writers who supported it for being too general. He preferred the visual horizon. See J.-M. Gérard de Rayneval, *Institutions du droit de la nature et des gens* (1803), p. 161.

[56] For the importance of the present treatise to subsequent diplomatic discussions of neutral rights, see E. Nys, *La guerre maritime: etude de droit international* (1881), p. 112.

[57] Nys, note 54 above, III, p. 432. Also see D. Simón Planas Suarez, *Tratado de derecho internacional public* (Madrid, 1916), II, p. 121.

[58] See on this point, quoting Gérard de Rayneval, H. Bargrave Deane, *The Law of Blockade: Its History, Present Condition, and Probable Future* (London, 1870), p. 22.

[59] L. de Sainte Croix, *La déclaration de guerre et ses efffets immédiats: étude d'histoire et de législation comparée* (1892), p. 139. Also see Nys, note 54 above, III, p. 45.

Gérard de Rayneval, the formalities of treaties ending war were no less important, a position widely shared by other writers and for which he was frequently cited.[60]

In Gérard de Rayneval's view, the freedom of the seas dictated the freedom of straits linking them. Straits, said he, are passages for communication from one sea to another. If the seas are free, the communication between them must be equally free; otherwise the freedom of the seas connected by straits would be a chimera.[61]

What in 1811 was still regarded as the classic British doctrine on neutral rights during wartime and claims to maritime jurisdiction, set out in the works of Jenkinson (Earl of Liverpool), Gérard de Rayneval undertook to refute point by point, to the general acclaim of many continental international lawyers.[62] It was his hope and expectation that the present work on the freedom of the seas would persuade Napoleon to unite with others in creating a "maritime code" that would lay down a just basis for the immutable freedom of the seas.[63] Calvo cited Gérard de Rayneval on the territorial sea, enemy goods on board neutral vessels, the right of visit and resistance to visit, and the role of treaties in beginning to produce results with respect to neutral rights.[64]

---

[60] See F. Menendez-Pidal y de Montes, *Manual de derecho internacional maritimo* (Madrid, 1923), p. 292.
[61] Note 53 above. Quoted with approval in P. Pradier-Fodéré, *Traité de droit international public Européen & Américain suivant les progrès de la science et de la pratique contemporaines* (1885-1906), II, p. 187. Also see L. Pézeril, *Des navires de commerce français dans les eaux étrangères* (1889), p. 116.
[62] See, for example, C. Calvo, *Le droit international: théorique et pratique, précédé d'un exposé historique des progrès de la science du droit des gens* (3d ed.; 1880), III, p. 504; (5th ed.; 1896), IV, p. 555.
[63] Cauchy, note 53 above, II, p. 356.
[64] Calvo (2d ed.; 1872), I, p. 315; II, pp. 431, 433; 618-619, 623, and 755.

The Translator

Peter Stephen Du Ponceau[65] was born at St-Martins, Isle of Ré, a small island off the port of La Pallice in the southwestern part of France, on 3 June 1760, the son of a French army officer.[66] By the age of five he had memorized a Latin and

---

[65] The name appears in various spellings: Du Ponceau, DuPonceau, Duponceau, du Ponceau, duPonceau, amongst them. If one is searching electronic data bases, it can matter which version one uses. Unless original usage requires otherwise, we shall refer to Du Ponceau throughout. Du Ponceau himself seems at one time or another to have used all versions.

[66] Du Ponceau deserves a thorough biography that gives full due to his achievements as a jurist and a specialist in languages. For this study I have consulted printed sources: *A Biographical Dictionary: Comprising a Summary Account of the Lives of the Most Distinguished Persons of All Ages, Nations, and Professions: Including More than Two Thousand Articles of American Biography*, ed. John L. Blake (Philadelphia, 1856), p. 391, s. v. "Duponceau, Peter S., LL.D."; *Appletons' Cyclopedia of American Biography*, ed. James Grant Wilson and John Fiske (New York, 1888), II: 263, s. v. "Duponceau, Peter Stephen"; *The Biographical Encyclopedia of Pennsylvania of the Nineteenth Century* (Philadelphia, 1874), p. 194, s. v. "Duponceau, Peter Stephen"; Gerard W. Gawalt, *American National Biography*, ed. John A. Garraty and Mark C. Carnes (New York, 1999), VII: 112-113, s. v. "Du Ponceau, Pierre Etienne"; James Mooney, *The Catholic Encyclopedia* (New York, 1909), V, p. 205, s. v. "Peter Stephen Duponceau"; Kurt H. Nadelmann, "Peter Stephen Du Ponceau", *Pennsylvania Bar Association Quarterly*, XXIV (April 1953), pp. 248-256; John Pickering, "Peter S. Du Ponceau, LL.D.", *Journal of the American Oriental Society*, I, no. 2 (1844), p. 167; *Nouvelle Biographie générale depuis les temps les plus reculés jusqu'a nos jours*, ed. Jean Chrétien Ferdinand Hoefer (Paris, 1862), XL, cols. 733-735, s. v. "Ponceau, Pierre Etienne du"; W. A. Tieck, "In Search of Peter Stephen Du Ponceau", *Pennsylvania Magazine of History and Biography*, LXXXIX (1965), pp. 52-78; *Philadelphia: A 300-Year History*, ed. Russell F. Weigley (New York, 1982); Thompson Westcott, *A History of Philadelphia, from the Time of the First Settlements in the Delaware to the Consolidation of the City and Districts in 1854* (unpublished version; 1886), V, pp. 1180-1198; Thomas I. Wharton, *The Lives of Eminent Philadelphians, Now Deceased Collected from Original and Authentic Sources*, ed. Henry Simpson (Philadelphia, 1859), pp. 329-333, s. v. "Peter S. Duponceau"; "Autobiography of Peter Stephen Du Ponceau", *Pennsylvania Magazine of History and Biography*, LXIII (1939), pp. 189-

French vocabulary. He began formal studies at a grammar school and was instructed at home by private tutors. Latin he studied with Father Raymond, later chaplain of the hospital La Charité, and a military officer, Mallorme. At a neighbor's home one day he accidentally found an English grammar and proceeded to undertake self-study of that language, testing his skills with English, Irish, and Welsh families quartered in the town. Soon he was devouring Milton, Thomson, Young, Pope, and Shakespeare.[67] As a student he shared a room with a young Irishman, Edmund Stack; they "spoke English together to our hearts' content".[68] Then it was the turn of the Italian language, which he acquired in the same manner and tested his skills with an Italian regiment quartered locally. Tutoring in other disciplines – mathematics, geography, history, and military science – he received from various recruits who volunteered their services to his father. Hopes for a military career were dashed by extreme nearsightedness.

Greek he acquired a bit, partly through self-study and partly through informal classes which he arranged with like-minded colleagues. Ultimately, however, he was sanctioned for this and never worked seriously with the language. As for Russian, this too he acquired, as he related in his *Autobiography*:

> While I was employed as Secretary to the learned Count de Gébelin at Paris, I became acquainted with a Russian nobleman, who was then on his travels through Europe. His name was M. Pisaroff, and he told me he was a nephew to Admiral Count Gleboff. He lived in great style, and was attended by several of his serfs. My acquaintance with him

227, 311-343, 432-461; (1940), LXIV, 97-120; 243-269. Du Ponceau figures frequently in *Documentary History of the Supreme Court*, note 4 above (1985-2007). Among manuscript sources, see the relevant holdings of the American Philosophical Society (hereinafter: APS), the Historical Society of Philadelphia (both of which enjoyed Du Ponceau's services as President), the Library Company of Philadelphia, and the Register of Wills, City of Philadelphia.

[67] Recounted in Robley Dunglison, "Biographical Sketch of Peter S. Du Ponceau," *American Law Magazine*, no. 9 (April 1845), pp. 1-33.

[68] See P. S. Du Ponceau, "Autobiography", note 66 above, LXIV, pp. 99-100, 102, 110.

> began in this manner. I was in a bookseller's shop, where I went to lounge almost every day, and where I found a grammar of the Russian language. I amused myself with copying a few Russian sentences in the proper character. M. Pisaroff, who was also in the habit of visiting the same shop, saw the paper which I had written, and was so pleased with it, that he desired the bookseller to introduce me to him, which he soon afterwards did. My Russian nobleman took a great fancy to me, and during five or six weeks that he remained in Paris, gave me lessons in his language in which I began to make some progress, and in return I gave him English lessons. He told me that he was going to Italy to finish his tour, and that if on his return he should find me in Paris, and I was willing to accompany him, he would take me with him to St. Petersberg and there obtain for me the place of teacher of the English language in the Imperial College of Cadets.[69]

His next formal education commenced at age thirteen at a Benedictine college, St. Jean Angely, where he excelled in philosophy and continued his studies of English. He left after eighteen months, at age fifteen, upon his father's death. Under a combination of maternal and clerical pressure agreed to enter a seminary ("took the tonsure," as he put it, and became *monsieur l'abbé*) on condition that he not be expected to enter the priesthood. Through the intervention of the Bishop of Rochelle, a friend of the family, the young *abbé* was appointed a regent in his episcopal college at Bressiure, in Poitou, where he instructed a much older class of students in the elements of the Latin

---

[69] Ibid., LXIII, pp. 443-444. This episode may help date the manuscript "Sea Terms" which Du Ponceau later presented to the American Philosophical Society. There are Cyrillic jottings, mostly the word "Louis" in Russian, rendered as "Ludwig" transcribed. No Russian materials dating from Du Ponceau's Paris period were included in his bequest of books to the American Philosophical Society. Pickering records that "in early life he had studied the Russian, which at that period was a *terra incognita* to scholars in general; and on his arrival in this country he kept his journal in the French language, written in the Russian character". Pickering, note 66 above, p. 168. In his will he left to the APS his Russian grammar and dictionary: Johann von Heym *Dictionnaire portative, francois-russe-allemand* (Riga, 1805); *Russische sprachlehre* (new ed., enl.; Riga, 1804).

language (for his period there he was credited with having received his bachelor's degree, having passed the examinations with distinction).[70] Bullying by the other regents and, at their instigation, students there persuaded him to leave. On 25 December 1775 he repaired to Paris to seek subsistence. Eventually he found freelance work by translating English works on a per sheet basis for other professed translators who sold his work as their own; he also translated commercial letters for merchants and tutored in the English and French languages. For several months he acted as secretary to the protestant minister, A. Court de Gébelin (d. 1784), a celebrated philologist.

He then found employment as secretary-interpreter with Baron Friedrich Wilhelm Augustus von Steuben (1730-1794)[71] and sailed with him from Marseilles to America, landing at Portsmouth, New Hampshire on 1 December 1777.[72] The Americans who greeted the Baron and his retinue found in Du Ponceau a "... dreamy-eyed, nearsighted, and hopelessly scholarly boy of seventeen ... possessed of an insatiable academic curiosity ... tougher than he appeared at first glance, with his pale complexion and tall, lanky frame, exaggerated by adolescent awkwardness".[73]

Because von Steuben spoke no English, Du Ponceau found himself obliged to cope with American English at once. After a few days in Portsmouth, von Steuben proceeded to Boston, where Du Ponceau, by now a stern republican, met John Hancock (1737-1793) and Samuel Adams (1722-1803). He then

---

[70] Du Ponceau relates the examinations with relish in his autobiography. See note 66 above.

[71] See Friedrich Kapp, *Life of Friedrich William von Steuben* (2d ed.; 1858), pp. 192-199; also see the useful exhibition catalog: *Steuben: Secret Aid for the Americans* (1981).

[72] Of this period there survives a little journal and notebook containing a variety of incidental materials, including scribblings, some poetry, small maps, and an account of the journey from Portsmouth to Yorktown. Although the text is mostly in French, Du Ponceau often has recourse to Russian, suggesting that he was resorting to code and also was studying some Russian on his own. This item is held by the Historical Society of Delaware. His notebook on "Sea Terms" also contained some Russian words.

[73] Paul Lockhart, *The Drillmaster of Valley Forge: The Baron De Steuben and the Making of the American Army* (2008), p. 49.

accompanied Baron Steuben to Yorktown, Mass., where they met General Horatio Gates (1727-1806). Upon von Steuben's request, Du Ponceau was appointed captain, by brevet, in the United States army.[74] On 19 February 1778 he and von Steuben went to Valley Forge, where, on 24 February, Du Ponceau was presented to General George Washington (1732-1799). It was at Valley Forge that Du Ponceau met his first American Indian. In time the Baron was appointed a major-general and the Inspector-General of the armies of the United States, in consequence of which Du Ponceau, as secretary to the Baron, also became aide-de-camp and, by courtesy, the rank of major. During his Valley Forge days, Du Ponceau befriended General Lafayette (1757-1834), a relationship that endured until the latter's death.

For four years he served von Steuben with the rank of captain. Among his tasks of international legal interest was to translate, see through press, and arrange the distribution of von Steuben's *Regulations for the Order and Discipline of the Troops of the United States* (Philadelphia, 1779).[75] This by all accounts was no easy matter. Skilled printers and engravers had abandoned Philadelphia to flee the British or to seek their fortune elsewhere.[76] Paper and ink were likewise in short supply.

---

[74] In due course Du Ponceau received a revolutionary war pension as a captain of infantry of the line until his death.

[75] A draft entitled *L'Exercise des Troupes* survives in the New York Historical Society. This, the first manual of discipline for the United States Army, was reprinted numerous times and amended from time to time. For his labors on the manual Du Ponceau was rewarded by Congress with the sum of $400 in addition to his pay. See Friedrich Wilhelm August Heinrich Ferdinand, Baron von Steuben, *Regulations for the Discipline of the Troops of the United States* (Philadelphia, 1779). Presented by Du Ponceau to the APS in October 1824 and inscribed by him: "By Frederick William Baron de Steuben, Inspector General of the American Armies. Original Ed." The Regulations contains passages which today we would recognize as part of international humanitarian law. There is no specific mention of the law of nations.

[76] Timothy Pickering (1745-1829), a member of the Board of War, explained to the Baron: "Here under the present scarcity of hands you can place no dependence on your workmen ... To-day they are with you, & tomorrow on board a privateer with hopes of making their fortunes". Quoted in Lockhart, note 73 above, p. 205 from the Steuben Papers.

The first engraver of the copperplate illustrations, John Norman, performed so poorly that he had to be replaced; only one bookbinder could be found, which exacerbated the delays. Whatever Du Ponceau's nascent legal skills and linguistic abilities, he was no taskmaster: "Effete and unprepossessing, the secretary was incapable of intimidating anybody, let alone rough-spoken Philadelphia artisans".[77] Richard Peters (1744-1828), despite his esteem for Du Ponceau, wrote to the Baron on 19 June 1779 that Du Ponceau was "... the worse person you could have left here as he was unacquainted with the Customs ... of our Country ... As to stimulating the Work*man* (for Work*men* we could not get) he was of no more use than if you had left him to observe an Ecclipse without a Telescope".[78]

In perhaps an ill-advised move, the Baron complained about the delays to the Continental Congress, which promptly rebuked the Board of War for delays that were beyond their control. A week later the production was finished. About 1,500 copies of the "Blue Book" were delivered by the Russian-born printer, Charles Cist (1738-1805), between June and August 1779 to the Board of War. The Continental Congress commissioned special leather-bound presentation copies for King Louis XVI of France and General George Washington.[79]

Ultimately, consumption ended Du Ponceau's tenure under Baron von Steuben. His doctors believed him to be incurable, a judgment which alienated him from the medical profession for the remainder of his life. He settled in Philadelphia and became on 25 July 1781 a citizen of the Commonwealth of Pennsylvania by oath. Seeking employment, he was recommended to Robert R. Livingston (1746-1813), sometime chancellor of the State of New York who had been appointed secretary for foreign affairs.

On 22 October 1781 Du Ponceau took up his duties as secretary to Livingston at a salary of $750 per annum payable in French crowns or *louis d'or* (the currency of the day). The house that Livingston occupied until his retirement from office became the house in which Du Ponceau resided from 1801 until his

---

[77] Lockhart, ibid., p. 205.
[78] Ibid.
[79] Ibid., p. 207.

death in 1844, at Sixth and Chestnut Streets in Philadelphia, literally around the corner from the American Philosophical Society.[80]

While recuperating, Du Ponceau set in motion a number of steps to consolidate his social and professional position in his newly-adopted country. On 14 February 1782 he petitioned Masonic Lodge No. 2 in Philadelphia, was elected to membership on 9 April 1782 and probably received the Entered Apprentice and undoubtedly the Fellow Craft on 14 August 1782. There is no information as to whether he proceeded to the degree of Master Mason, although in the eighteenth century it was common not to do so.[81]

When the War ended, Du Ponceau decided to enter the legal profession and studied law with William Lewis, whom he regarded as "the most celebrated lawyer in Philadelphia, and perhaps in the United States".[82] On 24 January 1785, upon the motion of Mr. Lewis, Du Ponceau was admitted as an attorney of the Court of Common Pleas and on the favorable report of the examiners, he was received. He had previously been appointed by the executive council as notary public; in 1791 he was made sworn interpreter of foreign languages. Success as a lawyer came rapidly; by September 1785 the court docket showed that he was counsel in twenty-one actions either for plaintiff or

---

[80] The house was diagonally opposite the State House. Du Ponceau purchased the house at a sheriff's sale, also acquiring at the same time the adjoining property to the rear along Sixth Street, described as a three-story brick tenement where Livingston had accommodated the foreign affairs office. Between the mansion and the tenement was a small low cottage that Du Ponceau used as his law office. Du Ponceau later rented out space to a bookseller who proved to be delinquent in his rent. See Tieck, note 66 above, pp. 59-60.

[81] See Julius F. Sachse (1842-1919), *Freemasonry in Pennsylvania 1727-1907 as Shown by the Records of Lodge No. 2, F. & A. M. of Philadelphia* (1912-13), II, pp. ix-xii, 26 (with portrait). Rumors persist that Du Ponceau was elected to membership in the Society of the Cincinnati. He assuredly qualified for membership, but no record of his membership can be traced in the Archives of the Society.

[82] Note 67 above, p. 17.

defendant.[83] On 28 January 1786,[84] once more upon the motion of William Lewis, Du Ponceau was admitted as Counsellor of the Supreme Court of Pennsylvania. On 8 February 1791 Du Ponceau was sworn in as Counsellor[85] of the United States Supreme Court.[86]

---

[83] There is some evidence to suggest that he may have formed a partnership with Maurice Desdevens. In September 1816 Du Ponceau presented a book to the APS which bore the inscription: "The Partnership of Peter Stephen Duponceau and Maurice Desdevens 8th September 1785". The book was *Case of Peter Du Calvet, esq. of Montreal in the Province of Quebeck . . .*, by Pierre Du Calvet (London, 1784). This may simply have been two lawyers assisting one another in a particular case.

[84] Du Ponceau shows this date in his own hand on the Certificate of admission to the United States Supreme Court, reproduced in facsimile in M. Marcus (ed.), *The Documentary History of the Supreme Court of the United States, 1789-1800* (1998), I(1), p. 548.

[85] The United States Supreme Court at this time distinguished between counsellors and attorneys, following English procedure and the practice of several states. Only counsellors could plead a case; attorneys could file motions and engage in other paperwork but not actually conduct a case before the Court. The rule was changed on 12 August 1801 to enable Counsellors to be admitted as attorneys on taking the usual oath. See ibid., I(1), p. 177, fn. 18. Pennsylvania was among the states which observed the distinction; Du Ponceau is shown as having been admitted to the Pennsylvania Supreme Court as Counsellor.

[86] There was some confusion on 7 February 1791 as to whether all the twenty-two individuals who presented themselves for admission in Philadelphia as attorneys or counselors had fully satisfied the requirements and what evidence was available to so confirm. On 7 February 1791 Edward Burd (1751-1833), the Prothonotary of the Supreme Court of Pennsylvania, and again on 8 February 1791, provided a Certificate affirming that the applicants were duly members of the Pennsylvania Supreme Court Bar for at least the minimum three years required for admittance to the United States Supreme Court Bar. Ibid., I(1), pp. 546-547. The Attorney General of the United States acted as the proposer for Du Ponceau and several others. Associate Justice James Wilson was the obstacle. Although he knew many of the candidates for admission personally, he was reluctant to act simultaneously as referee and judge in the matter. Six lawyers withdrew their application, and ultimately sixteen were admitted at this time. Edward Burd wrote of the affair to his brother-in-law, Jasper Yeates (1745-1817) on the same day, soon to be appointed an associate justice of the Pennsylvania Supreme Court. See L. B. Walker (ed.), *The Burd Papers: Selections from Letters*

He promptly found himself instructed to argue cases before the Supreme Court of the United States and eventually traveling to Washington for this purpose once the capital was established there,[87] together with other leading members of the Philadelphia Bar. Joseph Story (1779-1845) who, before his appointment in 1811, routinely observed the nation's high court and would drink and sup with the Justices, heard Du Ponceau argue and described him in 1808 as follows:

> Duponceau is a Frenchman by birth, and a very ingenious counselor at Philadelphia. He has the reputation of great subtilty and acuteness, and is excessively minute in the display of his learning. His manner is animated but not impressive, and he betrays at every turn the impatience and the casuistry of his nation. His countenance is striking, his figure rather awkward. A small, sparkling, black eye, and a thin face, satisfy you that he is not without quickness of mind; yet he seemed to me to exhaust himself in petty distinctions, and in a perpetual recurrence to doubtful, if not to inclusive arguments. His reasoning was rather sprightly and plausible, than logical and coercive; in short, he is a French advocate.[88]

Written by Edward Burd, 1763-1828 (1899), pp. 168-170. The text of the Parchment Roll of Counsellors is reprinted in *Documentary History of the Supreme Court*, note 67 above, I(1), p. 539.

[87] See, e.g., *Gorgerat, et al. v. M'Carty* 1 U.S. 366 (1788), *Quesnel v. Mussi*, 1 U.S. 436 (1789); *Vasse v. Spicer*, 2 U.S. 111 (1790); *Gorgerat, et al. v. M'Carty*, 2 U.S. 144 (1792); *Caignet v. Pettit, et al.*, 2 U.S. 234 (1795); *Vasse v. Balle*, 2 U.S. 270 (1797); *Glass, et al. v. The Sloop Betsey, et al.*, 3 U.S. 6 (1794); *The United States v. Richard Peters, District Judge*, 3 U.S. 121 (1795); *Talbot v. Janson, et al.*, 3 U.S. 133 (1795); *The United States v. La Vengeance*, 3 U.S. 297 (1796), *Cotton v. Wallace*, 3 U.S. 302 (1796); *Jennings et al. v. the Brig Perseverance, et al.*, 3 U.S. 336 (1797); *Jones v. Le Tombe*, 3 U.S. 384 (1798); *M'Ilvaine v. Coxe's Lessee*, 8 U.S. 209 (1808); *Rose v. Himely*, 8 U.S. 241 (1808). Du Ponceau is mentioned several times in passing in Warren, *The Supreme Court in United States History* (rev. ed.; 1937), vol. I. Du Ponceau described himself on the title page of his Bynkershoek translation as "Counsellor at Law in the Supreme Court of the United States of America".

[88] William Wetmore Story, *Life and Letters of Joseph Story* (1851), I, pp. 162-163.

With the benefit of time and contact, Story's appraisal of this French-born American improved markedly, as signaled by his expression of debt in correspondence to Du Ponceau in 1840: "To you and to Chancellor Kent I mainly owe whatever attainments I have made in foreign jurisprudence and the civil law".[89]

Although himself a democrat in matters of politics, he was well connected with republican merchants and often represented them in property transactions or litigation. His letterbooks for the period from 1792 to 1809 show that the majority of his clients were individuals of French-origin in the United States,[90] West Indies,[91] or France and that his "important suits" were concerned with issues of international, commercial, and maritime law.[92]

For a number of years he enjoyed a retainer from the French Republic. He considered intervention in a French prize claim against the frigate *South Carolina*, seeking documents to "... Determine if it is wise for the Republic to intervene in the case which is now pending before the supreme court, or if this action

---

[89] Correspondence to Du Ponceau, dated January 30, 1841. Cited in Richard H. Heindel, "Some Letters of Peter Stephen Du Ponceau," *Pennsylvania History* (1936), p. 199.

[90] About 1% of the white population in the United States were émigrés or refugees taking flight from the French Revolution in the metropolitan country or the slave rebellions in the French colonies. There were 5,000 in Philadelphia alone, or one-sixth of the population. See Allan Potofsky, "The 'Non-Aligned Status' of French Emigrés and Refugees in Philadelphia, 1793-1798", *Transatlantica*, no. 2 (2006).

[91] The flood of refugees in Philadelphia during the summer of 1793 from Santo Domingo and elsewhere in the West Indies impelled Du Ponceau and others to organize the Société Française de Bienfaisance de Philadelphie. More than two thousand arrived, and for some time Philadelphia became a tri-lingual city. See J. H. Powell (1914-1971), *Bring Out Your Dead: The Great Plague of Yellow Fever in Philadelphia in 1793* (reprint ed., 1993), p. 5.

[92] His Letterbooks are held at the Historical Society of Philadelphia, this data being drawn from Jennifer D. Henderson, "'A Blaze of Reputation and the Echo of a Name': The Legal Career of Peter Stephen Du Ponceau in Post-Revolutionary Philadelphia" (unpublished M. A. Thesis, Florida State University, 2004), p. 27.

would be likely to expose the republic to a Considerable expense without any benefit".[93]

In 1792 he became a founder and secretary of the Democratic Society of Philadelphia. In its founding documents adopted on 30 May 1793 the Society resolved "... to cultivate the just knowledge of rational Liberty, to facilitate the enjoyment and exercise of our civil Rights, and to transmit, unimpaired, to posterity, the glorious inheritance of a free Republican Government".[94]

His command of Roman and European legal concepts[95] and of international law, together with his language abilities, made

---

[93] See the Letter from Du Ponceau to Philippe de Létombe (d. 1833), the French Consul in the United States, dated 6 September 1796 and extracted in *Documentary History of the Supreme Court of the United States*, note 5 above, V, p. 482. Eventually Du Ponceau intervened in the case as *amicus curiae* and reported the outcome to Létombe on 21 February 1797. Ibid., V, pp. 487-489, 490-492. His intervention was decisive at the time in what was an exceedingly complicated affair. For a summary, see ibid., pp. 450-461.

[94] See Larry E. Tice, *The American Counterrevolution: A Retreat from Liberty, 1783-1800* (1998), p. 43. Known by friends and adversaries alike as the "Mother Club" of similar societies in the United States during the 1790s, the first President was David Rittenhouse (1732-1796), the Treasurer was Israel Israel, and the principal organizer was George Logan (1753-1821), physician, beekeeper, farmer, and United States Senator. Benjamin Franklin Bache (1769-1798) served as chairman of the Society's Committee of Correspondence. Members, following the French Revolution, addressed one another as "Citizen" – a practice that doubtless would have appealed to Du Ponceau. See Albrecht Koschnik, "The Democratic Societies of Philadelphia and the Limits of the American Public Sphere, circa 1793-1795", *The William and Mary Quarterly*, LVIII (2001), pp. 1-35.

[95] The Act to Regulate Processes in the Courts of the United States of 1789 provided in Section 12 that equity, admiralty, and maritime proceedings should "... be according to the course of the civil law, except where the Statutes of the United States otherwise provide". But except for practitioners in Connecticut and Massachusetts, where the civil law had been adopted during the Revolution for maritime cases, most practitioners in the United States were ignorant of and generally hostile to this and federal practice continued to follow English equity and admiralty procedure. Du Ponceau, being learned in the civil law, observed sardonically that this Act's reference to the "course of the civil law" was "well understood with us to be the course of the Courts of Equity and

him a natural advisor for European merchants, commercial agents, and diplomatic and consular officials. John Pickering (1777-1846) wrote of his law practice:

> [H]e was engaged in all the important causes, which then came before the courts of the State as well as of the United States. At that day the controversies which arose between France and the United States, and the position of the United States as a neutral power, while all Europe was at war, gave rise to questions of international law for which our lawyers, generally, were then quite unprepared; and his knowledge of the civil and continental law of Europe, which were easily accessible to him, by means of his native language – a language then studied, or read, by very few persons in this country – gave him many decided advantages at the bar in cases of the kind alluded to.[96]

Henry Hugh Brackenridge (1748-1816) reproduced two extracts from notes by Du Ponceau under the head of "allegiance" from the American edition of the *Edinburgh Encyclopedia*. High praise accompanied these notes: "... Mr. Duponceau, whom all will admit, I take it, possesses the greatest knowledge of general law of any, in the U. States, ... may be said to be the greatest universal jurist".[97]

Du Ponceau never sought public office after he left the employ of Robert Livingston. He devoted himself to private and professional business and scholarship, apparently becoming quite comfortable financially. Apart from his practice of law and his legal translations, scores of learned societies and organizations engaged the attention of Du Ponceau. Two of these, the Law Academy of Philadelphia and the APS, warrant special consideration in connection with his book collecting interests.

Admiralty in England and the United States before the adoption of the federal Constitution unless where Congress have by law declared it otherwise". See J. Goebel, Jr., *Antecedents and Beginnings to 1801* (1971), I, p. 535n.

[96] See Pickering, note 66 above, p. 164.

[97] See Hugh H. Brackenridge, *Law Miscellanies* (1814; repr., New York: Arno, 1972), p. 417.

Law Academy of Philadelphia

Despite its name, this was not a law school in the traditional American meaning of the word, but it was dedicated to legal education. In many respects it resembled an Inn of Court in England, which was perhaps no coincidence. The origins of the Law Academy are traced to 1783, when Du Ponceau, Bushrod Washington (later a Justice of the United States Supreme Court) (1762-1829), and John Wilkes Kittera (1752-1801), recently admitted to the Bar, formed the Law Society of Philadelphia.[98] Records are few, but apparently the members met occasionally to hear lectures upon legal topics or to engage in mooting. Various officers served from time to time, and possibly the name of the society itself changed.[99] In 1811 Du Ponceau was elected President of the Society, although by then he was 51 years of age.

In 1820 efforts were undertaken to create a permanent foundation for such an organization, and to this end the Society for the Promotion of Legal Knowledge and Forensic Eloquence was established by a group of judges and lawyers. The object of the Society, as articulated in the Preamble to its Constitution, was to "connect with the mode of instruction at that time exclusively pursued, a more scientific and academical system, whereby not only a greater degree of jurisprudential knowledge might be acquired, but the students might be exercised in the art of public speaking, so as to unite the talent of the orator with the science of the jurist". This group then invited an alliance with the Law Society, of which Du Ponceau was the President, and

---

[98] See George Sharswood, *The Origin, History, and Objects of the Law Academy of Philadelphia: An Address Delivered Before the Academy, March 13, 1883* (1883); William MacLean, Jr., *The Law Academy and the Growth of Legal Education in Philadelphia* (1900); For his own recollections of its founding, see Du Ponceau, *Address Delivered Before the Law Academy of Philadelphia on the Opening of the Session 1831-2* (Philadelphia, 1831).

[99] MacLean and Sharswood quoted sources who can document the existence of law societies during the period 1785 to 1811. Du Ponceau himself said he had "heard no more of Law Societies in this city, although some might have existed without my knowing it". Du Ponceau, note 66 above, p. 6.

suggested that the Law Society become a Law Academy as an appendage of the new Society and under its control. Du Ponceau was elected first Provost of the Academy.

The Law Academy formally opened on 21 February 1821 with what must have been a monumental address by Du Ponceau in the room of the Supreme Court before the Trustees and members of the Society for Legal Knowledge and Forensic Eloquence. On this occasion Du Ponceau referred to fledgling and unsuccessful efforts to persuade the University of Pennsylvania to establish a law school, noted the formation of law schools elsewhere, and strongly urged that a national law school should be created in Philadelphia.[100] The parent society soon came to an end (for essentially procedural reasons), but the Law Academy lived on well into the twentieth century (initially as an informal association, but incorporated by act of the legislature framed 14 April 1835).

Mooting was one activity of the Academy, the students being organized into teams and judged by legal professionals who actually produced a written opinion in judgment of the arguments presented.[101] Students also wrote dissertations on legal subjects, several of which the Law Academy deemed worthy of publication. One such dissertation by Antony Laussat, a student twenty years of age, achieved the approbation of John Marshall (1755-1835) and James Kent and became a standard work on equity.[102] Over the years the Law Academy published a number of works, including a seminal work by Du Ponceau

[100] The theme of a "national law school" comes up with some frequency at this period, also being encouraged during the 1820s by John Reed, who founded the Dickinson School of Law in Carlisle, Pennsylvania in 1833, now part of Pennsylvania State University. A close reading of Du Ponceau's address suggests that he believed a national law school was being created by the opening of the Law Academy.

[101] The Opinion Book, entitled "Opinions Delivered Before the Law Academy of Philadelphia by the Provost and Vice Provost," covering the years 1820 to 1822 and signed by Du Ponceau is preserved in the Manuscript Division of the American Philosophical Society, having been presented in 1862 by Robley Dunglison. (340.7 L41).

[102] *Essay on Equity in Pennsylvania* (Philadelphia, 1826).

himself on jurisdiction.[103] At some later stage the Law Academy established the Peter Stephen Du Ponceau Prize for an essay upon a subject, either legal or connected with the law, selected and proposed to the Law Academy by its Faculty for worthy works submitted anonymously. This "Duponceau Medal" was awarded to the best essay as the medal highest in value; the medal next highest in value was the Laussat Medal.[104]

In 1834 Du Ponceau published in Philadelphia another substantial monograph under the auspices of the Law Academy, this entitled *A Brief View of the Constitution of the United States.*[105] It enjoyed considerable success and was widely cited[106] and translated into French.[107] His interests in matters of jurisdiction and evidence led him to seek legislative change when he deemed this to be desirable. On 27 March 1826 he wrote to Congressman William Morris Meredith (1799-1873) at Harrisburg:

> [It was reported] in the *National Intelligencer* of last Friday that the House of Representatives on the motion of Mr.

---

[103] Du Ponceau, *Dissertation on the Nature and Extent of the Jurisdiction of the Courts of the United States* (1824); this volume appends Du Ponceau's opening Address to the Law Academy delivered in 1821. Cited in *Seminole Tribe v. Fla.*, 517 U.S. 44 (U.S. 1996); *Planters' Bank v. Neely*, 8 Miss. 80 (Miss. 1843). Also cited in James Kent, *Commentaries on American Law* (New York, 1826), I, p. 322. The book was reviewed in *North American Review*, XXI (1825), p. 104 (Charles S. Davies); *Thémis ou Bibliothèque Du Jurisconsulte*, VII (1825), p. 420 (Maurice-Parfait Daligny).

[104] See Article XII, *Charter, Constitution and By-Laws of The Law Academy of Philadelphia* (1867), p. 23. One noteworthy example of the award was the Medal for 1904 to George John Edwards, Jr. (1875-19?), of the Philadelphia Bar, for his work of lasting interest, *The Grand Jury: An Essay* (1906; repr. New York, London, Toronto: AMS Press, 1973; repr., Clark, NJ: Lawbook Exchange, 2004).

[105] Repr., New York: Da Capo, 1974.

[106] See, e.g., *Welch v. Texas Dep't of Highways & Public Transp.*, 483 U.S. 468 (U.S. 1987).

[107] Du Ponceau, *Exposé sommaire de la Constitution des Etats-Unis,* transl. by John d'Homergue (Paris, 1837). An abridged version printed in New York for distribution in Cuba and Puerto Rico appeared posthumously: *Breve Resena de la Constitución de los Estados Unidos* (1848).

> Livingston, of Louisiana, that the Committee of the Judiciary be instructed to enquire into the expediency of empowering the Consuls of the U. S. to take the acknowledgement or proof of Deeds & other writings, & also to take the affidavits and Answers in Chancery. Mr. Livingston is a Member of the Judiciary Committee, and I have no doubt that the Report will be favorable. Seeing that Congress are taking the lead in a measure which had been one Year before our Legislature, would it not be well, on the ground of an honorable State pride, that we should be before ... with them – the Act of Congress can only affect lands in the District of Columbia, and affidavits &c. in the federal Courts; it can have no operation on State laws; I therefore beg leave to bring this Subject again before you, & request that it may be attended to this Session, if possible.[108]

American Philosophical Society

Du Ponceau's contributions to the study of languages, particular those of the American Indians but also including Chinese and the Mexican heritage, were pioneering and immense, generating a larger secondary literature on this aspect of his life than his legal career.[109] They seem to have begun with his membership in the American Philosophical Society,[110] where he became the secretary of and prime moving force behind the

---

[108] Letter in the Manuscript Archive, American Philosophical Society.

[109] See Roy E. Goodman and Pierre Swiggers, *The American Philosophical Society and the Study of Language in the Early Nineteenth Century* (Leuven, 1993); Murphy D. Smith, "Peter Stephen Du Ponceau and His Study of Languages: A Historical Account," *Proceedings of the American Philosophical Society*, CXXVII (June, 1983), pp. 143-179; Pierre Swiggers, "Americanist Linguistics and the Origin of Linguistic Typology: Peter Stephen Du Ponceau's 'Comparative Science of Language,'" *Proceedings of the American Philosophical Society*, CXLII (March, 1998), pp. 18-46.

[110] Du Ponceau was elected to membership on 15 July 1791, serving on committees and acting as councilor, secretary, and vice-president before assuming the Presidency of the Society in 1827. Prior to joining he made a spectacular gift to the Society Library, reported on 6 March 1789, which included a Russian language version (Moscow, 1760) of John Locke's *Some Thoughts Concerning Education.*

Society's Historical and Literary Committee founded in 1815 (having been originally suggested by Du Ponceau in 1811). This was the seventh committee of the American Philosophical Society, adding the social sciences and humanities to what heretofore had been a purely natural science organization. The Committee was charged with, *inter alia*, quasi-legal interests, including "the collecting of original documents, such as official and private letters, Indian treaties, ancient records ...".

The impetus for the early expansion of the American Philosophical Society outstanding holdings of native American linguistic collections was generated by Du Ponceau and a Philadelphia wine merchant and bibliophile, John Vaughan (1756-1841).[111] During the first decade of the nineteenth century Thomas Jefferson (1743-1826) served simultaneously as the President of the United States and President of the American Philosophical Society, and in those dual capacities commissioned Albert Gallatin (1761-1849), assisted by Du Ponceau, to undertake a study of Indian vocabularies. Jefferson believed there were relationships between the Indian tribes reflected in the similarities and differences of their respective languages. Du Ponceau and Gallatin determined that there was a correlation between similarity of language and the duration of time that had elapsed since the tribes had migrated to other regions of North America. Du Ponceau recorded his own findings in a monograph on the grammatical system of Indian languages,[112] which on 2 May 1835 was awarded the Comte de Volney Prize of *Linguistique* of the Institut de France.[113]

---

[111] Vaughan had joined the American Philosophical Society on 16 January 1784 and was appointed librarian on 18 March 1803, a post which he held until his death in 1841. See Goodman and Swiggers, "John Vaughan and the Linguistic Collection in the Library of the American Philosophical Society", *Proceedings of the American Philosophical Society*, CXXXVIII (June, 1994), pp. 251-272. Apart from an astute acquisitions policy, Vaughan was generous to the American Philosophical Society with gifts of his own, itemized in ibid., p. 253, fn. 10. The Society preserves a printed version of its Library catalog from 1824 with interpolations of new acquisitions in Vaughan's own hand.

[112] Du Ponceau, *Mémoire sur le système grammatical des langues de quelques nations Indiennes de l'Amérique Du Nord* (Paris, 1838). A later

He then expanded his studies of language to encompass the Chinese system of writing by way of, in the main, a letter to John Vaughan, followed by appendices.[114] In assembling his materials on the American Indian languages he corresponded with individuals around the world. His correspondence with William Shaler (1778-1833) was published by the American Philosophical Society under the title "On the Language, Manners, and Customs of the Berbers of Africa,"[115] as were his letters to and from John Gottlieb Ernestus Heckewelder (1743-1823), a Moravian missionary in Ohio working with Indian tribes there.[116]

---

authority said that the Volney Prize had for Du Ponceau the effect of certifying him as "one of the few great linguists of the world." See Clark Wissler, "The American Indian and the American Philosophical Society," *Proceedings of the American Philosophical Society*, LXXXVI (1943), p. 193.

[113] Du Ponceau had unsuccessfully competed for the Volney Prize in 1825, having submitted an *Essai de solution Du problème philologique propose en l'année 1823 par la Commission de l'Institut Royal de France chargée de la disposition Du legs de M. le Comte de Volney*. The manuscript of the submission reposes in the Manuscript Division of the American Philosophical Society at 410. D921. See Goodman and Swiggers, note 109 above, pp. 18-19, 43.

[114] *A Dissertation on the Nature and Character of the Chinese System of Writing, in a Letter to John Vaughan, Esq. by Peter S. Du Ponceau, LL.D., President of the American Philosophical Society, of the Historical Society of Pennsylvania, and of the Athenaeum of Philadelphia, Corresponding Member of the Institute of France, &c. &c. to which are subjoined, A vocabulary of the Cochinchinese language, by Father Joseph Morrone, R. C. Missionary at Saigon, with references to plates, containing the characters belonging to each word, and with notes, showing the degree of affinity existing between the Chinese and Cochinchinese languages, and the use they respectively make of their common system of writing by M. de la Palun, Late Consul of France at Richmond, in Virginia; and A Cochinchinese and Latin dictionary, in use among the R. C. missions in Cochinchina* (1838). The book appeared as volume 2 in the *Transactions of the Historical and Library Committee of the American Philosophical Society*; reviewed favorably in *The North American Review*, XLVIII (1839), pp. 271-310 (John Pickering).

[115] *Transactions of the American Philosophical Society*, II (n.p.; 1824).

[116] Ibid., I (1819).

Contemporary scholars in retrospect believe Du Ponceau "can rightly be hailed as 'the father of American philology'" and his *Mémoire* "a pioneer work in language typology".[117]

In addition to the aforementioned learned pursuits, the silk industry stirred a passing enthusiasm in Du Ponceau, to which he devoted three years of his life and four thousand dollars in order to introduce the production and manufacture of silk into the United States. An Act of Congress being required, an appropriate bill submitted but not enacted. In the end he abandoned the project, "defeated in my patriotic design", but wrote two works on the subject, one general historical treatment and one recounting his experiences.[118]

In all, Du Ponceau was a member of forty-two learned societies, of which nineteen were abroad. The University of Pennsylvania conferred the degree of M.A. (Hon.) on him on 21 March 1782 at a ceremony attended by General George Washington, Baron von Steuben, and members of Congress, among others. Harvard University conferred the degree of LL.D. (Hon.) in 1820. He later became a trustee of the University of Pennsylvania. He was elected to the American Academy of Arts and Sciences and, in 1791, to the American Philosophical Society; served as Provost of the Law Academy of Philadelphia (1821-1844), President of the American Philosophical Society (1827-1844), President of the Historical Society of Pennsylvania (1837-1844), President of the Athenaeum of Philadelphia (est. 1814; 1844), and on 20 April 1827 was elected a Corresponding Member of the Institut de France.

Among his other works were *English Phonology; or an Essay towards an analysis and description of the component sounds of the English language* in *Transactions of the American Philosophical Society* (1817);[119] *A Discourse on the Early*

---

[117] Goodman and Swiggers, note 109 above, p. 41; Vilen V. Belyi, "P. S. Duponceau – the Father of American Philology", *Zeitschrift für Phonetik, Sprachwissenschaft und Kommunikationsforschung*, XXVIII (1975), pp. 41-49.

[118] P. S. Du Ponceau, *An Historical Review of the Rise, Progress, Present State and Prospects of the Silk Culture* (Philadelphia, 1831); and id, *The History of the Silk Bill, in a Letter to D. B. Warden* (Philadelphia, 1837).

[119] I, pp. 228-264.

History of Pennsylvania (1821); *Eulogium in Commemoration of the Honourable William Tilghman, LL.D.* (1827); *An Historical Discourse Delivered Before the Society for the Commemoration of the Landing of William Penn* (1832); and *A Discourse on the Necessity and Means of Making our National Literature Independent of that of Great Britain* (1834).[120]

A number of his legal writings which appeared as part of other works are among his most important. There is a certain poetic irony that his translation of passages from Huber should become available to the legal profession thanks to the United States Supreme Court, who in an otherwise brief opinion appended the extract that "was translated for, and read in, this cause."[121] His first major published contribution, entitled "A Summary View of the Law of France Concerning Bankruptcy," was inserted as an appendix to Thomas Cooper's treatise comparing American and English bankruptcy law.[122] Nadelmann describes the Cooper/Du Ponceau work as "the first comparative law book ever produced in the United States and also the first scholarly presentation in English of the bankruptcy law of France."[123] He contributed notes to the American edition of Butler's *Horae Juridicae Subsecivae* (Philadelphia, 1808). Following his translation of Bynkershoek in quick succession were Du Ponceau's translations of the French Commercial Code of 1808 and then the French Criminal Code.[124] For the

---

[120] All of the works in this paragraph were published in Philadelphia. The 1834 work is among the early American documents to undertake a comparative study of literature.

[121] Ulrich Huber was Cornelis van Bynkershoek's teacher. The passage concerned the conflict of laws and appeared in *Emory v. Grenough*, 3 U.S. 369 (1797). The translated work of Huber is not specified, but undoubtedly was *Praelectionum juris civilis* (1687). Pickering confirms that the translation was by Du Ponceau. See note 66 above, pp. 164-165.

[122] Thomas Cooper, *Bankrupt Law of America Compared with the Bankrupt Law of England* (Philadelphia, 1801; repr., Littleton, CO: 1992); Cooper wrote the book while serving a prison sentence for violation of the Sedition Act under the Adams administration. Du Ponceau added a translation of the Ordinances of Bilbao concerned with insolvency in Spain.

[123] Nadelmann, note 66 above, p. 249.

[124] Both appeared as appendices in the *American Review of History and Politics* (July and October, 1811).

Edinburgh Encyclopedia (American edition) he contributed the articles on "Allegiance" and "American Law."[125] When Kent's *Commentaries on American Law* appeared, he published a review of volume one.[126]

Among his earliest legal publications in the United States is a translation of Gerard de Rayneval's response concerning French assurances to the United States during the Revolutionary War.[127] His translation of Bynkershoek was greatly appreciated and prompted Joseph Story to observe that Du Ponceau should continue his translation contributions: "why will not Mr. Duponceau increase the public gratitude by translating the works of other learned foreigners, and by a critical account of the writings of those civilians who are best entitled to the attention and study of American lawyers?"[128]

Du Ponceau added notes and commentary to the translation that also influenced the state of the law as it existed when this American translation appeared:

> In his translation of Bynkershoek, he first suggested the application of the distinction between an *absolute* and a *qualified* neutrality, to the case of the United States and France; considering our neutrality not to be absolute, but qualified by the treaty with France, in 1778. His remarks (in

[125] Reprinted in *Port Folio*, VII (4th ser.; 1819), p. 267. Du Ponceau also wrote for Lieber's *Encyclopedia Americana* (Philadelphia, 1829).
[126] *American Quarterly Review*, I (1827), p. 162.
[127] Joseph-Mathias Gerard de Rayneval (1736-1812), *Observations on the Justicative Memorial of the Court of London* (Philadelphia, 1781), written in response to a similar work by Edward Gibbon (1737-1794).
[128] "Literature of the Maritime Law" in W. W. Story, note 88 above, II, p. 110. The American Philosophical Society holds Joseph Story, *A Discourse pronounced at the request of the Essex Historical Society, on the 18th of September, 1828,: in commemoration of the first settlement of Salem, in the State of Massachusetts* (Boston, 1828) with the inscription in the author's hand: "Presented to Peter S. Du Ponceau with respects of the author". Story sent to Du Ponceau an inscribed copy of his inaugural lecture as the Dane Professor of Law at the Harvard Law School: *A Discourse Pronounced upon the Inauguration of the Author as Dane Professor of Law in Harvard University: on the Twenty-Fifth Day of August, 1829* (Boston, 1829).

> the same work) on the doctrine of the *jus postliminii*, present some new and important views, which, if we rightly recollect, have been adopted by Mr. Wheaton, in his valuable work on International Law. We believe, too, that Mr. Du Ponceau was the first to announce the opinion, in the same work, that *piracy* might be committed on land as well as at sea; which principle was afterwards incorporated into the act of Congress on that subject.[129]

His translations of works on language and travel included: from the Swedish, Thomas Campanius Holm, *A Short Description of the Province of New Sweden. Now Called by the English Pennsylvania, in America* (Philadelphia, 1834); John Eliot, *A Grammar of the Massachusetts Indian Language. A New Edition with Notes and Observations by Peter S. Du Ponceau and an Introduction and Supplementary Observations by John Pickering* (Boston, 1822); from the English, John Heckewelder, *Histoire, moeurs et coutumes des nations indiennes qui habitaient autrefois la Pennsylvanie et les états voisins* (Paris, 1822); and from the German, D. Zeisberger, *A Grammar of the Language of the Lenni Lenape or Delaware Indians* (Philadelphia, 1830).

His activity as a translator, however, goes far beyond the fields of law and linguistics. Many papers submitted to the American Philosophical Society for possible publication were in foreign languages and required to be translated either for publication or for review by the publications committee. The records of the APS disclose, for example, that he translated, among others, the thermometrical observations of Peter Legaux; Pierre Samuel Du Pont's theory of winds; the last three volumes of *Hollandsche Maatschappij der Wetenschappen te Haarlem* (publications of the Dutch Society of Sciences); Italian medical works; and a Spanish paper on the analogy of Spanish and English.

On 21 May 1788 Du Ponceau married Anne Perry (1768-1792), of Massachusetts, the eldest daughter among eleven

---

[129] Pickering, note 66 above, p. 167.

children of a Presbyterian pastor, Rev. Joseph Perry.[130] After the death of her parents, she moved to Philadelphia, where she met Du Ponceau. There were three children: two sons who died in early infancy and a daughter, Louisa Frances (1790-1825). Anne died shortly after the birth of their third child. On 12 September 1794 Du Ponceau married Anne Latouche (1759-1817), of New York; there were no issue of this marriage.

His nearsightedness was legendary, and accompanied by and doubtless contributed to a habitual preoccupation which could amount to complete absent-mindedness: "He walked always in deep thought, and must needs be addressed or arrested to recognize a passing acquaintance".[131] He also was intensely American to a degree that goes far beyond the normal understanding of patriotism. Although he preserved a "tender attachment" for France, his country of origin, he took to the United States immediately upon arrival with a passion that intensified over the years. "My American Character," he wrote, "I prize above all things".[132] Although raised in the milieu of Catholicism, he formed an early attachment to the principles of the Reformation, notwithstanding having become "*monsieur l'abbé*". In Philadelphia he worshipped for more than half a century at the local Second Presbyterian Church, where at his wish he was buried.

---

[130] A manuscript ex-libris ("Anne Du Ponceau") appears with his on *Sea Terms in Different Languages*, a notebook apparently carried by him to record the meanings of marine terms, mostly in Italian, Portugese, and Spanish, but with some Russian jottings and Danish. Bound in are pp. 561-570 of an unidentified French marine conversation book. Presented by Du Ponceau to the American Philosophical Society and held by them in the Manuscript Division: 359.03 D92. It is not apparent which "Anne" signed.

[131] Quoted in Tieck, note 66 above, pp. 74-75.

[132] Ibid., p. 76.

The Manuscript

The manuscript translation of Gérard de Rayneval's *De la liberté des mers* apparently arrived at the American Philosophical Society in 1840 in the form of three oblong octavo volumes bound in sheep, since rebacked probably in the late 1930s or early 1940s. Externally, therefore, the volumes are in a "landscape" format. Internally, however, the text is in portrait format. In effect, the sheets were bound at the top and sturdily sewn by the binder. The paper consists of single sheets of varying thicknesses; each sheet is lightly ruled in pencil to guide the translator/calligrapher, with a substantial left ruled margin for marginal emendations, interpolations, or corrections – and extensively used for this purpose. Occasionally, there is text overleaf, signaled by the use of an asterisk or cross.

This would suggest that Du Ponceau himself arranged the binding of the volumes, and that, in turn, would further suggest that Du Ponceau placed the manuscript pages in sequence. The sheets are unnumbered, and they do not always follow the sequence of the original book in French. One plausible speculation is that Du Ponceau first completed the entire translation and later, when seeking to have the book printed or published, sought to abridge the text by deleting some of the documentary materials in volume two or moving some items from volume two into the first volume and integrating them with the narrative text. The footnotes – of extreme importance, as will be seen – are distributed separately at the back of segments of the manuscript to become veritable endnotes. They are jumbled and confused; some were eliminated in what appears to be an editorial exercise. Some were interpolated to express views of Du Ponceau himself.

This makes the manuscript something of a jigsaw puzzle. Subject to minor observations below, however, the manuscript appears to be complete once the pieces are property identified and placed. Another possible explanation, albeit in my view less likely, is that Du Ponceau, severely nearsighted from birth, experienced difficulty in ordering the manuscript. I consider it least likely that the binder interfered with the sequence of materials.

Although a binding of journeyman quality, half-sheep with marbled paper over boards, and bearing the bookplate of the American Philosophical Society that records the date of receipt/accession, the binding was carefully planned and executed. What in landscape format is the top of the book and in portrait format is the right edge has been exceedingly carefully collated and trimmed, such that the landscape top edge is even and no text is lost even though the calligraphic script goes right to the edge of the sheet. The bottom (landscape and portrait) is untrimmed. The binder cut the boards so as to leave ample space on all three open edges and preclude incidental wear or damage to the sheets (pages).

The text appears to be in Du Ponceau's hand, although the involvement of his wife and/or daughter cannot be excluded. The hand is accomplished, quite readable in most places once one is accustomed to the style; miniscule interpolated footnotes are a greater challenge, as are segments that appear to have been done in haste. Perhaps the firmness and clarity of the hand suggest the manuscript was completed earlier in Du Ponceau's life rather than later. The relevance of the text would assuredly have been greatest during the War of 1812, but whether the task was commenced and/or completed during those years is pure conjecture.

As for the Du Ponceau translation, it is a free translation of the original French; a literary translation, if you will, but by a jurist/linguist who possessed an intimate and specialist knowledge of the subject-matter. Notwithstanding Du Ponceau's protestations, it was most assuredly intended for publication. From time to time the main body of the manuscript contains underscoring of passages to designate italics; there are marginal instructions "print in Roman" that can only have been intended for the printer. If the conjecture is correct that the materials were reordered with a view to abridging the manuscript, that too would reflect an intention to see the work published in book form.

* * *

Joseph Mathias Gérard de Rayneval is regarded by historians as a man of "valeur veritable" who well represented the first generation of "cette glorieuse famille" in French diplomacy.[133] His credo of diplomacy and the role of international law is well expressed in a passage quoted by an American specialist on the law of the sea: "the victor should speak in the language of moderation; the defeated in that of dignity; if the latter is humiliated by facts, he ought not to be by words; no important matter of discussion should remain uncertain, no word ought to furnish any doubt as to interpretation".[134]

---

[133] Masson, note 4 above, pp. 21, 24. Also see Nys, note 54 above, I, p. 295.
[134] See C. H. Stockton, *Outlines of International Law* [Chicago, [1914]), p. 375.

ON THE FREEDOM OF THE SEA

Joseph-Mathias Gérard de Rayneval

Translated from the French by

Peter Stephen Du Ponceau

VOLUME ONE

Presented to the American Philosophical Society
by the Translator 17 July 1840
with the Original

This translation was not intended for publication. Translating is one of my methods of studying. It may serve those who do not understand the original.

I have not translated the Supplement at the beginning of the Second Volume. It is an answer to Selden's *Mare Clausum*.[1] After Grotius I thought that nothing more need be said upon the Subject.

PSD

Philadelphia 13th July 1840

[1] In fact, Du Ponceau did translate the entire Supplement. One may conjecture that at some point he contemplated abridging the work by omitting the item in question, perhaps on the grounds of excessive duplication. However, the entire work is present here – [WEB].

THE AUTHOR'S PREFACE

In pursuing this inquiry into the important question of the freedom of the seas, I have, as much as possible, kept clear of the difficulties in which it has been involved by the practice of nations & the opinion of publicists. I have set aside the versatile & arbitrary policy of governments as well as the systems of theoretical writers, and confined myself exclusively to the principles of the Law of Nature & nations, so far as they relate or are applicable to the ocean.

That vast element which surrounds, and by its ramifications divides the continent, is free; all have a right to its enjoyment, it is in short, the common inheritance of mankind. Few, however, take the pains to inquire into the origin, nature, extent and effects of that freedom; it is asserted by a kind of instinct and by the force of habit and prejudice, as much as from real conviction. Be it my task, then to produce and establish that conviction in the minds of men; a task which I the more readily undertake, that no French writer, that I know of, has yet attempted to elucidate this important point of the Law of Nations, in the true understanding of which, France, as a maritime and commercial power, has always been so essentially concerned; but it has on the contrary been left entirely to foreign writers, who have written upon it more or less at large, but never without some degree of partiality.[1]

I am induced to proceed in this investigation by a consideration of another kind. On a careful search into ancient history, I have found no trace of the maritime jurisprudence of modern nations in time of war.

The Egyptians, Phoenicians, Carthaginians, Greeks, Romans, in short, all the maritime nations of Antiquity, were more or less engaged in commerce, and had a greater or less number of vessels of war in their service. Yet history makes no

[1] I must, however, distinguish among others the work of *Lampredi*, entitled *Du Commerce des Neutres en temps de guerre* ["Of the Commerce of Neutral Nations in Time of War"]. We are indebted to Mr. Peuchet for a translation of it into French, with valuable additions.

mention of private armed ships, nor of the search, capture or confiscation of neutral vessels, and when the empire of the seas is spoken of, it is only meant figuratively to express the superiority of a particular nation on that element, or the great extent of her prosperity and commerce. Thus Tyre, Corinth, Carthage, the Rhodians, and the Romans were successively said to have acquired the empire of the ocean.[2] The navigation of merchantmen was only disturbed by pirates against whom the government waged a war of extermination. Everybody knows with what success the Great Pompey attacked those lawless robbers. The Roman Emperors never thought of arrogating to themselves the domination of the seas. Witness the answer of Antonius to the petition of one Eudaemon of Nicomedia: "I am, indeed, the sovereign of the earth, but the law is the sovereign of the sea". *Ego quidem mundi dominus, Lex autem maris*. The Emperor Augustus had before given a similar decision.[3]

The precise time when a change took place in ancient maritime jurisprudence is not known; it is to be supposed that it followed the natural course of human institutions, and that as manners changed, the laws changed with them. The most ancient document relative to the new system that we are in possession of is the compilation known under the name of *Il consulato del mare*; but notwithstanding the researches of a very learned writer,[4] its author, date, and authenticity cannot be ascertained. It is, however, presumed to have been written either at Pisa or Barcelona. Be that as it may, it is certain that the ancient collection has nowhere the force of law, and that it is only quoted as well as the writers who have adopted its doctrines, such as Albericus Gentilis, Bynkershoek, Vattel, &c., by those governments whose maxims it countenances; and therefore the British Government frequently appeals to its authority with great respect.

---

[2] The history and character of that dominion have been perfectly well delineated by Mr. Malouet.

[3] Dig. *De lege Rhodia*, l. 9.

[4] Mr. Boucher, who has translated the *Consolato* into French from the oldest manuscript extant, has prefaced his translation with a very learned dissertation on the maritime law and customs of the Middle Ages.

Certain it is that the change which the maritime law has experienced was effected in a slow and gradual manner. The sea in proportion as it became more known, and as it offered a wider field to avarice and ambition for amassing wealth and conquering or rather usurping distant lands, became one of the principal objects of the policy of governments; that element was made the theatre of hostile aggressions as well upon neutrals and upon enemies; in a word, the Ocean which connects together the most distant nations ceased to be free; it was made subservient to the arbitrary views of maritime powers, and would long ago have experienced all the revolutions which have so often changed the face of the continent, had not nature itself placed insurmountable obstacles in the way of its conquest.

While there is nothing in the whole universe that does not acknowledge some primordial regulating principle, nothing in short that is not governed by some fixed rules of legislation, the ocean alone seems abandoned to the caprice of nations, to the instability, exaggeration and abuse of their views, pretensions, and power. I have undertaken to combat this unnatural system of arbitrary violence; I mean to set reason, principles, and the general interest of mankind in opposition to their passions and to partial interests ill understood, whence have originated an infinity of abuses, suggested by ambition and avarice and supported and cherished by the tyranny of lawless power. I am well aware of the strength which those abuses have acquired, and of the difficulty of an attempt to eradicate them. But fortunately they have not been always and everywhere the same, they have varied and still do very with times and circumstances, they exhibit shades and gradations which may be laid hold of with advantage and help to bring men nearer to a correct understanding of their common interest, which must necessarily to be the result of a proper combination and conciliation of the rights of all, and consequently is the only true source of concord and harmony among nations.

In the execution of the task which I have imposed upon myself, I have thought it proper to establish as a preliminary proposition, the liberty of the seas, founded on the very nature of that element; such is the object of the first part of this work; and in order to enable the reader fully to understand the question, I have, before endeavouring to argue in favor of my opinion, exhibited in opposition to each other, two eminent writers of different sentiments on the same subject; the one is Grotius, who wrote in support of the cause of freedom, and the other is Selden, his antagonist, who endeavoured to overthrow that system and wrote solely with that view.

Selden is not satisfied with maintaining that the sea is capable of being subjected to exclusive dominion; but he also undertakes to prove that his own country is entitled to the sovereignty of all the sea which surround it, even as far as America and the Poles. His *Mare clausum* is a remarkable instance of the powers of a strong mind stimulated by vanity, interest, and national feelings. Selden flattered the opinions and asserted the maxims of his own Government; he dedicated his book to King Charles the first, who so eagerly adopted its principles, that in the year 1619 he desired Carleton, his ambassador at The Hague, to complain of the States General of the audacity of Grotius who had been bold enough to maintain the freedom of the seas, and to require than an example should be made of him to deter others from doing the like in future: *et tamen aicbatis legatus, mei infortunii exemplo terreri alios debere, ceam sententiam tuerentur*. The doctrine of Selden was also that of Cromwell and his Parliament, and was the occasion of a war between the English Republic and that of the United Provinces. England wished to compel the Dutch, who wanted to remain independent, to acknowledge her claim to the Supremacy of the Seas (see Part I, Chap. 11, Note 28).

It is natural enough that those who think differently from Selden should consider his doctrine and that of his adherents as absurd or at least as obsolete, but upon such a subject, the opinions of individuals ought to have but very little weight. All nations have a direct interest in this controversy, because its fate depends entirely on the will of their rulers, and those in whose favour Selden wrote, have certainly never given up his doctrine, be it ever so erroneous; they have not and never will acknowledge any prescription against their claims: their power alone is, and ever will be, the measure of their rights, pretensions, and conduct.[5]

And let not what I have said be considered as the language of exaggeration. Grotius wrote his *Mare liberum* merely with a view to prove that Dutch vessels had a right to navigate freely in the Indian Seas: and yet that some nation, about twenty years ago, claimed the right of prohibiting the Spaniards from sailing to the Philippine Islands round the Cape of Good Hope. The Portuguese once pretended to exclude the Europeans from navigating the African Seas, towards the Bissago Islands; Queen Elizabeth of England caused some Hanseatic vessels to be seized in the very harbor of Lisbon for having dared to sail around Scotland without her leave; the Doge of Venice did solemnly wed the Adriatic, the Genoese boasted of being Lords of the Ligurian Sea, as far as the Island of Corsica. Would not Spain have assumed the exclusive dominion of the Sea of Mexico and even of the Pacific Ocean, had she been sufficiently strong to assert those pretensions with effect? Would not the Dutch have cut off the communication between the Moluccas and China? I do not speak of the wish so often manifested to transform the Baltic into a *mare clausum*.

---

[5] Can Selden's doctrine be looked upon as obsolete or abandoned by the Government of England, when we see William III assert it in a manifesto in which he reproached Louis XIV with having suffered his subjects to violate the sovereign rights of the Crown of England over the British Seas: "We have already shown what was understood under that pompous denomination."

And under the reign of Charles II, an English writer expresses himself as follows: "The ancient dominions of the King of England were, first England, and all the seas round about Great Britain and Ireland, and all the isles adjacent, even to the shore of all the neighboring nations; and our law saith, The Sea is of the liegance of the king, as well as the land; and as a result thereof, all ships of foreigners have antiently demanded leave to fish and pass in those seas, and do at this day lower their top sails to all the king's ships of war; and therefore children born upon these seas (as sometimes hath happened) are accounted natural born subjects to the King of England and need not any naturalization, as other born out of his dominions". *Anglia notitia, or The Present State of England.* By Edward Chamberlayne, Part I, B. 2, C. 2.

The peremptory assertions by which Selden endeavours to prove the pretended maritime dominion of England have not been refuted by any French writer, either contemporary or modern, that circumstance has induced me to analyse his dissertation, altho' of ancient date. Besides, I have thought that such a subject was more worthy of discussion than the true meaning of an Egyptian hieroglyphic, an ancient inscription, or an obscure passage from some Greek or Latin poet.

I hope, however, that the reader will forgive the length of the extract which I have made from Selden's work, as well as that of my notes. Having to contend with a celebrated author the avowed advocate of a particular doctrine, I thought myself bound to omit nothing by which that doctrine might be fairly tested; at the same time, I thought that impartiality required on my part the most scrupulous fidelity and exactness in the exposition of his facts and arguments, for Selden justly ranks among the first class of those writers who have been distinguished for their learning, acuteness, and ingenuity.

After all, whatever may be the opinion of the British Government on the subject of the maritime dominion which this writer ascribes to it, it is impossible to deny that it is in consequence of the extension which it has given to his doctrines that the principles relative to the natural freedom of the sea have been lost sight of, and to that we are to look for the primary cause of all the variations which those principles have experienced, and of the obstacles that have been placed in the way of neutral navigation in time of war. The geographical position of Britain between the Northern and Western seas, and the advantage which she enjoys of being entirely separated from the continent enable her to pursue without restraint the arbitrary measures which her political views, her commercial interest or her jealousy may suggest.[6]

To be convinced of this truth, it is only necessary to turn to the ancient as well as modern commercial treaties, and above all to the various ordinances, regulations and proclamations which

---

[6] It is evident that the measures which the British Cabinet is pursuing in the course of the present war are founded on this implied principle of maritime dominion or, rather, are that principle itself carried into practice.

every war has successively produced. It is certainly in that labyrinth that are to be found the principles on which rest the freedom of the sea and the rights of belligerents and neutrals. It is even impossible to discover there the traces of any certain fixed usage among nations. The law of treaties, or as it is called, conventional law, is as uncertain and variable as the source from whence it springs. Nor is its practice less subject to the same inconvenience; a practice which fluctuates with ever varying circumstances, and as the consciousness of power or the impulse of fear alternately prompt. Besides, if a power were disposed to adopt just and liberal principles, it would be diverted from its purpose by the fear of aiding the views or promoting the interest of its enemy. Thus the shackles and impediments of commerce gradually increase, all the seas are thrown into disorder and confusion, and transformed into a theatre of spoliation and plunder. For surely no other name can be given to that multitude of depredations which are daily committed at sea, and are attempted to be justified by ordinances and proclamations. In the vast solitude of the ocean, where power is not afraid of the accusing eye of witnesses, it freely gives a loose to its rapacity, the last shadow of suspicion or doubt, real or imaginary, is sufficient to justify its proceedings, by which the innocent navigator is made the victim of avarice under colour of the exercise of a just and lawful authority.

If in the actual state of things maritime jurisprudence is more uncertain, intricate and arbitrary than ever, and if it seems difficult to bring it back to its first principles, it is at least a laudable undertaking to endeavour to restore them to their primitive purity by separating them from the alloy which usage, treaties, circumstances and the passions of governments have amalgamated with them; for usage, however general, may be vicious, it may be the result of erroneous maxims. As to treaties, they are but partial stipulations, arising from the will of the contracting parties, and are but too often the result of superiority on the one side and weakness on the other. I do not speak of the influence of circumstances and passions, because it has no bounds. If I should be told that this is an idle undertaking because governments never will acknowledge any other guide but their power and interest, and that it is in vain to remind them of just principles, I answer that on this supposition the mariner's compass is a useless instrument to the unfortunate navigator exposed to the fury of a storm, for in that situation he cannot steer the course to which it points. The tempest which the conduct of governments has raised is the result of violated principles, therefore it is an additional reason at least to preserve them from total oblivion, to exhibit them to the world in their genuine purity, and to explain and develop them as fully and clearly as possible, for if they do not now produce fruits, circumstances may at some future day occur which will at least restore them to some degree of efficacy.

Such are the considerations which have induced me to write on maritime law, as far as it is connected with war; that will be the subject of the second part of this work, and as I have already observed, I have set aside all treaties, customs, partial laws and edicts, and even practice. I have confined myself to those principles of the law of nature and nations that are applicable to the sea; they are in my opinion the science to which we must necessarily recur, to be able to decide on the rights of nations and the conduct of governments, the law of nature is the key to that important science, and leads to it as certainly as arithmetic does to the most abstruse parts of geometry.

Undoubtedly, most of the principles which I have set forth are notwithstanding their self evidence, more or less in opposition not only to the law which customs and treaties have introduced, but also to most of the systems established by those who have written upon that subject. I also confess that they do not afford to a lawyer entrusted with the defense of a maritime cause, a fixed and invariable rule on which to ground his opinions and arguments. I know that he must look for those in the text of treaties and either diplomatic acts, or in the usage of nations. But if public documents are silent or equivocal, or if the case before him has no precedent in usage or has not been ruled by authoritative decisions, if the facts are intricate, complicated or obscure, if they are qualified for attenuating or aggravating circumstances, or if their real character cannot be easily defined, from what source shall in the case the lawyer draw his arguments? Where shall the judge look to for the grounds of his decision? And where are those to be found, if not in the law of nature and in the dictates of reason? Where will the physician perplexed by the intricacy and uncertain symptoms of a disease seek for a light to guide him but in the theory or fundamental principles of his art? If he has no resource left but practice or the usual routine of his profession, his patient will be in great danger of falling a victim to his ignorance.

As to the statesman, he must be well acquainted with the fundamental principles of social order and judge of things, not from facts merely, but from their nature. Saving such deviations as public interest or other important considerations may imperiously require, unless he pursues this method, how will he be able to decide upon the rights of belligerents and neutrals? How will he undertake to affirm that such a national aims at usurping the dominion of the sea, and that an author is endeavouring to maintain its freedom? He will have no rule to go by but arbitrary will and caprice, and his government shall bear the blame of his incapacity.

It will, no doubt, be remarked that I do not quote any authors in support of my doctrine. The reason is that the truth or fallacy of principles lie (if I can so express myself) in the principles themselves. Genuine principles are self-evident propositions, and whatever is not so, falls within the circle of hypotheses, systems, and opinions, about which men may either agree or differ, and may dispute for a thousand years, without understanding or agreeing with each other. I thought it best, therefore, to lay down my doctrines, without calling to my aid those who have written before me, that is today, without an affected display of erudition which the reader does not stand in need of to induce him to adopt truths which naturally occur to every man capable of reflection, who is free from prejudice and has sufficient courage to enter upon and pursue the analysis of principles; but I thought myself bound to notice and combat some of those writers who have opposed the freedom that I contend for, or at least who have narrowed the sphere of its effects, such as Bynkershoek, Vattel, Jenkinson, &c. If I have quoted Valin, the commentator of our ordinance of 1681, it was merely to correct an error into which he has fallen. I pass over in silence several of very estimable foreign writers, because wherever they serve from the principles which I have laid down, they fall in with the opinions of the authors above cited.

The reader will also observe that I have taken particular pains to refute the opinions of the Right Honorable Charles Jenkinson, afterwards Lord Hawkesbury, and since Earl of Liverpool. I have undertaken that task because his doctrines are those of the British Government and are in direct opposition with the principles that I maintain. And that I may not be suspected of weakening his arguments, I have thought proper to give a literal translation of his discourse at the end of my work, to which I have subjoined some notes. Thus the reader will be able to judge of my impartiality with a thorough knowledge of the subject, as well as of the merits of my refutation; and the partisans of the English system of jurisprudence will have no reason to charge me with having kept back or weakened any of the facts or arguments on which it rests.

I am well aware, after all, that my opinions will have no weight or influence whatever on their governments whose views or interest they may thwart, but they will at least help to enable others to judge of their conduct, and it is not altogether impossible that the constant repetition and wide spreading of good principles, may prepare a happy revolution in the maritime system of Europe. The French government had once begun to lay the principle foundations of such a system; but those foundations have been unfortunately destroyed.

Napoleon, by his wisdom and power has decided the fate of the continent; he has destroyed all the germs of dissentions and wars: the only kind of glory which yet remains for him to acquire is that of being the author of a maritime code which shall firmly establish the liberty of the seas, on a just and immutable basis, and afford complete security to navigation and commerce in the four quarters of the globe.

OF THE FREEDOM OF THE SEA

PART I.

OF THE FREEDOM OF THE SEA GENERALLY CONSIDERED

Chapter 1.

Of this Pretended Right of Dominion of the Sea – Opinions of Grotius and Selden – Refutation of the Latter

Among those who have been engaged in the discussion of this important question two eminent writers of the seventeenth century are deserving of particular notice: Grotius, who asserted the freedom of the Seas, & Selden who endeavoured to destroy it, doubtless because he was persuaded his System favoured the political views of his own country.[1] I have therefore thought

[1] Grotius and Selden — I only quote the doctrines of these two writers, because they were the first who thoroughly investigated the subject. Those who followed them were but their commentators. For the same reason, I make no mention of Puffendorf nor of Bynkershoek. The former in his discussion betrays much indecision and, of course, does not rest his argument on any of those fundamental principles to which all questions relative to the law of nature and nations are to be traced back as the only source from whence their solution naturally flows. Sometimes he sides with Grotius, sometimes with Selden, and introduces political considerations into a discussion to which State policy is a stranger. True

proper to exhibit at the head of my investigation the opposite opinions of these two writers. I begin with Grotius, and in order that his doctrine may be clearly and fully understood, I state it here in his own words (*De jure Belli ac Pacis*. L. 11, c. 2, §3):

"We affirm", says that celebrated author, "that none can have a property in the Sea, whether considered in the whole or in respect to its principal parts; and because some people are willing to allow this with regard to private persons but not with regard to States & nations, we will prove the contrary; first by an argument drawn from moral reason, which is that the cause which obliged mankind to desist from the custom of using things in common has nothing at all to do, in this question, for the Sea is of so vast an extent, that it is sufficient for all the uses that

---

policy, indeed, when directed by justice and not by jealousy, rapacity, and ambition, is but a corollary of the genuine principles of the law of nations. As to Bynkershoek, he rather inclines to Selden's system, he admits the possibility of the private dominion of the sea and lays considerable stress upon its utility.

It may not be amiss to say something of two other writers who advocated Selden's doctrine. Welwood, an Englishman whose book is entitled *De Dominio maris juribusque ad dominium spectantibus*; and Hurgus, an Italian, who in imitation of this prototype, wrote a treatise on the dominion of the sea in general, with a view to assert the claim of the Republic of Genoa to that of the Ligurian Sea, which he extends as far as the Island of Corsica. The title of his work is *De Dominio Serenis Genuensis Reipublicae in mare Ligustico.* I ought also to mention Albericus Gentilis, whose doctrine Selden adopted and enlarged. I do not analyze the works of these writers because they repeated the arguments of each other. I cannot, however, help observing that Welwood grounds particularly his opinion of the divisibility and dominion of the sea on several passages of the Holy Scriptures and almost would have been considered an article of faith. What is still more singular is that he accuses of avarice all those who oppose his favorite doctrine. His anathema falls particularly upon the Dutch nation: "I except", says he, "only one nation, which tho' her native land abound with milk, is nevertheless indebted to other countries for all other necessities and is even enriched and become haughty with the spoils of all nations, having despised all distinctions in her free or open sea, *in mari suo libero*, and has even had the boldness to style herself invincible". Chap. 1, p. 9. This censure is in contradiction with the pretended aspect of all the nations of Europe on which Selden so strangely relies.

nations can draw from thence, either as to water, fishing, or navigation: the same might also be alleged of the air, if we could put it to any use without being placed ourselves on the surface of the earth. But this is necessary in order to enjoy the benefit of it, and therefore fowling, for instance, is permitted so far only as the owner of the land thinks fit".

"There is also", continues Grotius, "a physical reason which forbids that the Sea, thus considered, should be anybody's property, because possession can only be taken of things that are limited but liquids having no bounds of their own, can never be possessed, unless they are enclosed by something else, as lakes and ponds; thus rivers are capable of being reduced into possession, because confined within their banks. But the sea is not contained in the earth; for it is equal to it, if not greater; as the ancients believed, and therefore affirmed, that the earth was contained within it".[2]

This writer goes still farther in his treatise entitles *Mare liberum*. I give his own expression: "We ground our opinion on that most certain, self-evident and immutable principle of the primitive law of nations, that very nation has a right to resort and trade to other countries. God himself proclaims this truth by the voice of nature".[3]

---

[2] *His positis, dicimus mare sumptum aut sub ratione integri, aut sub ratione praecipuarum partium, in proprium jus abire non posse, quod quia de privates quidam concedent, non de populis, probamus primum ex morali ratione: quia causa ob quam a communion discessum es, hic cessat: est enim tanta maris magnitude, ut ad quemois usum omnibus populis sufficiat, ad aquam hauriendam, ad piscatum, ad navigationem: idem dicendum esset de aere, si quis ejus usus esse posset, ad quem terrae usus non esset necessaries u test ad aucupia; unde illa legem accipiant ab eo qui in terra imperium habet.*

Est et naturalis ratio quae mare consideratum ut diximus, proprium fiery vetat: quia occupation non procedit nisi in re terminate: liquida, quia per se non terminantur, occupari nequeunt, nisi ut contenta in re alia, quomodo lacus et stagna occupata sunt, item flumina, quia ripis continentur. Mare vero terra non continetur, pars terrae, aut terrae majus: unde terram mari contineri voters dixere.

[3] *Fundamentum struemus hanc juris gentium quod primariam vocant regulam certissimam, cujus perspicua et immutabilis est ratio: licere*

Therefore, according to the opinion of Grotius, neither the whole, nor the principal parts of the sea, can become the property of one or more sovereigns; for the motive derived from the principles of moral reason which induced mankind to give up the possession [of] the earth in common, is not applicable to the ocean. Indeed, the extent of that element is such, that it is sufficient for the wants of all nations. The same might be said of the air, if it could be made use of independent of the earth. There is moreover a physical reason which militates against the doctrine of the dominion of the sea; and that is that nothing can be exclusively possessed, but what is limited and immoveable; but the waters do not come under this description unless they are bounded like ponds, lakes, and rivers, while the sea cannot be so limited, being as extensive and perhaps more so than the land which it surrounds. Such is the doctrine of the Dutch writer.

I shall not exhibit in opposition to it, that of his antagonist, but I do not intend to follow him in all the arguments that he makes use of in support of it, lest I should find myself bewildered in a labyrinth of erudition which I think unnecessary as a subject on which reason alone must decide. I shall confine myself to giving the substance of his elaborate work.

Selden divides natural law into two branches, one which he calls obligatory or imperative, and the other potential or permissive. The former commands and prohibits, the latter neither prohibits nor commands, but permits. The earth and the sea are within this last predicament, and therefore the earth, which originally was possessed in common, may lawfully have been divided and partitioned into separate estates. The same principle, he contends, may be applied to the sea.

It is true that the Scripture, when it speaks of the division of the earth among the descendants of Noah, does not particularly mention the sea; but it says nothing that militates against the principle for which Selden contends, and there are even some passages which favour it. The rules and principles of the permissive law of nature, respecting the dominion of the sea, must be sought for in the customs and laws of the most

---

cuivis genti quamvis alteram adire, cumque ea negociari. Deus ipse hoc per naturam loquitur.

celebrated and most civilized nations, ancient as well as modern. Now we find that those laws and customs, far from being opposed to the dominion of the sea, do on the contrary admit of it. Of this, the fabulous ages offer numerous testimonies. The Greeks, as well as the Eastern nations, acknowledged the right of possessing the sea, and so did the Carthaginians and Romans. Similar instances are to be found among modern nations; the Venetians claimed the dominion of the Adriatic, and the Genoese that of the Ligurian Sea. The Tuscans, the Roman States, and the Portugese, not only admit the right of acquiring the dominion of the sea, but even have positive laws by which they pretend to attribute to themselves that of the Sea of Guinea, India, and Spain considers the sea as common to all, yet several Spanish writers maintain that it may become the property of one or more States. Neither the written nor the customary law of France militate against the right of acquiring this dominion; and lastly, that right has been sanctioned by Denmark, Sweden, and the Ottoman Porte.

After this long enumeration of precedents, Selden proceeds to answer objections.

[*First objection*]. The first which he takes notice of is founded on the right of passage which merchants and others freely exercise over the sea. This universal freedom of navigation, it is said, flows from the very nature of that element. It is sanctioned by the authority of publicists, necessarily excludes the idea of private dominion.

Answer. In answer to this, Selden acknowledges that the laws of humanity, indeed, enjoin the exercise of hospitality towards strangers who ought not to be interrupted in their lawful voyages; but in this opinion, this condescension does not derogate from the principle of the dominion of the sea because the right of navigation is to be assimilated to those servitudes, rights of way, passage, and the like which are attached to the tenure of landed property and to those passages which are sometimes granted by sovereigns thro' parts of their territories and yet do not militate against the right of private dominion on land, but rather serve to confirm it; for those special rights, or to speak more properly, easements, are common subject to such restrictions as the sovereign of the country chooses to impose, [for example, the Alps or the Pyrenees].

Second objection. The sea from its very nature is incapable of private dominion, as well because of its fluidity, from which results a state of perpetual motion as of the impossibility of establishing fixed bounds and limits on its surface, without which the extent of private property therein cannot be ascertained. Besides, the sea, from its vast extent, is always sufficient to supply the wants of all mankind.

Answer. Rivers are considerably more fluid than the sea; there is a declivity in their beds which makes them constantly run forwards towards it, and the sea, compared to them, appears in a manner to be still and immoveable. But admitting the sea to be ever so fluid, it is certain that its bed remains always stationary, altho' its waters are constantly shifting and are indeed in a state of perpetual motion. The same may be said of rivers, and yet it has never been pretended that the fluidity of their waters did in any manner impair the right of exclusive dominion over them. The beds of rivers are everywhere considered as belonging to the respective sovereigns of the countries thro' which they flow, altho' their waters are freely conceded to public use.

It is the same with the bed or bottom of the sea. Hence, as island rising on its surface belongs to the first occupant, altho' the sea and the land that it covers belonged before to the generality of mankind. Thus, the dominion of rivers having never been disputed, on what ground can that of the sea be contested? For the sea is but a river or a lake differing from others only in extent, which makes no difference with respect to the question of dominion. The same reasoning is applicable to air which in fact is infinitely more fluid than water and is continually changing. But the space which it occupied belongs to the owner of the soil, and his right to raise his buildings as high as he pleased, is unlimited; hence the legal adage: *Cujus est solum, ejus est usque ad calum.* Finally, says Selden, the subtleties which are opposed to the doctrine of the dominion of the sea were first invented by those philosophers (particularly Heraclitus and Epicharmus) who taught that everything is so changed, altered, and renewed every moment that nothing in the world continues at this instant the same that it was the moment before.

Third objection. The nonexistence of boundaries in the sea, its vast extent, and inexhaustible abundance show that it cannot be the subject of private dominion.

Answer. In order to give a clear answer to the first branch of this objection, the sea must be considered in a twofold point of view; first with respect to its shores, and next with regard to the main ocean. I cannot see why the shores should not be reputed lawful bounds, whereon to ground separate rights of dominion in the sea, as well as ditches, hedges, mounds, and other similar things used by surveyors in the boundaries of landed estates. It is true than an eminent writer, Grotius, says, that according to natural reason, the sea cannot become the subject of private property, because nothing can be occupied that is not bounded; and liquid things, not being bounded of themselves, cannot be possessed except when contained within some other thing, as lakes, ponds, and rivers, and the sea being equal in size and even larger than the earth, cannot be said to be contained or bounded by it, so that the ancients have even said that the earth is contained within the ocean, as if it were an island.

But even admitting that the sea is contained within the earth, I do not see, continues Selden, why the thing containing should not in truth be bounded by the thing contained, as well as the thing contained by that which contains it. May not a lesser body that is spherical or of any other form when contained by a greater which is every way contiguous to it be said to bound and limit the concave of the greater body, as well as this to limit the convex of the lesser? For thus concave and convex bodies do mutually bound and limit each other. Such was Scaliger's meaning, when he said, speaking of the sea: *Non ab altero alterum ita continetur; quin illud quoque contineat.* The one is not so contained by the other, but that it also contains it. The sea and land mutually embrace each other with crooked windings and turnings, this with peninsular and promontories butting forth, and creeks bending inwards, that washing up its waves about are the passages of its vast body. So that it is evident that the one indifferently sets bounds to the other, not otherwise than ponds, lakes, rivers, and their respective banks and shores. This is made still more evident by the Caspian and Mediterranean Seas. Since Hercules or, as the Arabians say, Alexander the Great, did by cutting the mountain, let in the Atlantic Ocean thro' the Straights of Gibraltar. The same idea is still more clearly expressed in holy Scripture: *Circumdabat mari terminum suum, et legam ponebat aquis, ne transirent fines suos.* "He surrounded the sea with its limits and gave his decree unto the waters, that they should not pass their bounds" (Prov. §29). Nor is there more difficulty in assigning limits to the main ocean than to those seas which we have just mentioned. Everywhere it exhibits high rocks, shelves, promontories, and islands scattered up and down, from when as well direct lines, as crooked windings and turnings and angles, may be made use of for the boundary of a territory in the sea.

We have moreover the experience of the mariner's compass, the degrees of latitude and longitude and the doctrine of triangles arising therefrom. In the American colonies, the degrees of latitude and longitude determine the limits of the respective possessions. The same method might be adopted as to the sea, for without recurring to other instances, we have a treaty made in 1630 between Great Britain and Spain, in which the equinoctial line is the appointed boundary in the sea. Thus, the promontories of Sarpedon and Calycodonus in Cilicia, were recognized as boundaries of maritime dominion in a treaty between the Romans and Antoichus, being of Syria. Similar limits were assigned by Pope Alexander the Fifth between the Spaniards and the Portugese. A line was supposed to be drawn from pole to pole, and that imaginary line was to separate the conquests made by the Spaniards from those made by the Portugese. Again, even those who contend for the freedom of the sea admit the right of exclusive dominion over it to a certain distance from the shores. Bartholus extends it to one hundred miles and Bodin to sixty. Now the extent of dominion can only be bounded on one side by an imaginary line, and this mode of limiting the sea must either be admitted or every pretension to jurisdiction beyond low water mark must be entirely abandoned.

As to the argument which is drawn from the vast extent of inexhaustible abundance of the sea, it is, continues Selden, of very little weight in solving the present question. For, says he, admitting the sea to be inexhaustible, so that he, who shall appropriate it to himself can receive no damage from other men's using it, the same thing may be said of fire, which is not denied to be a proper subject of exclusive property. And surely it cannot be said to impair in the last the right of the owners of a fire or candle that another should light his from it. He nevertheless still remains the sole and only lawful owner of his fire or of his candle. But even if it were otherwise, it is not the less certain that the sea by reason of other men's fishing, navigation, and commerce, becomes the worse for him that owns it, and for those who enjoy it in his right. So that less profit accrues to them than they might otherwise receive, which most evidently appears in the use of those seas which produce pearls, coral, and other similar things. The abundance of and the productions of those seas is lessened every hour no otherwise than that of mines of metal, quarries of stone, or gardens when their treasures and fruits are taken away. This is equally applicable to fisheries of every description. The sea is no more inexhaustible than the rest of the globe, however extensive and abundant, it is still but a part of the whole. Therefore, there are not arguments which at all mitigate against the right of dominion over the sea. Nor can this right be denied unless we also call in question that of the Roman Emperors to universal Empire and reject the ancient inscription made in honor of Augustus: *Orbe mari et terra pacato, Jano clauso &c.* Peace being restored to the world by sea and land, he shut up the Temple of Janus &c.

Having thus exhausted his subject on the ground of principle, as well as of precedent, Selden concludes with undertaking a direct refutation of the doctrine of Grotius. But as that refutation consists of the same arguments that he had already deduced, and which he again sets forth somewhat more at large, a refutation of them would be as useless as tedious. We think it right, however, to insert here literally the concluding period of his argument.

"Upon the whole, and after duly weighing all that we know of the customs of different ages and nations, and of the civil as well as conventional law of a great number of them, no one, I think, will question but that there remains not either in the nature of the sea itself, or in the law, either divine natural or of nations, anything so militating against the dominion which I contend for, as to show that it is not to be admitted on the clearest principles of law, and that all seas whatever are not on every principle capable of being subjected to private dominion, which is what I had undertaken to demonstrate".[4]

It cannot escape observation on comparing the works of Grotius and Selden that the former in his defense of the liberty of the sea is remarkable for the beauty and plainness of his argument, while the latter in his answer seems to have exhausted all the means which art, ingenuity, science, and erudition could supply him with. The reason of it is evident; the one found his doctrine fully proved and easy to be established by the law of nature and the usages of nations, while the other, having a more difficult task to perform, was obliged to have recourse to extraneous aids which his adversary did not stand in need of; this sufficiently accounts for the differing length of the one and the comprehensive brevity of the other.[5] We shall now

---

[4] *Caeterium universis quae hactenus extat saeculorum gentiumque moribus, de jure tam plurimorum civili quam communi seu interveniente deprumpta sunt, rite perpensis, nemo (puto) dubitavit quin neque in natura ipsius maris, neque in jure sive divino, sive naturali, sive gentium quid maneat, quod ita dominio ejus privato reluctetur, ut id non jure omni modo, atque exploratissimo queat aditti; adeoque quin jure qualicumque dominii privati capax sit qalecumque mare, quod erat demonstrandum.*

[5] For this observation I have Selden's own authority. He says in his Preface that he was obliged to search for authorities into private and public libraries and among the records of Parliament and those that are deposited in the Tower of London. He carried his investigation back to the times which preceded the conquest of England by Julius Caesar and, in short, laid under contribution poets, philosophers, and historians; Lucan, Virgil, Seneca, Cicero, Pliny, Tacitus, &c. Prolixity cannot be avoided when a pre-established system which does not carry conviction along with it must be supported by authorities drawn from so many sources. I say a

endeavour to enable our readers to form a correct judgment between these two writers. And that we may not appear guilty, at least, of willful omission, we shall trace the subject back to the origin of things, for that is also the origin of the rights of mankind with respect to the land as well as the ocean.

But before we enter upon this important discussion, we ought to observe that Selden has principally drawn his doctrine from the customs and usages of various nations, ancient as well as modern, which customs he assumes to have been founded on the principles of universal law and thence infers that the right to acquire and preserve the exclusive dominion of the sea is proved beyond controversy. But altho' he appears to have ransacked history for precedent, he has not been able to shew that his doctrine is at all supported by general usage or the customary law of nations; for usage cannot be inferred from scattered insulated facts, even supposing them to be accurately stated. Nations cannot be bound unless the general assent concurs with the frequency of precedents. These principles are immutable and shall be our apology for not entering into a discussion of the facts cited by Selden, altho' it would not be difficult to prove that he has misconstrued and misapplied them. But let us enter at once into the consideration of our subject.

In the beginning the earth and the sea were common to all. The land gradually ceased to be so because man compelled to cultivate the earth justly wished to appropriate to himself the spot of ground which his labour had made productive. Such is the origin of exclusive property, which after having occasioned many contests, gave birth to civil society and laws. The same thing could not happen with respect to the sea, which by its nature is not susceptible of cultivation or improvement. The same reason therefore which originally gave a joint title to the exclusive possession of portions of the earth is not applicable to the ocean. Nature has done everything for that element, and man cannot improve it by art or labour; its spontaneous productions are formed, grow, and increase without his aid; he has nothing to do but to take and gratefully to enjoy.

---

pre-established system, for Selden calls it so himself in his dedication to King Charles I.

Among the various gifts which the sea bestows on mankind, fish was undoubtedly the first which attracted their attention and which they were eager to partake of; but the inexhaustible abundance of that nourishment which the sea constantly affords, must have taught them that the exclusive possession of that element, even tho' they might have believed it as easy to be secured as that of the land, offered to them no object of real utility; for they must have observed that fish reproduced itself without the assistance of man, while the earth, without cultivation, refused to yield its treasures.

The nature of things, therefore, was the cause that the earth was progressively divided into separate estates and that the sea remained common. We are now to consider whether it is possible to change that primitive state of things with respect to the ocean and admitting that it could be done, whether it would be useful or expedient?

The earth, as it appears, is a fixed immoveable solid body and therefore is capable of being meted and bounded and actually permanently occupied. Were its surface of a different nature from that of its bottom, or detached from it, or were it moveable, fluid, erratic like the waves of the sea, it could not be parceled out, inhabited nor cultivated, and such is the physical state of the ocean. It presents an immense surface in constant motion and agitation. It does not afford to man a safe dwelling or asylum, a regular supply of aliments, nor the means of obtaining it by cultivation. Hence it is natural to believe that the sea was at first abandoned on account of its sterility, and that it was even looked upon as dangerous and likely at some time or other to submerge the land and its inhabitants.

But men[6] in the process of time accustomed themselves to that element, and they must at length either by this effect of chance or of some other circumstance have discovered its destination and its use. From this twofold source we shall endeavour to draw the solution of the problem which we are

[6] I do not take here into consideration the knowledge which was revealed to the first man and which he transmitted to his posterity. I am only considering the probable progression of the human mind by natural means alone independent of the aid of revelation.

now discussing, and not like Selden, from the equivocal usages and customs of nations either ancient or modern.

We must in the first place inform ourselves that we only mean to speak of the open sea and not of those parts which wash the coasts of the continent and islands; for it is generally admitted that those parts are dependent on territorial jurisdiction This principle has been introduced by the usage of nations and is an exception to the general rule, which establishes the freedom of the sea, but it does not militate against it because the waters which wash the shores being capable of permanent protection, are likewise capable of being exclusively owned.

As to the high sea, Selden endeavours to prove that it may be divided into separate dominions by fixed and immoveable limits. And the means that he points out for that purpose are rocks, sand banks, promontories, and islands, lines and triangles, degrees of latitude and longitude, the mariner's compass, and the immobility of the bottom of the sea. We must willingly admit the use that may be made of all these for the mensuration of the sea; we will even concede that the ocean may be partitioned off with mathematical precision, nay, we will go so far as to agree that the dominion of the sea may be secured with as much facility as that of the fast land: but after this being admitted, we must next inquire what fair and honest advantage may be drawn, not by mankind at large, but by a particular State or country from an established dominion upon a portion of the high sea? I cannot suppose that the securing of an exclusive trade with distant countries, or the right of laying foreign ships under contribution, or compelling them to purchase licenses, will be contended for as legitimate objects. I shall not therefore take into consideration the monopoly that would result from that order of things. I shall seek for other objects of public utility in the exclusive dominion of the ocean, which I shall for that purpose consider in a threefold point of view, to wit, in relation to its surface, depth, and bottom.

The only advantage that the surface of the sea offers is navigation, or the means of a direct intercourse between the different parts of the globe. That, indeed, is one of the greatest blessings that the Almighty Lord has bestowed upon mankind. Navigation brings nations nearer to each other and enables them to partake of the various productions of all countries and climates. Without navigation, what would be the relations of Western Europe with Africa, India, and China? What communication would the vast continent of America have with the rest of the world? How would the Northern nations be able to carry their produce and manufactures to those of the Western and Southern regions? But great and invaluable as are the advantages which the surface of the sea offers as a means of intercourse between the inhabitants of remote countries, there is none to be derived from its exclusive possession. The sea is of such vast extent, that it is impossible for the ships of one nation to be an obstacle to the navigation of those of another; it may even be affirmed that all the large and small vessels of the four parts of the globe might navigate at the same time on the surface of the ocean without disturbing or even, perhaps, meeting one another. It is clear, therefore, that as far as respects navigation, the exclusive dominion of the open sea offers no object of advantage or utility that any nation or government will be willing avowedly to contend form. If anyone, however, should be to regard less of character as to venture to assert a claim to exclusive navigation for the sake of securing to itself a monopoly of trade, I would say to that ambitious nation, "Take then the whole sea to yourselves, if nothing less will suffice to satisfy your unbounded rapacity, but be sure that you are able to protect it in such a manner as to maintain it against all the world, which, if you can effect, you will, indeed, by the tyrants but not the lawful sovereigns of the sea; you will only have a precarious possession founded on nothing but your superior force, which a storm may at any time annihilate, and hurl you in a moment from your usurped throne, for know that the winds and waves are combined in close and perpetual alliance against you".

But, it will be said, that the bosom of the ocean offers in the fisheries an invaluable source of profit and riches and that of these, at least, exclusive possession may be obtained. I grant that the fisheries are an object of immense value, but I do not see in that a reason why they should be exclusively possessed. I might rest my argument on the eternal, immutable principle of natural law, that it is not lawful to derive a profit to ourselves from the detriment of others. But I have no need of recurring to first principles so long as it is not proved that some advantage is to be derived from the exclusive right of fishing or that some detriment will result from competition. You should make it appear that it will either hinder you from fishing, that it will destroy the fish, or at least lessen its quantity and thereby deprive you of the means of subsistence. But fishing has been practiced ever since the seas have been frequented and it does not appear that any species of fish has been destroyed or even diminished. The most important fisheries are those of the code, whale, and herring. Those species of fish abound in particular latitudes and nowhere else. The codfish is caught on the banks of Newfoundland and in the Gulf of St. Lawrence. The principal whale fisheries are in the seas adjacent to Greenland in Hudson's Bay and along some of the coasts of South America; and altho' that fishery be open to all nations, it has not yet appeared that the quantity of that species of fish has experienced any diminution; on the contrary, it is the number of whalers which has decreased in consequence of the little profit which that employment affords. As to herring, it is so very abundant and prolific that were it not for the quantity which is daily taken and many other causes of destruction, it would at last encumber the sea. Besides, the herring is a wandering fish, which often shifts its course, and it is not even known from what climates it proceeds in columns towards the South. What nation then could intercept it, so as to secure that fishery to itself exclusively of all others?[7] And what would be the effect of that exclusion, if it could be carried into effect, but to diminish the quantity at market of a valuable article of food at the expense of all Europe. We do not speak of any of the other species of fish which are taken along the coasts by their respective inhabitants for immediate use, but only observe that foreign fishermen are permitted to come and catch fish without any difficulty, and that

---

[7] Everybody is acquainted with the controversies in which the Dutch were involved by Great Britain on the subject of the fishery on the coast of Scotland; the fishery itself was not the real cause of those quarrels; they were but a pretext to cover the jealousy which the activity, industry and prosperity of that nation had excited. It would have been better for the English to imitate than to disturb them.

it has not yet been thought necessary to expel them for feat of a scarcity: which would however be very natural, if their concurrence were detrimental to the national fishery. A particular remark occurs here on the subject of the cod fishery. It is as I have just observed, principally carried on off the banks of Newfoundland, at no great distance from that island which belongs to Great Britain; yet notwithstanding their proximity to the British shores, England has never claimed them as a part of her exclusive dominions: it would not, however, be very difficult for her to draw an imaginary line from the island to the banks.

I proceed now to consider what advantages may be derived from the exclusive possession of the land which the sea covers, or, in other words, of the bottom of the sea, from thence mankind draws coral, pears, and some other articles of a similar nature. Selden pretends that competition could produce a diminution of the quantity of those articles and, of course, would be detrimental to the exclusive possessor of the soil on which they are found. This assertion is certainly not founded in fact, but if it were, it is to be observed that coral and pearls are not necessaries of life, but articles of luxury, which cannot furnish an argument in favor of destroying the inalienable rights of the human race upon the ocean. What! Because some parts of the sea feed the insect which produces coral, or furnish the oyster which produces pearls, are navigation and fishing to be converted into monopolies? Such an assertion is surely not worthy of a serious refutation, for it proves that its author was not anxious to discover truth, but endeavoured by every possible subtlety to support his pre-established system. But, after all, admitting even the whole of Mr. Selden's argument as applicable to fisheries of every description, admitting that they can only be carried on to advantage by means of an exclusive monopoly, it may still be asked how that argument is to be applied to navigation in general and in support of the doctrine of the dominion of the sea? The greatest number of those who are engaged in navigation, whether merchants or seamen, have nothing to do with fishing. Their object is not to catch fish, but to carry on commerce, or fight their enemies. They cannot therefore do any injury to or lessen the quantity of the fish and other productions of the sea. And consequently there can be no motive or pretence for interrupting or subjecting the sea, as far as respects them, to exclusive dominion.[8] We do not mean to apply these observations to those parts of the sea which are considered within the territorial limits of maritime States; we only contend for the liberty of fishing and navigation on the high sea, beyond all legal, jurisdictional limits.

Having as we believe sufficiently refuted the arguments founded on the utility[9] of the dominion of the sea, we will now proceed to consider that dominion in a more general point of view without regard to its utility or expediency.

We will, for the sake of argument, suppose that the high sea is capable of exclusive dominion and will ask by what means such dominion may lawfully be acquired between independent nations? The first step, no doubt, must be to occupy and establish an actual firm possession with an intent permanently to retain it. I admit that such a possession of solid land will give a title by usucaption and finally by prescription; but what are the means by which a nation amidst storms, winds, and waves may obtain such a firm, permanent, uninterrupted, undisturbed possession of the fluctuating elements as will amount to usucaption? And if it should success so far, what Code shall sanction and what tribunal shall enforce the prescriptive title? Let us remember that the right of navigating the sea, as Selden himself acknowledges, is merely permissive (*jus permissivum*); that consequently a nation may use it or not without waiving her right, or without being presumed to have abandoned or transferred it to the first occupant. Thus, the plea of prescription would be defective in its very foundation because it supposes not only a bona fide possession, but likewise a real or at least presumed waiver on the part of those who were equally entitled? Now as to such rights as are only permissive, a mere presumption of waiver or consent is inadmissible by the civil law and much less between independent nations, who neither

---

[8] The northern seamen do not go into the Mediterranean to gather coral, nor do those of the south go into the Baltic for yellow amber. This reflection was alone sufficient to dispel Selden's fears on this account.

[9] Utility is the great and irresistible argument adduced by Bynkershoek in favor of the exclusive dominion of the sea.

acknowledge the civil law nor the doctrine of prescription, and who have no common judge. We will put a case: France, by virtue of the Treaty of Utrecht, and all the other subsequent treaties, has the right to fish on the coasts of Newfoundland. Let us suppose that the French for several successive years or during such a long space of time as you may be pleased to imagine abstained from the exercise of that right; can it be for a moment believed that the British Government would think itself authorized to expel them from that fishery on the ground of prescription? Most certainly it could not entertain such a preposterous idea, or else, if it should commit any aggression, it would provoke a war evidently unjust. And yet it would act in conformity with Selden's principles. Not long ago (in 1786) a discussion of that kind took place between Spain and the United Provinces of the Netherlands on the establishment of the Company of Philippine Islands. The Dutch attempted to prevent the Spaniards from sailing to the East Indies round the Cape of Good Hope; they rested their pretended right not on the principles of the English writer, but on treaties and the repeated assent of the Spanish court. But both these grounds were so evidently unfounded that the claims of the Dutch could not be admitted; they were of course rejected, not only because the treaties were wrongly interpreted, but also because it was attempted to apply them to one of the largest portions of the Atlantic.

Perhaps it will be said that a nation may maintain her dominion over the sea by laws and penalties, but it must be observed, first, that such dominion (admitting it to be physically possible), if it is not assented to by the other nations, can only be maintained by force, and that force may destroy it. In the next place, in order to be able to inflict the punishment, the offender must be taken in the very act; it is therefore necessary to have always and everywhere ships stationed on the high sea to prevent other nations from transgressing the imaginary limits of lines and triangles. But a storm will be sufficient to drive away the guard ship from her station, and open a free passage to the prohibited vessels. Thus it is that a vicious principle never fails to lead to absurd consequences.

To make an end of this difficulty, we say that the natural rights of mankind are the foundation of the law of nations, that whenever some parts of those rights have been given up, it has only been in favor of public authority and for the sake of maintaining peace and social order; with this single exception individuals and nations have preserved their primitive rights. But social order does not necessarily require that nations should renounce in favour of one another the right freely to navigate on the high seas and to take fish, coral, and pearl oysters. If such a renunciation is not necessary, if it would not be productive of any real advantage or utility, it cannot therefore be presumed, and every attempt against the freedom of navigation and the universal right of fishing would be an act of violence, an usurpation, and a lawful cause of war.

All that we have said in refutation of the theory of Selden and his adherents seems to render it unnecessary for us to examine into the possibility of partitioning the high sea and dividing it by fixed metes and bounds. We think, however, that it will not be useless to offer some remarks upon the subject.

Our author, as we have already observed, speaks of elevations, promontories, islands, the mariner's compass, lines, triangles, the degrees of latitude and longitude, and pretends that it would be as easy by those means to draw a straight line from one continent to the other, as between two fixed points on *terra firma*. Let us, then, suppose a line thus traced with mathematical precision, for instance, from Cape St. Vincent, in Portugal, to Cape Horn, at the extremity of South America. What security will it procure to the sovereign who will have imagined it? Will it prevent vessels from sailing beyond that imaginary mark? Shall ships of war be stationed at certain distances or forts erected to cause it to be respected?

It is evident that no nation would undertake a task so very difficult and at the same time so little efficacious to establish a permanent occupation, the *sine qua non* of dominion. Again, let us suppose that the sovereign of the Island of Ceylon should draw a line from that island to Cape Comorin, on the one side, and to the northernmost point of the island of Sumatra, on the other; is it to be believed that he will prevent the Europeans from transgressing it and sailing in the seas of India and China?

Selden, in support of his imaginary lines, quotes the famous Bull of Pope Alexander the Sixth; but we must observe that by the said Bull a straight line is supposed to be drawn from pole to pole, not for the purpose of restricting navigation, or dividing the dominion of the sea, but to establish the limits of the continental conquests, or rather usurpations of the Spaniards and Portuguese in America and Asia. The Bull establishes its imaginary line at the distance of one hundred league at sea, west of the Azores and Cape Verde islands, but that line was so uncertain, that it produced the warmest discussions between Spain and Portugal; the point at last could never be settled, the parties could not even agree about the maps which should be made use of for that purpose. The two powers made several provisional treaties, which never were carried into execution. And the question after being the cause of many ruptures was only finally decided in the year 1777, by the mediation of France without any regard to the imaginary line.[10] It is then possible that governments will be so blind or so unwise as to consent to such an ineffectual mode of partition? And, after all, let us draw lines and triangles in every direction, let us divide the sea into square portions, as might be done on *terra firma*, let us distribute those square portions among the maritime nations: what will be the result of that grand geometrical operation? What advantages will it procure to the partitioning powers? What effect will it have as to the general tranquility of the world? The obvious answer to all these questions sufficiently demonstrates, if it stood in need of demonstration, the absurdity of the hypothesis on which they are founded, and makes it unnecessary for us to dwell any longer on this idle and impracticable system of imaginary boundaries.

But, says Selden, we must lay aside the fluid element, that is to say, the whole map of waters of which the sea is composed, and only turn our attention to its bed or bottom which is immoveable; to that bottom, and not to the surface the right of property attaches, precisely as it is with rivers, which are still more fluid than the sea. We might decline answering this

---

[10] This controversy is fully explained in my Institutes of the Law of Nature and Nations, Book 2, C. 2.

proposition, as merely theoretical, and incapable of any application in practice, and consequently not bearing in the least on the question before us: we will, however, undertake to discuss it, not on account of its importance, but of its singularity and of the great celebrity of the author; for it is well known to what degree mankind are led away by the magic of a name and that they will often adopt paradoxes merely because they have been advanced by a celebrated writer. Besides, Selden's proposition is in his own eyes an irresistible argument in favour of his system of imaginary limits.

We observe in the first place that the pretended similarity between the high sea and rivers is inadmissible, for everyone knows that rivers are capable of certain improvements which are impracticable on the sea, and require the aid of the land, such as bridges, dykes, mills, aquaducts, &c. Besides, the beds of rivers are dug across the land and embanked within it, the course of their waters may be changed, not only by nature, but also by the hand of man. Therefore, as Grotius says, rivers are *res terminata*; they are capable of being protected; consequently, their beds cannot be considered as *res nullius* or *res communis*; they are, on the contrary, by their situation, the property either of the Government, or of the owners of the adjacent land. Therefore, rivers may be made inaccessible to foreigners, because their entrance can be defended.

To make matters perfectly plain, we are willing to assimilate rivers to the sea adjoining the coast, which to a certain distance is considered as a continuation of the land. In this point of view, it is evident that they are subject to public or private dominion, but in order to favour it, it is not necessary to distinguish between the bed of a river and the water by which it is covered. But let us return to Selden's proposition.

In order to acquire a property in something, it is not sufficient to describe it, to point out the precise spot where it lies, and to group and hold it by the mere force of imagination; there must be *occupatio*, *possessio continua*, and *animus retinendi*; that is to say, an actual firm permanent occupation, coupled with an intent to keep and maintain it. Rivers, undoubtedly can be thus possessed, but how is it with respect to the bottom of the sea? How is that firm possession to be obtained? By what specific act is it to be evidenced? You will take possession of the land which the sea covers, by laying hold of a watery surface, which is indeed in contact with but not adhering to it, and which belongs, moreover, in common to all the world, and then you will claim that surface as identified with the ground below. But how will you perform your operations, on a fluid, incoherent element, shifting continually from place to place, and carrying along with it everything that it finds in its way? And if you should even be able to overcome that difficulty, on what principle will you appropriate that surface to your exclusive use? Because you will say, it lies on your own soil; but observe that the water and your rocky solid land at the bottom are not at all homogeneous substances, that the sea cannot be considered as a production of the land that it covers, or as a derelict, that it is an element specifically distinct, that it does no more adhere to the land than air to the convexity of the globe; that not a single portion of that water rests continually on your land, but that it is constantly flowing from place to place while the ground remains fixed and immoveable. Will your rights of property follow in their rapid course those ever shifting parcels of which the surface of the sea is composed? In that case, you may at last become the sovereign of the entire ocean. And on the wings of Chimera by the incessant pursuit of your fugitive dominions you will enjoy and protect your imaginary Empire.

The sea, as has been already observed, may be compared to the air: those two elements are equally fluid, in contrast with the land, always in motion, and always displaced. Will it be said that an aeronaut flying through the air in a balloon, which is a kind of vessel, altho' it has neither masts or guns, may take possession of the uninhabited or derelict lands over which he passes. No, he will alight, take actual possession of the land, and make a settlement on it, which he could not have done while he remained suspended in the air, even tho' he had drawn imaginary lines and triangles and had with the greatest precision ascertained this latitude and longitude of the lands which he coveted; by so doing he would at least attain an useful object, for he would secure to himself an habitation and the means of subsistence, and would still be surrounded by his proper element without which he could not live. But with the navigator dwell under water? Will he there build himself a house and procure the necessary means to support his existence?

Let us now reverse the question and consider what rights the owner of a piece of ground has over the column of air placed directly over it: is he the sole Lord and owner of that mass of air? It is certain that he has only an exclusive right to displace it by raising buildings in the space which it occupies; but he cannot prevent other men from enjoying it; they may peep through it as freely as the clouds. And, indeed, it would be absolutely impossible for him to intercept their passage. Let us now apply these truths to the sea; it rests as well as the air upon a solid bottom, of which it constitutes the surface; now, altho' they differ in weight, water and air are both fluids and both in constant motion, and thus they are both alike in relation to the earth with which they come in contract; the sea, therefore, even supposing its bottom to be private property, is as free as the air, and the dominion of neither of those elements can be acquired by usucaption. And if it were otherwise, it is clear that the dominion of the useful element would give the command over that which is inert or so unproductive; it is thus that the land commands the air, and that the waters command the ground over which they flow. You are, however, at liberty to build, if you can, an edifice at the bottom of the sea; you may raise it as high above the water as you are able, and in that case, you may be sure that everyone will respect it as your sole and undoubted property.

Selden himself seems to acknowledge the truth of these principles when he says that the dominion of the bottom of the sea would not be an obstacle to the freedom of navigation, that nations would enjoy it by grant as freely as they do by virtue of a natural right, and precisely in the manner as ways, passages, commons and other similar servitudes are enjoyed on the land. Be it so; but why is the title to be changed when the possession remains the same. Why abandon a title that is positive and independent of every human power, for an imaginary one, depending altogether on the will of man? Surely, the nations of the earth never will consent to so singular an exchange; they enjoy in their own right all the advantages of navigation; and if in spite of nature any one of them should acquire the property of the ground which the sea covers, the others would still continue freely to enjoy the surface without requiring any permission or grant. Thus we have disposed of Selden's most powerful argument in favor of the dominion of the sea. And such is the ultimate result of his system of lines and triangles.

The same author, in support of his doctrine, goes so far as to apply to the sea all the principles relative to property in land. Thus he contends that the exclusive dominion of the sea may be lawfully acquired by occupancy and by prescription in the same manner as newly formed islands in the bosom of the ocean. Before we proceed to the discussion of these two points of law, let us consider for a moment how the matter stands in point of fact. We know of no part of the vast expanse of the sea of which any particular nation possesses the exclusive dominion either by right of occupancy, prescription or conquest; we know no spot where Europeans do not or may not freely navigate. I am speaking only of the high sea, and not of gulphs, bays, the harbours, or of what are called the jurisdictional waters of a maritime State, altho' it is not by the effect of prescription or dereliction that those waters are considered as private property, but by virtue of an established rule of the law of nations which recognizes the sovereign of a certain portion of the adjacent sea because he may give it an effective and permanent protection. As to newly formed islands, Selden argues that they are a part of the bottom of the sea and yet that they become the property of the first occupant.[11] Nothing is so easy as to refute this boasted argument. From the moment that an island appears on the surface of the water, it ceases to be part of the bottom, or bed of the sea, as being no longer covered by its waters; it is now a limited thing (*res terminata*), it forms a solid body and has determinate bounds, it is susceptible of being inhabited, cultivated, and actually permanently possessed. It may therefore be subjected to all the laws applicable to land, of which it has assumed the character. If it were possible that there should exist an island without these characteristics, it would not, I am sure,

[11] This assertion is incorrect. Newly formed islands, if in the waters of a State, belong to it of full right. Those islands alone which are formed in the open sea become the property of the first occupant.

tempt the ambition of any power. Let us now pass on to the question of law.

The civil law and the law of nations agree in this, that a permissive right is never presumed to be lost by mere *non usus*, but there must be direct, or at least circumstantial proof of an actual waiver or renunciation. The rights of navigating and fishing are permissive, they cannot therefore according to the civil law be forfeited for *non usus*, and it is so *a fortiori* among nations which acknowledge no other law than that pointed out by natural reason and treaties. This being granted, what becomes of the right of the first occupant? How is the prescription to operate? Wherever the sea is free, that is to say, where it does not make a part of the domain of the territorial sovereign, it is subject to the permissive right of all mankind to use it, and cannot be appropriated to the exclusive use of any nation, for the reasons that have been already mentioned, and therefore no one can claim it by right of prior occupancy. As to prescription, it neither does nor can exist between nations. It is a creature of municipal law, by which governments do not consider themselves bound, nor if they were, is there any authority by which it might be enforced. The common legislator of nations is natural reason. But where is the judge legally invested with competent powers to compel an unjust nation to obedience? Force is the tribunal which usually decides between nations and enforces its decisions so long as it preponderates, but the right of appealing from them cannot be barred by any lapse of time. At any rate, there must be a possession to ground the plea of prescription on, but how and in what manner can the high sea be possessed? No land mark, crop, post, or inscription can be set up there, as is done in taking possession of solid dry land; therefore, even admitting the fantastic idea that there may be a right of property in the ground which the sea covers, it would be impossible to set up any permanent mark upon it. I do not say to secure that property, but even to point out where the estate lies. If nations should voluntarily submit to acknowledge such a dominion and establish its locality by means of imaginary lines, all reasonings are at an end and there will remain nothing to consider but the wisdom and utility of such a submission, for as to its obligatory force: *volenti non fit injuria*.

Finally, Selden in order to remove all the difficulties which militate against his system, contends that the ocean is bounded by the land, and not the land by the ocean, and thence he concludes that the ocean is *res terminata*, and consequently capable of dominion as all other things which have determinate bounds. This question appears to us very indifferent in itself, for however it may be decided, the nature of the sea will remain the same. And indeed, it makes no kind of difference whether the sea bounds or is bounded, or (to make use of a comparison introduced by Selden himself), whether a spherical body swimming in a fluid is limited by the spherical body. But our author was bent on refuting Grotius, who had asserted that the sea is *res terminata*. Whether he has or not successfully refuted him, we leave to the reader to decide after attending to the following observations.

It cannot be denied that the sea and the land are contiguous to each other, but it is equally true that the ocean, considered as a whole, is of the same and perhaps of a greater extent than the earth; that it encompasses and encircles it as the ancients said, as if it were, with a zone; that is presses upon the land, but the land cannot press upon it. Now, can it be said that the thing which is surrounded is limited by that which surrounds it? Is a vessel filled with water limited by the liquid that it contains? Is a circle limited by the space within it? It may be also observed that the extension of the waters of the sea is variable, as appears from the variations of the tides and it often happens that sometimes in one region the sea recedes from its bed, while in another in encroaches upon the land. Where then is the certainty, stability, and immutability of its limits? Therefore, let us say with Grotius, that the limits of the sea are undetermined. It is the same with all rivers, which altho' they have a regular channel, do nevertheless frequently overflow it. We shall only instance the great inundations of the Nile, to which mountains alone are an effectual surround. It is true that the freshes of our European rivers do not appear in the same regular succession and are not productive of the same advantages; but it is not the less true that it is impossible without erecting immense works which no Government will be at the expense of undertaking to assign to them fixed and immutable limits. Let us add that according to general usage, rivers are designated as boundaries to the adjacent lands and not the lands as limiting the rivers. Why then should a difference be made with respect to the ocean? And where are its limits to be found around the poles? We shall now sum up and conclude this argument with the following observations.

The right of property cannot be acquired by the mere operation of the mind, nor by corporal acts of a transitory nature, unaccompanied with the consent of those who have adverse claims, and much less can it be obtained by the exercise of force and violence. Therefore the dominion of the sea cannot be acquired by laws, ordinances, diplomas, or instructions. If force is resorted to, it is necessary to have armed ships; those ships must be stationed in that portion of the sea of which the dominion is to be secured, and then, all that can be done is a solemn taking of possession by proclamation, as when the Doge of Venice wed the Adriatic. But in this solemnity, if it is not interrupted by the fury of the elements, there will still exist a radical defect, for an empty ceremony is not sufficient to confer a right of property. There is therefore no legal seizing and consequently nothing on which to ground afterwards a claim of prescription. Besides, an armed vessel occupies in reality the column of water on which she stands, and by extension that over which her guns may reach and no more, as long as she remains stationary. She enjoys the sovereign command of all that space, and no one could displace her without doing her an injury. But that momentary empire vanishes at the very instance that the vessel either removes voluntarily or is compelled by the elements to abandon her station and the space which she just now occupied is again become free.

Such is the nature of things that are common to all, and such are the principles relative to the fugitive waters of the ocean. These principles must not be considered as arbitrary rules, or as the wanderings of a heated imagination, misled by abstract ideas of fancied freedom; for it is sufficient to contemplate the sea with an unprejudiced eye, to become sensible of their correctness and to be fully convinced that no part of its vast expanse can be momentarily occupied but its billowy surface and not its bottom, which is immoveable and can at most be reached by sounding or diving. Are these sufficient means to reduce it into possession? If so, the fisherman with his line, his net, and his fishing boat may acquire the dominion of the sea in as valid a manner as the most powerful fleets. At least, his would be a bloodless conquest and he would not be reproached with having made use of lawless force, either to make or to secure it.

But it will be said that the dominion of the sea may be acquired by virtue of treaties and therefore it is not as we contend a mere non-entity. Before I answer this objection, I think it necessary to quote what Montesquieu has very concisely said upon the subject: "One nation may resign the sea to another as well as the land. The Carthaginians forbade the Romans to sail beyond certain limits, as the Greeks had obliged the King of Persia to keep as far distant from the sea coast as a horse could gallop" (*Spirit of Laws*, B. 21, c. 17).

It will be observed that the author lays it down as a principle that one nation may make a cession of the sea to another. If before venturing on that decision he had pursued the subject a little farther, and enquired by what right such a cession could be made, he, most certainly, would have fallen upon this incontrovertible truth, that the sea is the common property of all and belongs to no one exclusively and from thence he would have inferred that a nation cannot cede what does not belong to it and that it may only renounce its own right to the use of it in favor of another country. This conclusion would have been perfectly consistent with true principles and with the two historical facts on which he founds his proposition – the Carthaginians and Romans were implacable enemies to each other, but they could not come in contact together except by sea, that is to say, with the assistance of their fleets; now fleets by quickening the motions of armies, facilitated surprises and exposed the navigation of the Carthaginians to incessant interruptions. It was then very natural that the victorious power should take advantage of his superiority in order to secure himself against such inconveniences and in this manner provide for his own safety. Thus the Carthaginians required of the Romans whom they had vanquished, that they should bind themselves not to navigate beyond certain limits. Most certainly the Romans did not by that act of submission give to their enemy the dominion of the sea. They only renounced the use of that element in particular latitudes, probably near the coasts of Sicily. In time of peace, that restriction was of little importance to the Romans, because, as Montesquieu well observes, they cared very little about navigation and were jealous of commerce. The same remark may be applied to the case of the King of Persia; we only think it necessary to add that as the coasts are only mentioned, it cannot be considered as applicable to the high sea. Let us therefore set aside the dictum of Montesquieu and consider in what other point of view the private dominion of the sea may become the object of a treaty. The more we sift this question, the less we are able to discover the slightest pretence for a cession of that element because, as we have already remarked, nothing can be ceded which is not possessed, and no nation nor individual is in possession of the ocean; and consequently, it is not in the power of anyone to cede or transfer it. All mankind have a right to enjoy it; any portion of mankind may renounce that right, either because they choose to do so, or in order to secure the tranquility of others. This is the only case in which the sea can be the object of a treaty. We are willing, however, to admit that if all nations joined in investing a single power with the dominion of the sea, that is to say, with the exclusive enjoyment thereof in addition to the right of expelling others from it, that act would be equivalent to the most absolute and unlimited dominion, and in that case, the doctrine of Selden would be established; but we must wait until that event takes place before we decide on its effects and, above all, before we believe its possibility.

Such are the preliminary observations which we have thought necessary to make in order to establish the doctrine of the freedom of the sea; we will now conclude with one single reflection which flows from the nature of the subject, and appears to us to throw considerable light upon it.

According to Selden and his followers, such as Welwood, Burgus, Bynkershoek, and others, the sea is from its very nature capable of being brought under exclusive dominion, that is to say, of being exclusively the permanently occupied, possessed, and preserved; that exclusive right of property may be claimed and enjoyed by prescription, and the assent of other nations is no more necessary in this case than in that of a desert and newly discovered country; in short, utility alone is a sufficient ground to justify a similar acquisition.

If those principles are correct, how then does it happen that in the course of so many centuries, and amidst so many revolutions, no part of the main ocean has yet afforded a single instance in support of the doctrine which I oppose, and that all the sea in the world still remain free? It will not be said that the element has escaped the ambition of conquerors; no, the only thing which can be said to have escaped them is the idea that it could be conquered, seized, and occupied. Neither will it be contended that the Greeks and Romans were unacquainted with the use of the sea and its advantages, and yet there is not a single historical fact, a single law, a single monument to shew that they were possessed of the exclusive dominion of the sea, altho' there was nothing to prevent the Romans, the absolute masters of Asia, the coasts of Africa, and all the west of Europe, as far as the British islands, from asserting such a claim. The exaggerations, the flattery of courtiers and poets, and the interpretations which commentators have made of some of the laws of the Digest[12] cannot be cited as historical proofs. In modern history we find but three nations to which the pretended dominion of some parts of the sea has been attributed, viz. Great Britain, Genoa, and Venice. The two republics have vanished with their imaginary dominion; as to England, her maritime power has progressively increased, and is now preponderant on the ocean; yet, notwithstanding the diplomas of her Admirals and the arguments of her writers, there is no part of the ocean on which her exclusive dominion has been, I will not say acknowledged, but even established *de facto*, much less *de jure*. Nevertheless, the pretensions which she is supposed to have, and the importance which is attached to the name and to the opinions

---

[12] Mari, quod natura omnibus patet, servitus imponi private lege non potest. D. B. 8, tit. 4. ... p. 54. The sea, which by the law of nature belongs to all mankind, cannot be subjected to private dominion. This law is clear and precise, and the advocates of maritime dominion have taken great care to keep it out of view in their discussions of this subject.

of Selden warrant us in believing that it will not be useless to analyze and discuss the arguments by which in the final part of his *Mare clausum* he attempts to support the claims of his own country to the dominion of an extensive portion of the ocean. That discussion, therefore, will be the subject of Volume Two below.

PART II.

OF THE SEA IN TIME OF WAR

Chapter 1.

General Observations

§1: Importance of this Subject

The question of the freedom of the seas in time of war is of such high importance that no pains ought to be ignored to investigate it thoroughly and to establish its principles on a firm and immutable basis. The necessity of carrying light into that obscure labyrinth will be the more strongly felt when it is considered that the greatest diversity has at all times existed in practice, as well in the treaties as in the jurisprudence of maritime States; and yet all pretend to justify their conduct by the rules and principles of the law of nations, altho' it is probable that they have only consulted their partial interest, their political views or some circumstances of momentary concern.

§2: Nations are Bound by Fixed and Certain Rules

There are, however, fixed and certain rules by which the conduct of nations towards each other ought to be regulated. Whatever may be their policy, they are bound towards each other to the fulfillment of reciprocal duties on which the preservation of the general peace and the very existence of nations depends; duties which, however, avarice, ambition, and power may violate them, can never cease to exist and be obligatory on mankind.

§3: Reason – the Supreme Law of Nations

Those duties are indelibly recorded in the primitive code of mankind which is no other than natural reason, the supreme law of nations. It is reason which decides on the justice or injustice of human actions, from that source and from that alone. I have drawn the principles which I am about to establish. The consequences to which they will inevitably lead shall serve to appreciate the pretensions of powers at war, on the one hand, and the rights of neutral nations, on the other. In developing those principles, I shall set aside custom as well as treaties, and the opinions of writers I shall merely take notice of them as far as to compare them with the positive rules which I shall establish and to shew how far they have deviated from them. Not but that I am sufficiently aware of the weight of precedents and the authority of those writers who sanction them with their approbation and praise; but what do precedents exhibit to us, but a series of versatile and contradictory actions, the abuse of power on the one side, and on the other submission and weakness? What are treaties but compacts made, altered and violated according to the suggestions of a momentary interest? Whoever will cast a look on the maritime history of Europe shall find there the proofs of this melancholy truth. And as to writers, whose doctrines are only founded on custom or precedent, and who attempt to establish a law of nations founded on usages or treaties, they ought to be read and consulted with the greatest circumspection; for they may fairly be suspected of partiality and may well be presumed to have had no other intention than to support the system adopted by some particular governments; so that they have been obliged to make principles bend to the cause which they had to defend. Those, therefore, who consider them as authorities are in great danger of being misled by them, and on a subject of such high importance, their errors may lead to the most fatal results.[13]

---

[13] Can there be more striking instances of it that the writings of Selden, Welwood, Vattel, and before them of Albericus Gentilis? I may also add those of the Earl of Liverpool, formerly Mr. Jenkinson, whose opinions I shall examine in the course of this work. Welwood goes so far as to say

Chapter II.

Mutual Independence is the Foundation of the Law of Nations

§1: Nations are Independent of Each Other

It is the first and most undeniable principle of universal law that nations are independent of each other, and that, like man in a state of nature, they possess above all things the right of preserving their own existence. As self-preservation is the first care, so it is the first right of all mankind in or out of civil society. National independence, therefore, is the true foundation of the law by which nations are governed in their relations with each other.

§2: Right and Duties Arising Therefrom

Every nation has rights which are inseparable from a state of independence. Those rights authorize her to provide for her safety, welfare, and happiness, to receive laws from nobody but herself, and to repel every aggression or encroachment on her absolute freedom. At the same time, she is bound to allow to other nations the same rights which she claims for herself, and on no account to violate them. The reciprocity of rights and duties operating upon and modifying each other, is the foundation of the relations established between the different political socictics and thc invariable rule by which they are to be governed; it maintains peace and concord between them, and its violation produces a state of war, which is the disposition of social order. In these few words is summed up the whole of what is called the *law of nations*. It is derived from natural reason and is as ancient as the first formation of man into civil societies.

---

that those who maintain the system of the freedom of the seas are only instigated by avarice and that they wish to excite wars, that they may profit by them.

Property was the first cause and object of those associations; for it was to defend and protect it that men, by forming themselves into a social body, combined together with their wills and their united strength. Independence is the most precious property of nations; it is the basis of all others, and without it no nation can properly be said to exist.

Chapter III.

The Principles of the Law of Nations Applied to the Sea

§1: The Sea is Free and Common

The same independence that each nation enjoys within her own limits she retains upon the sea because that element is free (see Part One). The effect of that liberty is: that the sea is not the property of anyone, that it is common to all nations, that they all have an equal right to it, that they may use it with the most absolute freedom, which cannot be restrained without violating their independence. The reader will be sensible that the use of that freedom must be inoffensive, that it ought not to encroach upon the rights of others to their own self-preservation.

§2: Application of the Principle in Time of Peace

This doctrine, founded on the first elements of natural reason and which also constitutes the universal law of nations, has its full execution in time of peace. All nations whose territory bordered freely on the ocean freely navigated thereon, and no one has a right to interrupt or impede their navigation. To guard against such attempts and to prevent all mistakes, the distinction of flags has been introduced. Every nation which frequents the sea has a particular one; it designates the country to which the vessel belongs and thus secures her independence. This is commonly called the immunity of the flag. The vessel which has displayed hers is out of all foreign jurisdiction; it has the absolute and exclusive enjoyment of the place which it occupies; it is the mansion or dwelling of those who are on board which no one has a right to enter; in a word, the place where it remains stationed is considered for a time as the dominion of the sovereign whose colours it bears, and justice is there administered in his name. When we consider the insulated situation of a ship sailing on the high sea, we must be sensible of the necessity of establishing the most severe and precise principles to protect her against outrages which might be aimed at her liberty and safety. The least relaxation in this respect will necessarily produce disturbance and quarrels; invite rapacity; open the door to arbitrary pretensions; and of course to an arbitrary system of jurisprudence which each power will enforce as may suit its convenience. It will be easy to be convinced of this truth by taking into view the many impediments thrown in the way of the navigation of neutrals. They are the necessary result of the neutrality and diversity of the rules which belligerent powers arbitrarily adopt under the exaggerated pretence of self-preservation.

Chapter IV.

First Exception in Time of War with Respect to Belligerent Powers

§1: The Ocean a Field of Battle

The absolute immunity or inviolability of the national flag is, however, subject to some modifications in time of war.

The whole surface of the vast ocean which surrounds the globe is a wide field of battle on which the belligerent nations pursue, attack, and destroy each other wherever they can meet. The slightest quarrel in Europe stains the waters with blood, and neutral waters are only respected from motives of conveniency.

Chapter V.

Second Exception with Respect to Neutrals

§1: Exorbitant Pretensions of Belligerents

The freedom of the navigation and commerce of neutral nations is always contested by belligerents in a greater or lesser degree. They claim the rights of restricting it as suits their interest and convenience: under pretense that this right is given to them without limitation by the law of war, they assert a supreme jurisdiction[14] on an element which they themselves acknowledge not to be capable of it, while they deny the same right to neutrals, and yet, what is war itself to be made the foundation of such exorbitant pretensions? Its cause or pretext, often nothing else than the most trifling incident, some equivocal pretension of claim, or the violation of some

[14] *Lampredi*, in his treatise on the commerce and navigation of neutrals, finds fault with the application of the word *jurisdiction*; but I ask what other name can be given to the detention and seizure of a vessel, to its trial and final adjudication to the use and benefit of the captors? I ask whether those are not proper acts of jurisdiction, or the exercise of the *jus coercendi*? To say that those things are done by virtue of the law of war, and are merely the exercise of belligerent rights, is only playing upon words, and does not make any difference as to the point in controversy, for what matters it as far as respects the present question whether the authority which is exercised is derived from the law of war or from municipal law? The adjudication of a prize under the law of war is as much an act of jurisdiction as the trial of a private controversy under the local law of a particular country, and the seizure of a vessel at sea by a ship of war or privateer, but virtue of a commission from the belligerent sovereign, may be in like manner assimilated to a seizure at law by a ministerial officer of justice, acting under a precept from the municipal authority. Undoubtedly, the jurisdiction which belligerents exercise at sea upon neutrals is irregular, but it is the same with everything which is relative to a state of war; and the independence of neutrals being subordinate to that state of things, it must necessarily suffer from the irregularity of those proceedings. I am speaking here of things as they are in fact, not as they ought to be, according to the true principles of law, which are no longer attended to.

insignificant right; the least offense is transformed into a serious aggression. I say nothing of those wars which avarice or ambition has provoked; the moment that war exists, no matter from what cause or for what motive, the belligerents claim the right to violate at their will and pleasure the most important and indisputable rights of neutral nations. They think themselves entitled to inflict upon them a kind of treatment which they would not themselves suffer from the nation against which they have taken up arms.[15] Neutrals deny the justice of such

---

[15] In order to be fully convinced of the truth of our assertions when we speak of the arbitrary pretensions of belligerents, it will be sufficient to read the Convention between Great Britain and the United Provinces, signed at London on the 22nd of August 1689. Those two nations had just declared war against Louis XIV.

In the preamble of that remarkable instrument, the parties set forth: "That whereas it behooves the said King of Great Britain and the said Lords, the States General, to do as much damage as possibly they can to the common enemy, and as it is necessary for that end that they should make use of all their forces and order matters so as effectually to interrupt and break off all trade and commerce with the Most Christian King's subjects, his said Majesty of Great Britain and the said Lords, the States General, the better to attain that end, have ordered their fleets to sail towards the coast of France and to block up all the ports, havens, and roads belonging to the Most Christian King".

The second Article stipulates: "That as several kings, princes, and States in Europe are already engaged in a war against the Most Christian King and have already prohibited, or will in a short time prohibit, all commerce with France, it is agreed between his said Majesty of Great Britain and said Lord the States General that if during the course of the war the subjects of any other kings, prince, or State shall undertake to traffick, or have any commerce with the subjects of the Most Christian King; or if their vessels or shipping are met with in their passage to the ports, havens or roads under the obedience of the Most Christian King, the said vessels, shipping, merchandise, or wares shall in the case above mentioned be attacked and taken by the captains of men of war, privateers, or other subjects of the King of Great Britain and the Lords the States General, and shall before proper judges be condemned for lawful prize".

"The said King of Great Britain and the said Lord the States General shall as soon as possible notify this treaty and convention to all the kings, princes, and States of Europe that are not in war against France; and that the said kings, princes, and States shall at the same time be informed that if the ships or vessels of their subjects are found before this notification is

pretensions and from this controversy arises the question which I have undertaken to investigate. The reader must be sensible that I do not mean to speak of neutrals who have renounced their rights by particular treaties or stipulations. Their engagements are the law which they have enacted for themselves. Those general principles of the law of nations which they thus have waived no longer concern them so far as they have consented to be governed by different rules.

§2: Equality and Reciprocity – the Foundation of the Law of Nations

According to these principles, equality of rights and reciprocity of conduct are the fundamental rules of the intercourse between nations, they should not assume to the

---

given, at sea, making their way for the ports, havens, or roads under the obedience of the Most Christian King, they shall be obliged by the ships of the King of Great Britain and of the Lords, the States, forthwith to turn back; and if the ships or vessels appertaining to those kings, princes, and States, or to their subjects, shall be met with sailing from the said ports laden with the merchandise or commodities of France, the said ships or vessels shall be obliged to sail back to the said ports and there to leave the said goods and merchandise, upon pain of forfeiture; and in case the ships or vessels of those kings, princes, and States or of their subjects shall after the notification be found at sea and sailing towards the ports, havens, or roads under the obedience of the Most Christian King, or from the ports of the said King, they shall be seized and forfeited together with their cargo, and be reputed good prize".

That Convention is a remarkable monument of maritime despotism, a notorious abuse of the law of war, a wanton and shocking violation of the rights of neutrals. And what is still more striking is to see the Dutch participate in that act of tyranny, when they owed their prosperity to the freedom of commerce and still more to the favors which France had granted to them. But they were under the yoke of William III and could not well help themselves. It will be particularly remarked of that Convention that it has a strong feature of that system of general blockade, by means of which England has in our own times entirely subverted every principle of maritime law.

Note: The Convention above mentioned is to be found in a collection of treaties in three volumes, printed at London in 1785.

prejudice of the right of doing to others what they will not suffer others to do to their own prejudice, and consequently a neutral nation who will not take part in an existing war is bound to abstain from every offensive act against either of the belligerent parties, and as a further consequence she must not give assistance to the one to the detriment of the other, for she would not suffer it to be done to her own detriment in a similar juncture. The right of the belligerent nation to oppose it is founded on the perfect right which she has to act hostilely against her enemy; to give him aid and assistance is to become associated with him and a party in the war. Therefore neutrals are strictly bound to observe impartiality, which is the essential characteristic of neutrality. It remains now to ascertain the precise meaning of that word, and of the duties which flow from it.

Chapter VI.

Of Impartiality

§1: Impartiality, What It Is

Impartiality is a word of most extensive import and meaning. It comprises all the duties of neutrals toward belligerents, and is in fact the sum and substance of them all. In this discussion, however, we shall not consider it farther than as it relates to the navigation and commerce of the subjects of a neutral State with those of the powers at war. We shall endeavour to lay down its precise extent and limits in relation to the subject before us, and to discriminate with accuracy between the real duties of neutrals towards belligerents in matters of trade and navigation in time of war and those unjust restrictions which force alone has established and which are, in our opinion, to be considered as direct infringements of neutral rights.

§2: The Freedom of the Sea is a General Principle, All Exceptions to It are to be Strictly Construed

In order to proceed with method in our argument, we must recur to the primary and fundamental principle which we have already established, that nations are independent of each other at sea as well as on land, and that it follows, as a necessary inference from this plain and undeniable proposition, that the sea is free and common to all mankind. And as a further inference, it also follows that all the restrictions to which nations may be subjected in the exercise of their independent rights are so many exceptions to this general rule. This being admitted, it must be acknowledged likewise that all exceptions, whether founded on general law or special contract, are to be strictly construed and never can be extended by interpretation beyond their precise object. Now the avowed object of the exceptions that we are going to speak of is to prevent neutral nations from doing that which endangers the safety of the powers at war. Danger is the watchword on which belligerents have founded their various restrictions and prohibitions on the commerce and navigation of neutrals. We shall proceed to consider how far these several prohibitions are justifiable in this particular point of view.

Chapter VII.

Of the Prohibition of Arms and Ammunition, and Incidentally of Money

§1: Neutrals Cannot Favour One of the Parties, so as to Endanger the Safety of the Other

It is then freely admitted as a principle of the law of nations founded on the undeniable right of self-preservation that neutrals cannot carry on in favour of one of the belligerent nations a branch of commerce which may endanger the safety of the other, because the former would thereby be enabled more or less to hurt her enemy; they would therefore cease to be impartial and consequently would no longer be neutral. But in what does this danger consist? In the correct application of the word lies the whole difficulty.

§2: Arms and Ammunition

It is pretended that there is danger when the neutral trader supplies one of the belligerents with such articles, as are of immediate use in war, such as instruments of destruction, among which are included arms and warlike ammunition of every kind; therefore a neutral is not free to furnish such articles. Such is the law established by usage, which has been borrowed from the jurisprudence of the Romans: *damnum emergens*.

But we may be permitted to think that it is in general more thro' habit than fear that governments have hitherto adhered to this prohibition. To be convinced of it, we need only take a general view of all the States of Europe, great as well as small; almost everywhere we see foundries of cannon and manufactories of arms: there does not exist a small city honoured with the title of Republic which has not its arsenal and military apparatus. If we circumnavigate Europe, from Archangel to the extremity of the Mediterranean, where shall we find that power which is obliged to procure from abroad cannon, guns, bayonets, halberds, pikes, saltpeter, saddles, belts, &c? Let us fix our attention on the two first and greatest maritime powers, France and Great Britain. Will anyone honestly maintain that either of them may impede the military operations of the other by preventing neutrals from supplying them with arms? If either nation was to be reduced to that only resource, she would clearly have no alternative left but to submit to her enemy and receive the law from his pride or his generosity; for unquestionably, the arms which she might receive from foreign countries would afford her but very little relief and let it not be said that belligerent nations might at any moment purchase arms and ammunition from neutrals, for these articles are nowhere an object of commercial speculation; they must be bespoken beforehand. The Northern States furnish copper, iron, &c., but where are their warehouses and manufactories of arms? Where are the necessary capitals to enable the merchants to purchase upon speculation large quantities of those articles and expose them to the dangers of the sea and to all the other rigors of a commercial adventure? And why are halberds and pikes included in the list of contraband goods, when they are now no longer in use? Why are saddles, belts, and other articles of a similar description? Are those capable of attracting the attention of a Government about to engage in war? I enter those details because I am persuaded that too much cannot be said against a prejudice that has no real object, a prejudice so contrary to the rights of nations and which in every maritime war is the fruitful source of a variety of incidents which were it not for particular circumstances would nearly produce a general war.

§3: Contraband of War Difficult to be Concealed

Besides (and this remark is well worthy of consideration) it is so true that the prohibition of arms and warlike stores is without a rational object that nothing is less common (if even it ever happens) than to find such articles concealed on board of neutral vessels, and indeed, nothing is more difficult than such concealment. Yet it is made the pretence for searching and rummaging neutral ships from one end to the other, for putting the crew in a manner to the torture, in order to discover concealed arms or ammunition. And if by a lucky chance the privateer finds a few pounds of gunpowder, or a few rusty arms, belonging to the people on board, it is considered a sufficient ground of suspicion to capture, or at least to ransom the unfortunate vessels.

§4: Its Prohibition Useless as well as Unjust

We do not therefore hesitate to say that however positive the principles may be, abstractly considered, and however general may be the custom which has established it, the application which is now made of it is a wanton and useless violation of that fundamental principle of the laws of nations, the independence of neutrals. And it is truly astonishing that all governments do not unite in condemning and abolishing it. Nor let it be thought that this opinion is founded on abstract theory, or is the mere result of philanthropic feelings, as I am persuaded it has no foundation in the nature of things and is, above all, confirmed by experience. I shall never be able to conceive how a nation for the sake of removing a few obstacles or some trifling inconvenience can think itself authorized to set at nought the most clearly established rights of all, without which no nation can exist; and but for the acknowledgement of which the world would still be involved in chaos and confusion, and exhibit a perpetual scene of war and plunder. Whatever latitude may be allowed to policy and self interest, governments are still bound, if not to be just, at least to abstain from useless acts of injustice; and they will do so, whenever they shall have courage enough to reflect coolly and calmly upon the subject, forget for a moment their power and greatness, and set aside the odious maxims of a selfish policy, which can never succeed, but by the unhallowed means of force and violence.

However, it may be, the prejudice still subsists and governments rigorously adhere to it. It is sanctioned by almost all the commercial treaties[16] and must therefore of necessity be considered a part of the conventional or customary law of nations.[17]

---

[16] Frederick II, the late King of Prussia, did not consider that prohibition as of very great importance. In his Treaty of Commerce with the United States (10th September 1785) it was stipulated that neither arms nor ammunition should be considered as contraband and that it should only be lawful to stop such vessels and articles and to detain them for such length of time as the captors might think necessary to prevent the inconvenience or damage that might ensue through paying, however, a just compensation therefor to the proprietors. The captors might also retain the articles, paying to the owners their full value, to be ascertained by the current price at the place of their destination.

[17] There is, in our opinion, but one single exception to all that has been said above; it is the case of a rebellion breaking out in the dominions of a sovereign. To furnish the rebels with arms and ammunition may certainly be considered as a participation in the crime; because not having any of their own, they could not maintain themselves in their rebellion without foreign assistance; therefore, the danger resulting from such assistance is sufficiently evident; the party which affords it is liable to be treated as an abettor or accomplice, or as a violator of the law of nations. A similar discussion once arose between the Courts of Versailles and London before the breaking out of the American War. The French merchants did clandestinely furnish arms and ammunition to the Americans and their shipments were for the most part disguised by means of passports given to them for the West India Islands, or those of St. Pierre and Miquelon. The English Ministry complained of those shipments, and were answered that the Government had no share in those transactions of the French merchants and that all it would so was to forbid the exportation of arms and ammunition and to take strict measures to prevent it, and that besides if the British cruisers should meet and capture on the American coast any French vessels laden with prohibited articles, the Government would not interfere. But the court of London considered that answer as evasive, they suspected that there was collusion or connivance in the case; and relying on the weakness of the French Ministry, they ordered the capture and detention of French vessels not only on the high sea and in the latitudes of our West India Islands, but also on our coasts and at the entrance of our rivers. It is true that the clandestine trade was carried on with great activity. But all that England had a right to do by the maritime law and general custom was to capture French vessels in the waters of North America which at that time was still considered as a part of the British dominions. The arbitrary conduct of the Court of St. James contributed not a little to the determination which that of Versailles took at last to treat

§5: Whether Money is Contraband of War

It is asked whether money is to be included among what is called contraband of war? The treaty signed in 1656 between England and Sweden stipulates the prohibition thereof, but the Treaty of Commerce made in 1677 between France and Great Britain expressly declares that gold and silver, either coined or in bullion, shall be free. I confine myself to these two instances to prove that there is no generally established rule upon this subject.

As to the question itself, I think it may be thus considered – money, whether coined or in ingots, is nothing more than a medium of exchange, the representative sign of everything that is used or consumed by man. If the prohibition were well founded, it should be extended to all the productions of nature and art, for armies are in want of everything that money can represent or procure. Besides, money will circulate in spite of every prohibition. It may as well be attempted to stop the circulation of air and water, or to prohibit the wind from blowing from a particular quarter. I grant, however, that there is a distinction to be made. Either the money shipped on board of a neutral vessel belongs to individuals, or to the government of the enemy. In the first case, there is no doubt that it must remain free, but in the second, its capture appears lawful because money in the hands of a government is, as is commonly said, the principal sinew of war. There can be no difficulty if the money is sent as a subsidy; as that alone would be sufficient cause of war, it may *a fortiori* be considered as a legitimate cause of confiscation.

---

with the American commissaries and acknowledge the independence of their country.

Chapter VIII.

Of Naval Stores

§1: Are Naval Stores Properly Contraband of War

There are governments which extend the prohibitory system so far as to include timber, hemp, cordage, sails, tar, copper, and all other articles comprised under the general denomination of *naval stores*. Are they justifiable in so doing?

§2: Question to be Considered on Abstract Principles

This question to be correctly solved must be considered abstractedly from any connection that it may have with the various interests of belligerents and neutrals; the doctrines to which it has given rise are to be tested only the eternal and immutable principles of right and wrong, and not by those fluctuating systems suggested by self interest and expediency which have constantly varied with times and political circumstances. Nor are we to look for its solution in treaties, the stipulations of which are various and often in opposition to each other, and after all are only binding on those nations which are parties to them.

§3: Naval Stores Not Prohibited on the General Principles of Neutrality

That neutral commerce is liable to certain restrictions in time of war is a principle which I have already admitted and am not therefore disposed to controvert, but it does not follow from thence that those restrictions are arbitrary and that their sphere may be extended or narrowed at the will and pleasure of the belligerents. The freedom of neutral trade knows no limits but those which are set to it by the duties of neutrality – Thus, I have already observed that impartiality is a duty to which neutral nations are strictly bound. That duty obliged them either to deny everything equally to the belligerent parties, or to favor them alike. On this principle, it is plain that if a neutral nation supplies one of the belligerents and not the other, with timber, hemp, &c., it violates by such preference the primary duty of impartiality; but if, on the contrary, it supplies both the belligerents, or leaves them equally at liberty to purchase such articles. I cannot see that either of them has a right to complain. That equality, indeed, may not suit alike the convenience or interest of the contending powers; but the law of nations has nothing to do with their interest or convenience. Claims that rest exclusively upon similar grounds can only be supported by the *sic volo* of power or the obligation of treaties, which for the most part are produced by the ascendancy of force over weakness in violation of the rights and laws of neutrality.

§4: Objection. Naval Stores are Dangerous. Answer

But say the advocates of the restrictive system (and that is the argument on which they principally rely) by supplying my enemy with timber, cordage, tar, copper, &c., you enable him to build ships, cast cannon, manufacture firearms, swords, &c. You put my safety in danger and consequently do me an injury. I have therefore a right to prevent it by all the means in my power and to intercept your trade with my enemy in articles dangerous to my very existence and, of course, unlawful according to the acknowledged principles of the law of nations.

This might, perhaps, be conceded if it were possible with a conjuror's wand to transform naval stores into ships already fitted out and armed; but the age of miracles is past; we have no faith in supernatural influences; we only calculate on the nature of things; we do not say: a thing may be injurious and therefore it is so. We abide by the maxim taught by Aristotle and common sense: *à posse ad actum non fit argumentatio*.

§5: Same Subject Continued

But let us argue seriously. We admit that those articles which may do immediate injury in the state in which they are dangerous; and for that reason, arms and ammunition, and even saddles and bridles for horses, have been prohibited. But can the same thing be said of the raw materials? These cannot without much preparation and labor be transformed into implements of war, nor even into instruments of husbandry or other innocent articles. There is certainly a very great difference between unwrought copper and iron, and cannon, muskets, sabres, and bayonets; between a man of war and pieces of square timber, hemp, tar, &c. There is even a great interval of time between the moment when those articles are shipped in America and that when the men of war built out of them are in readiness to sail. All the materials which I have described are common articles of trade; has war the power of changing their nature? Corn feeds the laborer in his cottage; must it be prohibited because it also nourishes the soldier and the sailor? In that case, you must prohibit all nature if it stands in your way; you may accumulate all possible scourges on mankind, for the sake of a doubtful controversy, or to satisfy your rapacity and ambition.

§6: Argument Summed Up

Here, then, is the true principle on which the decision of this important question entirely depends. Certain and immediate danger to the belligerent may be a lawful ground of prohibition, but it is not the same with a mere possibility that an article of trade may after being combined with other articles and undergoing a variety of mechanical processes, be ultimately employed to the prejudice of the prohibiting power. For there is nothing in nature that may not in some shape or other, mediately or immediately, be applied to the purposes of war. And if the abstract principle of danger to the belligerent, however uncertain or remote, be once admitted, there is an end forever to neutral trade.

§7: Treaties

For these reasons, were we disposed to argue from the almost uniform tenor of treaties, we would say that mankind (Great Britain herself not excepted) have in general agreed to consider naval stores as articles of free commerce, but opponents would contend that those stipulations are exceptions to the general rule and would not fail to retort our own remark upon us that treaties are only binding on those who made them, and thus the question would remain precisely where it stood before. We will not imitate them by flying from principle to precedent and from precedent to principle as either may suit our purpose; and therefore we again frankly declare that however favorable it may be to the rule which we are contending for, we do not mean to rely on the authority of treaties. Yet altho' we do not avail ourselves of that authority in point of law, we cannot entirely overlook the great support which it gives to our argument in point of fact. When we view the multitude of existing stipulations in favor of the free commerce of neutrals in naval stores, we cannot help enquiring where is that danger which belligerents so industriously hold up to view, and which is the professed basis of the doctrine of our adversaries? It is not, after all, so great or so imminent, that it may not be lost sight of for certain particular considerations; the prohibitory rule is not therefore founded on the eternal principles of right and wrong. It is the mere offspring of human conventions and is raised up, modified or annihilated at pleasure. But we must repeat that the interest or convenience of nations at war cannot make the law for neutrals, nothing but superior force can induce them to renounce their incontestable right and the lawful advantages which they derive from it. Let it not be forgotten that while the danger to belligerents from this particular branch of trade is so much exaggerated this identical trade is allowed to neutrals by almost every commercial treaty; so that the pretended general rule, if it ever existed, has in fact become the exception and the exception, the rule.

§8: The Prohibition of Naval Stores is of Modern Date

But, there is so little foundation for this pretended rule, that those who contend for it are compelled to admit that it is of modern date and that formerly naval stores were considered as articles of a dubious nature.[18]

If the great majority of commercial treaties which sanction our principle does not shew that the doubtful question has been decided in our favor by the assent of nations, it, at least, affords evident proof that the modern rule, as it is called, never was, if at all, but partially adopted, and consequently cannot be considered as binding on those who have not agreed to it. For no usage can be introduced so as to become a part of the law of nations, but by the general assent of the civilized world. The most that can be said, therefore, by our adversaries is that the question still remains doubtful on the grounds of usage and conventional law, and of course that it cannot be decided otherwise than on general principle. On this solid basis we have taken up the discussion of the subject and flatter ourselves that we have satisfactorily established the strength of our cause and the weakness of that of our adversaries.[19]

---

[18] The celebrated Sir William Scott, the oracle of the Court of Admiralty of England, has acknowledged the truth of this assertion in his judgment in the case of the Maria, Poulson, commonly called the case of the Swedish convoy. That magistrate is too enlightened not to have been sensible that the cause which he had to adjudicate was at least doubtful and in such a case a judge who is not allowed to have an opinion of his own must support his decision as well as he can. In that case, he must have felt himself under peculiar embarrassment for he had not merely to decide on the legality of the conduct of the captors, but of the Lords Commissioners of the Admiralty themselves, who had issued a special order for the capture of the Swedish ships.

[19] *Valin*, the Commentator of the French ordinance of 1681, likewise confesses that formerly naval stores were not considered as contraband; but he affirms that they have been so considered since the beginning of the 18th century. We do not know on what authority he took upon himself to express his opinion in so direct and positive a manner. Something more than assertions is required to prove the abolition of an ancient usage founded on the genuine principles of the law of nations, some public acts ought to be shown, not mere ex parte documents, but such as may properly be considered as constituting a part of the conventional or customary law of nations; but the French commentator does not cite any document of one or the other description. If Mr. *Valin* had only consulted treaties, he would have hesitated at least before he emitted an opinion so contrary to the facts which they evidence. His example affords a sufficient

§9: Contrary Opinions. Vattel

There are, however, several estimable writers who have entertained on this subject a different opinion from that which I have expressed. Among them, Vattel requires to be particularly noticed, as he goes the whole length of the modern British doctrine as to what constitutes contraband of war. According to him, not only arms and ammunition, but ship timber and naval stores of every description, horses, and even sometimes – provisions are to be considered as prohibited goods and may lawfully be captured and confiscated by a belligerent when found on their way to the ports of his enemy (*Law of Nations*, Book 3, §§3 and 112).

As the question whether naval stores are contraband of war was by no means settled at the time when Vattel wrote, it might have been reasonably expected that he would have adduced some special reasons for including them within that denomination. But he takes the rule at once for granted, and undertakes to assert by the same course of argument and without any discrimination the right of the belligerent to seize and confiscate all the different kinds of goods which he thinks proper to include within his list of prohibited articles, I shall take a cursory view of his reasoning on the subject, and endeavour to

---

proof of the great circumspection that ought to be used in laying down the rules and principles of the law of nations.

In order to be fully convinced of *Valin's* mistake, it is sufficient to consult the commercial treaty made in 1674 (seven years before the publication of the ordinance of 1681) between Great Britain and the United Provinces. In that treaty, naval stores of every description are expressly excluded from the list of contraband articles. And since the publication of the said ordinance, the commercial treaty between France and Great Britain, signed at Utrecht in 1713, also acknowledges the freedom of naval stores. That treaty as far as relates to contraband and free goods is the model on which all the subsequent commercial treaties have been framed. England has likewise excepted naval stores from the list of contraband articles by the second article of her commercial treaty with Russia made in 1766 and in the third article of the convention signed in1801. We shall abstain from further quotations in order not to fatigue our readers; we have shown enough to enable them to appreciate Mr. *Valin's* pretended modern jurisprudence.

shew its general inconsistency and its inconclusiveness as to the question before use.

He begins with admitting that neutral nations have a full right not only to sell to the belligerents within their own country, contraband articles of every description, but even to carry them for sale to enemy's ports. "For", says he with great truth, "they are under no obligation to abandon their accustomed trade, for the sake of a war in which they have no concern, and in doing so they only exercise a right which they are under no obligation of sacrificing to either party" (*Law of Nations*, Book 3, §111).

But, on the other hand, he contends that there is a *co-existing right* in the belligerent to seize and confiscate the contraband goods which the neutral is carrying to the ports of his enemy and that both those rights may be exercised, that is to say, the neutral may carry the goods and the belligerent may seize them without either having cause to complain of the other. "If", says he, "after I have notified to them my declaration of war against such or such a people, neutrals will run the risk of supplying them with things relative to war, they cannot complain if their goods fall into my hands, any more than I can declare war against them because they attempted to carry such goods. They, indeed, suffer by a war in which they have no concern, but it is accidentally. I do not oppose their right, I only make use of my own" (*Law of Nations*, Book 3, §111).

§10: Answer

Nothing in my opinion can be more absurd than this reasoning, and in order to test it fairly, we need only apply it to a more familiar subject. Suppose one man were to say to another: "I acknowledge that you have a right to speak, but I have also a right to shut your mouth by force and prevent you from speaking, nay, I may punish you for uttering a single word, and in so doing, I do not oppose your right, I only make use of my own". Everybody must perceive at once that this language is fraught with the most irreconcilable contradiction. It presupposes two rights standing in direct opposition to each other, both of which may be exercised at the same time; and yet one of them may destroy the other. Nor does even the author contend that one of those rights is of a superior nature, for then the inferior right would, of course, give way before one of superior degree and its exercise in opposition to it would cease to be right and become wrong. But, on the contrary, he places both rights on the same footing of perfect equality. It is plain, therefore, that they will remain perpetually balanced, at least, until the external agency of force comes to destroy the equilibrium in which they must otherwise forever stand in with respect to each other. Thus Vattel's doctrine opens the way for a struggle between force and right, which is an inexhaustible source of controversy, violence, and war.

Not satisfied, however, with attempting to maintain his proposition by argument, this author endeavours to illustrate it by examples. He contends that nothing is more frequent in war than similar collisions of opposite rights. "When", says he, "I exhaust a country from whence you draw your subsistence, when I besiege a city with which you carried on a large trade, I doubtless injure you, I cause losses and inconveniences to you, but it is without design of hurting you, I only make use of my rights, and consequently do you no injustice".

A very simple and natural distinction will easily shew that these examples do not at all justify or support the doctrine for which Vattel contends. It is undeniably true that by the law of nature every man is at liberty to pursue his own happiness and welfare, and is not to be blamed even tho' injury to his neighbor by the *consequence*, but it is not lawful for anyone to do injury to another in the first instance, as the *means* thro' which he is to derive benefit to himself. Thus, a shopkeeper or a mechanic may set up his shop or his trade in the neighbourhood of another of the same profession and thus draw to himself a considerable part of his customers, but he may not lawfully seize his rival's goods, or shut up his shop by force, because it interferences with his own profits. In the same manner a belligerent may besiege an enemy's city or lay waste an enemy's country, careless of that loss or damage which a neighbouring neutral nation may suffer in consequence of it, but it would be absurd to suppose that he may besiege or blockade a neutral city, to prevent his enemy from carrying on with it a profitable trade, or exhaust a neutral territory, in order to starve that enemy, who, perhaps, may derive from it his principal means of subsistence. This distinction is so obvious, that it needs only to be pointed out, to command the assent of every man who is not absolutely blinded by passion or prejudice. Leaving, therefore, Mr. Vattel's illustrations, we return to his principles.[20]

§11: Vattel's Doctrine Further Considered

It may be, we believe, laid down as a clear and undeniable proposition that if neutrals possess the right to supply one of the belligerents with certain articles, the other belligerent cannot legally forbid its exercise and punish the violation of his prohibition by the confiscation of the obnoxious merchandise; if,

---

[20] Those who deny this proposition will probably cite as an instance of opposite rights existing at the same time that of two independent nations to make war upon each other. Each of them, it will be said, has a right to make war upon its adversary, and those two rights are in direct opposition to one another. But the right of making war, considered as merely permissive, exhibits no such contradiction. It belongs to all nations and may be exercised by two or more at the same time. By its exercise, indeed, nations are set in opposition to one another and by the same means pursue contrary objects, which both claim as incontestable rights so that in the exercise of the right of war, that is when two nations are engaged in it, there exists in appearance two opposite rights. But it is not so in fact, for in that case there can be but *one right*, that of the power which is engaged in a just war, whether offensive or defensive. Its adversary does not exercise a right, but makes an ill use of it by converting it into a wrong; it commits an act of violence condemned by the most positive principles of the law of nations; for according to those principles, the right of making war has, and can have, but one object which is to put a stop to injustice. Therefore, it can only be lawfully exercised by that sovereign who is in the last predicament, or rather, it exists for him alone; his enemy makes a wrongful use of it, and as I have already said, is guilty of violence of which his superior power alone can secure the impunity, but which neither power nor success can legitimate. It is easy to make the application of these principles to belligerents and neutrals. If the former are entitled to carry on a particular branch of trade, the latter have no right whatever to forbid it, and if they do, they do not exercise a lawful right, but commit a wrongful act. Such is the true state of the question – which sophistry and party spirit may indeed misrepresent but can never change.

on the contrary, the belligerent has a right to issue such prohibition, the neutral cannot be innocent in disobeying it and this act of disobedience to a competent authority cannot be called the exercise of a lawful right. For certainly the same thing never can at once be lawful and unlawful between the same parties and under the same circumstances. This is so true, that while moral cause which compels the rights of the neutral, tho' equal to that of the belligerent to yield to it in every case. Vattel, well aware of this difficulty, has at last recourse to *necessity*, the ever ready plea of power when every other source of justification fails. "If", says he, "our rights clash with and reciprocally injure each other, it follows from the effect of an *inevitable necessity*" (*Law of Nations*, Book 3, §111). Here then, after pursuing them thro' a cloud of sophistry which has no other object but to conceal the real state of the argument, we find the ultimate ground on which our adversaries rest danger to the safety of the belligerent and the consequent necessity of warding off that danger. But we have already shewn that even this hackneyed plea, this *ultima ratio* is not admissible in the case before us. We have shewn the wide difference which exists between arms and ammunition and timber and other articles necessary for the building and fitting out of ships, that the proper and direct use of the former is to do *harm* and consequently to obstruct the full exercise of a positive right, and that the same cannot be said of the latter – and by a reference to the greatest number of modern treaties, we have proved to a demonstration that naval stores are not so dangerous to the safety of belligerents as is pretended, for if they were real obstructions to exercise of the right of self-preservation, which is the true foundation of war, it would be absurd to stipulate their freedom in treaties, and those very stipulations most incontestably prove that the contracting parties do not consider articles of this description in so very alarming a point of view.[21]

---

[21] There is an enumeration of contraband articles which consists entirely of warlike implements, and which are to be considered as all other merchandise declared free. It is true that by a special convention made in 1658 naval stores are also declared to be articles of contraband, but it is sufficient to read that declaration to be satisfied that in that instance the

§12: Argument Summed Up

The pleas of *danger* and *necessity* being thus shewn not to be founded in fact, and the pretended right to seize and confiscate naval stores being proved to be neither founded on treaties nor on general usage, nothing remains but to turn back to first principles and here we find that of the independence of nations in full force, which must be the rule, unless it is admitted that with powerful governments, justice is a mere matter of opinion, that their duties are to be measured only by their interest, that because they are strong they may lawfully do anything which is convenient to them; in a word, that they have over the weak an arbitrary jurisdiction, which they would not venture to exercise over their own subjects, and which they would not permit others to ascribe upon themselves. Let us not lose sight of this important truth, that so long as the policy of great nations shall be directed by their exclusive interest, the whole universe is doomed to be a bloody scene of disturbances, war, and usurpation.

§13: Grotius

Grotius has also discussed this question. He distinguished between three species of things; some that are necessary only in war, such as arms, others that are of no use for purposes of hostility or defence, and lastly others which are of a mixed nature and are useful both in peace and war; as for instance, money, provisions, ships and their appurtenances. In speaking of arms, he says, that the nation which supplies them is to be

---

Protector imposed that restriction upon Sweden by the terror of his superior power. Besides, the convention was only to have its effect during the war then existing between Spain and Great Britain. And the freedom of naval stores is expressly stipulated in the following treaties, among others, to wit: 1st between France and England in 1655, 1667, 1713, 1786. 2nd between England and Holland in 1668 and 1674. 3rd between Spain and France in 1659. 4th between France and Holland in 1713. It would be too tedious to recite all the treaties in which a similar stipulation is contained.

considered as an enemy.[22] Those that are of no use for war present no difficulty. As to the third species, I shall quote his own words: "As to the third sort of things that are of doubtful or equivocal use, we must distinguish the actual state of the war. For if I cannot defend myself without intercepting those things which are sent to my enemy, *necessity* will give me a good right to them, but upon condition of restitution, unless I have just cause to the contrary".[23]

The doctrine of Grotius, as far as it relates to articles of the first description, is entirely conformable to the ancient system and therefore has over that of Vattel at least the advantage of consistency. If it be admitted that supplying enemies with arms or implements of war is a crime or offence against the law of nations, the right of seizure and confiscation by way of punishment, follows, of course. But Vattel was surely not aware of the extent of this concession which he made, when he excluded the furnishing even of warlike articles from the list of crimes in which it had stood so long almost without contradiction, he there gave up a vantage ground, the loss of which all his ingenuity has not been able to supply, as it left him no plea but *necessity*, the *caput mortuum*, as we have shewn, of all his arguments which his artful web of sophistry is insufficient to conceal.

In the same predicament Grotius finds himself when he comes to treat of the third species of merchandise, of those that are useful in peace as well as in war. Unwilling to class them among those which it is criminal to supply, but desirous nevertheless to find a plea on which to justify their seizure, *necessity* again is the only one which appears to have occurred to him, the only one at least which he pretends to make any use;[24] he does not, however, like Vattel, attempt to colour it, and

---

[22] In primo genere verum est dictum Amalasuinthae ad Justinianum, in hostium esse partibus qui ad bellum necessaria hosti administrat. *De Jure belli ac pacis*, Book III, c. 1, §5.

[23] In tertio illo genere usus ancipitis distinguendus erit belli status. Nam si tuere me non possum, ni quae mittunter intrecipian, necessitas jus dabit, sed sub onere restitutionis, nisi causa alia accedat. Ibid.

[24] I think it proper to enquire here into the real meaning of the word *necessity*. This subject has long been considered as exclusively within the

by artful reasonings to divert the attention of its readers from its naked deformity; with laudable candor he at once confesses that necessity alone can justify the seizure of articles of doubtful or equivocal use, and that unless some other cause appears they are not to be confiscated, but restored to the owner.

---

range of what is called State policy, but I am of the opinion that it properly belongs to the law of nations. *Necessity* as applied to States may be said to exist in those cases in which their safety or existence is directly involved; in such extreme cases everything must give way, every engagement, every obligation is at an end. Such is the doctrine taught us by the primordial principles of natural law. But if that absolute, that extreme necessity, is not evident, if the word is only made use of as a cover for mere expediency, to facilitate some political design or to ward off some partial damage, it cannot in such case justify the breach of any engagement, or violation of the rights of another party. This question is highly important to neutrals. The freedom of their navigation and commerce is founded either on the rules and principles of the law of nations, or on some special treaties. To restrict it at the will of one of the parties would be a violation of positive law, and consequently of public faith, which is the bond of nations. This is especially true when there exists formal engagements. If a power under the pretence of necessity could break them at her sole will and pleasure, then treaties would be idle and nugatory; they would be snares fraught with the mischief which they appeared intended to guard against; the tranquility of nations would be at the mercy of powerful States, and every kind of confidence and security would be at an end.

But, will it be said, when I contracted engagements, they were relative to the then existing order of things which was to be considered as a tacit condition thereof, that order of things is changed, therefore my engagements are no longer binding upon me, for had I foreseen what has happened or had things been in the same situation that they now are, I would not have contracted them; and this is what is called the reason of State. If it should be indefinitely admitted, expediency will be the only rule of policy; it will maintain or break engagements according to the point of view in which affairs may be considered. Thus a treaty of peace or alliance which was thought useful at the time when it was made shall be performed or violated as it shall be thought to have continued or ceased to be so. The whole of the question resolves itself into this proposition: if the performance of your engagements endangers your safety or existence, they cease to be in force; in every other case, they are binding upon you even tho' by their fulfillment, you should suffer detriment or damage.

The correctness of this last principle cannot be called in question. If necessity compels you to lay hold of the property of an innocent friend, and divest it from its intended course, you have no right, at least, to inflict on him the punishment of confiscation. Where there is no guilt there can be no punishment. On the principles of Vattel, fairly construed, belligerents can have no right to confiscate even arms and ammunition, since that writer fully acknowledges the right of the neutral to carry them to an enemy. This argument applies with still greater force to those articles which we have now under consideration, and which not only Vattel, but Grotius and all other writers, as far as we know, admit to be innocent from their mixed and doubtful nature, and if we have shewn that no necessity exists for intercepting the neutral trade in those articles, we have fully made out our principle that they ought not even to be liable to seizure and we have done it without disturbing the long agitated question "whether necessity can in any case be a just plea for meddling with the rights or property of others", a question which has long since been settled in municipal jurisprudence, but will, we are afraid, for ever be considered as a problem in the law of nations.

§14: Conclusion

Let us therefore upon the whole conclude that there can be no just or honest plea for the seizure and confiscation of naval stores found on board of neutral vessels in time of war. Grotius admits that they cannot be lawfully confiscated and justifies their seizure only in cases of necessity which knows no law. Vattel contends for the right both of seizure and confiscation, but his very argument shews the futility of his doctrines. He was led astray by his predilection for Great Britain; his work was composed and published in the capital of that Kingdom.

Chapter IX.

Enemy's Property under a Neutral Flag

§1.

The third restriction which belligerents assume to impose upon neutrals concerns goods belonging to an enemy. They contend that neutrals have no right to carry such goods and when taken on board of their vessels, they consider them as lawful prize.

§2.

The advocates of that protection argue in the first place that a belligerent may take the property of the enemy wherever he may find it.[25] They say, moreover, that those who carry enemy's goods favour the commerce and industry of the hostile nation and supply her with the means of continuing the war, that this is prejudicial to the belligerent, and therefore that he has a clear right to prevent it. Hence the old adage: *que la robe amie ne sauve point la merchandise ennemie*, that a friend's property does not cover that of an enemy, and on that principle a neutral cannot lawfully carry enemy's goods, whatever may be the place of their growth, shipment or destination, and if he attempts to do it, he is punished by confiscation, and even mere presumptions are interpreted against him (See C. 16, §12).

§3.

But this protection is clearly not justified by the exception above mentioned, which relates only to the carrying of articles that are of *immediate use in war* because there are the only ones that may be considered as *dangerous*; that exception therefore

---

[25] To avoid repetition I will indicate here that I shall examine or refute below the views of Messrs. *Jenkinson*, *Bynkershoek*, *Barbeyrac*, *Lampredi*, and others. [WEB]

cannot be farther extended without the consent of neutrals, and if the extension that is pretended to be given to it were admissible, every neutral nation that should carry on trade, even by land, with an enemy would necessarily be guilty of an offense against the other belligerent who, if he could neither intercept the enemy nor the merchandize, would be authorized to consider the neutral nation as an enemy for every violation of the law of neutrality is an injury to one of the belligerents, and every injury is a cause of war. The absurdity of the last proposition sufficiently demonstrates the absurdity of the first.

A neutral nation that durst recur to first principles, I mean, if it was sufficiently strong to maintain them with success, might address a belligerent in this manner: "If in order not to endanger your existence I give up a part of that liberty to which I am entitled by the law of nature, I neither care nor ought to do so for any other cause: I cannot, I will not for our sake interrupt my navigation and commercial relations to the prejudice of my own subjects. All that I can and ought to do to maintain my impartiality is to take your property as well as that of your enemy under the safeguard of my flag. That is the only obligation which my neutrality imposes upon me. If as you pretend that industry of your enemy is injurious to you, why, then go and destroy it in his own country which the law of war gives you a right to invade; lay his lands waste, ruin his manufactories, carry away his money and even his subjects. Send forth your complaints to Heaven that the sun shines for him as for you, but respect the high seas, which neither belong to you nor to me, respect my flag, for it is not under your jurisdiction, but under my own; do not interrupt and harass my navigation which puts no obstacle in the way of your military operations; bear with my industry as I bear with yours. If I do you an injury by carrying the goods of your enemy, I would injure you still more were I to purchase them, for then I would procure him an immediate supply of money; and yet you do not carry your pretensions so far as to deny me the right of purchasing. After all, nothing is so easy as to elude the rigour of your pretended law, a few simulated documents will do the business, and such will in the end be the result of your abuse of powers if I cannot maintain my right by agreement or force.

Besides, if you possess the unlimited right of obstructing my navigation and commerce with your enemy under the specious pretence that it injures you, you may also, you even ought to prevent me from selling to him grain, wool, ashes &c., in a word, you may break up all my commercial intercourse with him and prohibit my vessels from entering his ports. All that you may do lawfully by a fair application of your principle, but you do not require so much, you do not pretend to prevent me from carrying the natural productions of my soil nor the produce of my industry. I therefore may with justice conclude that your system cannot be defended before the tribunal of reason and that it is only supported by the superiority and abuse of your powers, but abuse of power never can convert injustice into a lawful right. You have no objection to my trading with you; you even wish it, and you favour as much as you can our commercial intercourse; nay, you are well pleased to see your merchandise secure from capture under the protection of my flag, just so as I deal with you, I think proper to deal with your enemy; were I to act otherwise I would do him an injury, for I would be partial to you and consequently would cease to be neutral, and thus I would involve myself in war entirely for your sake".

§4.

Our opponents rely very much on an antiquated book called *Il consolato del mare*,[26] and on some other authorities among which are two treaties made in 1661 between England and the Courts of

[26] That compilation so little deserves to be quoted as an authority that even its date is uncertain, and nobody has as yet been able to discover the name of its compiler, the legal authority from whence it issued, nor the place where it was first enacted and put in force. But whatever may be the origin of the *Consolato*, and whatever may have been its authority in ancient times, it is now only to be considered as a mere collection of opinions or as a monument of the ancient jurisprudence of some countries bordering on the Mediterranean. It may be placed on the same shelf with the writings of *Albericus Gentilis* and *Selden*, with the laws of the Goths and Lombards and those of Rhodes, Oleron, &c.

Stockholm and Copenhagen; the former authorizes the capture of enemy's goods, but the second says nothing about it.[27]

§5.

It is pretended, it is true, that the true doctrine of the law of nations is to be found in treaties and in books of long established authority, and that all stipulations to the contrary in modern treaties are only exceptions to the ancient rule; but admitting this to be true, when the exceptions are very numerous and there remains but little room for the application of the old principles, are we not authorized to say that those exceptions are now become rules and constitute the common law of nations? Now, this freedom of enemy's goods under a neutral flag is stipulated in almost all the treaties made by England herself, from her treaty with Portugal in 1654 up to that which she entered into with Russia in 1797. I take no notice of the conventions signed in 1801 and 1803 between the three northern powers and Great Britain because they were the result of extraordinary circumstances, and in such cases, policy generally gets the better of principle. In proof of this assertion, I shall only cite one instance: in the commercial treaties made in 1766 and 1797 between Russia and England, it is stipulated that free ships shall make free goods, and on the contrary, the capture of enemy's goods on board of neutral ships is authorized by the convention of 1801. We must observe that the freedom of the neutral flag had been established by the armed neutrality not only by virtue and on the authority of treaties, but also as a necessary inference from the principles of natural law, and that the three northern crowns as well as almost all the other maritime powers adhered at the time to that convention and that France recognized its principles by the 27th Article of her commercial treaty with

[27] Those two treaties as well as the *Consolato* are principally cited and relied upon in England. There are some other similar treaties which were made in the fifteenth century, to wit: in 1406, 1446, 1460, 1468, 1486 between England, the Dukes of Burgundy, and Brittany and the Republic of Genoa. That made in 1716 between France and the three Hansa Towns also prohibits the transportation of enemy's goods.

Russia in the year 1787, and it is that almost general agreement of nations which is at this day pretended to be only an exception to the universal rule!

§6.

In order to determine whether a particular doctrine is a positive rule or only an exception, it is absolutely necessary to recur to the fundamental principles of natural law: now, one of those principles is that of perfect equality between nations, and the foundation of that equality is independence. Such is the general rule; and everything by which it is either restricted or modified can only be considered as an exception. Some of those exceptions are sacrifices which weak nations have consented to for the sake of peace; others are founded only on particular conventions or private interest, or have no other foundation than the exercise of lawless power.

This subject will be examined and considered more at large in Chapter XXII.

Chapter X.

Neutral Property under an Enemy's Flag

§1.

The fourth restriction imposed upon neutrals is the inverse of that which I have just spoken of. It is pretended that they are prohibited from shipping their goods on board of enemy's vessels.

§2.

This again is one of those questions on which neither principles, practice, or treaties are uniform. My intention is not to state all that has been done by the different governments in relation to this subject – much less to analyze the different treaties which have sanctioned the one or the other rules: for however absurd their stipulations may be, principles must bend to them and are of no avail against superior force. I shall therefore confine myself to stating and discussing the principles of the law of nations, where the only true solution of this question is to be sought for.

§3.

I already have shewn the correctness of the principle that free ships make free goods. It would seem at first view that in the present case the proposition ought to be reversed, for in the first case the neutral or hostile character of the goods is determined by that of the vessel; it might therefore be said that in the second the same rule of decision ought to take place, as an enemy's ship can offer no protection against an enemy, but that of superior force. According to general usage, the captured vessel is a lawful prize, and the property which her flag covers ought to share the same fate.

But this reasoning cannot be admitted.

If the neutral flag covers the enemy's goods, it is because it evidences the neutral character of the ship and because that ship is not amenable to any other jurisdiction than that of her sovereign; from whence it follows that a stranger cannot forcibly enter her without violating that jurisdiction and, of course, the independence of the sovereign to whom she belongs. There is no other exception to this principle but in the case of arms and warlike stores. It is not the same with the enemy's flag; it is not entitled to any of the advantages secured by the law of nations; it can claim no privilege, no immunity, no right resulting from national independence against its enemy; it is under the empire of force which may lawfully be employed against it. When captured, it is lawful prize, but not so the neutral goods, which are on board, because it preserves its original character notwithstanding the hostile character of the vessel, which cannot in any manner affect it. To explain these two propositions in a few words, I say: in the first case the neutral ships protects the enemy's property because the belligerent has no rights to enter or search her (see Chapters XVI and XVII); in the second, the neutral goods are safe on board of the enemy's ship because their neutral character is not affected by their being there.

§4.

It is on this last principle that in a continental war, neutral property is respected as tho' it be found in an enemy's city. No legal fiction can alter the nature of that principle, no supposition, no subterfuge can make the goods of neutrals be considered as belonging to any enemy; there is but one case in which such a thing may be presumed without direct proof, it is when the neutral property is not satisfactorily evidence by the usual documents, and then, all that is found on board of the vessel is presumed to belong to her owner. I even look upon that presumption as so conclusive that in my opinion no after proof can be admitted to rebut it. Shippers ought to be acquainted with the laws and usages of the sea, and to know that particularly in time of war all their requisites ought to be strictly and rigorously complied with; otherwise, that the vessel which they employ is liable to be seized and confiscated, and consequently that it is incumbent upon them to comply with the requisite forms, in order to prevent their property from sharing the fate of the vessel. If commerce and navigation were always carried on fairly and without fraud *ex post facto* proofs might certainly be admitted, but unfortunately such frauds are too frequent, especially in time of war not to employ every means to prevent or punish it.

It has been gravely said that the neutral merchant knows beforehand, or is presumed to know, the danger to which his goods are exposed by being shipped on board of an enemy's vessel and that consequently he can impute their loss only to himself. Certainly a man who knows that a wood is infested with robbers or voracious animals and who nevertheless ventures into it can accuse nobody if he is robbed or devoured; for the same reasons the navigator is alone to be blamed if he puts himself in the way of pirates and is plundered or even carried into slavery by them, because those men know of no law nor authority, or rather robbery and plunder are their supreme law. But it is not the same thing with civilized nations who maintain an intercourse with each other, who have common interests and are bound by the same law: they are subjected to the observance of strict rules; they cannot violate them without being guilty of injustice and giving just cause of retaliation and revenge.

Such is the point of view in which this question is to be considered. The goods of a neutral, wherever they may be found, are still his property and must be treated as such unless by his own act, or by some special treaty or agreement, he has impressed upon it a different character. This is the plain, unsophisticated principle of law and we must presume that it is respected by all governments. If there are some who violate it, they only can do it with impunity with respect to those weak nations that are forced to submit to every injury and think themselves happy if they are left in the possession of a shadow of political existence. But those that have the means of asserting their rights, know how [to] support them in an efficient manner, or if they neglect them, or from particular considerations are induced to give them up by positive agreement, it is to be supposed that there are powerful reasons which compel them to be silent, or to enter into such positive stipulations. But these stipulations founded on their personal interests and political views concern nobody but themselves and can have no effect on those States who have not subscribed to them. Perhaps an argument may be drawn from the acts and proclamations of governments, by which they declare the conduct which they mean to pursue in the course of an existing war. I shall hereafter examine the import and effect of these documents (see Chapter XV).

Chapter XI.

Of the Extension of Neutral Trade in Time of War

§1.

It is pretended that the commerce of neutrals is not lawfully capable of any extension in time of war, and that neutral nations are not then allowed to carry on any trade from which they were excluded in time of peace. This doctrine owes its origin to the ingenuity of the British Government who have maintained it with a considerable degree of warmth. We shall now bring it to the test of reason and principle.

Every nation has an unlimited right to navigate the seas, but the right to trade with others is not thus indefinite; it depends on the will of those with whom commerce is to be carried on. A nation is at liberty to open or shut her ports as she thinks proper; she may with respect to her dominions make laws or regulations as her interest or convenience requires; she may punish or prohibit the entry into her ports the importation of foreign goods, or the exportation of its own produce. On this subject she is not accountable to anyone and retaliation is the only measure which the law of nations allows to those who think themselves aggrieved by her conduct.

If from motives of mere municipal regulation a government may be induced to enact prohibitory laws in time of peace, the circumstances of war may induce it to repeal or suspend the prohibition.

§2.

It is asked whether neutrals may avail themselves of the permission thus granted by one of the belligerents, without being guilty of a violation of neutrality? And whether the other belligerent may lawfully prevent them from doing it?

All commercial relations as well between nations as between individuals are voluntary and are not founded on any general principle of the law of nations. Nothing demonstrates this truth more clearly than the numerous treaties of commerce by which the contracting parties settle and regulate according to their will and pleasures the kind of intercourse and advantages which they mutually grant to one another. They are not accountable to society at large for the favours they grant, receive or refuse and do not in any other cases infringe the obligations imposed upon them by the law of nations. War makes no alteration in that state of things between nations in amity with each other; it makes no alteration in their rights, relations, and reciprocal freedom; the one may grant favours and the other receive them without doing an injury to other nations, whether friends or enemies. No doubt the belligerent who grants means thereby to benefit her trade and to elude the obstacles which the war puts in the way of her own navigation and the neutral who receives is instrumental in promoting that design. But all this they may both lawfully do and no earthly power has a right to prevent them; such a power, if it existed, would be the absolute master of all the others and from that moment there would be an end to national independence, or we would be obliged at once to acknowledge that the whole universe is bound to obey the law which belligerents are pleased to dictate. This would certainly be a simple and expeditious mode of cutting short every difficulty; it would put an end to controversies and establish peace universally thro' the world; but what kind of peace, I leave the reader to judge.

§3.

But, will one of the belligerents say (see Chapter XXII) if a neutral undertakes to carry on the commerce of my enemy who can no longer carry it on himself, he thereby affords him an inestimable advantage, for he promotes his prosperity and enables him to carry on the war for a larger period; therefore, he ceases to be impartial, he violates his neutrality, he acts hostilely against me, particularly so, as this new branch of commerce is only allowed to him on account of the war, and with the direct view of serving my enemy and consequently of doing me an injury.

§4.

It is true, and I repeat it, that if everything was to bend to the laws of war, and to the interest of the belligerents; if the rights and independence of nations were to weigh nothing in the scale against that interest, the pretensions that I speak of would be a matter of course. Belligerent governments would decide in the last resort of the rights and duties of neutrals; a simple declaration would be sufficient to make known their supreme will and to command obedience: *et nutu totum contremuit orbem*. But such supremacy has never been admitted and never have belligerent nations been allowed the rights of universal monarchy. The truth is that in time of war, neutrals preserve all their rights, faculties, and relations; they may extend them and avail themselves of all the advantages which the war puts in their way, as a dealer in corn takes advantage of the scarcity of provisons and to deprive them of that right is to destroy their independence. This general principle, as I have already observed, admits but of one exception, that of contraband of war, properly so called, and it cannot be extended farther. It is well known that neutrals commonly grow rich at the expense of belligerents, who, on the contrary, are ruined by war, but they knew it would be so before they engaged in hostilities. And it is to be wished for the sake of humanity and public quiet, that this consideration had more influence on the minds of men, and that the immense loss which belligerents suffer in their commerce should be put in the balance together with the expense of blood and treasure which war necessarily occasions and weighted against the uncertain advantages which are expected from it.

§5.

Undoubtedly the neutral who carries on a commerce of exportation and importation with one of the belligerents may in a indirect manner injure the other. But on the one hand such neutral is answerable for it unless he should refuse to carry on the same trade with the other belligerent, which is not to be supposed; on the other hand, it is known that the industry of a nation cannot prosper, even in time of peace without injuring more or less the competitors. It is a cause of rivalship, envy, nay, of considerable displeasure, but not a wrongful injury; otherwise, as there never is a time in which nations do not more or less injure each other in that way, there is an ever subsisting lawful cause of war. But let us return to our subject. You that are a belligerent pretend to prevent me from engaging in a branch of trade which I did not carry on in time of peace. By what right, by what authority, do you set up such a pretension and do you impose such a law upon me? Have I bound myself to it by my treaties with you? I have only to tell you in a few words that you were not the cause that I did not carry on that particular trade in time of peace, nor that I am permitted to carry it on during the war; with you have absolutely nothing to do; I am exercising an inalienable right and your pretension goes to destroy it; nay, according to your own construction it goes to compel me to concur in the destruction of your enemy with whom I am at peace and to do an injury to my own subjects. It is true your interest requires it, but interest never was sufficient to create a right; when taken as the only rule of conduct, it generally produces nothing but injustice, controversies, and wars.

§6.

The question which I am discussing exhibits a truly remarkable contrast. The neutral renounces a branch of commerce to which he is accustomed because the belligerents considered the objects thereof as dangerous, and the endeavour to prevent him from carrying on a lawful commerce for the only reason that he is not in the habit of carrying it on in time of peace. These two contradictory prohibitions can only be reconciled by the argument of expediency which reconciles everything because it subjects everything to the power of force and under such a mode of argumentation, reason, law, and justice are of no avail.

§7.

I shall conclude this article with the following remark. The neutral is obliged to abstain from supplying a belligerent with such articles as are of immediate use in war: the merchandise that he carries in consequence of the new direction of his commerce is not of that description; therefore, it is not and cannot be included within the prohibition. The principle of which that prohibition is founded is an exception to a general rule and all exceptions to general principles are to be strictly construed. They therefore cannot be enlarged by arbitrary interpretations.[28]

Independent of the several restrictions which I have mentioned, there are other points which are insisted upon by belligerents which are the source of much vexation to neutrals

---

[28] That doctrine was broached for the first time by the English Government at the beginning of the war of 1755. France allowed neutrals to ship provisions in her ports, such as flour, wine, brandy, etc. for its own colonies, and to bring back in exchange colonial produce. England ordered all those vessels to be captured on the outward as well as on the homeward voyage. She thus secured to herself a monopoly of colonial produce and procured at a cheap rate the flour which she stood greatly in need of. It must not be believed that her intention was to famish the French colonies, for her own vessels carried provisions thither and purchased their produce in order to enhance its price at their will and pleasure in Europe. That is what the English writers call the pure principles of the law of nations. But now, let us set England herself in opposition to her own doctrine. Everybody is acquainted with her famous Navigation Act; let us suppose her to be in the same situation in which France was during the war of 1755; that is to say, that her navigation and commerce are interrupted in consequence of the war, is it to be believed that she would let her colonies in a fate of penury and starvation? That she would not invite neutrals to supply her inability? That she would not for a while repeal or modify her Navigation Act in their favour? Any one of our readers may easily answer these three questions, and the Court of London itself would undoubtedly in such a case answer them conformably to our principles.

and occasion frequent controversies and much injustice. The first that I shall notice is the pretended rule by which everything is presumed against neutrals.

Chapter XII.

Of Presumption with Respect to Property Shipped on Board of Neutral Vessels

§1.

No presumption can arise but where found or irregularity may be supposed to exist. We are going to consider what ought to be the effect of it in either case.

§2.

Fraud is guilt; therefore it cannot be presumed, it must be made out by satisfactory proof. This is an undeniable principle, and we have already had occasion to apply it elsewhere.

§3.

The presumption that we speak of is an inference drawn from particular facts. Goods are shipped on board of a neutral vessel, but some of the ship's papers point out their owner or the consignee. If the merchandise is lawful and the sovereign of the cruiser admits the principle that free ships make free goods, there can be no difficulty in the case whatever may be the destination of the vessel. But if the goods are contraband, they may be seized if the neutral vessel is met with near the coasts of the enemy, altho' she be bound to a neutral port, because the natural presumption is that her master intended to put in there under a fraudulent pretense unless he had been forced to alter his course. If the vessel is met on the high seas and is bound to a neutral port, the want of a bill of lading does not authorize the seizure even of prohibited goods, because it is to be presumed that they have the same situation with the remainder of the cargo.

§4.

But the question becomes more intricate with respect to those States which do not admit the principle that free ships make free goods. It is asked whether in that case the want of a bill of lading is sufficient to induce a presumption that the goods on board are enemy's property and whether in consequence thereof they are liable to seizure as is asserted by those States which I have just mentioned?

I observe in the first place that those goods may as well belong to a neutral as to an enemy. Secondly that the flag indicates the neutrality of the vessel and that all the property on board is under its safeguard and participates in its immunity. This is the only principle that can be admitted. Therefore the master of such a vessel has a right to say: this merchandize, if lawful, is entitled to the privilege of my flag; this principle is undeniable, its effect cannot be destroyed by a mere presumption, the offspring of your avidity.

Such a declaration is certainly more to be favoured than the presumption of the cruiser; for it cannot be too often repeated that we are speaking of lawful goods. If the master's declaration be false, it at least tends to a legitimate object, that of avoiding injustice, whilst the suspicions of the cruiser lead to no other object than an odious spoliation.

§5.

Let us suppose, however, that the master makes no other declaration but that he took the goods in a neutral port and that they are bound to another of the same description; but that, as it frequently happens, he is ignorant of the name of their owner, what inference is the cruiser authorized to draw therefrom? Is the ignorance of the master sufficient to induce a presumption of fraud and to charge it upon the shipper? but in that case, on which ground shall that presumption rest? Presumptions are conjectures with respect to doubtful things, they ought to result from circumstances and probabilities that often occur, they are, in short, the anticipated judgment of common sense founded on what most frequently takes place. The Civil and Common laws acknowledge several kind of presumptions, but they consider them all as inferences drawn either from a law or from antecedent facts; in a word, inferences at least require a great probability. As to laws, there are none in the ordinary sense of the word between nations. They acknowledge none but natural reason and the treaties. but reason tells us that fraud cannot be presumed. Nor are there in the case before us any antecedent facts on which to found such a presumption. For let us suppose that the Shipper A had made a fraudulent consignment; it does not follow from thence that the Shipper B has acted in the same manner. Besides, an accidental solitary fact is not sufficient to induce a presumption; it can only arise from such facts as are of frequent occurrence.

§6.

For all these reasons, I think that I may lay it down as a certain maxim that whenever innocent goods are found on board of a neutral vessel, they are to be considered as neutral property and that the contrary presumption founded on a particular fact is inadmissible. Let us not forget that this presumption of guilt is odious and is not to be favoured.

§7.

It will perhaps be objected that with the help of this maxim, neutrals with impunity carry on all the commerce of the enemy; that such a thing cannot be tolerated by those belligerents who confiscate enemy's property tho' under a neutral flag, and that it is precisely with a view to prevent it that they have declared that all goods, the real ownership of which does not appear on the face of the ship's papers, should be confiscated.

But I have already refuted that doctrine and shewed it to be in opposition with the elementary principles of the law of nations; it is itself an injustice which is in the case made use of to justify another. At any rate, that rule can only be applied to those nations who from interested motives, or in consequence of forced engagements, or from a sense of their own weakness, have submitted to a system of jurisprudence which is subversive of the most self-evident principles of the code of nations, and I acknowledge that in such a case no more need be said about rights or wrong; submission, whether the result of interest or compulsion cuts short all difficulties as well as all pretensions; it is the supreme law, and subjects must bend to the policy of their government.

§8.

But even admitting the legality of the system in question, it does not follow that lawful goods are liable to confiscation, because their ownership does not appear on the fact of the ship's papers. The principle that I have laid down still remains the same; the presumption is in favour of the flag, therefore it must protect the goods, altho' it be not ascertained to whom they belong. But what support can the master of a vessel expect from a sovereign that has given up or rather sacrifices the rights of his nations; he will be obliged to submit to force and remain silent, and at a future day his case will be cited as a precedent, and as evidence of the customary law of nations.

§9.

As to the fear that neutrals should carry on all the commerce of one of the powers at war, it cannot legalize a doctrine which is in itself illegal: experience shows that there is so little ground for this apprehension that it can only be considered as a practice. But even if it were well founded, it would not follow that belligerents have therefore a right to obstruct the navigation. and commerce of neutrals. I know very well that power makes use of a different and more irresistible logic, but mine is founded on principles only and not on the law of the strongest.

§10.

There is no doubt but that a belligerent sovereign sees with reluctance his enemy sell the produce of his soil and industry and receive in exchange the articles which he stands in need of, but his feelings have nothing to do with the law of nations; it is not a principle of law that everything must yield to the private interest of the belligerents that neutrals must submit to their will and sacrifice to them the interest of their own subjects. War undoubtedly confers great privileges, but are they to be exercised on those who have nothing to do with the controversy, or on the sovereigns who have thought proper to wage an inconsiderate and perhaps an unjust war, and who, to support it, violate all the obligations of social order? That idea is so shocking that it is difficult to conceive how it can still remain a problem.

Chapter XIII.

Of Presumption with Respect to Neutral Goods on Board of Enemy's Ships

The maxim which I have established concerning doubtful goods found on board of neutral ships is also applicable to goods of the same description found on board of enemy's vessels. The presumption is in favour of the flag, and therefore the merchandise found on board which the ship's papers do not shew to be neutral, shares the fate of the vessel and is, of course, lawful prize. It is, as I have already observed, of very great importance that this rule should be strictly enforced, in order to compel shippers to observe a greater regularity in their shipments; they ought to know the dangers to which a hostile ship is exposed, and they were well acquainted with the rapacity of cruisers; it is therefore incumbent upon them to take all necessary precautions for the preservation of this property. If they neglect those precautions, they must lay the consequences to their own door; their government cannot protect them nor procure them an indemnity.

Chapter XIV.

Of Neutral Vessels Deviating from Their Direct Course

§1.

Neutral vessels are sometimes confiscated for putting into a port not mentioned in the clearance.

§2.

This question depends entirely on the usages of the sea; now, it is a fact evidenced by general practice that the master of a vessel, even tho' his passport mentions only one port of destination, is at liberty to put in into other ports. It but too often happens that a vessel cannot find a return cargo in the port mentioned in her clearance and that she is obliged to seek a lading elsewhere. The nation alone on whose coasts she sails has a right to visit her, because she may be loaded with contraband articles, or suspected of attempting to defraud the revenue by a fraudulent landing of the goods on board. She may be suspected from the very circumstances of setting her course. But a nation that has not the same interest has no right to control her navigation and cannot attempt it without violating the freedom of the seas. The cruiser may undoubtedly ascertain the character of the vessel in those places where he may lawfully exercise the right of search, but if there appears no irregularity in that respect, he has not a right to enquire any farther. It is well known that in general the passport of a vessel serves only for our voyage, but that limitation does not prevent her from touching at another place. The voyage is at an end as soon as the vessel has returned to the port from whence she had sailed and if she sails on another voyage without taking a new passport, she is, in peace as well as in war, considered as a pirate.

Perhaps it will be said that the rule which I have above established cannot be admitted in time of war, because at such time every formality must be strictly pursued, everything is liable to suspicion, and the least irregularity is an evidence of fraud.

§3.

But where is the foundation for that extreme rigour? The right supposed to belong to belligerents to trespass on the freedom of the seas and to search and confiscate neutral vessels is founded on a mere exception to a general rule, that is to say, on the necessity that there is to punish a dangerous fraud. If the master of a neutral vessel by touching at several ports commits such fraud, he may incontestably be detained and punished for it. But if he is not in fault from the course of his vessel and the nature of her cargo no danger is likely to result to the belligerent, I ask on what principle she can be detained and what views of necessity or even of utility can be promoted by her detention? That the passport does not mention the name of the places at which she may accidentally touch can only induce a suspicion of guilt, in case the nature of her cargo or the place in which she was met should concur in assisting it: I mean of the cargo consisted of real contraband articles or if the vessel were met in a place where she might lawfully be searched?

Those governments, however, who wish to be just acquit the master in such cases, unless they are coupled with very aggravating circumstances. Among those we must include that of a vessel laden with prohibited goods and bound to a neutral country but which without being forced to it by stress of weather or otherwise steers a false course and is met with within jurisdictional waters. For instance, in the event of a war between France and Great Britain, a neutral vessel apparently bound to Spain approaches without necessity too near the coasts of France. The English cruisers in such a case would be clearly authorized not only to examine her papers, in consequence of the suspicion induced by her apparent deviation, but also to detain her if she were laden with contraband goods; for it could then be no longer a mere case of suspicion or of mere apparent intention, but she would be taken in the very act of violating the law and her punishment would be so much the more just that her master must have known that he was attempting to do an unlawful act and to commit not only a breach of the law of nations, but of the engagement which he had taken with his own sovereign when he received his clearance. The same thing would take place if the neutral vessel were met on the coasts of England by a French cruiser, but if she should be met in neutral waters, the cruisers of the power at war have not even a right to ascertain her neutral character and still less to inquire into the nature and destination of her cargo. But let us speak frankly, the rapacity of cruisers far exceeds the avarice of neutral merchants, but belligerent governments think it their interest to encourage and protect the former; hence the extraordinary favour which is shewn to them, and favour, when the interests of a third party are concerned, is real injustice. Upon the whole, the true state of the matter is this: the cruiser wishes to enrich himself with the spoils of others, and the merchant ventures his stock and industry to improve his fortune; the former employs all his art and ingenuity to discover offenders, and the latter does the same to escape from the grasp of lawless power.

Chapter XV.

Of Declaratory Edicts and Proclamations

§1.

Those governments who restrain the freedom of navigation and unjustly assume the right of regulating it according to their own interest believe that an Edict or proclamation issued by a belligerent is sufficient to compel all nations to submit to it: they allege in their justification similar acts of their own and of other nations (see Chapter XXIII). They have even found pliant civilians who have not shrunk from the defense of their cause.

§2.

Necessity first introduced similar edicts and usage has sanctioned them, and indeed but for them, all would be uncertainty and confusion, for every one settles, interprets, and applies the principles of the law of nations according to his own interest; the neutral maintains with great reason that being ignorant of the war, he neither could no ought to have taken precautions for the safety of his flag and of the absolute freedom of his navigation and trade. Declaratory edicts at least prevent neutrals from being taken unawares by informing them of the existing state of the war and of the rules and line of conduct which the belligerents intend to pursue with respect to them.

§3.

But those edicts, to be entitled to their full effect, ought not only be notified in due form to the neutral States, but also to receive their assent in as much as their interests are concerned, for no one has a right to prescribe rules to them or to restrict navigation against their wills. If they keep silence, it may be construed into a tacit consent, altho' it is but too often the effect of inability to resist or of a timorous policy.

§4.

Experience has taught, moreover, that similar edicts, as well as treaties, obtain respect only from weak governments; and that those powers which are in a situation to assert their rights and dignity either recognize or reject them as suits their situation and their political relations; while those who make such edicts always find some pretence to extend their operation derived from the particular motives and circumstances of the war. During those of 1740 and 1755 between France and Great Britain, the latter power, then superior to the rest of the world at sea, dictated to neutrals. During that of America (1778), France that in her turn had the maritime superiority, altho' she did not take advantage of it, shewed them considerable favour, and they, by the Treaty or convention of 1780, called the armed neutrality (See Chapter XXV), adopted her principles which had been before made known by a declaratory Edict.[29] That convention,

---

[29] Edict of France of the 26 July 1778. For the satisfaction of our readers, we think it proper to insert this Edict here at full length. It is as follows:

Art. 1st. All vessels of war are prohibited from arresting the ships of neutral powers and bringing them into the ports of the Kingdom, even tho' they should come out of or be bound to the ports of an enemy, excepting nevertheless those that might be carrying succours to blockaded, invested or besieged places. With respect to neutral vessels that might be laden with contraband articles and bound to the enemy, they may be arrested and the said contraband articles shall be seized and confiscated, but the vessels and the remainder of their cargo shall be liberated, unless the said contraband articles should amount to two thirds of the value of the cargo, in which case the ship and the whole cargo shall be confiscated. His Majesty further reserving to himself the right of revoking the liberty mentioned in the present Article if the enemy powers shall not grant the same in like manner within six months from the publication of this regulation.

Art. 2d. The masters of neutral vessels shall be bound to make proof at sea of the property being neutral, but exhibiting their passports, bills of lading, invoices, and other ship papers, one of which at least shall expressly and precisely certify the property to be neutral; and as to such charter-parties and other documents as shall not be signed, they are to be considered as null and of no effect.

Art/ 3rd. All vessels taken, of whatever nation they may be, whether neutral or allies, from which it shall be proved that papers have been thrown out, or otherwise suppressed or put away, shall be declared lawful prizes together with their cargoes, nor shall it be necessary to examine what there papers were, by whom they were thrown overboard, or whether there remained such other papers on board as might sufficiently prove that the vessel and her cargo belonged to friends or allies.

Art. 4th. No passport or clearance shall serve more than one voyage; every such passport or clearance shall be considered as null and void, if it be proved that the vessel to which it was granted was not at the time of granting the same within the dominions of the prince from whom it issued.

Art. 5th. No regard shall be paid to the passports of neutral powers when those who shall have obtained the same shall not have complied with or shall have acted contrary to the directions thereof, or when the passports that contain a different name of the vessel from that which shall appear by the other ship papers, unless those papers shall contain the proof of the alteration of the name and of the identity of the vessel, and unless they are attested by the public officers of the place of her departure, and registered by the principal public officer of the same place.

Art. 6th. No regard shall likewise be paid to the passports granted by neutral or allied powers, either to the owners or masters of vessels, subjects to the States in enmity with His Majesty, if they have not been naturalized or have not resided within the dominions of the said powers three months before the commencement of hostilities; nor shall the said masters or owners so naturalized enjoy the effects of their naturalization if since obtaining the same they have returned into the dominions of the States in enmity with His Majesty to carry on their commerce.

Art. 7th. No vessels built in an enemy's country or who shall have been owned by an enemy shall be considered as neutral or as the property of allies, if there shall not be found on board some authentic documents attested by public officers that may ascertain the date of the sale, and prove that it was made to a neutral ally previous to the commencement of hostilities; and if the said instrument of sale or transfer shall not have been duly registered before the principal officer of the place of departure, and signed by the owner or his attorney.

Art. 8th. With respect to enemy-built vessels which shall have been captured by His Majesty's ships, those of his allies or subjects during the war, and shall afterwards have been sold to the subjects of allied or neutral States, they shall not be considered as lawful prize, if there shall not be found on board instruments of writing in legal form duly attested by public officers authorized for that purpose, proving the sale to have been made to neutrals or allies, either in the ports of France, or in those of neutral or allied powers, in default of which documents proving the capture as well as the sale, such vessels shall be ajudged lawful prize.

Art. 9th. All foreign vessels on board of which there shall be a merchant, supercargo, clerk, capitain, or mate (*officier major*) of a country

the principal object of which was to assert by force of arms the treaties already subsisting between the contracting parties and the two powers at war, and to establish their stipulations as principles of natural law, was principally the work of Catharine II. Most of the other States acceded to it, and namely the United Provinces of the Netherlands, after having refused to comply with the demands of the British Government.[30]

---

in enmity with His Majesty, or the crew of which (exclusive of the officers) shall be composed beyond one-third of the subjects of enemy powers, or who shall not have on board the roll or list of the said crew (*role d'equipage*) attested by the public officers of the neutral place from whence such vessel sailed, shall be adjudged lawful prize.

Art. 10th. Excepting nevertheless from the preceding Article such ships, the captains or masters of which shall be able to prove by documents found on board that they were obliged to take such foreign officers or mariners in ports which they might have put into in order to replace their own neutral officers or mariners who had died during the voyage.

Art. 11th. It is His Majesty's will that no documents which may be produced after the capture shall receive credit or be of any use, either to the owners of the said vessels or to the freighters of the goods laden therein, but on all occasions regard shall only be paid to the papers found on board.

Art. 12th. No neutral vessel cleared out of the ports of the kingdom and not having on board any goods or merchandize, except what they shall have shipped here, shall be arrested by French vessels of war or privateers or brought back into the ports of the kingdom on any pretence whatever.

Art. 13th. If any privateer shall act contrary to these regulations, the vessels and cargoes by them taken (except goods liable to confiscation) shall be restored, and they shall be decreed to pay damaged to whom it may concern.

Art. 14th. His Majesty intends that these regulations shall apply to such vessels as may be shipwrecked on the coasts of his dominions.

Art. 15th. His Majesty further orders that the Title of the Marine Ordinance of 1681, relative to captures shall be executed according to its form and tenor, inasmuch as the same is not derogated from by the present regulation, which shall be read, published, registered &c.

The Executive Directory during its ephemerical government found that Edict too mild to be continued in force. But the Consular Government thought differently and revived it by a Decree made in the Year XI.

[30] I think it proper to relate here what took place on that subject in Holland. France had communicated her Edict to the States General, as

During the war occasioned by the French Revolution, Denmark and Sweden (after the death of Gustavus III) were the only powers that observed a kind of neutrality; but those two powers were compelled to submit to the tyrannical mandates of England, who pretended that the singularity of the then existing circumstances authorized her to adapt to them her maritime system of jurisprudence, and those who were at the head of affairs in France were no longer in a situation to aid or set them in motion, notwithstanding their immense quantity of paper money. The Emperor of Russia, Paul I, began with being one of the most ardent champions of the antigallican coalition. Particular causes, which history will one day bring to light, brought on a misunderstanding between him and his two allies,

---

well as to all the other maritime powers. The Court of London with a view to prevent the Dutch from supplying France with naval forces, as they were permitted to do by the commercial treaty of 1674, between the United Provinces and Great Britain, proposed to them to alter that treaty. The Court of Versailles on its part declared that those cities which should adhere to the demand of Great Britain should be deprived of all commercial advantages in France. The demand was rejected, the United Provinces determined to accede to the armed neutrality, and sent orders to their Minister at St. Petersburg to sign the instrument of accession. They at the same time gave a convoy of some ships of the line to a fleet of merchant men laden with naval stores. The British in order to defeat or prevent the accession of the Dutch to the armed neutrality and before it was completed by their ratification attacked and captured the whole fleet of Dutch vessels with the men of war that convoyed them. The three Northern Courts then deliberated as to what they should do to maintain their dignity and the honor of their convention. But they at last abandoned the Dutch under pretence that their accession to the armed neutrality was not complete. This was precisely what the Court of St. James wanted. In that situation the United Provinces sacrifices by a weak and timorous policy had nothing else to do than to break openly with Great Britain and make a common cause with France.

Those details from what we have said elsewhere about the versatility of the principle by which belligerent powers are actuated, and shew how much they are governed by motives of expediency and self interest. As to the Northern Powers, the weakness which they displayed on that occasion, while it greatly lessened their influence and respectability, gave a severe shock to the system which they had endeavoured to establish, and which a little more firmness on their part would probably have consolidated.

and principally with England, and determined him to withdraw from the coalition and reconcile himself with the new government of France. That change of policy operated another in the measures which the Russian monarch adopted with respect to navigation; he again adhered to the armed neutrality of 1780 and even enlarged its provisions. The new convention was signed in 1800 by the Courts of Stockholm and Copenhagen, which at that time were engaged in serious controversies with that of London on account of the capture of some Swedish merchant man under convoy of men of war. The Court of Berlin acceded to that new convention, but England being at liberty to direct her force whithersoever she pleased in consequence of the weak state of the French Navy, hastened to break that union which she considered as hostile with respect to her. She ordered the bombardment of Copenhagen and her undertaking was effectually seconded by the unforeseen death of Paul I, and by the want of assistance on the part of Russia and Sweden. Those two events were followed first by a suspension of arms and afterwards in 1801 by a convention with the Emperor Alexander, to which the courts of Copenhagen and Stockholm successively acceded. That of Vienna without taking any part in the above convention published an Edict in 1803 in which it is referred to.[31]

§5.

I have thought it useful to take notice of all the above facts; for, independent of the event which I have related, it appears to me necessary to show the inconveniences and danger which may result from the uncertainty of the jurisprudence of nations with respect to neutrals, and the critical situation in which they may be placed by declarations, principles, and measures in which all do not agree. It is certain that nations ought to place a mutual confidence in each other's justice, good faith, and general conduct. But neutrals on the one hand are too easily led by

[31] All the documents relating to the armed neutrality are to be found in Martens' collection of treaties, vol. 9.

cupidity, whilst belligerents will acknowledge no law but what arises from their situation, wants, embarrassments, and political views. Amidst that conflict of opposite interests, the common law of nations, the law of reason and nature is forgotten, and the peace and happiness of mankind depends on the versatile views and opinions of the rulers of nations, often even on their silence, while a frank and candid declaration made beforehand of the rules and principles intended to be pursued would at least serve as a guide more or less to direct the conduct of the parties concerned.[32]

---

[32] During the war of 1740, the Court of Berlin adopted the prudential measure which I here recommend. Before the Prussian flag ventured to appear on the high seas, an explanation was asked of the British Government as to the manner in which it was intended to treat it. The British Ministry gave an answer, but that answer was expressed in general terms and gave no precise explanation of the real system of Great Britain; it merely promised that the Prussians should enjoy all the advantages granted to neutrals. At Berlin, they were persuaded from verbal assurances that those advantages would be the same as those expressed in the commercial treaties then subsisting between England and other States; but it was not so understood at London. The verbal declarations were disavowed, and a great number of Prussian vessels laden with merchandise belonging or presumed to belong to French or Spanish subjects were captured. Frederick II did not submit to those arbitrary proceedings. After having applied in vain for redress, he retaliated by the sequestration of the principal and interest of a certain debt which the Prussian Government owed to British subjects and for the payment of which the revenues of the Duchy of Silesia had been pledged. That high-handed measure produced a lively altercation between the two courts, but for political reasons it was at length terminated in favor of Prussia during the war of 1756. It is to be remarked that the Court of Berlin, in the arguments which it adduced in its defense, after briefly touching on general principles and on the verbal answers of the British Ministry, chiefly insisted on the true meaning of a preposition which had been made use of in the written answer of the British Ministry. They had raised a distinction between neutral nations who were in possession of commercial treaties with Great Britain and those which had none. After establishing that distinction, they said, that the Prussian flag should notwithstanding (*nonobstant*) be treated as favourably as that of other neutrals. From the proposition *notwithstanding* it was inferred at Berlin that all the advantages expressed in the commercial treaties would be extended to the Prussian flag; but that construction, altho' it was very much insisted upon,

Chapter XVI.

Of the Right of Search

§1.

The impediments which I have already spoken of are not the only cause of the numerous controversies which arise on the subject of the navigation of neutrals. There is another still more important and of a more serious nature; it is the practice of visiting or searching neutral vessels. It cannot be denied that it s sanction by treaties as well as usage; but for want of suitable precautions, it has introduced an arbitrary and vexatious system of jurisprudence, a system which is subversive of the freedom of the seas and entirely opposed to the true principles of the law of nations. I am fully aware of the difficulties which I shall have to encounter in attacking so inveterate a custom which is at the same time such a fruitful source of arbitrary proceedings, vexations, plunder, and litigation; and I foresee that those who are interested in maintaining that order of things and who are in the enjoyment of its sweets will accuse me of what is called *modern philosophy*.[33] But that accusation shall not deter me from my honest purpose, convinced as I am of the truth of the principles on which I ground my opinion. I do not hesitate to submit it to the censure of the most zealous opponents of the freedom of the seas.

---

was not so strong an argument as those which were drawn from the principles of the law of nations. It may even be said that it was not entitled to any consideration, because, besides that it was easy to perceive that the insertion of the word *notwithstanding* was a mere clerical mistake, the conclusion of the phrase left no doubt as to the true meaning of the Court of London. And if the Prussian Court had had nothing else to rely upon than the forced interpretation which it gave to the word *notwithstanding*, it would have had no just right to retaliate, but its claim was justified by the law of nations, and Frederick II had so much the greater right to enforce its principles that he was not in that respect shackled by any treaty.

[33] The Englishman, Dr. Scott, in his report of the capture of a Swedish convoy in 1799.

§2.

I shall in this discussion keep custom and treaties entirely out of view, considering the subject as *res integra*, and as if it had never before been discussed. If in imitation of other writers I had taken treaties and other public acts as my only guides, I would have had nothing to do but to class them in regular order, which would have produced an Index or digest, not of the principles of the law of nations, but of that peculiar system of public law of each separate State. But, it is evident that it is not from such sources that we are to draw rules and principles obligatory upon all nations that have not otherwise bound themselves by special treaties.

§3.

The right of search now exercised by the belligerent powers consists in arresting neutral merchant men wherever they meet them; examining their papers to ascertain their neutrality, origin, destination, and the nature of their cargoes; in detaining them if they have on board goods said to be prohibited; in searching for evidences of fraud on the slightest ground or even pretence of suspicion, which the avidity and impunity of cruisers seldom leaves them at a loss to find. This is certainly a clear, positive exercise of jurisdiction,[34] unless we choose to call it an act of arbitrary power which cannot be otherwise defined.

---

[34] *Lampredi* asserts the contrary. "It is evident", says he, "that when a privateer detains and searches a neutral vessel on the high sea, he does not exercise any jurisdiction, he only exercises his lawful right acknowledged as such by neutral nations and which they have bound themselves to respect". (*Du commerce des neuters en temps de guerre*, p. 174). In rejecting the word jurisdiction, *Lampredi* ought to have substituted another, by which the act might be as clearly defined.; and had he taken the trouble of attending to the consequences of a seizure, he probably would have been convinced that the captor exercised the first act of jurisdiction which leads to the judgment which either condemns the prize or acquits it and condemns the captor in damages. But, after all, since *Lampredi* objects to the use of the word *jurisdiction* and attributes to the rights of the cruiser a peculiar character of their own, I believe it is

§4.

To determine the nature and extent of the right of search, it is important to distinguish between the high sea and the jurisdictional waters of belligerent and neutral States.

1° The high sea is the dominion of no one, and all nations have an unlimited right to enjoyment. These primordial truths are axioms of the law of nations, and it follows as a direct consequence from them that any vessel sailing on the high seas is out of all foreign jurisdiction and preserves the free and independent character of the nation to which she belongs. Therefore, her flag when properly made known is inviolable, and all kind of restraint laid upon it is a violation of its independence.

2° That absolute independence ceases to exist when the vessel is in the waters of a neutral State, but only with respect to that particular nation; as to all others, it remains in full force; therefore, belligerent cruisers have not a right to detain a neutral vessel in neutral waters, nor even to force her to exhibit her papers. They are so far from having such a right, that the ships of war of hostile powers dare not pursue each other, nor commit the least act of hostility on the coast of a neutral State, else they would be guilty of a violation of territory. *A fortiori*, the offense would be the same if a belligerent should there presume to detain and search a vessel over which the law of war does not

---

necessary that I should further analyze his doctrine. The question is too important not to be closely investigated. I shall not, however, so much attend to the denomination or to the thing itself.

I ask then by what right a cruiser detains a neutral vessel? Clearly by virtue of the commission which he has received from his sovereign; without it, he would be guilty of an act of piracy and deserve death. He, therefore, does not act in his own right, but in right of his sovereign. Therefore the neutral who has just cause of complaint applies for satisfaction to the latter who by his judges (who are his proper representatives) passes a formal sentence awarding damages and costs of suit. Now, is not all this a clear and direct exercise of jurisdiction? Is it not *jus dicere*? And is not the seizure the first step of these proceedings, as in civil cases the service of a summons or writ of arrest by an officer of the court?

give him any kind of right. These rules are so strictly observed that when a ship of war of one of the belligerents has put in into a neutral port at the same time with a vessel belonging to its enemy, the former is allowed to depart only twenty-four hours after the latter has set sail, and if she attempts to transgress that prohibition, she is fired at from the ports or land batteries. The same thing takes place if an enemy's vessel happens at the time to be at anchor in the roads.

3° But as soon as a neutral vessel is found on the coast of the enemy, the cruiser has a right to require the exhibition, not only of her passport, but of all the requisite documents to ascertain the nature of her cargo; and if it should consist in whole or in part of contraband articles, he seizes them, altho' destined for a neutral port, because in that case there is a strong presumption of fraud, unless by stress of weather or some other inevitable accident, the vessel had been forced to deviate from her course, or unless her passport allowed her to touch at an enemy's port lying in her way. But the cruiser has no right to search the vessel unless there is some evidence of fraud?

§5.

All that I have said concerning neutral vessels sailing in jurisdictional seas presents no great difficulties either in theory or in practice, but it is not the same with respect to the high seas. Controversies in the latter case are so much the more frequent that there exists in that respect, as I have already observed, an ancient practice which has been strengthened by a long series of treaties; and indeed, if we were only to look to those two sources for the solution of the problem before us, it would be readily found; each nation would only have to consult its own engagements and execute them more or less strictly and she would in vain complain of abuses. But as I have already observed, I am not investigating the rules which treaties have sanctioned or usage established, but those which ought to exist according to the true principles of the law of nations free from all the alterations which the routine of practice or stipulations dictated by peculiar circumstances may have introduced therein.

In conformity with those principles, I lay it down as a fundamental maxim of the maritime law of nations: *that on the high sea the independence of that neutral flag is unlimited, and that consequently it cannot be there subjected to the right of search.*

§6.

I am very sensible that the world is so accustomed to the indefinite use of that right and that the doctrine which establishes it is so deeply rooted in man's mind, that it has been for a long time considered as a positive, irrefragable principle of the law of nations, and that the stipulations of treaties were intended merely to provide for its application. Matters in this respect are even carried so far that the mere suspicion of the cruiser and often even the most frivolous pretence are sufficient causes to detain, search, and molest neutral vessels on the high sea, as if they were in an enemy's port, and that their cargoes are confiscated if they are in contravention with the treaties, or even with the Edicts of the powers at war.

Such an abuse of power, such an odious violation of the law of nations, cannot be too much resisted; in a word, it cannot be too often repeated, all treaties, political interests, and authorities to the contrary notwithstanding, that a neutral vessel, while sailing on the high sea, has no other duty to fulfil than to prove that she does not belong to an enemy, and that her flag is genuine, and that everything being regular in respect to these two points, she is not liable to be searched or detained, whatever may be the nature of her cargo; everything done to the contrary is a violation of her independence, of which she alone can restrict or modify the exercise. It is in this point of view that all the existing treaties on the subject of commerce and navigation in time of war are to be considered; being only exceptions, they only bind those who are parties to them. The same may be said of usage; it only binds those States that have acknowledged it; all others are to be governed by the general principles which I undertake to establish. Force alone can compel them to submit to other rules.

§7.

In order to do away the force of those truths, it is said that a neutral must be impartial, that the belligerents have the right to ascertain whether he conducts himself according to that rule, and that can only be done by exercising the right of search. Such is undoubtedly the opinion that force has introduced and which habit has maintained; but I cannot too often repeat it, it is entirely opposed to the dictates of sound reason. According to those, that partiality which amounts to a violation of neutrality and consequently which may be considered as hostile can never be presumed, and therefore it cannot be required of a neutral that he should himself furnish the proof of it by suffering his vessel to be searched, and that he should thus become his own accuser. Such is, however, the true and direct object of what is called visiting or searching neutral ships, of that strange custom by which a cruiser is authorized to ransack a vessel in order to discover therein prohibited goods not mentioned in the ship's papers, or some evidence which may lead to a suspicion of the neutral character of the cargo or destination of the ship, notwithstanding the precise tenor of her documents. Such an inquisitorial mode of proceeding is hardly practiced at land under the must arbitrary governments, and yet among civilized nations it is considered as a thing of course on an element which is essentially free, on which no one has a right to dictate laws? No partiality can be supposed to exist without clear and satisfactory evidence either direct or circumstantial; and in such case, that partiality must appear to have assumed a character manifestly hostile; then, and then only, the right of self-preservation may authorize the taking of measures to prevent its effects; but that can only be done in strict conformity with the rules of the law of war, or in the exercise of a competent jurisdiction. But you the belligerent are not at war with the neutral nation to which the vessel belongs that you are pleased to consider as suspicious, you are therefore not authorized to offer her any kind of violence. It must be observed that the merchandise whatever it may be is accounted neutral property as long as it remains in the possession of the master of the vessel. Therefore, it enjoys of all the rights belonging to the neutral flag which protects it, and the belligerent who seizes it on the high sea does himself infringe the law of neutrality by violating national independence. But it will be said that the neutral by supplying the enemy with prohibited goods, commits an act of hostility and consequently is himself guilty of breach of neutrality. This is true, if he really does supply the enemy or if his intention so to do manifestly appears. But neither the one nor the other can be imputed to him so long as he is sailing on the high seas. The intention, as I have already observed, can never be presumed and even if proved, is not equivalent to the fact, except then the vessel is found on the coasts of an enemy.

As to a right of jurisdiction, no nation can claim it over another on the high sea; this fundamental principle makes an end of the difficulty, unless there are stipulations to the contrary. In a continental war, whatever may be the cause of complaint of one government against another, it has not a right to enter upon the other's territory before it has in vain demanded satisfaction and formally declared war. Thus, altho' you may suspect a neutral vessel sailing on the high sea, you are not on that account authorized to violate the immunity of her flag; you may, if your choose, keep her in sight, follow her, and detain her as soon as she enters your jurisdiction; these precautions are all lawful, but all others are prohibited by the rules and principles of natural law.

§8.

Those writers who contend for the right of search on the high sea draw their strongest argument from the right of self-preservation, which I have above mentioned. It is true that nations are thereby authorized to do all that is necessary for the preservation of their existence and of their just rights, and that they may exercise it in peace as well as in war. This truth is derived from nature itself, and may be called the cornerstone of the law of nations. But how easy it is to misapply it. How frequent the false interpretations given to it by ambition and avarice! How often has mere expediency been disguised under the pompous words necessity and danger! Not to wander from my subject, I ask whether it is not extraordinary that governments should represent their existence as exposed to the most imminent dangers, that they should obstruct all commercial relations between the rest of the world, transform the freest of elements into a scene of robbery and plunder and expose Europe to a general conflagration, because an imprudent neutral may by chance supply one of the powers at war with some of the articles that are so emphatically proscribed by commercial treaties; because a sadler, an armourer, or a horse dealer may have made some petty mercantile speculations; because they are or pretend to be very much afraid lest their enemy should be supplied with some firearms or a few barrels of saltpeter, or lest a few bales of lawful merchandise belonging to that enemy should be carried by neutral vessels from one port to another.

§9.

Let us, however, allow to the right of self-preservation as much latitude as possible; will you conclude from thence that you may exercise your right of search or seizure wherever you may think proper? You will undoubtedly answer that you have a right to exercise it wherever you may meet with the object which you consider as dangerous; and if I should deny a proposition so evidently false, you will beg the question by calling to your aid the law of war, which you will without scruple apply to neutrals, because, to be sure, the interest of the whole world must give way to ensure your safety; you would even be offender if your right and the justice of your cause were to be called in question. To cut the matter short, I say that you can only exercise your rights where the danger is imminent and actually exists. But it does not exist on the high sea, for, I repeat it, the presumed intention of the master of the vessel does not constitute danger. And yet it is all that can be imputed to him while he is not on the coasts of your enemy; therefore, you cannot exercise an authority over him; otherwise you may for the same reason enter the ports, magazines, manufactories, arsenals, and waters of the neutral State, the very moment that you know or suspect that there are arms destined or presumed to be destined for your enemy. Intention, however, certain, is not equivalent to an act, nor is fear t be construed into danger, except when the neutral vessel is found in the waters of your enemy; there you may detain, seize, confiscation her; nay, if necessary, sink her, because you are there the master and have a right to the exercise of jurisdiction; I will even go so far as to admit that you have the same right on your own coasts, if deceived by his confidence, the master of a neutral vessel has been unfortunate enough to approach them. But on the high sea, every attempt to search, every restraint, is an act of hostility, nay of piracy.[35] I think that I may reduce the whole question to the following proposition: If on the high sea I violate the immunity of your flag, I do you a wrong and an injury. The same thing must therefore be said of you, if you violate the immunity of my own. Now, you are guilty of such a violation if you forcibly enter a vessel which

---

[35] Everybody knows the origin of the war of 1755. Everybody knows that England under cover of a feigned negociation captured several French vessels of war and a great number of fishermen before the war was in any manner declared. The Court of London endeavoured to justify its conduct by alleging that the two nations were then in a state of hostility towards the Ohio, and that the French ships bound to America were suspected of hostile designs, but that pretence did not justify it in the public opinion and history has recorded its conduct as an act of perfidy and lawless violence.

The principles laid down in our text were maintained by the ancient government of France before it took an active part in the American War. Many shipments were made in the ports of France for America, then in a state of insurrection; they were principally composed of arms and ammunition besides various kinds of lawful goods, and in order to escape the English cruisers, the masters commonly cleared out for the West India Islands and the Islands of St. Pierre and Miquelon. The English Ministry had spies in all the French ports and was minutely informed of all the articles that were shipped. The British cruisers captured the French vessels even in our harbours and at the mouths of our rivers. The Cabinet of Versailles complained in vain of such a manifest violation of the law of nations, and after war had broken out, it clearly made it appear in its answer to the justificative memorial of the Court of London that England had not a right to capture French vessels whatever might be their cargoes either on the coasts of France or on the high seas, that she could only exercise that right in her own waters, either in Europe or in North America. The irregular conduct of Great Britain and her refusing to make satisfaction for her violations of the French territory was not only the least motives which determined France to declare war against her.

bears that flag and gives sufficient proof of its being her genuine national colors. This comprises in a few words the whole maritime law of nations, and it follows from thence that on the high sea you are bound to respect my flag, as you require that I should respect your own. There is no medium between these two propositions, unless you mean to establish as such the irresistible power of your cannon.

§10.

But it will be said that the right of search incontestably belongs to every cruiser because otherwise the neutral character and lawful destination of ships and merchandise cannot be ascertained, nor can it be known without searching whether the vessel is loaded or not with contraband goods and all the treaties consider that right as pre-existing and only regulate the mode of exercising it. It is true will it be added that its exercise requires force, but it is a force not unlike the execution of civil process under the municipal law; consequently, it cannot be lawfully resisted. The interests of the neutral sovereign cannot destroy the right of the belligerent; in short, all opposition is the exercise of unlawful violence against a legal right (Dr. Scott cited above).

If the reader will take the trouble to analyze those arguments and compare them with the principles which I have maintained, I am confident that he will be convinced that the pretended legal, incontestable right of search is nothing else than the elementary principles of the law of nations and which has nothing but expediency to support it; he will be sensible how ill applied the epithet legal is to an usage which is founded, not upon the general laws or universal consent of nations, but on mere metaphysical reasonings and on motives of self-interest; an usage which is applied to an element which is not capable of dominion nor jurisdiction; he will above all wonder at the avowal which is made that that usage is exclusively maintained by force, which is preposterously called a legal force, and assimilated to the execution of the warrant of a judge for the arrest of a person charged with the commission of a crime against the law of his own country.

I shall, however, take the liberty of adding the following reflections: it will be remarked that such a latitude is given to the right of the cruiser that not even the slightest suspicion is required to search a neutral vessel, but it is plainly said that were it not for that precaution, it could not be ascertained whether she had or not contraband goods on board; so that her papers are useless, the seal of the sovereign by which they are authenticated does not deserve any credit, and the neutral master is himself obliged to furnish evidence of the imaginary offense, because it is believed possible. Thus it is lawful for a cruiser, for such an unhallowed purpose, without the least previous suspicion, to subvert the plainest elementary principles of natural law, morality and common sense, and to violate the freedom of the seas and the independence of nations. Doubtless a cruiser may do all this by force, but to give the name of legal force to such proceedings is a new interpolation into the code of nations and a new test to be commented upon by civilians.

It is to be observed that the doctrine which I am impugning is laid down as a general principle of the law of nations, and not merely as a rule founded upon treaties, on which ground alone it might be justified if treaties really did sanction it; but on the contrary, they disavow it, for they all require no more than the exhibition of the ship's papers, and search is permitted as an auxiliary means when there are actual proofs or strong indications of fraud. But the opponents of maritime freedom, to crown all their paradoxes, assert that the rights of war are unbounded, and from thence it is inferred that belligerents have an unlimited dominion at sea and that such dominion extends to the trade and navigation of neutrals. I shall not waste time to discuss so erroneous, dangerous, and exaggerated an opinion, even as between enemies, but I shall refute it as far as it is meant to be applied to neutral nations.

My argument is extremely plain: neutrals have nothing to do with the war; consequently, the rights which it confers cannot extend to them. If, however, the neutral puts your existence or our right in jeopardy, he is not longer a neutral, he is your enemy. But if in making use of his rights, he only stands in the way of your commercial advantages, of your political views or of your fancied supremacy, if he resists exactions that are unjust in themselves or which would work to his own disadvantage, he does not offend you by his resistance; therefore, you have no right to recur to hostile measures against him. Your right, I repeat it, to pursue your enemy, however unbounded you may suppose it to be, cannot be exercised upon neutrals without trespassing upon their own rights. I have already applied these truths to their trade and navigation; therefore, I shall abstain from repeating the same arguments in this place.

§11.

But even setting aside the illegality of the practice of searching neutral ship on the high seas, a single reflection will suffice to show how odious it is in itself. Who is to be the first and the only judge to determine in the first instance whether there is or not probable ground of suspicion against a neutral vessel? The cruiser whose interest it is to find the master in fault, that he may enjoy the fruits of his spoliation. He often is unable to read or understand the documents exhibited to him, and in that case his very ignorance becomes an additional if not the only ground of suspicion. To him those papers naturally appear mysterious, for to him they are unintelligible; it is therefore the safest course to suspect them as well as those which he discovers on a thorough search of the vessel and crew; but he is presumed to have fully understood them, for they are the evidence of the fraud, or what is called in law *corpus delicti*. On this he detains the vessel, turns her away from her course, and involves her in a long and expensive suit and often comes off in the end by saying that he was mistaken, and even when the neutral master by good luck happens to be acquitted, he remains saddled with a heavy and irreparable loss in the damage which he has sustained and the costs and expenses which he has incurred, for which he is never to be indemnified, for belligerents delight in giving credit to the good faith, honesty, and purity of intention of their cruisers.

§12.

It must not be supposed that the doctrine for which I contend is a mere philanthropic speculation or what is in derision called modern philosophy, or at least that it is an exaggeration of the principles relating to the freedom of the seas. I find the elements of that same doctrine in a treaty which was made at a time when modern philosophy was not as yet in vogue. I mean the treaty made at Utrecht in 1713 between France and Great Britain.[36] After enumerating the goods which are and those that are not to be considered as contraband, it proceeds to point out the mode of examination to be pursued with respect to a ship's papers. The text is so remarkably clear and precise that I think proper to insert it here literally. It is as follows:

"Art. 6. But in case the ships of the subjects and inhabitants of both their most Serene Royal Majesties, either on the sea coast or on the high seas, shall meet with the men of war of the other, or with privateers, the said men of war and privateers, for preventing any inconveniences, are to remain out of cannon shot, and to send a boat to the merchant ship which has been met with, and shall enter her with two or three men only to whom the master or commander of such ship or vessel shall show his passport, concerning the property thereof, made out according to the form annexed to this present Treaty, and the ship which shall exhibit one, shall have free passage, and it shall be wholly unlawful any way to molest her, search, or compel her to quit her intended course".

Can there be any thing more positive than the provisions of this Article? Is it is possible to show a more explicit regard for

[36] I might also quote the treaty of the Pyrenees. The 17th Article contains in substance that in case French vessels shall meet on the high seas any Spanish men of war or privateers, the said men of war or privateers shall remain out of the reach of cannon shot and shall send only two or three men on board of her to whom the master shall show his passport to which credit shall be given. But I confine myself to the treaty of Utrecht, as having been made with that power which alone contends for the rigorous principles of suspicion and search. I might also instance the treaty between England and Spain, signed at Utrecht in the same year with the former.

the true principle of the law of nations? Not only the masters of vessels belonging to the subjects of either of the two contracting powers are not bound on the high sea to make known their destination or the nature of the cargoes, but they are not even obliged to do so when along the coasts; the master proves the property of his vessel to show that she neither is a pirate nor an enemy, and that being done, nothing more can be required of him; the vessel must be left at liberty to pursue her voyage and no suspicion whatever can authorize her search or detention.

It is true that the same treaty establishes a modification to the general rule: it says (Article 24) "that a merchant ship of the other party which intends to go to a port at enmity with the other confederates, or concerning whose voyage, and the sort of goods on board there may be just suspicion, shall be obliged to exhibit, either on the high seas, or in the ports and havens, not only her passport, but her certificates, expressing that they are not of the kind of prohibited goods which are specified in the 19th Article".

This exception gives rise to three remarks: 1°. That a vessel not bound to an enemy's port is not in general obliged to make known the nature of her cargo; 2° That a vessel bound to an enemy's port and met with on the high seas is only subject to the formality of exhibiting her manifest or clearance in case there is just reason to suspect the legality of her voyage or the lawful character of her cargo; 3° That such suspicion has no other effect than to produce the exhibition of the ship's papers, and that it does not authorize to search the vessel to ascertain the veracity thereof, and still less to seek for proofs by ransacking her and examining the people on board. The 26th Article positively confirms these remarks, for it only mentions prohibited goods and real contraband, appearing on the fact of the ship's papers; the word suspicion as authorizing the search is not even mentioned. The provision which I have just spoken of is confirmed by an additional convention which immediately follows the Treaty. The 7th Article is in these words: "and whereas the quality of the ship, master, and goods will sufficiently appear from such passports and certificates, it shall not be lawful for the commanders of men of war to exact any other verification under any title whatsoever". Here then is the doctrine of suspicions and presumptions literally so far as it relates to the searching of neutral vessels, and everybody knows that that doctrine is the inexhaustible source of the vexations which neutrals daily experience.

I am therefore warranted to assert on the authority of two great naval powers that the searching of neutral vessels on the high sea, such as it is practiced at this day, is not founded on a general or permanent custom; that it is still less conformable to the true principles of the law of nations; that when exercised by belligerents merely of their own authority, they commit an act of violence; that the example of nations which submit to it, either in pursuance of treaties or for any other cause; that is to say, those who sacrifice one of the most valuable prerogatives of national independence for the sake of paltry, selfish considerations, cannot be adduced as evidence of a general rule, and that when there exists no stipulation to the contrary, resistance becomes lawful and that right is founded on the first elements of natural reason and of the law of nations.

§13.

I foresee that certain critics who consider usage as the supreme law and who believe that the rights of war are paramount to all the other rights of mankind, will oppose my doctrine on the subject of the pretended right of search not as immoral but as impracticable, and that to prove their assertion they will affirm that without it, fraud would always remain undetected and unpunished, and they will add that belligerents have as good a right to provide for their own safety as neutrals to defend their liberty and independence, and that they would be exposed to that most imminent danger were it not for the right of searching neutral ships wherever they meet with them, even tho' that right be not acknowledged or secured to them by a treaty. To this I answer: 1°. Notwithstanding the precautions stipulated in treaties, the practice of cruising is still fraught with a great number of abuses and vexatious proceedings; the cruiser never meets a neutral vessel whithersoever bound without exercising upon her the right of search, not to detect fraud, but to seek for it; he wants neither previous proofs nor probable cause; he creates both at his pleasure, his cannon finish the business, and where are the witnesses to accuse him? If such practice is just or reasonable, if it reconciles the contending rights of the parties; in a word, if it is necessary for the safety of the belligerents, I have nothing more to say on the subject: neutrals must be sacrifices above all if they are not able to make any resistance. 2°. As to the protection which it is said that my theory would afford to fraud, I cannot discover it. A merchant vessel is bound to some particular port, the cruiser is informed of her destination by the examination of her papers, the exhibition of which he has a right to demand; if notwithstanding their regularity, he entertains any doubt about the legality of the cargo, he is at liberty to follow the vessel until she is in the waters of his enemy, and there he has an indisputable right to search her if he has probable grounds to suspect fraud. I see no impracticability in that mode of proceeding and I think that it is less inconvenient to adopt it than to expose a neutral vessel to be searched on the high seas, unless the trifling inconvenience experienced by the cruiser be considered as extremely important, or unless it be said that the independence of nations and the dignity of their flag are more metaphysical ideas which have no existence when opposed to political interest. 3°. The safety of the belligerent ought incontestably to prevail over the rights of neutral merchants, and even over their existence; but how is that safety endangered because neutral vessels are not to be searched on the high seas? It is in danger, say our opponents, because a neutral not being afraid of being searched at sea will with impunity ship articles of a dangerous nature, that is to say, arms and ammunition and even naval stores. But such a thing cannot be presumed, because, in the first place, it is improbable to ship cannon in a clandestine manner; it is no where an article of commerce, and it is impossible to suspect that the neutral sovereign will supply it from his arsenals. It is the same with gunpowder, the manufacturing of which is not free. As to firearms, swords, &c., what maritime power, as I have said elsewhere (see Chapter VII), is under the necessity of procuring them from abroad? I say nothing of naval stores, which cannot be secreted in the hold of a vessel. Still, if an idle fear of danger is to prevail over sound reason, let the cruiser pursue the pretty that he is so anxious to grasp; let him pursue the vessel, search her, and if she carried contraband goods, capture her in the waters of his enemy and let him employ the same means, if without necessity, she deviates from her direct course. 4°. The right of searching neutral vessels wherever they may be found is neither admitted nor admissible; it is contrary to the first principles of the law of nations; it is in opposition with even the laws of war. The neutral flag must be respected whenever it is not in the dominions of the belligerent nations. If the vessel is not a neutral port or harbor, the belligerents have not even a right to require the exhibition of her papers. 5°. As to the power of violating treaties, nothing need be said upon the subject.

Chapter XVII.

Of Resistance

§1.

It is true that the right of resisting search of which I have already spoken is called in question and has not long since given rise to serious controversies.[37] It is contended that a neutral vessel can in no case resist the search of a cruiser, and that if she does, she becomes *ipso facto* liable to forfeiture. Let us see whether that doctrine is founded on any correct principle.

§2.

Before resistance to search can be construed into an offense, some law ought to exist declaring it to be such, for it is certain that it is not in itself more criminal than resisting a robber or a murderer. There are only two sorts of laws between nations: treaties and the principles of the primitive law of nations. The former impose a formal, direct, and voluntary obligation; the latter an indirect and consequential one, resulting from the fundamental principles of social order. Those principles, as I have already shown, are independence and reciprocity. Without the former, no nation can exist as such, and without the latter, mankind could be perpetually engaged in war and destruction.

§3.

There is not in any existing treaty a direct, express stipulation concerning the resistance of neutrals to the exercise of the right of search; there are clauses which restrict the unlimited freedom of the seas, and admit the right of search as a means to enforce these restrictions. But it is only by inference

[37] Case of the Swedish convoy in the year 1799.

from the existence of that right that resistance is considered and punished as an offense.

§4.

In order therefore to have an exact idea of resistance, its true character must be defined with relation to its object and circumstances.

The engagements that a sovereign has entered into undoubtedly bind his subjects; if therefore he has agreed to the indefinite right of search, he has thereby indirectly but necessarily prohibited resistance to it, and every violation of that implied prohibition is, of course, an offense. But if the right in question is not indefinite, if it is only admitted in certain specified cases, and if except in those cases the sovereign has not acknowledged the legality of search, he has by a similar implication prohibited it, and it can only be considered as an act of violence; it is clear therefore that resistance is a legal right, particularly as the neutral sovereign by permitting his vessels to be searched, has indeed been willing to subject their masters to a vexatious proceeding and even to an eventual punishment, but he could not mean to consent to its arbitrary and unlimited application and he incontestably retained the right of repelling unauthorized violence.

For instance, I suppose that a neutral vessel sailing on the high seas is met by a cruiser of the belligerent power to whom his sovereign is bound by a treaty; the cruiser is authorized to require the exhibition of his passports to ascertain that she neither is a pirate nor an enemy; I even suppose that he has the right to examine the documents which prove the nature and destination of her cargo. The master of the neutral vessel complies with all these requisitions and the papers as well as the cargo are found to be regular, therefore he ought to be left at liberty to pursue his intended course. Nevertheless, the cruiser thinks it proper to allege that he suspects fraud, and will not give credit to what appears on the face of the papers, and therefore of his own authority and on the strengthen of his own opinion, he assumes the right to search the vessel, that is to say, to ransack her from one end to the other in order to discover proofs of the fraud that he suspects. The neutral master has in that case a right to resist the illegal attempt of the belligerent, and owes it to the dignity of his flag to make, if he is able, an effectual resistance, and if he is compelled to yield to a superior force, it is a duty incumbent on the sovereign of the cruiser to chastise his subject, for this violation of the treaty and of the law of nations, for it is an important truth, which ought never to be lost sight of, that the right of search cannot be legally exercised unless there is some preexisting proof of fraud, and that a vessel ought never to be ransacked and the master and crew put to a kind of torture, merely for the sake of obtaining such proof. If these principles are once abandoned or deviated from, there is an end to the liberty and independence of nations; the weak must bend before the strong and submit quietly to the yoke.

§5.

There are governments who regulate by edicts and ordinances and sometimes by declarations and proclamations the conduct of their men of war and privateers in time of war, but those are all acts of municipal authority which only bind the subjects of the governments that free them and are no part of the law of nations. Sovereigns do not acknowledge the authority or jurisdiction of each other, nothing but the abuse of force can make them submit to it, and prevent the effects of a legitimate resistance. If those acts, however, are made known to the neutral States, and they expressly or tacitly acquiesce in them, they are equivalent to treaties and produce the same rights and obligation.

§6.

But if there exists no treaty nor anything that is equivalent to it, the original principles of national freedom are the only law of neutrals as well as of belligerents. Now, according to those principles, cruisers and ships of war have no other right on the high sea but that of ascertaining the character of the neutral vessel; anything they may require beyond that formality is evidently illegal, unless it is authorized by a positive treaty. In vain is custom alleged and relied upon; it binds none but those who have voluntarily acknowledged its authority; beyond that it is nothing but the apology of the strong for oppressing the weak. The doctrine which we contend for is all important for the preservation of peace and social order which are certainly more beneficial to mankind, than a few cases of fraud or the escape of a few miserable ships from capture can be hurtful. Power may reduce reason and duty to silence, but never annihilate them. From all that I have said, it may be safely concluded that the right of resistance to search cannot be called in question.

§7.

In order to give an exhibit together with the three preceding distinctions in one point of view, I say: 1°. That when the right of search is acknowledged, it can only be exercised in conformity with the precise text of the instruments by which it is granted, that to extend it in any way is unlawful and resistance becomes a matter of right; 2°. That when there is no treaty or agreement, the right of resistance is inherent to independence, and that to contest the one is to contest the other. 3°. That no general custom or usage can be alleged because custom binds only those who have acknowledged it, or who have not the means of resisting it.

§8.

Besides, I am not ignorant that those who are opposed to the right of resistance insist upon it, that a neutral vessel which resists the exercise of the right of search is *ipso facto* liable to be seized and confiscated, that that principle has at all times been universally admitted; that the right of search necessarily results from a state of war, and that treaties do no more than modify and limit that pre-existing right.[38] Those assertions deserve to be

[38] See Mr. Pitt's speech in Parliament, 2 February 1801.

examined and I entreat the reader to forgive me if to answer almost every proposition of my opponents I am obliged to recur to first principles.

§9.

It is said that the right of search is generally admitted. I grant it, but does it follow from thence that it must be exercised in an arbitrary manner, that it is unlimited in its application as well as in the mode of exercising it? Surely, no one will be found bold enough to make such an assertion. No treaty admits the right of search as a general indefinite right, they all on the contrary determine the cases in which it may be exercised and the mode which is to be pursued. As long as the cruiser keeps himself within that double limit, every resistance offered by a neutral is an offense. In the contrary case, this latter is not bound to anything, and it is lawful for him to resist all illegal attempts. But, it is said, that treaties are merely intended to modify and limit the free existing right of search. This amounts to an assertion that the right of search is unlimited in its nature and that it exists of itself independent of all stipulations. If so, our adversaries must show from what source it is derived, and how far that pretended right extends. They say that it is founded on the law of war, that their rights which war confers are unlimited, and therefore the right of search must be so likewise. I am willing to grant that the rights of war are undefined, but it does not follow that they are unlimited. The object of war is to obtain from an enemy by force of arms the satisfaction which he denies. The power who take up arms to obtain such satisfaction makes use of the means which circumstances require, so far, that is to say as far as respects the mode or manner of making war upon his enemy, his rights are indefinite. Still they do not extend beyond the limits which I have above pointed out, and in that respect it may be said that the rights of war are circumscribed. Besides, those rights cannot operate either in the one case or in the other on a third party who is an utter stranger to the controversy; such third party cannot be restrained against his will in the exercise of his own right without violating his independence. Belligerents must then be driven to the plea of necessity which, indeed, when it really exists, supersedes all law. But who made those sovereigns the exclusive judges of the application of that formidable word necessity? Must it depend upon their caprice or convenience? Is their decision final and without appeal? But no, I would say to them, you are not entitled to avail yourselves of the plea of necessity, except your existence should be in danger. I grant that I as a neutral power ought to abstain from doing that which might protract or increase that peril; for that reason I acknowledge that I am bound not to furnish soldiers, arms, or warlike stores to your enemy. Beyond that, I owe you nothing, and all that you may require besides you can only obtain by force, that is to say, by an open violation of my rights. Such are, I believe, the true principles of the law of nations concerning the subjects that I have been treating of. The right of search presupposes the existence of fraud in violation of an open acknowledged duty; resistance repels an unjust suspicion or an act of violence. In the first case the neutral, in the second, the belligerent is guilty. And yet in both cases, it is the neutral who is punished. What a strange perversion of the plainest rules of jurisprudence!

Chapter XVIII.

Of Vessels Under Convoy

§1.

The observations which I have made in the preceding chapter may help to throw some light on a new question, which has become important in consequence of the events that it has occasioned; I mean to speak of the rights belonging to a man of war convoying merchant vessels. I have shown that nothing can be required of a merchant vessel on the high seas, altho' sailing alone than to exhibit the proof of her neutral character, unless it is otherwise stipulated by particular treaties. This principle being admitted, it is asked whether the presence of a ship of war dispenses the merchant vessels under her protection from undergoing that formality and whether the declaration of the commanding officer can supply its place? And finally, whether the merchant man in that case is exempt from search?[39]

---

[39] I say that this question is modern because no mention is made of convoys in any treaty anterior to the Convention of 1800; and even that convention only declares (Art. 4) that squadrons shall be fitted out by the contracting powers for the protection of their respective merchant men, and which shall be employed in convoying them; but it does not assign to them any other duty, the right of search is left precisely as it stood under former treaties. The first that I know of in which the verbal declaration of the commanding officer of a convoy is mentioned was made in 1782 between Russia and Denmark; and that provision was afterwards inserted in all the commercial treaties of Russia, except that which she made with England in 1797. It is also inserted in a convention made in 1800 between France and the United States of America; but we must confess that in all those treaties the stipulations are expressed in such general terms, and in so concise a manner, that no provision is made for the various incidents which may take place, and which the negotiators did not foresee. Besides, how could the contracting parties imagine that they might be *ex parte* stipulations between themselves, bind the other governments, which were not parties to them and introduce into general use a new mode of proceedings, however just and useful it might be? This course is not at all consistent either with the law of nations or the civil law, and much less

§2.

The object of ships of war in convoying merchant men is to protect them against all arbitrary acts, vexations, proceedings, plunder, and in a word, against the rapacity of cruisers. It is the direct and only object which the commanding officer of the convoy has in view. It is, moreover, his duty according to the modern practice to attest the regularity of the ship's papers and certificates of the cargoes and thereby to remove all suspicion of fraud and prevent any further examination or inquiry. He is the immediate organ of his government; it is in his name that he fills his station, that he acts, protects, and attests. Therefore, if being on the high sea and after having made himself known in due form he attests in the name of his sovereign that all the vessels that he convoys are neutral and that their papers are regular, conformably to the treaties or general usage, this respect which sovereigns owe to one another, as well as the respect that it is in their interest to secure to their navy, require that faith be given to such declaration, which is the less to be suspected that the commanding officer by his attestation only confirms by virtue of a positive authority and after taking all due precautions, what his sovereign and the proper officers have already attested by the ship's papers. His commission and his rank are a pledge of his

---

with the policy of States. Force, therefore, was necessarily to be resorted to either to compel the adoption of the new system or to resist it; and force, of course, was effectually employed for the latter purpose. It is well known that in the year 1799 a fleet of Swedish merchant men, altho' convoyed by a frigate, was captured by English men of war and that a short time afterwards, two Danish fleets met with the same fate. The Court of London, in order to justify her proceedings, alleged that they were conformable to usage and treaties; both parties became highly incensed and (as is always the case) the negotiations which ensued were carried on in a tone of bitterness and reproach. That state of things accelerated the new maritime coalition, occasioned the bombarding of Copenhagen, and gave birth to the convention of 1801, which in a great degree decided the question in favor of the Court of London, for the right of search was maintained notwithstanding the protection of convoying ships of war, it was only stipulated that it should not be exercised by privateers. The reader will find the details of those events as far as they have been made public in Martens' collection of treaties, vol. 9.

honor and veracity, his declaration is certainly of an equal value with that of the custom house officers, or of any other agent of government; it is a further proof of their accuracy, and to call it in question would be offering them a wanton and voluntary insult; it would, at least, be an unwarranted adherence to the latter of treaties, without even the semblance of a lawful motive; it would be in short a clear deviation from the only path pointed out by reason and decency.

§3.

To the above considerations, I think I may add the following: the ship of war which has the convoy under her protection has the supreme dominion for the time over what may be called her waters, that is to say, that portion of the sea which is within reach of her cannon; no other vessel can enter that circle without her permission, there she exercises a right of exclusive jurisdiction, and that jurisdiction ought to receive the same respect from the armed vessels of the belligerents which they expect to be paid to their own. Hence it results that the ship of war at the head of a fleet of merchant men is inviolable, and so are all the vessels placed under the protection of her cannon. If this principle be correct, as I believe it to be, the consequence which naturally flows from it cannot be denied. The only duty incumbent on a neutral ship of war which meets one belonging to a belligerent power is to fire a gun under her proper colors, according to the usage established at sea, and the belligerent ship is bound to do the same. Whatever the neutral may do beyond this, must be considered a mere courtesy. Thus, and thus only, she transmits to the belligerent commander the assurance that the vessels they she convoys are neutral. In this manner the neutral officer does more than his duty requires, he supersedes the necessity of a search by giving an equivalent satisfaction to the cruiser who ought to be satisfied with it. Such is the only practice consistent with the honor of the flag and the best calculated to preserve peace between sovereigns. If anyone should object that the law of war confers more extensive rights on the belligerent, I answer that such a law is the law of the strongest and that of power of equal or defensive force will never submit to it. Besides, the objection would be so much the more odious, that an extension of belligerent rights would in this case be without a reasonable object, because the declaration of the neutral commander ought to do away all suspicions respecting the character of the vessels which he convoys. It is tantamount to an oath and leaves no room to presume fraud, unless military honor should be considered as no longer having any existence.

§4.

But if notwithstanding the assurances given by the commander of the convoy and the precautions taken by him and his government, the belligerent satisfies him that there are not merely suspicions or indicia, but evident proofs that the property of some of the vessels under his convoy is masked or covered or that there is fraud in the nature of the cargoes or place of destination, or that enemy's vessels are disguised under the neutral flag, may he in that case with propriety insist on the dignity of his own flag and on the uncontrovertible veracity of his declaration? May he authoritatively assert that the proofs exhibited to him are false? Or will he overlook them? Or, in short, will he protect the offender who has imposed upon him, who has deceived his government and violated his oath?

It is necessary to establish here a distinction which appears highly important. Either the existing treaties do or do not authorize searches or suspicions on the high sea. In the latter case, the commander of the convoy need not listen to anything; he has fully complied with his duty by attesting the neutrality of the ships under his convoy.

But if in cases where there are proofs or well grounded suspicions of fraud, a search is authorized by the existing treaties. I think that the commander of the convoy has no right to reject those proofs, for he would then violate a formal engagement of his sovereign, his own character would suffer, and his honor would be suspected; and if he was not accused of conniving at the fraud, he would at least be justly taxed with imprudence and, in short, he would commit both the belligerent sovereign and his own. The former by a proper application to the latter, which he would be authorized to make, would undoubtedly obtain from him that redress which the commander of the convoy had unjustly denied; for, no sovereign can be presumed to be willing to protect fraud, when he is bound by his engagements to employ the most severe measures to prevent it. He wants and ought to protect a lawful trade, but not a criminal cupidity. His object in granting convoys cannot be supposed to be to defeat his own measures and render them illusory, the bare suspicion of such a design would be an injury. Therefore, it seems that justice as well as decency require that the commander of the neutral convoy should take into consideration the denunciations of the belligerent. If they are vague, insignificant, mere presumptions on anonymous information, they do not deserve to be attended to; for such are not admitted either by the treaties or by sound reason; and are more deserving of suspicion than of credit. But if they are founded on evidence and positive proofs, I see no reason or justice in rejecting them, either on the ground of conveniency, dignity, or any other. However, at the same time that the commander of the convoy is bound to admit those denunciations, he ought himself to proceed to ascertain the truth of them and cannot permit it to be done by the cruiser, for if he gave up that point, he would compromise the dignity by permitting a stranger to exercise an act of authority where he alone has the right to command.[40] All that he may and even ought to permit is that an officer from on board the cruiser be present at the verification. If from a mistaken point of honor, he should refuse so to do, he would run the risqué of committing himself by occasioning an unavoidable quarrel and perhaps even some violent measures, the consequences whereof cannot be foreseen.

---

[40] The Convention between Russia and England gives that right to the commander of the belligerent ship of war and not to the commanding officer of the convoy. See Chapter XXVII.

§5.

But notwithstanding the mode of proceeding and precautions that I have just pointed out, there are two cases which it seems may produce some embarrassment, as well as to the belligerent as to the neutral commander, if the two governments are not previously agreed: which are: 1st, when the cargoes of the convoyed vessels are enemy's property;[41] 2nd, when the belligerent considers as prohibited those goods which the neutral considers as lawful. The instructions given to the two commanding officers are conformable to the principles of their respective governments; therefore, they are necessarily in opposition to each other and in such a case how can they be reconciled? It seems then that force alone can put an end to the conquest. But it is evident that whatever may be the result, the belligerent sovereign will have supported a cause which the law of nations disavows, and the impropriety of this conduct will be so much the more evident (independent of the breach of the usages which are observed between ships of war) that the cause of neutrals is not merely founded on principles, but is supposed by so many commercial treaties, that they may in some manner be considered as constituting the common law of nations, while the few which lay them under some restrictions in that respect, are only to be considered as exceptions to the general rule.

---

[41] This question occasioned a very serious dispute between the Courts of London and Berlin. During the war of 1740, Prussian vessels either did carry or were suspected of carrying goods belonging to French and Spanish subjects, those two nations being then at war with Great Britain. The English cruisers captured a considerable number of them which were declared lawful prize. The British Government contended that by the law of nations, it is not lawful for neutrals to ship enemy's goods on board of their vessels. The Prussian Government asserted the contrary. I have related, in a former note, the issue of that controversy. A statement of the facts relating to it, with the documents, will be found in a work of Frederick Böhmer, entitled *Observations du droit de la nature et des gens, touchant la capture et detention des vaisseaux neuters, etc.* (Hamburg, 1771).

§6.

But let us precisely establish the fate of the question.

If there exists a treaty, it is the law both of the neutral and belligerent commandeer. If there is none, it is to be enquired whether there have been edicts or declarations officially communicated and approved of. In the latter case, the belligerent and the neutral have also a law common to them both. If there are neither treaties nor edicts, the law of nations must have its full effect, and the parties are bound to act according to its full principles; whoever deviates from them, commits an act of injustice which the other has a right to repel by force. There can be no question here about custom or usage, because there exists none. The proof is in the great variety of stipulations to be found in treaties and in the different conduct of different governments. Besides, an independent nation is not bound by any usage, but such as it has recognized.

§7.

Upon the whole, I do not hesitate to say that if maritime powers would blot out from their Code the odious chapter of suspicions and presumptions, if paying due respect to each other, they would agree to be satisfied with the inspection of the ship's papers, there would be an end to controversies, or at least they would be extremely rare, and the question respecting the immunity of the flag on the high seas would be settled in fact as it is in law; indeed, there would no longer be any motive or pretence for violating it; for it is natural to suppose (excepting, however, treaties which nations are mutually bound to observe) that neutrals would consider themselves as bound in honor to watch with a most vigilant eye over the regularity and correctness of their ship papers and the legality of their cargoes. And that they would be careful not to attest anything under their national seals which was not strictly conformable to truth. But if governments should persist on the one hand in considering as dangerous the exemption of neutrals from all kind of control and restraint on the high seas, and if on the other hand the advantages of an undisturbed navigation should be preferred to the unlimited exercise of the rights belonging to independence, the Treaty of Utrecht offers the means of reconciling the reasonable pretensions of all parties: by the exhibition of the ship's papers which should not only sufficiently prove the neutral ownership of the vessel, but also the nature of the cargo when bound to an enemy's port; but that being done, there should be an end to every further enquiry, no detention, no search ought to be permitted. This precaution would be sufficient to induce neutral merchants to be cautious and would save the dignity of governments which is evidently committed by the searches, visits, inquisitions, and examinations which take place notwithstanding the exhibition of the documents delivered in their names and authenticated by their seals. And why should not the sovereign of the neutral master detected in the act of fraud inflict upon him a personal punishment, besides the confiscation of his ship or goods? For he is guilty of a twofold offense; the one against the belligerent sovereign, and the other against his own government, whose engagements he has violated, and whose good faith he has surprised by a false oath? If all governments were to agree to adopt this mode of proceeding, it would become a part of the conventional law of nations; and by the slight sacrifice of the unbounded freedom of the seas, they would put a stop to, or at least greatly diminish, the source of the controversies occasioned by the odious right of search; no more would be said about that strange right, so improperly called legal force, and the proposed mode of proceeding would be the more effectually maintained, if (while private armed ships continue to be tolerated) they were to be enjoined to confine themselves to the capture of enemy's vessels. The measure which I propose would be a blessing to mankind, and even supposing that a few abuses might take place, they could be but very insignificant. Surely the evil which would result from them, let it be ever so much exaggerated, cannot be compared with that which is occasioned by the vexatious proceedings which are made use of to prevent it.

Chapter XIX.

Of Sieges and Blockades

§1.

A place is in a state of siege when it is invested and the cannon of the enemy can reach it. It is blockaded when the enemy only invests it is such a manner that nobody can enter or go out of it. Therefore, the blockade of a town by sea as well as by land has no other object but to invest it so that no reinforcements or supplies may be thrown into it and thereby compel the enemy to surrender to avoid famine.

It is asked whether a blockade may be extended to an harbor, a shore, or a coast? The most natural answer is found in the meaning of the word itself. The object of a blockade is to cut off all communications with the place that is so invested. Anything therefore which may contribute to that end constitutes a part of the blockade; and whatever does not tend to that object cannot be so considered. This explanation requires to be further developed.

§2.

A town may be blockaded by sea when it is situated on the sea coast, at the bottom of a bay or creek, or near the mouth of a river. In these three cases, the enemy who intends to blockade the place must place in its vicinity a sufficient stationary force to prevent its being approaches, and that force he may distribute on all the points which are best calculated for the accomplishment of his object. Beyond that line, the law of blockade and the rights which it confers on the blockading belligerent have no force, and neutral, on the contrary, are entitled to the full exercise of all their rights. Hence it follows that portion of the sea coast and harbours placed without the circumference occupied by a blockading force cannot be considered as blockaded, and that neutrals have a right to sail thither and from thence unmolested, saving to the belligerent cruiser the right of searching their vessels by virtue of his transitory jurisdiction while they are in the waters of his enemy.

§3.

It will be said that in this case the belligerent who is cruising near the enemy's coast has a right to intercept the navigation of neutrals and to prevent every kind of communication with the hostile country, but that inference is not correct. In order to be entitled to rights of any kind over a particular dominion in time of war, it is necessary to have a real and not a fictitious possession thereof, and a ship of war on a cruise has not and cannot have such real *bona fide* possession; she only rules over that portion of the sea which is within the reach of her cannon. All beyond that is free, and this is so true that the jurisdiction of a country over the waters which wash its shores extend no further than they can be reached and protected from the coast, and so far, and so far only, they are considered as a part of the national territory. But a cruiser cannot do that so long as the coast itself is not in his power; he therefore has no right to claim as his own the dominion which belongs to his enemy. It follows from thence and from the principles of the law of nations that you, the belligerent, cannot prevent me who am neutral from navigating and carrying on a lawful commerce with your enemy; that the only right you possess is to take legal measures, prevent my supplying your enemy with men or prohibited articles. Thus far and no farther can neutrals be made to feel the scourge of maritime war. This positive principle is sanctioned by usage as much as treaties, and never yet has a just government presumed to call it in question.

§4.

Therefore, a blockade in order to command respect must exist *de facto* and not be a mere creature of the mind, for it is impossible to rule over or conquer any portion of the sea or land without occupying it, and being able to defend it. A mere proclamation is not sufficient; there must be stationary cannon to give it effect; otherwise, I repeat it, a government might blockade all the rivers and coasts of Europe, nay, of the four parts of the globe, without putting a single ship in motion; nothing more would be required that the mere will to make conquests on the continent.[42]

§5.

It ought, moreover, to be observed that due notice of sieges and blockades must be given to neutrals before the rights resulting from that state of things can be exercised upon them. The law strictly requires this previous formality. And it cannot in any manner be dispensed with. But after notice given, every neutral vessel found within the circle of the blockade is liable to capture.

[42] This subject has given rise to serious discussions between France and Great Britain which are still subsisting. But the particulars thereof are too long and complicated to be explained here. All that can be said is that the Court of London has by its declarations of unlimited blockade subverted every principle and usage and that it has in a most unjustifiable manner violated the rights of mankind and the first principles of the law of nations. Can she after all this complain that she is accused of aiming at the universal dominion of the seas and of procrastinating the war with a view to consolidate that dominion?

Chapter XX.

Of the Competent Judge of Prizes

§1.

After having discussed the principles which relate to the searching and capturing of neutral vessels, the next object of consideration is the competency of the judges whose duty it is to take cognizance thereof. This point is so much the more important, that nothing can be compared to the excesses which in time of war are committed on the ocean; rapacity and ferocity appear to be let loose upon that element, and the mischief which they produce is still increased by the immense number of lawsuits which they necessarily occasion. I say nothing of the numerous acts of injustice which proceed from the policy of governments and the uncertainty of their legal principles.

According to the generally established practice, a captured vessel is adjudicated by the government of the captor; and that universal usage may be considered as a part of the customary law of nations. I believe that it may be useful to enquire into the grounds and reasons of that practice, and also into the character, functions and proper rule of conduct of those who are trusted with the exercise of that important branch of jurisdiction.

§2.

It is true that at first view the usage in question seems opposed to the primitive law of nations, which is well known to rest on the fundamental principle of mutual independence to the enjoyment of which all civil societies are entitled at sea as well as on the land. It is well known also that there can be no common judge between them, and that war is the only remedy that one nation has against another which has dealt unjustly by her. But let us analyze these truths and trace their application to the navigation of neutrals.

§3.

A neutral vessel when on the high seas is out of every foreign jurisdiction; and the slightest attempt upon her freedom is an offense. Such is the general, positive, incontestable principle of the law of nations in time of peace.[43] But as I have already showed, that principle is subject in time of war to some modifications with respect to those governments who wish to remain in a state of peace. There is one from which all the others are derived; it relates to those things which are considered as dangerous to one of the belligerent parties. It is agreed that neutral States could not furnish them[44] without violating their neutrality; consequently, they ought to abstain therefrom, and this prohibition is a modification of the unlimited independence of neutral vessels. The articles attended to are arms and warlike stores of every description.

§4.

There is no doubt that very few controversies would arise if all the sovereigns were agreed on the principles relative to commerce and navigation in time of war and if the conduct of belligerents and neutrals were entirely guided by honesty and good faith. But on that subject each power has its particular system of jurisprudence which each accommodates to its own interest and situation; they never take into consideration the principles of the law of nations, except when they favour the

---

[43] Everybody is acquainted with the long and serious controversy which the violation of this principle by the Spanish *Guarda-costas* in America occasioned between the Courts of Madrid and London.

[44] To furnish means to carry, to deliver. This explanation is necessary in order not to confound the sales which a neutral makes at home with the transportation of goods by sea and their delivery abroad. Neutrals are at liberty to sell goods of any description to either of the belligerents in their own country, but they cannot lawfully carry and deliver them to the belligerents elsewhere. Mr. *Lampredi* has thrown considerable light upon the question in his work entitled *Du commerce des neutres en temps de guerre*. Part 1, c 5, p. 49.

system which they have adopted or when they can twist to answer their purpose by exerting all the powers of an insidious logic and, indeed, the diversity which exists in that respect, well deserves to be attended to. It often happens that those governments which are bound by treaties, respect them only as they find it expedient under the existing circumstances; and thence arise two serious inconveniences. On the one hand, the neutral owner confiding in the system and relying on the protection of his government, makes the shipment accordingly and the thirst of gain often induces him to make some which are equivocal and perhaps fraudulent. On the other hand, the belligerent cruiser has no wish but to make captures, privateers especially are fitted out for that only purpose, the slightest pretence is sufficient for them to detain, search, and molest neutral merchant men; they go as far as they can beyond the letter of their instructions, which are unknown to the neutral trader and not seldom in contradiction with the principles of the neutral government. Thus a merchant vessel, on the least suspicion of fraud, nay, for the sake of a mere irregularity is diverted from her intended course, and must submit to long and expensive proceedings, whether in the end she is to be released or condemned.

§5.

To detain a neutral vessel on the high seas and carrying her into another port than that to which she was bound is certainly an act of violence and a violation of the immunity of her flag. However, since the right of search is acknowledged by treaties in certain cases, and since there is a possibility that fraud may exist, there ought also to exist some means of repressing it; for the independence and immunity of the neutral flag are not intended to enable merchants to commit fraud with impunity. On the other hand, it happens but too often that the captor is guilty of an act of violence, of an infraction of treaties, or at least of an unlawful detention of the neutral vessel and in all those cases, he ought to be punished.

§6.

There are but two modes between nations for the repression of fraud and violence. They are war and negotiation or some other amicable mode of settlement. Nobody will surely maintain that the first mode ought to be preferred, for in that case the least dispute would become the subject of war. A milder remedy has been adopted, which is, on the one hand, the confiscation of the property of the fraudulent neutral and, on the other, the punishment of the captor who has exceeded the bounds of his authority.

§7.

But in order to inflict that twofold penalty, the existence of the fact must be ascertained and the punishment must be legally awarded. There must be a judge somewhere by whom these functions are to be exercised. Shall that power then be vested in the government of the captor, or in that of the captured?

All this is out of the ordinary rule, and no doubt, is subject o many inconveniences; for in general governments act the part of protectors more than that of impartial judges. Some encourage privateering while other strive to promote navigation and trade. The object of the former is to restrict the freedom of the seas, while the latter wish to maintain it in all of its integrity. Be it as it may, it is but too true than in war everything is irregular and that war itself is the subversion of all social principles. The effects of that order, or rather disorder of things, are more or less felt by neutrals, particularly on that element where friends and foes meet unobserved and where cupidity finds its most precious resources. Therefore, it is not in the strict principles of the law of nations that we must expect to find the solution of the problem before us; it is only to be solved by recurring to analogy, or rather, by reconciling those principles with the necessity of preventing, if possible, the abuse of force on one side, and fraud on the other, without having recourse to the violent remedy of arms.

§8.

In order to be able to decide this question, we must establish some preliminary points. In the first place, the fraudulent trader has assessed the character of an enemy and committed an act of hostility for which he deserves to be punished according to the rigour of the law of war and thus has knowingly placed himself at the discretion of the State which he has offended; now, the severity of the law of war is mitigated by substituting to it the seizure and confiscation of the instrument of the fraud. On the other hand, the captor may have been guilty of any act of injustice or lawless violence, or otherwise have exceeded his powers, and in that case, he also is deserving of punishment. Here then are two objects of investigation: the legality of the capture and the conduct of the captor. Some competent authority must exist to pronounce judgment on both those points. In whom is this authority to be vested? Let the nature of the facts itself decide the question.

The seizure takes place on the high seas or in the waters of the sovereign of the captor, or in those of a neutral State. In the first case, if it is not authorized by a treaty between the two sovereigns, it is clearly vexatious and illegal, being made in a place which is out of all human jurisdiction. In the second case, the jurisdiction of the belligerent in his own waters in incontestable, and in the third case, the jurisdiction, of course, belongs to that sovereign whose territory has been violated. We shall therefore only consider this question as in relation to the first case; admitting for the sake of argument the legality of the seizure of neutral ships on the high sea.

According to usage and treaties, an armed vessel duly commissioned for that purpose is authorized to visit on the high sea a vessel justly suspected of fraud and to capture her, if she is really in fault. In conformity with his instructions, the cruiser ought to endeavour to secure his prize by sending her into a port of his own country, or in case of necessity into that of a neutral State. But the mere act of seizure is not sufficient to vest in him the property of the prize; it may be illegal, unjust, or vexatious; it must therefore undergo a process of adjudication. We must not forget that the first and principal act to be tried is done by the cruiser at the moment of the capture. He is either a trespasser, or he does a lawful act in the execution of a special authority, for which he is responsible to his government as well as to the captured, while they latter is merely passive and acts only in his own defense. The Government of the captor therefore is the only competent judge of the legality of his conduct and of the manner in which he has executed the authority committed to him. He is the only one who has a right to punish him for transgressing the bounds prescribed to him by his instructions. At the same time, we must observe that in the judicial investigation which takes place after the capture, the captured is in fact the complainant or actor, demanding restitution of his property illegally captured. Here then the axiom of reason and law *actor sequitur forum rei* finds its natural and proper application. It would therefore be interverting the natural order of things to propose to the captor to go and answer for his conduct to the tribunals of a foreign sovereign who has no jurisdiction over him because the act complained of was not done within his territory or limits. And let it be particularly observed that the captor may not only have been guilty of an illegal capture, but also of other trespasses deserving a particular punishment; that he may have seized the neutral vessel out of more wantonness and caprice; that he may have plundered her, committed murders, batteries or other criminal acts, and occasioned her considerable damages. Who is to pronounce sentence upon these facts? Shall it be another sovereign than that of the accused captor? That sovereign has no right to punish him, and if he had, how would he be able to secure his person? And if he should award restitution and damages, how will he be able to carry his judgment into execution? Privateers are obliged to give security, but that security is taken in their own country, and no foreign judgment can be executed there. Will it be said that the captured vessel must be brought back to the country to which she belonged? But on what principle of law can this be required of the captor and where are the means of compelling him to do it? How can it be expected that he shall dispossess himself of his prize, which he already considers in a manner as his property, and that forsaking his natural judge, he shall exhibit himself as a defendant and perhaps as a culprit before a foreign tribunal? Let us suppose, for instance, that a French, Spanish, or English armed ship captures a neutral vessel in the Mediterranean, say a Hamburgher, a Dane, or a Russian, can it be required of the captor that instead of carrying his prize into Toulon, Cadiz, or Gibraltar, he shall send her into a port of the Baltic or Northern Ocean; that he shall run all the further changes of war and the elements, for the sake of submitting his conduct to the judgment of a foreign tribunal? It would be too much to require that of him, nor would the requisition ever be complied with for his own sovereign neither would nor ought to enjoin it upon him; for, after all, he might with propriety answer: I am in possession of my prize, I took it by your permission and under your authority, I am ready to prove before you that the capture is legal, and that I strictly pursued the instructions which you was pleased to give me, but in the name of all that is just, do not compel me to submit my rightful claim and what is more, my honor and my character to the judgment of a foreign power that never had, nor can have, any authority over me.

It may indeed be objected that the government of the captor which is to decide on the legality of the capture is at the same time a judge and a party, and that its judgment will, of course, be partial. It is certain that in matters of prize the government is the sole judge and this councils or boards of commissioners which it appoints for that purpose are only its agents or representatives, that they have none of the characteristics of the ordinary judicial authority because they are not appointed by virtue of the law, but of a mere mandate revocable at pleasure, that they are not bound to decree according to law but according to edicts, ordinances, proclamations, and treaties; in short, that their acts are more of a ministerial than of a judicial nature. but it would be the same thing if the proceedings were to take place before the government of the captured neutral, and therefore the objection in this respect deserves no consideration. Partiality may exist on one side as well as on the other, and as to corruption and prevarication, it is too serious a charge to be made against any government, and neither can nor ought to be suspected or presumed. Prepossession, indeed, is inherent to all human assertions, and it may easily be conceived that a belligerent government will naturally favour a class of men which it is endeavouring to stimulate by the allurement of profit, to expose their lives and fortunes in the support of its cause, and that a neutral government on the other hand will feel favorably inclined towards its merchants thro' whose industry and exertions the country flourishes and prospers. But, after all, on so serious a subject, where everything is out of the ordinary course and where light is in a manner to be elicited out of chaos and darkness, there is an essential point of which the whole argument rests and which must never be lost sight of. There must be some certain means of trying and punishing officers of the description that we are speaking of; the sovereign of the captor and he alone possesses those means; he alone, therefore, ought to be constituted the judge in such cases.

Besides, and it cannot be too often repeated, it is in a great measure the fault of neutrals that there are so many captures and so much litigation in matters of prize. They claim, as may well be expected, the freedom of their trade and navigation, and the belligerent endeavours to restrain it. In that conflict, abuse of power, trespasses, tortious acts of every description, and consequently complaints, cannot be avoided. The only way of preventing, or at least lessening, all those inconveniences would be for neutral nations to concert with each other and agree upon certain uniform principles which should serve as a general rule and upon the means of maintaining them with effect; for if that cannot be done, the weak must needs submit to the strong. But in the latter case those who are obliged to bend under the imperious law of necessity ought at least to give order to their merchants not to expose themselves to ruinous, certain and irreparable losses.

Let me be permitted to make here some remarks on the habitual carelessness of most governments respecting the subject that I am treating of. During a peace, they forget the disturbances and inconveniences which their trade and navigation experienced in time of war, and take no steps whatever to prevent them for the future, as if the millennium was already come and a perpetual peace was to reign forever; and as soon as war again takes place, they hasten to draw their profit from it by making what use they can of the liberty of the seas, while the belligerent powers are endeavouring to restrain or favour it, or their interests require; how, then, is it possible to negotiate and come to an understanding in the midst of such confusion and tumult? Both parties therefore remain in a state of uncertainty; everything is precarious, or rather arbitrary; hence innumerable complaints, contestations and lawsuits, the issue of which is naturally as uncertain as the rules by which they are to be determined. Most certainly, the principles of the law of nations are not equivocal, but what are principles when opposed to the interests or views of governments? Policy ever has and ever will mould them its own way; reason is a nose of wax which may be twisted into any shape. Besides, in time of war, governments act more than they argue, and negotiations are gone thro' with the rapidity of military operations. Power and danger only calculate the interest of the moment, and the neutral often yields at the expense of his dignity and rights.

After having carried our investigation thus far, we are next to consider who is the competent judge of a prize carried into a neutral port? Is it the neutral sovereign, or the national judge of the captor?

It appears to me that this question ought to be decided on the principle that in personal causes the cognizance belongs to the judge within whose jurisdiction the fact happened. Therefore, if the vessel was captured in the waters of the neutral State into whose port she is carried, that government is the only competent judge of its validity and ought to declare it illegal and void. This principle is so much the more certain that that very Government has a right to demand satisfaction for the violation of its territory. Nay, even if the captor had carried his prize into a port of his own country, the neutral sovereign into whose waters the capture was made would not only be entitled, but in duty bound to claim its restitution; otherwise he would be responsible to the State to whose subjects the prize belonged at the time of the capture.

But if the vessel was captured on the high seas, she can only be adjudicated, as I have already observed, by the sovereign of the captor; and that of the port into which she might have sought an asylum would have no right to interfere. The reason is that the capture took place out of his jurisdiction and that the circumstance of the prize being temporarily within his dominions must transfer to him the right of jurisdiction already vested in another.

I shall conclude with a few observations on the legal effects of a judgment given respecting the validity or invalidity of a prize.

It is certain that the competence of a judge being once acknowledged, his judgment must be allowed to have its full effect; it becomes the law of the parties and cannot in any manner be evaded. Such is the incontrovertible rule, with respect to domestic tribunals in causes between subjects of the same State; but is that rule equally certain when it is to be applied to a foreigner, in a matter thus complicated, so fraught with contradictory principles and on which policy has more influence than the ordinary rules of justice. Has not the sovereign to whose subject manifest injustice been based a right to complain of it, and if his complaint should not be listened to, and he has in his power the means of redressing the wrong, is he not authorized to do himself justice?

This question is extremely delicate. It requires to be considered in a legal and in a political point of view. In the latter aspect, the relations which subsist between the governments sometimes determine their mode of proceeding, and there have been instances of sovereigns who, after they have been convinced that a judgment was manifestly unjust, instead of annulling it by an act of arbitrary authority to the prejudice of a third party, or when the constitutional laws of the country did not allow of a similar measure, did of their own accord grant an indemnity to the injured party. But when that does not take place, what is the neutral sovereign authorized to do, whose subject has been spoliated by the unjust sentence of a foreign tribunal?

It may be said that as soon as the competency of the tribunal is acknowledged (and it is so when the parties appear and submit their controversy to its decisions), its judgment becomes necessarily binding on those who have thus recognized its authority and there is no further remedy after going thro' the degree of appellate jurisdiction. The sovereign of the party condemned has himself indirectly acknowledged the competence of the court by allowing his subject to appear and solicit judgment. How then is it possible that he should after that exclaim against that sentence and take measures to prevent its legal effects? That mode of proceeding appears evidently contradictory and the quarrel of private individuals would be thus transformed into a matter of State, the consequences of which might lead to a war.

Still, nothing is more difficult to be borne than injustice, and the want of power alone can induce resignation under it. That truth is of the greatest importance to the rulers of nations; it ought to convince them that the cupidity of doing justice to others ought to outweigh in their minds every other consideration. The law imposes silence on the citizen who has been aggrieved by the judgment of a municipal court because that is absolutely necessary for the maintenance of good order and the public peace. But between nations, there is a supreme tribunal called *ultima ratio Regum*. It is that awful tribunal which governments should always keep before their eyes.

Therefore, when a government does injustice to the subjects of another, it ought to foresee that complaints will be made and even that measures will be taken to obtain effectual redress; and it is impossible to find fault with those proceedings, for a government is the natural protector of its citizens and ought to make use of the means in its power to obtain that justice which has been denied them; it becomes the supreme appellate tribunal from an iniquitous sentence, nor can an objection be made from its express or tacit consent to the proceedings which took place, for that consent was grounded on its confidence in the equity of the judges, and that confidence was deceived.

There are some publicists who are of opinion that the concerns of private persons have nothing to do with the political interests of the State and consequently that they cannot be made the subject of discussion between two governments; but it is evident that such opinion is erroneous and in contradiction with the fundamental principles of social order. And indeed, why have men associated together and submitted to civil government? Have they not deposited their individual rights in the hands of their rulers and united together in a political body that by their joint force those rights might be more effectually protected? Governments represent not only the body of the nation, but every individual of which it is composed, and it follows from thence that the sovereign is in the obligation of protecting not only what is called the interest of the State, but also that of every individual member of the political body. Therefore if an individual in injured in a foreign country, if injustice is done him, his sovereign is in duty bound to undertake his defense; were it not the case, how could he be said to owe protection to his subjects.

These truths may easily be applied in the cases which happen at sea. A merchant cannot fit out a vessel without a passport from his sovereign and without displaying the national flag; she is in consequence thereof under the immediate safeguard and protection of the State. So that if any violence is offered to her, it is not only a violation of the right of private property and of the freedom of the sea, but it is an outrage offered to the sovereign himself, because by the contempt shown to his flag and passport, his rights and dignity are violated.

In that state of things will it be said that a sovereign has not a right, nay, that he is not absolutely bound to interfere so that justice may be done? Such interference does not, as is pretended, make him a party in his subject's cause; he only acts as his supreme protector, taking care that the law of nations or the existing treaties are duly observed. Hubner[45] does not properly discriminate between these two characters when he asks by what right a government can assume the exercise of a sort of jurisdiction over neutral sovereigns.[46]

---

[45] *De la saisie des batimens neutres*, Vol. I, Part 2, c. 1, § 4, 5, 6.

[46] *Lampredi* (*Du commerce des neutres*, p. 173) refutes this opinion of Hubner, and contends that he misapplies in this instance the word *jurisdiction*; and in order to avoid the application of that word, he gives a definition of *capture* which is neither clear nor correct and which is otherwise liable to a variety of objections. He says: *that a privateer who detains and searches a neutral vessel does not thereby exercise an act of jurisdiction, but only exercises his lawful right acknowledged as such by the neutral nations themselves.* And he adds that if after searching the vessel, considering her to be lawful prize, he should carry her into port and afterwards discover that he had committed a mistake, he would be excused on paying the damages and that there would be nothing in his conduct *evidently unjust*. All this is very well for the privateer; he may commit a mistake, carry a neutral vessel arbitrarily out of her course, occasion with or without design the failure of a well planned and widely

extended speculation on paying damages, the whole mischief is atoned for. But amidst this system of jurisprudence what becomes of the safety of neutrals, of the freedom of the sea, of the independence of nations? The privateer, says again *Lampredi*, exercises a right acknowledged by neutrals themselves; but the general assertion is inaccurate, for the consent of neutrals is conditional; it is restricted either by the letter of the treaties, by custom, or by natural reason. Treaties require either positive proofs or at least strong presumptions of fraud. When there are positive proofs, there can be no difficulty; the question is decided at the very moment of capture, but the case is quite different when there are only suspicions. If they are admitted, they must at least amount to strong circumstantial evidence, or what the civilians call *semi-plena probatio*, that proof must have been acquired before the search and not merely the result of it; in short, they must be such as to satisfy impartial judges of the *bona fides* of the captor; otherwise, he has acted as a pirate, he has committed an arbitrary act of violence, and his conduct is manifestly unjust. Such are, in my opinion, the reflections which *Lampredi* should have made, but it does not appear that they even occurred to him. He seems to have forgotten that the captor acts by virtue of a commission and not in his own right. Custom which governs when treaties are silent also sanctions the principles which I have laid down. As to natural reason, it decided that if I allow you to pass over my lands, I do not thereby authorize you to destroy or ruin my crops.

As to what *Lampredi* says on the subject of jurisdiction, it is a mere dispute about words which has nothing to do with the main point of the question. The cruiser, altho' acting for his personal benefit, does not act in his own name, but in the name of his sovereign. If the letter does not authorize him to exercise an act of jurisdiction in the strict sense of the word, he authorizes him to exercise an act of power, to be tried afterwards by a tribunal of his own appointment. That tribunal, or ministerial board, however it may be constituted, undoubtedly exercises an act of jurisdiction. Now that act of jurisdiction is a consequence of the capture, which alone has given rise to that proceeding and is its sole object and motives. Therefore, it must be considered as a point of it, more particularly as being done by virtue of a special commission from the sovereign authority. Certainly, every similar act of power, whether lawful or not, is properly to be considered as an exercise of jurisdiction. Neutrals have granted that right of jurisdiction to belligerents as to vessels taken in the act of committing fraud, for they have given them a right to seize and capture them and to try the validity of the capture. Now, it is perfectly indifferent whether this is called *jurisdiction* or *authority*, but one of the two words must certainly be made use of.

Chapter XXI.

Of Reciprocity and Reprisals

§1.

Reciprocity in my opinion consists in this: it requires that a neutral should obtain from one of the belligerents the same degree of freedom which is allowed to him by the other. If he does not obtain it, the former belligerent is no longer bound to anything, but is authorized to adopt the system of his enemy. By not adopting it, he would injure himself and benefit the hostile nation.

§2.

It may perhaps be objected that such reciprocity cannot take place when there exists a treaty between a belligerent power and a neutral State because the objectives of the two contracting parties are determined by the said treaty and they are not at liberty to deviate from its stipulations. This question deserves to be thoroughly investigated.

In most commercial treaties, provision is eventually made for the case in which one of the parties should be involved in war, and the effect of such stipulations when the *casus foederis* takes place, is the question now to be determined.

It is asked whether a belligerent power, bound by a treaty with a neutral State, may restrict the stipulations thereof in case the latter should not obtain the same advantages from the other belligerent? We will put a case in order the better to elucidate this question.

Suppose that France is bound by a commercial treaty with one of the Northern Powers in which the rule *free ships, free goods* is stipulated on both sides. Suppose afterwards that France is engaged in war with Great Britain and that the latter power confiscates all French goods found on board of neutral ships, not excepting those of the nation to which France is bound by the above mentioned commercial treaty. May in that case the

French Government notwithstanding her positive engagement with the neutral State adopt the principle of her enemy and on the ground of reciprocity confiscate the English goods found on board the vessel of the neutral nation?

It may be said on the one side that the case in question is presumed to have been foreseen when the freedom of enemy's goods was stipulated; that the stipulation was absolute and unlimited, and not conditional: that it is not lawful to insert ex post facto a condition which is not expressed in the instrument, and which it is not a necessary inference from what is expressly stipulated, or from the nature of things; and therefore that the contract must under all circumstances have its full and entire execution. It may, indeed, be prejudicial to the belligerent power, but it is a chance which it ought to have foreseen and which does not arise from the fault of the neutral. Consequently, it is not a sufficient reason to destroy a formal obligation; otherwise, the execution of treaties would be submitted to the arbitrary will and pleasure of the contracting parties, and the slightest pretence would be sufficient to annul them.

But, on the other side, there are important considerations to be attended to. The belligerent who has stipulated with the neutral the freedom of enemy's goods on board of his ships may address him as follows: when you carry the goods of my enemy and refuse to carry or protect mine, you depart from the line of impartiality; for you favor my enemy to my prejudice. The case is the same if altho' you do not ship my enemy's goods you refuse or abandon mine because by acting thus, you do me an injury in order to comply with unreasonable demands of my adversary; but impartiality is the first duty of neutrals, nothing exempts them from its binding force. I cannot be supposed by a tacit engagement to have authorized you to injure me, but you are presumed to have taken upon yourself the contrary obligation. Obtain then from my enemy equal advantages on both sides, or suffer me to establish that equality by adopting his own system of jurisprudence, or else, if you require me to fulfil my engagement, I require you to fulfil yours, that is to say, to take proper measures that your flag may afford an effectual protection to my goods. If you want either the will or the power to do it, the confidence which I showed when I entered into treaty with you has been deceived; the contract made between us is a leonine partnership in which you have the lion's share; I have therefore a right to rescind it. In a few words, I say, that I cannot have agreed with you that you should have a right to injure me and favor my enemy; I ought on the contrary to have supposed that you would have obtained from him the same acknowledgement of your rights which you have received from me, or that you would effectually have maintained them against him. This last observation is founded on the following principles. The freedom of the neutral flag is a necessary inference from the first principles of the law of nations, and the neutral flag cannot be free unless it affords an effectual protection to the enemy's property that it covers (see Chapter IX). Therefore, when that freedom is stipulated by a treaty, that stipulation is not a grant or favour from one party to the other; it is merely declaratory of an incontestable pre-existing right. So that, after all, the whole question is reduced to this: may a neutral renounce the exercise of an undoubted right in favour of one of the belligerents and exercise I to the prejudice of the other? The answer is plain and clear: the conduct of the neutral in this instance is an act of partiality and consequently hostile. I may then conclude that in the case which I have supposed, the neutral is bound to protect the goods of the power with whom he has contracted, or renounce that freedom which this latter has by his treaty acknowledged?

§3.

Reprisals precede hostilities and belong to that political branch of the government. They consist in seizing the property of any member whatever of a nation whose government has been guilty of injustice to a foreigners, or denied satisfaction for an act of violence committed by one of his subjects. Thus, the innocent is exposed to suffer for the guilty. This mode of proceeding is founded on the joint and several responsibility supposed to exist between all the members of the same political society who are jointly and severally responsible for one another as is acknowledged by the law of nations. Therefore, if a sovereign is under the necessity of complaining of an injury suffered, he is authorized in case of a denial of justice to exercise the right of reprisals and by that means procure an indemnity to his inured subject; but it will be easily conceived that the injury must be manifest, that all the means of conciliation must have been tried and exhausted, before such a measure be adopted, for reprisals are a sort of hostility, even tho' disguised under the specious name of indemnification[47] and easily lead to an open rupture. Therefore the same cause which would justify a declaration of war will also justify reprisals; from whence it must be inferred that the case must be of a serious nature, the motives very urgent, and the injury clear and manifest before a power has recourse to the latter extremity. Belligerents when deciding on matters which involve the interest of neutrals ought always to have it before their eyes, and consequently to calculate the possible effects of an act of injustice.

In order to explain my ideas on so intricate and important a question with all the precision that I am capable of, I shall put the following case: a power is engaged in war, and sends to sea his men of ear and some privateers to watch over the navigation of neutrals; he either has or has not made known to the latter the rules and principles which he had adopted or meant to adopt with respect to them. In the first case they ought to conform to those rules if they have not disclaimed them. In the second case, they are authorized to follow the general principles of the primitive or customary law of nations at their election. If those principles are opposed to those of the belligerent, and if the latter in consequence thereof should violate the immunity of the neutral flag, the neutral government ought to make his complaints in proper time, decline the foreign jurisdiction, declare the principles on which his pretensions are founded, and protest beforehand against all judicial proceedings to the contrary, or at least declare that he will not be bound by a sentence contrary to the principles which he considers to be just; thus it will not be pretended that he is bound by a formal or tacit

---

[47] As was done in 1793 by the Court of Berlin in its discussion that that of London. See the Note to Chapter 15, § 5.

acquiescence. If, on the contrary, after being informed of the capture and consequent proceedings he authorizes his subject, the owner of the captured ship, to appear and claim before the tribunal, if he should suffer sentence of condemnation to pass and be carried into execution without making any complaint, he is presumed to have given his assent, and in that case, how could he justify his tardy measures for the indemnification of his subject? It appears evident that he could have no right to issue reprisals and that if he did, he would run the risk of provoking an unjust war. But lately, if the principles of the belligerent government being avowed or at least known in a manner sufficiently authentic, the sentence of the tribunal should be in contradiction with them, then the neutral would have just ground for complaint, notwithstanding his admission of this jurisdiction of the Court, because he had confided in the equity of the judge, and his confidence had been deceived; and if in that case, injury be not redressed, he has a right to take measures to redress it himself and consequently to make reprisals. Policy will then decide whether the measure is rash or precedent.

§4.

I shall conclude this article with an observation which has some analogy with the question of competency.

Captures are to be considered in two different points of view. Some vessels are seized because the neutral owners have either violated treaties or the principles generally adopted; others because the cruiser has conformed himself to the system of jurisprudence of his own country, and to the instructions of his own government, while that of the captured had adopted an entirely opposite system. In the first case, the government of the captor has but one line of conduct to pursue; its decision must be conformable to the tenor of treaties, or to the rules and principles generally adopted, or in default of such, to the principles of the primitive law of nations. If it should deviate from that line, his proceedings are subject to be reviewed by the sovereign of the captured; for he is bound to afford protection to his subjects and to complain of the violation either of treaties, usage, or the law of nations.

It is not the same thing when the neutral and the belligerent sovereign act upon different principles, for in that case, there is no common rule between them on which the latter may ground his decision. He cannot decide according to his own system, the subject matter is foreign property; nor can he adopt that of the other government because he has not a right to apply it to the captor, who is his own subject and who has only obeyed the instructions which he had received from him.

I shall venture to give my opinion as to what ought to be done amidst those conflicting principles, jurisdictions, and interests. I do not wish to cut the difficulty short, but to solve it, if possible, according to the rules of justice and the neutral respect which nations owe to each other and which alone can maintain peace and harmony among them.

Captures are made either on the high seas or in the waters of the captor, or of his enemy, or in those of a neutral State. Let us consider those three different cases:

1°. I have already observed, and think demonstrated, that on the high seas, according to treaties and usages, the search of neutral vessels cannot lawfully take place, except there is a well grounded suspicion that she is laden with contraband goods. That case excepted, searches are irregular and vexatious, nay, are real acts of violence. If the suspicion is well founded, the detention and seizure are so likewise and ought to be acquired or condemned according as the fraud is or is not established by evidence.

§5.

But in order that things may go on in this way, there ought to be an agreement between the two governments respecting the right of search and what is to be considered as prohibited and fraudulent. This is done commonly by commercial treaties or mutual declarations, and when there are neither, the general usage is to be followed. But if there exists no such document and if the two governments act upon opposite principles, what ought they in that case respectively to do? It is evident that the belligerent cannot without violating the first rules of justice decide according to his own laws, because they cannot be applied to a foreigner, nor to a fact which happened on an element which is out of his jurisdiction. In that case, would it not be both equitable and fraudulent for him to abstain from pronouncing any judgment on the capture and to endeavour to settle the matter by negotiation with the neutral State? For, after all, this is no longer a controversy between private individuals, but a contest between two governments; the decision whereof belongs to the law of nations and consequently to the political and not to the judicial branch of the government. This mode of proceeding appears to me so much more adapted to the circumstance, that the neutral government has an indisputable right to interfere and complain, not as the mere protector of his subjects, but as having a direct interest in maintaining his own system of jurisprudence, his own dignity, and the rights inherent to his independence; and if matters cannot be thus accommodated, and the belligerent sovereign still persists in adhering to his principles, the neutral has an incontestable right, not only to retaliate, but to make reprisals.

2°. When the neutral vessel is in the waters of one of the belligerents, she is under his jurisdiction and therefore she is obliged to respect the rules which he has established concerning trade and navigation. Hence he has a right to search her in order not only to ascertain whether she is *bona fide* neutral, but also to examine into the nature of her cargo, because she may be suspected of intending to defraud the revenue or to violate some prohibitory law of the State and is liable, even in time of peace, to be searched, seized, tried, and confiscated on that only account. But the question is to know whether she may be so on account of goods of a doubtful character which the local government has thought proper to include among prohibited merchandise? I believe not, if both governments do not agree on that point, because in that case, as in the preceding one, the controversy is of a political and not of a forensic nature. But powerful States make no account of this difficulty and do not hesitate to cut it short by exercising their authority.

3°. If a neutral vessel met with on the coast or in the waters of an enemy, she is undoubtedly liable to be searched. But as that question belongs to the subject of sieges and blockades, I refer my readers to what I have said above, Chapter XIX.

Chapter XXII.

An Examination of the Doctrine of Mr. Jenkinson (Earl of Liverpool)

After having laid down the true principles of the law of nations respecting the rights and duties of belligerent as well as neutral powers, it will not be uninteresting, but on the contrary, will greatly contribute to the full elucidation of the subject, to show in what manner it is understood by those governments whose policy consists in laying the most extraordinary restrictions on the freedom of neutral trade. Among these powers, Great Britain stands foremost because of all the European powers she has been at all times the most attached to the restrictive system; her principles, therefore, are of all the others the most deserving of our attention. I shall not take notice of her edicts or other public acts because they are only the result of which they exhibit, as it were, in action, but without affording a sufficient development of the theoretical doctrines on which they are founded. It is the writings of her publicists only that that development is to be found, and among those there is one who deserves particular attention, as well on account of his personal character and of the reputation which he has long since enjoyed and also on account of his intimate connexion with the English administration at the time when he wrote. I mean to speak of Mr. Jenkinson, afterwards known by the title of Earl of Liverpool. In the year 1757, when France admitted neutrals to trade with her colonies, he wrote a pamphlet[48] under the title of *A Discourse on the Conduct of the Government of Great Britain in respect to Neutral Nations*. Such a work may well be expected to contain as full a development as the author thought necessary to make of the maxims and principles of his Government, in order to justify the application which they made of them to other nations; indeed, he employed all his sagacity, learning, and erudition to

---

[48] It will be found at large in the Supplement, with Notes. He was at that time Secretary of War.

set them forth in the most favorable light and I cannot but acknowledge that his opinion has considerable weight. But we are not so much to consider the name or reputation of a writer, however celebrated he may be, as the real merits of the doctrine which he maintained. Besides, it but too often happens that an author suffers himself to be swayed by national prejudice or by other equally powerful motives. The reader will himself decide whether Mr. Jenkinson did yield to some external impulse or whether he wrote with that impartiality which the importance of the subject required. I begin with the translation of a passage from his work which contains in substance nearly the whole of his system.

"The right of protection (says he) must then have its foundation in some law and where considered in relation to any particular case, it must be founded on that law, by which the interests of the parties concerned are generally determined and which hath force in that place, where the right of protection is claimed. Thus in the present case, if neutral nations have any rights to protect the property of the enemy, it must take its rise from those laws, which are the established rules of conduct between nations, and particularly on that element where this right is supposed to be exerted. No civil or municipal institutions, and much less the privileges arising from them, can here take place; they have no force but under the dominion of those who agreed to their establishment. The question then is – *How far according to the law of nations does this right of protection extend*?

To answer this clearly, we must observe that governments can have succeeded to no other rights, but such as their respective numbers enjoyed in a state of individuality; that that one nation is now to another, as it were in a state of nature, that is, in the same condition in which man was to man before they entered into society; the right therefore of protection, which individuals would have enjoyed in such a situation, is the same which government can claim at present. An individual then in a state of nature would have had an undoubted right to protect his own person and property against any attack.

But if I am engaged in contention with another, would he then have a right to protect him against me? Most certainly not, since he thereby would deprive me of a right with the law of nature, for my own security, would in such a case give me, of seizing the property of this my enemy and destroying his person; if he thought my conduct manifestly injurious, so as to call for general resentment, he would, on that account, become my enemy himself; but as long as he calls himself a neuter, to act in this manner against me would be no less absurd than unjust. Such therefore, and no more, is the right of protection which governments enjoy at present in those places, to which their own dominions do not extent; they have descended to the rights only of their respective members, and by consequence those alone can protect.

But it will be asked from whence there arises the right which governments always enjoy of protecting the property of the enemy within the precincts of their own country? It is a consequence of the right of dominion, unless, therefore, their dominion extends over the ocean, the right of protection cannot there take place; dominion gives a right of enacting laws, of establishing new jurisdiction and of making all (whether its own subjects or those of other countries) submit to these, who come within the pale of its power. Here then the trial which the law of nations gives, is, as it were, superseded; and any proceedings upon it would, of course, be unjust; but as soon as you are out of the range of this particular jurisdiction, the laws thereof and the privileges which attend them cease at once, and the general laws of nations again have their force: here the property, even of an ally, hath no other protection than what these laws allow it; being joined, therefore, to the goods of an enemy, it cannot communicate its protection to these since the same law which gives sccurity to the first allows you to seize and destroy the latter. These reasonings are exemplified by a common fact: within the precincts of the dominion of any government, you are not at liberty to search the ships of any country; but is not this liberty universally and immemorially practiced over all on the main sea? And therefore is this search made, but that, according to the law of nations, all are here answerable for what they may convey".

In order to analyze this long passage and to refute with precision the remarkable doctrine which it contains, we have thought it best to divide it into simple propositions, that they may be better understood and that the reader may be the better enabled to judge of their correctness and application.

FIRST PROPOSITION

"The right of protection must have its foundation in some law relative to the particular case in which the parties are concerned".

OBSERVATION

This maxim is clearly and undeniably true; but it is important that it be not misconstrued in its application. The question here is not of individuals living under the municipal law of their countries, but of nations who know of no other law than the dictates of natural reason, which, above all things, enjoins upon them to maintain their respective independence and attend to their self preservation. It is from that law which is common to all nations that results what Mr. Jenkinson calls the right of protection. The application and development of this principle will be found in the sequel.

SECOND PROPOSITION

"If neutral nations have any right to protect the property of the enemy, it must take its rise from those laws which are the established rules of conduct between nations, and particularly on that element where this right is supposed to be exerted".

OBSERVATION

To protect is a word of very extensive meaning. It is supposed that the author only meant to apply it here to the shipping of enemy's goods on board of a merchant vessel and placing them under the protection of the neutral flag. We shall therefore direct our observations to this specific point.

As soon as the property of an enemy is shipped on board of a neutral vessel, it is considered to be within the territory of the State to which she belongs. This truth is a consequence of the independence of the flag and of the principles relative to the unlimited freedom of the seas. Now, Mr. Jenkinson himself acknowledged that the property of an enemy cannot be taken in the dominions of a neutral State because it is under its jurisdiction that nobody will dare to infringe. A neutral vessel altho' on the high sea is also under the same jurisdiction and acknowledges no other. The master alone by delegation from his own sovereign has a right to exercise it over the people on board, as far as the law of his own country authorizes him so to do. But the belligerent who accidentally meets her on the common element has no right whatever to molest her or to attempt to exercise any kind of power or authority over her.

In order to explain myself with the greater precision, I must repeat what I have already said, to wit: independence is the basis of the law of nations, and the source of all their rights and duties towards each other. This fundamental principle is applicable to the sea, as well as the land, that element is acknowledged to be free, it is common to all and belongs to none. The nations who frequent it, preserve upon it their independence and impart it to their flag which is hoisted upon their ships. Such are the true and genuine principles of the maritime law of nations; the belligerent himself claims and enjoys the benefit of that law, for he will not suffer his vessel to be entered against his will, nor to be searched or ransacked; he takes care not to submit to any violation of his independence, of the immunity of the flag or of his right of property. If he is legally authorized thus to conduct himself with respect to me, I have, of course, a right to follow his example and to respect him by force if he should attempt to enter my ship in order to ascertain the nature of her cargo. This argument appears to me not to admit of any reply and is in my opinion a sufficient refutation of Mr. Jenkinson's proposition, in the sense in which he meant it to be considered.

THIRD PROPOSITION

"How far according to the law of nations doth this right of protection extend? Governments can have succeeded to no other rights but such as their respective members enjoyed in a state of individuality; and our nation is now to another as it were in a state of nature. The right of protection does not at present extend beyond that of the individual in a state of nature. Such individual then in a state of nature would have had an undoubted right to protect his own person and property against my attack, but if I had been engaged in contention with another, he would not have had the right to protect him against me. I have the right of seizing the property of this my enemy and destroying his person; he who protects him ceases to be neutral. Such therefore is at present the right of protection in those places to which the dominion of governments does not extend: governments can only protect their subjects".

OBSERVATION

The right of protection is inseparable from independence, and nations are as independent of each other as sea is within their territorial limits; consequently, the right of protection also extends to that limit and, indeed, as I have before observed, the place occupied by a vessel so long as she occupies it, is considered as the territory, the dominion, of the nation to which she belongs. This principle cannot be disputed, at least as to the vessel itself, and, of course, everything that she contains is under her protection as participating in her independence. A ship of war extends her dominion, and consequently her protection and jurisdiction, as far as her cannon can reach, and whatever vessel happens to be within this circumference of that line is according to the common expression, in her waters. A merchant ship has a more circumscribed line of jurisdiction; she holds it by as sure a title and is as independent within it as a ship of war: this latter has no advantage over the merchant man but her force, by which she is enabled to command respect. These maxims are not controverted in time of peace; they ought therefore to apply with equal force in time of war; otherwise, we must call in question the independence of nations and the freedom of the seas; and in that case, determine to whom the supreme dominion of that element belongs: undoubtedly to the strongest, but no one dares to acknowledge it.

In support of his system, Mr. Jenkinson says that governments are, with respect to each other as individuals in a state of nature, and from thence he draws the following inference: an individual in a state of nature had a right to protect his own person and property, but not to protect another against a third who was engaged in a quarrel with him. This is going pretty far back for an argument; it is beginning, as it were, with the creation of the world, as a period when mankind were actively uncivilized and before they had even an idea of property, at a time when there was not law, but that of the strongest, at an era, in short, which probably never existed except in imaginations of metaphysicians. Let us, however, consider what would be the rights of an individual in a state of nature with respect to another individual with whom he had a quarrel. Those rights are simple and not at all contested. The savage may pursue the person and property of his enemy, which property will probably consist of a few wretched moveables and of the produce of his labour. If a third person not concerned in the quarrel takes a part in it by protecting one of the two contending parties, he undoubtedly becomes by his own act the enemy of the other. If, on the contrary, he remains a passive spectator, he naturally continues his relations with both, because their enmity is indifferent to him; he may receive the one and the other in his hut, and there they will be safe. Let us suppose (to come nearer to the point contended for by Mr. Jenkinson) that the neutral party has received in his hut some fruits, game or other articles belonging to one of the two contending parties; has the other a right to come and take them away and make them his own? Certainly not, for it is evident that in so doing he would commit an act of violence, assume an unjust authority over the neutral and destroy his liberty by entering his dwelling against his will. Let us, moreover, suppose that one of the hostile parties having some fruits or game to share interests the neutral to carry those articles to a relation or friend; that the latter while on his errand is stopped in the way by the other enemy, who endeavours to get possession of the things that he is carrying and not being able to succeed by other means, at last employs force. What will naturally be the conduct of the assaulted party if he chooses to sand upon his right? He will resist, he will call the aggressor a robber; he will observe to him that the thing which he is carrying have nothing to do either with him or with his quarrel and that he is determined to defend them, even at the peril of his life. Will the aggressor be able to make any reply, except that he is the strongest and that force must be submitted to? Shall he say that the things which he wishes to carry away belong to him, because they are the property of his enemy? That would, indeed, be a miserable argument and far from putting an end to the contest, and the aggressor would, on the contrary, be considered as a plunderer and as a disturber of the peace of the savage tribe. Instead of one enemy, he would then have a hundred to contend with. Thus would these things happen between individuals living in a state of nature, that is to say, according to the law of natural justice unshackled by Codes, edicts, and regulations, and in a word, free from the whole apparatus of modern public law. Thus ought they to happen, according to Mr. Jenkinson himself, between nations, when he acknowledges them to be to each other as individuals in a state of nature. A neutral has a right to defend the thing which has been entrusted to him as if it were his own; violence alone can take it out of his possession; but violence never could establish a right, nor stamp legality on any proceeding. Undoubtedly, as Mr. Jenkinson well observes, an enemy may seize on the property of his enemy and in case of necessity destroy his person, but he cannot do either within the jurisdiction of a third party without being guilty of a violation of his rights. Therefore (that I may not lose sight of man in a state of nature) a man who is engaged in a quarrel with another has not a right to enter the dwelling of a third person, of me, for instance, who have nothing to do with his quarrel in order to take away the person or property of his enemy; and if I resist his attempt, I most certainly only make use of my undoubted right; I neither commit a partial nor a hostile act; and yet what I do is clearly and positively an act of protection. The neutral vessel from the moment she has displayed her flag is as sacred as the hut of the man in a state of nature; this principle, however, has been in some degree modified by modern nations. I have already shown how and for what reasons, but those reasons I have not drawn from the same source whence Mr. Jenkinson derives his system. I do not say with him that a belligerent may exercise at sea a right of jurisdiction over neutrals, as the same that he denies to the latter the use of the same privilege. On the contrary, I maintain that the sea, free to all nations, is not and cannot be subjected to the jurisdiction of anyone and that every act in opposition to this fundamental truth is also in opposition with the nature even of things that are negatively common and that it ought to be considered as a manifest violation of the law of nations. And, I add, that impartiality is the essence of the neutral character; that it is a violation of it to supply one of the enemies with dangerous things; that it is on that ground that neutrals must abstain from supplying them; that in not fulfilling that duty they make an ill use of their freedom to the prejudice of a third party; that they act hostilely towards him; that he is therefore authorized to repel that hostility conformably to the laws of war, I mean by force of arms. Confiscation is the mildest remedy, and if it cannot be obtained, the belligerent has a right to call on the delinquent neutral sovereign and make him responsible.

FOURTH PROPOSITION

"If governments have the right of protecting the property of the enemy within the precincts of their own country, it is a consequence of the right of dominion and of the jurisdiction which emanates therefrom. Now, their dominion does not extend over the ocean, here then the trial which the law of nations gives, is, as it were, superseded and any proceedings upon it would, of course, be unjust; the general laws of nations again have their force; consequently, all right of protection ceases at once".

OBSERVATION

Mr. Jenkinson's maxims are undoubtedly true, but it is unfortunate that the consequences which he draws from them are entirely false. If he had adopted a more logical mode of reasoning, there would probably be no difference between us.

Our opponents endeavour to get over the force of our objections and even think that they make their doctrine perfectly legal by saying that the sovereign of the captor must pay to the neutral master his freight and damages for his detention; but if a principle is essentially bad, it will remain so, however it may be modified. The evil may be thus lessened, but it is not destroyed. Besides, if the carrying of enemy's goods is prohibited, it is, of course, a criminal act, and the offender, instead of being indemnified ought to be punished. If on the contrary, the act is lawful, the capture is illegal and no indemnity can make it otherwise. Nothing is more dangerous than thus to attempt to modify principles and palliate their violation. Those writers who pretend to be impartial ought to abandon that resource to State politicians whose peculiar province to it is to mould principles so as to fir them to the view and interest of their governments and to the circumstances of the times without troubling themselves much about justice and the rights of others.

I must also take notice of an explanation by means of which it is endeavoured to justify the confiscation of enemy's goods, found on board of neutral vessels. It is said that the belligerents after taking those goods still leave the neutral at liberty to carry on his trade with the enemy and to hire out his vessels to him.[49]

I confess that I have no idea of this distinguishing away the rights and privileges of nations, nor do I understand how a neutral may charter his vessels to an enemy when he cannot protect them against capture. I shall not dwell any longer on such palpable contradictions, but shall express my own sentiments in plain and intelligible language. I say then, that the words "*free trade*" imply the liberty of buying, selling, and bartering every description of merchandise and that by *free navigation* is meant the freedom of carrying all sorts of goods

[49] *Lampredi*, § 10, p. 137.

(contraband only excepted); every attempt to narrow that freedom is a violation of the rights of neutrality. It is a manifest abuse of the principle of self preservation which is the source from whence proceed the rights granted to belligerents with respect to neutrals. If our opponents had sufficiently attended to the proper definition of those words *self preservation*, I am persuaded that they would have give less latitude to the rights which they are pleased to allow to belligerents.

At sea, as I have already observed, the rights of territory and dominion are inseparably attendant on the national flag. There the sovereign is as independent as in the midst of his continental possessions; there he exercises an exclusive jurisdiction over the vessel and her crew; no one has a right to displace her, to give her orders or to enter her. The law of nations protects her against force, and if it should be employed, it is a violation of ever principle and an offense against all independent nations. And you, who deny my jurisdiction on the high sea, are you not by the very act, claiming it for yourself and endeavouring to set yourself in my place? On what ground, then, do you pretend to that superiority over me? Would you permit a foreign vessel thus to molest your own? Would you not employ force to repel her aggression and in so doing, would not you think that you were exercising a lawful right? Surely, it is not your cannon which constitutes that right, its only use is to assert and enforce it. The neutral merchantman has indeed no cannon, her only protection is public faith and by violating it you set yourself up at once for the master and the tyrant of the seas.

But let us go a step farther. A vessel tho' on the high sea belongs to somebody; otherwise, she would become the prey of the first occupant as *res nullius*. Such would undoubtedly be her fate, according to Mr. Jenkinson's doctrine; and in case of violence where is the tribunal that would afford her redress? But the fact is that the vessel is manned by members of an independent nation who obey a commander placed in authority over them, to rule and govern them according to the laws enacted by their common sovereign. That sovereign, therefore, exercises at sea by his delegate a clear, positive jurisdiction in the same manner as he does at home in the midst of his dominions. Now that jurisdiction is essentially exclusive as well over the vessel as over the space which she occupies, therefore no other nation has a right to exercise it. And the cruiser who is lying in wait for a neutral vessel, but what authority does he arrest her? Is it not in obedience to the orders of his sovereign? His sovereign therefore also exercises a real act of jurisdiction on the high sea. These very plain reflections overthrow all the edifice of Mr. Jenkinson's system and that of the maritime jurisprudence of Great Britain. Finally, the sovereign of the neutral vessel may say, if my jurisdiction over the ship which carries my flag is paralyzed on the high sea, that which you pretend to arrogate to yourself must be likewise. Therefore your pretended rights resulting from a state of war can have no effect or validity; we are both of us with respect to each other as if transplanted into another world, where man acknowledges no law, but lives altogether in a state of nature.

FIFTH PROPOSITION

"Within the precincts of the dominion of any government, you are not at liberty to search the ships of any country, but the liberty has been universally and immemorially practiced on the main sea, because, according to the law of nations, all are answerable for what they may convey".

OBSERVATION

This is a plain and direct assumption of the very point in controversy. It is generally acknowledged by all maritime powers that the flag is the token of the national character and independence of the vessel, and that the space which she occupies is temporarily considered as a part of the territory of her sovereign. Whoever therefore presumes to search there for the goods of an enemy is guilty of a violation of the neutral territory and of an encroachment upon its jurisdiction and consequently upon its independence in the same manner as if he forcibly entered the proper territorial possessions of the neutral government.[50] It follows from them that a neutral vessel is not bound to give an account of her cargo, nor is she answerable to anyone for what it may consist of. I have already shown the only exceptions that this general rule admits of, as well as the particular motives on which those exceptions are founded. Their application cannot be extended farther than is warranted by the usage and consent of maritime nations; and without such consent, Mr. Jenkinson's doctrine can never be considered as law. But in so far as from having received the assent of other nations, that there is not one northern nation that does not protest against it and that would not, if it had the power, as it has the right and as its interest would require, employ its utmost efforts against it.

I do not here speak of France, Spain, nor of the late Batavian Republic, because their system of jurisprudence on that subject has always been and ever will be variable. But that versatility itself proves that the most evident principles of the law of nations are almost always subordinate to those which State policy creates, and it would have been better for Mr. Jenkinson frankly to have acknowledged this truth than to have made painful and vain efforts to give the sanction of the law of nations and even of natural law to a system which has no other foundation or object than the decided interest of his government; but he would at the same time have been obliged to maintain that that interest ought to predominate over all others, that it must be the law for all nations who carry on maritime commerce, he would, in short, have been compelled to take the bold ground that the sea belongs exclusively to those who are sufficiently powerful to expel others from it.

Let us now oppose to Mr. Jenkinson the opinion of one of his countrymen. The conduct ascribed to the Spanish *Guarda costas* stationed in the Bay of Mexico to prevent the British from carrying on a contraband trade with the Spanish-American colonies gave rise in 1738 to very serious discussions between the Courts of Madrid and London, which in a short time ended in a war. In the parliamentary debates will be found among

[50] Some writers have thought proper to consider this doctrine as absurd, but the unprejudiced reader will easily appreciate their opinion.

others the speech of Lord Delaware, Earl of Cholmondeley, on the subject of the right of search which was the principal grievance complained of by the British Cabinet. Lord Delaware in the course of his argument, which was grounded in part on a treaty which had been made between the two powers in 1697, spoke as follows:

> Supposing (said he) an English ship had prohibited goods on board, yet the Master of the Spanish *Guarda costa* has no right to rummage his hold or to ransack the vessel; for the fact of having or not having prohibited goods on board is to be taken upon an inspection of the English master passes and sea letters. The authority of these passports and sea letters and the proof of their being genuine, must depend upon the bare word and credit of the master of the English vessel; and after such passports and letters are produced, and averred by the master of the English ship to be genuine, the ships is to proceed unmolested on her voyage, because by the latter part of this article, entire credit and faith shall be given to such passports and letters when produced. But tho' by these letters and passports it should appear that prohibited goods are on board an English ship, tho' it should appear that such a ship is bound to, or, is sailing from a port at enmity with Spain, and has goods on board that, in the sense prescribed by the Articles of the same treaty, are to be deemed contraband, yet even these circumstances can never justify the confiscation of the whole ship and cargo.

This passage requires no commentary, for the reader will easily perceive the difference between the doctrine of Lord Delaware and that of Mr. Jenkinson. The only observation which we think proper to make is that the former argued in 1738 in favor of what was then the commercial interest of his country, while the latter maintained the contrary doctrine because at the time when he wrote it was of great importance to Great Britain, then the mistress of the sea, to destroy the commerce of neutrals with France, not only in the European seas, but also in the West Indies, where France admitted them to trade. Thus it is that the principle of maritime law will not unanimously adopt the fundamental principles of the freedom of the seas and the immunity of the flag, so modified and combined as to secure the real interests of nations. But let us return to Mr. Jenkinson.

He relies in support of his own reasoning on the authority of publicists, and among others quotes *Albericus Gentilis*, the *Consolato del mare*, *Grotius*, *Bynkershoek*, *Barbeyrac*, *Vattel*, &c. The testimony of such grave and respectable writers, whose names and just acquired reputation give in a manner to their opinions the stamp of authority, was alone sufficient to make me pause and cold have overborne me altogether had I found that their sentiments had been drawn from either of the only true sources which are the primitive law of nations and the unanimous assent of the interested parties. But I felt my courage revived, as soon as I had observed that those writers have done nothing but copy one another and that they have been satisfied with the bare affirmation or denial of the proposition which they had to consider, instead of entering into a full and elaborate discussion of their merits, instead of trying usage and practice by the test of principle and forming their opinion on the whole, not merely by referring to treaties but by recurring to the infallible rules of natural reason.

Not to entangle my readers in a tedious maze of erudition and quotations, I shall only attend to the author form whom Mr. Jenkinson has shown a particular predilection. I mean Bynkershoek. I copy his own expressions: "And on rational grounds (says he) I cannot see why it should not be lawful to take enemy's goods, altho' found on board of a neutral ship; for in that case, what the belligerent takes is still the property of his enemy, and by the law of war belongs to the captor."[51]

It is thus that he states his opinion, and he argues as follows in support of it: "It is lawful to detain a neutral vessel in order to ascertain, not by the flag merely which may be fraudulently assumed, but by the documents themselves which are on board, whether she is really neutral. If she appears to be such, then she is to be dismissed; otherwise, she may be captured". The author

---

[51] *Ratione consulta, non sum qui videam cur non liceret capere res hostiles, quamvis in nave amica repertus; id enim capio quod hostium est, quodque jure belli victori cedit. Quest. juris publ.*, Book 1, *de rebus bellicis*, c. XIV.

can see no reason why that rule should not extend to the goods which a neutral ship may have on board, and if there should be found merchandise belonging to an enemy, why it should not be captured and condemned by the law of war. He even declares it to be his opinion, that the owner of the neutral vessel should in such a case lose even his freight.

Notwithstanding my respect for Bynkershoek, I acknowledge that I am not convinced by his logic, and that I find neither similarity nor analogy between the two cases which he considered as identically the same. In time of war the genuineness of the flag is ascertained because enemy's ships often attempt to pass under the disguise of the neutral flag. On the other hand, it is necessary to ascertain whether independent of the flag the vessel has otherwise conformed to the requisites of the maritime law and whether she is a regular merchantman or a pirate.

But the right of ascertaining the genuineness of the flag does not give that of searching the vessel and still less of seizing the goods on board, altho' they should belong to an enemy; on the contrary, the flag when acknowledged places beyond dispute the independence of the vessel and that independence secures to her all the rights appertaining to neutrality and consequently the immunity of her cargo. The only exception which is not contested and is to be found in all the treaties is that which applied to contraband articles. But it cannot be too often repeated that the seizure of such articles is an exception agreed upon between nations and therefore should not be extended beyond its object.

The argument upon which the Dutch writer founds his opinion is truly remarkable: "The law of war (says he) authorizes me to take what belongs to my enemy; consequently, I may seize enemy's goods, even on board of a neutral vessel".

Mr. Bynkershoek does not take notice that in the second case, in order to come at the goods which belong to an enemy and are under the protection of the neutral flag, it is necessary to violate its immunity and consequently the property and independence of the vessel; he does not observe that in order to exercise the right which he so generously attributes to belligerents, an injury must be done to a friendly nation. Now I ask with confidence whether such a proceeding is regular, whether it is tolerable, and whether it is not an infraction of neutrality and of the first principles of the law of nations?

It is truly singular to observe with what zeal the writer whom I have quoted pleads the cause of belligerents and argue against the freedom of the seas. And does not the fatal law of war already confer sufficient privileges on those who have arms in their hands? Is not war itself productive of sufficient mischief? What! Because two sovereigns obstinately persist in making war upon each other, must social order be disturbed in every part of the globe? Must every intercourse between men be interrupted? Must the labourer, the mechanic, the navigator of countries at peace bear the pain of the belligerent's obstinacy? Must those countries give up all their enjoyments? No, the prerogatives of war ought not to be extended farther than the flames which threaten to devour a city. It is so much the more important that they should be kept within bounds that every restriction upon them tends to shortening the duration of the war. Therefore, those who raise their voices against the arbitrary extension of those privileges are the advocates of humanity and of mankind. We shall now return to Mr. Jenkinson.

Chapter XXIII.

Of the Authority of Precedents

§1.

To complete his system, Mr. Jenkinson labours hard to show that it is consistent with the practice of most of the European governments. I do not mean to contest any of the facts which he adduces nor any of the edicts or ordinances which he quotes; but, I say, that precedents, however numerous, unless they are generally and above all freely adopted as a rule, do not constitute the law of nations. And that, on the contrary, the law of nations is the test by which they ought to be tried and according to which they are to be approved or condemned. The law of *wreck* was formerly almost generally established; will it be contended on that account that it was just or that it was founded on natural reason? It was in ancient times the universal custom to make slaves of prisoners of war, and is not that custom generally reprobated at this day? The scalping of prisoners is an established *usage* among the American Indians; is it therefore to be justified? I quote these instances in order to show that usage can only sanction what is just and that those who appeal to it without sufficient consideration are in danger of being led into very great errors. And if their mistakes and misrepresentations should happen to influence the conduct or decisions of a government, it may be induced to take false steps which will be as prejudicial to its reputation as fatal in their consequences.

§2.

I grant, however, that precedents are *prima facie* evidence of usage, and even may constitute what is called *customary law*, but in order to produce the latter effect, they must be acknowledged by all the interested parties; otherwise, they produce partial obligations which, like treaties, only bind those who have subscribed to them; therefore, those sovereigns whose system is founded on the restriction of neutral trade, may allege their interest and call to their aid all the ancient and modern edicts and ordinances; neutral nations will never comply except when they are not strong enough to resist. But neither the silence nor the inactivity of neutrals can stamp legality on pretensions that are essentially unjust. Policy or the consciousness of their want of power may induce them to yield or dissemble for a time, but a change of circumstances will not fail to work alteration in their conduct; so soon as they cease to feel the pressure which bore them down, their legitimate rights will resume their sway.

Chapter XXIV.

Of Edicts and Treaties

Let us, however, adopt Mr. Jenkinson's principle, let us for the sake of argument admit with him the full force of precedents, and let us see on which side the scale will preponderate. The documents which the writer relies upon are edicts and treaties.

The *ex parte* edicts of sovereigns are of no account in the law of nations. They are properly municipal laws which from their very nature can have no effect beyond the limits of the jurisdiction of the sovereign who issued them, and if respect should be paid to them abroad, it is by no means because they are considered as obligatory. This transitory effect is produced by necessity or some other accidental cause; in a word, nations adopt or reject them as their interest, convenience, or situation dictate. But what consistent system of jurisprudence may be collected from a series of documents that are ever variable and in contradiction with each other? The edicts of France, for instance, are generally more or less favourable to neutrals, while the object of those of England has always been to confine their rights within the narrowest limits. In which of these opposite systems is to be found the evidence of the customary law of nations?

Treaties alone may be quoted as precedents because they are public acts of the number of those which constitute the conventional law of nations. Now, if we attend to treaties, without going farther back than that of the Pyrenees, we find that most of them stipulate the freedom of naval stores and of enemy's goods on board of neutral ships. To several of those treaties England herself is a party and all those which have been signed within the last twenty years (that made in 1794 between Great Britain and the United States of America only excepted) contain these very stipulations. Therefore, if we are to take treaties as a rule, if they are to be the evidence of the common law of nations, it is sufficiently shown that on the two points in question it is conformable to the principles which I have laid down. But I must again repeat it, treaties, whatever they may stipulate, do not constitute the law of nations; they are but the expression of the will and pleasure of the contracting parties, and the law of nations is independent of the will and pleasure of any sovereign. They are analogous to contracts made between individuals; when there is no express contract, the common law decides, and among independent States, there is no other common law than the law of nations.

Chapter XXV.

Of the Convention of 1780, Known under the Denomination of the Armed Neutrality

Among modern treaties, I think it proper to notice the convention which was signed in 1780 (see Chapter XVIII, notes) because it excited at the time the general attention and was considered as the first step towards a uniform system of maritime law.

This convention was preceded by an edict of Catharine II, Empress of Russia. It was founded upon the commercial treaty of 1766 between that country and Great Britain and *on the clear and incontestable principles of the law of nations.* It recommended to Russian subjects the observance of the most scrupulous neutrality and, in consequence, they were prohibited carrying contraband goods consisting of arms and ammunition. All other kinds of merchandise, even enemy's property shipped on board of Russian vessels, were declared free, but in order to prevent every kind of dispute or misunderstanding,[52] the subjects of Russia were to avoid shipping any property on board of vessels belonging to one of the belligerent powers. Every Russian vessel must be provided with a passport and a clearance; nothing was provided on the subject of convoys.

That edict was communicated to the three powers then at war, to wit: France, Spain, and Great Britain.

France was very much pleased with the Empress's system, as it was perfectly consonant with her own principles, according to which the freedom of neutral ships is a direct inference from the dictates of natural law, the safeguard of nations, and even a relief to those who are laboring under the scourge of war.

The answer which Spain gave was analogous to the sentiments of France. She declared that the conduct of the British navy, whole subversive of the received rules among neutral powers, had obliged her to follow their example, but that

---

[52] This was avoiding the great question concerning neutral goods on board of enemy's ships. See Chapter X.

she would respect the neutral flag of all the courts that had consented or should consent to defend it until she should find what part of the British navy would take and whether they would together with the privateers keep within proper bounds.

The answer of Great Britain contained in substance that her conduct to neutral powers would be conformable to the clearest principles generally acknowledged as the law of nations (see Chapter XXII), being the only law between powers where no treaties subsist and agreeable to the tenor of her different engagements with other powers which had altered that primitive law by mutual stipulations.

The consequence of these three declarations was that France maintained her Edict of 1778 which had served as a text to that of the Empress of Russia, that Spain, at the same time that she acknowledged the true principles, kept herself within the line of reciprocity which Great Britain had compelled her to adopt; and finally that England professed to adhere strictly to her treaties without explaining the meaning or extent which she attached to the principles of the primitive law of nations. Everything therefore remained in *status quo*.

In order to give effect to the above declaration, the Empress of Russia entered into the convention already mentioned with the Court of Copenhagen. I think it will not be amiss to give it here in substance.

By that first article, all trade in contraband articles is prohibited. The second article declares that the meaning of the word *contraband* shall be determined by the treaties subsisting between the contracting parties and the belligerent powers. The provisions of those treaties are to be applied to the powers with whom there are not treaties, as being a consequence of the law of nature and nations, and in order to prevent in future arbitrary interpretations respecting the rights of neutrals, the following general principles were laid down.

Art. III. 1°. Every ship may navigate freely from port to port or along the coasts of the nations at war.

2°. Effects belonging to the subjects of the belligerent powers are free on board of neutral vessels, with the exception of contraband articles.

3°. A port is understood to be blockaded when the assailing power has taken such a station as to expose to imminent danger any ship or ships that would attempt to sail in or out of such port.

4°. No neutral vessels shall be stopped without a material and well grounded cause.

By the fourth article the contracting parties stipulate that they will fit out squadrons for the protection of the trade and navigation of their respective subjects and, when necessary, of the subjects of each other. But the fifth article provides that under the occasion of such required assistance and protection, no contraband shall be carried on nor any prohibited trade contrary to the laws of neutrality.

The King of Sweden acceded to that convention as well as the States General, the King of Prussia, and the courts of Vienna and Lisbon.

On examining all these conventions it will be found that they rest on two grounds: in the first place on the existing treaties, and next to them on the law of nature and nations, and that both are considered as founded on the same principles and leading to the same consequences. On this twofold basis, the contracting parties consider nothing as prohibited or contraband but arms and ammunition. Enemy's goods under the neutral flag are declared free; but neutral merchandise on board of enemy's ships is not at all mentioned. The right of searching vessels on the high seas is maintained, not, however, on mere suspicion but for material and well grounded causes, or, in other words, on clear and evident proofs. Convoying ships, or military escorts, are only to protect against vexatious proceedings; no mention is made of the verbal declaration of the commander of the armed force, nor of the form or mode of search in his presence.

Therefore, everything well considered, the convention of 1780 (except that it prohibits searches on mere suspicions) has made no alteration in the system of maritime jurisprudence of the powers bound to each other by treaties, but it has declared that the stipulations which it contains, are direct inferences from the principles of natural law and has consequently applied them to all nations without discrimination. This is the most important point of the convention of 1780.

Chapter XXVI.

Of the Conventions of 1800 and 1801

I have already observed that the Emperor Paul of Russia, having withdrawn himself from his alliance with England and Austria, returned in 1800 together with the two other Northern Powers, to the principles of the armed neutrality of 1780, and I pointed out what were the consequences of that new coalition (see Chapter XVIII). It was dissolved by the bombardment of Copenhagen, and the courts of St. Petersburgh and London signed a particular convention in 1801. In that new instrument the commercial treaty of 1797 was in part confirmed. The trade and navigation of the subjects of the contracting parties was declared free, with the exception of war contraband goods and enemy's property. Naval stores were not included among contraband articles. It was, moreover, agreed that merchant vessels could not be detained without just and sufficient cause; that the right of searching them, when under convoy, shall only be exercised by the commanding officer of the man of war of the belligerent power and never by the privateers. The forms to be observed in searching vessels were also settled, and lastly, it was stipulated that the provisions of that treaty should be considered as permanent and should be the rule of the contracting powers in every future war. The courts of Stockholm and Copenhagen acceded to that convention.

The reader will observe: 1st, that the new convention is derogatory to that of 1780 in as much as it prohibits the carrying of enemy's goods which is declared free by this latter; 2nd, that the presence of convoying ships does not exempt neutral vessels from being searched.

Chapter XXVII.

Of the Right of Pre-emption

§1.

Not long after the convention of 1801, Sweden signed a separate treaty by which she granted to England the right of pre-emption with respect to several kinds of naval stores which had been declared free by the preceding conventions, as well as by most of the commercial treaties. We shall not make any comment on that stipulation, because we are unacquainted with its motives; we must suppose that they were of a very powerful nature. It is but too well known that in the course of human events governments are not unfrequently compelled to yield to the pressure of particular circumstances and to sacrifice to them not only principle but every consideration of dignity and self-respect.

§2.

But setting policy aside, let us consider the subject in itself and without regard to the contracting parties. What is the right of pre-emption? It is the right of purchasing by force and in preference to all others goods belonging to and shipped for the account of a third party. Such stipulation evidently affects the commercial relations existing between the sovereign who grants the right and the other powers because it is only a subterfuge to avoid the word *prohibition*; and certainly the power which it prejudices may consider it as an act of partiality.

Chapter XXVIII.

Of the Rights and Duties of Privateers

§1.

There is no question here concerning the morality, legality, or advantages of privateering; that practice has long since been established and will probably continue as long as there are maritime wars. My only object is therefore to point out the principal rules by which it ought to be governed.

§2.

The commander of a privateer is but the agent of his sovereign; from him alone he has received the authority to cruise on the seas, intercept the trade and navigation of the enemy, and prevent neutrals from carrying on a fraudulent trade.

§3.

Therefore the rights which the commander of a privateer is authorized to exercise, as well as the obligations which he has to fulfill, result from his commission or patent and the instructions with which it is accompanied. Those documents are his Code, from which it is not lawful for him to deviate.[53]

A privateer on meeting a merchant vessel ought to hoist her flag and fire a gun, conformably to received usage. The latter must do the same thing, and if she is an enemy her capture is legal and requires no formality; her flag is sufficient to ground

[53] A modern writer (*Lampredi*) denies this proposition and says "that a vessel on the high sea or in free waters cannot be considered as making a part of the territory of its sovereign, and therefore that when a belligerent and neutral ships meet each other they are bound by no laws but those of natural justice, modified by the state of war in which they are placed". We shall abstain from making any comments upon this passage.

her condemnation upon. But if she is neutral, the privateer must keep himself at the distance of cannon shot and send two or three persons on board to ascertain her character; that is to say, that she is neither an enemy nor a pirate. Therefore he has a right to demand the exhibition of her passport or sea letter. Usage, moreover, requires that even on the high sea the neutral should prove the property and nature of his cargo by clearances from the custom house and bills of lading. If all those documents are regular, the neutral ought to be left at liberty to pursue her intended course, and any further search is prohibited.

§4.

However, as it is possible that fraud might exist, either thro' the connivance of the custom house officers, or by a surprise on their vigilance, there is a case in which notwithstanding the regularity of the papers, custom has authorized the searching of the vessel and that case exists when there is a strong presumption of fraud. But that presumption must be founded upon evident proofs previously obtained and must not be the result of the search made on board[54] and still less be procured by interrogatories or by some act of violence. This point is so much the more important that privateers go to sea with the only view of enriching themselves by captures and being but too often guided by the mere impulse of their avidity, they presume fraud where there is no ground to suspect it, and the hope of being supported by their government encourages them to vex neutrals, intercept their navigation, and make them undergo the uncertainty of a trial, which, however favorable the result, may be never can indemnify them; and in general there is such a disposition to trust in the honesty and good faith of privateers and to give credit to their hypocritical assertions, that neutrals are well warranted in not placing too great a reliance in the justice of belligerents. Let the reader but follow in imagination the unfortunate neutral from the time of his capture to that of the

[54] The convention of 1801 between Russia and England is the most precise upon this subject. It says, Art. 3, §5 "that the ships of neutral powers shall not be stopped but upon just causes and evident facts".

final judgment which he is obliged to solicit in a foreign country; let me consider the loss of time and expense that he is put to, the stagnation of his capital, the maintenance of his crew, the interruption of his commercial operations, and he will easily be convinced how important it is for governments to put a stop to the cupidity of privateers, to their arbitrary and vexatious proceedings, and above all to the length of judicial proceedings in prize causes.

§5.

In order to simplify the question we say that nothing is to be left to the judgment of privateers, that their conduct ought to be fully and clearly pointed out by their instructions, that those instructions ought expressly to state that they may stop any vessel at sea in order to ascertain her real character; that they may likewise according to general usage ascertain the nature and destination of her cargo by the examination of her custom house documents; but that those two points being found regular, that they are prohibited from making any further search, that they are, however, allowed to search a vessel if the cargo should consist in whole or in part of prohibited articles or if there should exist sufficient evidence of fraud, but that except in those two cases, every search is a trespass and a violation of the primitive and conventional law of nations.

There is nothing easier to ascertain than the neutral character of a vessel and of her cargo, for it requires nothing but the examination of her papers. But when mere suspicion is attended to, there is a great danger of arbitrary proceedings, for then, the opinion of individuals is substituted for proofs and that opinion takes its colour from the interest of those who are made judges as well as parties. All belligerents, therefore, who wish to be just ought to turn their attention to this particular subject; they have in their power the means of preventing abuses of power, and the spoliations which result from them; and they need but to enjoin strictly on their privateers not to search neutral vessels unless they have sufficient evidence of fraud and to reject all proofs obtained by searching the vessel and interrogating the crew.

That is the only remedy against arbitrary proceedings, and the only way to repress the numerous complaints which they occasion. In a word, it is only by such measures that the rights of neutrals and those which true or false necessity attributes to belligerents, may be reconciled. If the latter choose to adopt for themselves an arbitrary system of jurisprudence, they ought at least not to put its execution in the hands of privateers.

§6.

From what has just been said, it appears that the authority given to privateers with respect to neutral vessels is graduated into three distinct successive acts, to wit: stoppage, search and seizure. The first of those steps presents no difficulty because its object is only to ascertain the neutrality of the vessel and cargo. Search is to be made according to the rules which we have pointed out. Seizure or capture is a consequence of the illegal nature of the cargo, or of such strong presumptions, such as we have already explained?

§7.

Seizure is the first judiciary act; it is followed by carrying the vessel into a port of the sovereign of the captor and there the validity of the capture is submitted to legal adjudication. There are some writers who improperly confound stoppage or detention with seizure or capture, whereas they are acts essentially distinct from each other.

§8.

It is here, I think, the proper place to speak of the interrogatories which are administered to the master and crew of the captured neutral vessel. Is that custom grounded on the principles of the law of nations, natural justice, or treaties?

Interrogations are admitted by the civil law in criminal cases, but that jurisprudence is not applicable to prize causes;

because the proceedings in the latter case do not relate to an offence, either against natural or municipal law, but, to a mere political offense which itself results from an exception to a positive right. I am going to be more explicit.

§9.

Navigation is free by its nature and by usage. Policy has introduced some modifications to that freedom in time of war. Those modifications are the law of neutrals as well as of belligerents. If neutrals transgress it, they are punished by the confiscation of their property; if the belligerents, by being bound to indemnify the injured party. But how is the transgression to be ascertained? Usage, as well as treaties, proscribe the exhibition of the passport and other custom house documents. If there is a well-grounded suspicion of fraud resulting from evident proofs, search is in that case authorized. Such is the almost length to which treaties authorize cruisers to carry their proceedings; not one of them gives the authority to administer interrogatories; they admit of nothing but clear and positive proofs, and that alone is sufficient to show that the kind of inquisition which is exercised with respect to the master and crew of a neutral vessel, is not legal. If there are proofs of fraud, they are to be weighed at the trial, and not be the subject of interrogatories on which nothing is admitted to, but the confessions of the examinants and their denials are of no force. If the latter are not admitted, neither ought the former. I pass over the danger of making the fate of a vessel depend on the statements made by her crew and passengers to an individual who is not authorized to require them. Besides, parole testimony cannot be admitted in those cases which require pre-existing positive proofs and, above all, when the law by virtue of which you act does not admit it. If usage is relied upon, I answer that it is an ill custom, which is neither founded on law nor on treaties; if it should be alleged that such is the practice in all criminal cases, I answer that it is so in consequence of the express directions of municipal law which has nothing to do with matters of prize.

§10.

I conclude this article with a few observations on the security to be given by the cruiser to answer for his conduct.

The commanders of Government vessels do not give any because their respective sovereigns are their immediate guarantees and alone are responsible for their acts.

It is not the same with a privateer, besides that he is not properly an officer of his government; he fits out his vessel at is own risk and expense; he does not expose his person and fortune in the service of the State, his only object is to enrich himself; he is in wait to kidnap merchant vessels and such is the whole extent of his military exploits. It cannot therefore be required of him that he should be inspired with that same spirit which animates offices whose only incitements are honour, glory, and the service of their sovereign, and who promotion is not the reward of rapacity and of an inordinate threat after plunder and riches, such as characterizes privateers men; in a word, every profession has its particular principles, education, and feelings. It is for that reason that the officers of the Navy do not and ought not to give any security as a guarantee for the legality of their conduct, while privateers require such a powerful curb to keep them in check.

That precaution cannot on any account be dispensed with and the security must be such as to cover all the damages that the privateer may occasion to a neutral. We even go so far to say that in the case where the security should not be sufficient, justice as well as policy requires that the government should itself make up the deficiency.

ON THE FREEDOM OF THE SEA

Joseph-Mathias Gérard de Rayneval

Translated from the French by

Peter Stephen Du Ponceau

VOLUME TWO

Volume 2 comprises an Appendix to the original work consisting of State papers showing the manner in which Great Britain succeeded in warding off the bloc which was aimed against her by the convention of the armed neutrality.

Introductory Observations

We have treated above (Chap. 25) of the armed neutrality agreed upon in 1780 by the three northern powers and pointed out the most important political event which results therefrom, which was the accession of the United Provinces to that celebrated league. We have shown that the accession became ineffectual in consequence of the intrigues of the British Cabinet[1] and the weakness of those of St. Petersburgh, Stockholm, and Copenhagen. That weakness, it must be acknowledged, destroyed and even turned to the advantage of England a system well calculated to secure the establishment of the fundamental principles of the freedom of the seas and which might have become the basis of a maritime code for all the European States. By sacrificing Holland to their fear of committing themselves with the British Government, they brought their system into discredit and their convention descended into a mere experiment.

The British Government, well aware that that system affected their dearest interests and was in direct opposition to what politicians call *arcanum domus*, endeavoured from the beginning to subvert it. And the accession of Holland afforded them a ready opportunity to effect that purpose. Artifice and perfidy were the means which they employed; the northern courts fell into the snare, and their interests and dignity were sacrificed. When they agreed on their convention, they had lost sight of the important principle that before into an undertaking,

---

[1] See the work entitled *Mémoire sur la neutralité armée maritime*, par le Comte de Goertz (Paris, 1805).

it is necessary to calculate the means and to count the cost: *quid valeant humeri …*

That our readers may be enabled to decide on the merits of that important cause, we have thought proper to lay before them the principal documents relating to it. They are: 1st, the Memorial presented by the States General by the English Ambassador Sir Joseph Yorke, by which he demanded the reformation of the commercial treaty of 1674 and the succours stipulated by that of 1678; 2d, the Manifesto or Declaration of War of Great Britain against the United Provinces; 3d, the Counter-Manifesto of the States General. These documents essentially belong to the political history of the eighteenth century and particularly to that of the British Government.

By analyzing those documents it will be seen on the one hand with what insincerity the British Ministry misconstrued a solemn treaty in order to make it subservient to their views, and, on the other, with how much dexterity and how little candour they endeavoured to evade the true state of the question. The British Government consistent with its policy laid unjust accusations to the charge of the Dutch nation, which were not in the least connected with the armed neutrality in order to furnish to the three northern powers, who not only had agreed to but had provoked the accession of the States General, if not solid arguments, at least specious pretences to elude the fulfillment of their engagements. It cannot be too often repeated that the conduct of the Court of London on that occasion is a classical model of cunning and perfidy, which that of the three northern crowns exhibits a striking instance of weakness and inconsistency. It will appear upon the whole that those powers after proclaiming with great pomp their philanthropic convention to an expecting world, rested satisfied with the inefficient expression of their wish for maritime freedom while if they had firmly persevered in the line of conduct which they had agreed to pursue, they would in the then existing circumstances, have dictated the law and saved their reputation. Denmark was the victim of a system which was well conceived, but ill digested and still worse supported.

OF THE DOMINION CLAIMED BY GREAT BRITAIN OVER CERTAIN PARTS OF THE SEA

ANALYSIS AND REFUTATION OF SELDEN'S ARGUMENT IN SUPPORT THEREOF

We proceed now to this discussion of the pretended rights of dominion which Selden ascribed to Great Britain over the seas by which that island is surrounded.

We are obliged to confess that the dexterity with which that writer avails himself of obscure partial acts and documents and exhibits them to the world as solemn testimonials of acknowledged rights, his methodological and apparently logical manner of reasoning, and the consummate skill that he displays in construing his evidence and applying it to the purpose that he has in view are well calculated to mislead those of our readers who attend only to results without sufficiently analyzing arguments or recurring to the sources from whence they are drawn. It shall be our endeavour to destroy the magic of those illusions.

We will not here repeat what we have already said in the preceding chapter or to demonstrate the right which all nations have in common to the free use of the sea. We look upon that right as completely established and as an axiom of the law of nature and nations. We shall therefore, for the present, confine ourselves to the examination of the system which the English writer has endeavoured to substitute for that universal right and by which she strikes at the freedom of the ocean in order to establish on its ruins the exclusive dominion of his own country.[1]

Selden includes within his system all the seas generally which come in contact with the Kingdom of Great Britain and the islands belonging. Such are the Northern Seas, the Western or Atlantic Ocean, the seas of Germany, and Norway, and particularly the British Channel. In order that we may be able clearly to follow the course of his argument and at the same time not to divert the attention of our readers, we shall give in regular succession and with all the precision and accuracy that impartiality requires the series of his proofs, reasoning, and inferences and throw all our observations together at the end in the form of notes.

Our author divides the whole ocean into four parts, after the four cardinal points of the compass. According to his opinion, the dominion of Great Britain in the Western Sea not only included St. George's Channel, the sea which divides Great Britain from Ireland, but also all that part which lies to the westward of that kingdom in a northern direction. It further extends over all the hyperborean sea in which are the Orkney Islands, Thule or Iceland, Greenland, &c. The western part includes the German ocean and particularly that part which lies between Great Britain on one side and Norway and the Netherlands, on the other. And towards the south, the British dominion includes nearly all that part of the ocean which borders upon France, down to the frontier of Spain. Let he hear Selden himself on this last point: "All that was called the British

---

[1] There are persons who consider Selden's doctrines as antiquated and obsolete. He published his book in the reign of Charles I and traces the pretensions of England back to the time of Richard I. But how can we consider those pretensions as obsolete when we attend to the tenor of the commissions given by Charles II in which the English High Admiral is styled *Angliae et Hiberniae et Aquitaniae ac Dominiorum et insularum earundem, villae Calesioe et marehiarum ejusdem, Normandiae, Gasconiae et Aquitaniae Magnus admiralis*, etc. This formula is still in use.

Sea which extends itself like a half moon along the French shore, thro' the Bay of Biscay into the northern coast of Spain. For this we have the testimony of Mela, who says the Pyrenean promontories do butt out into the British sea. Yet every man knows it is called likewise the French, or Cantabrian or the Aquitanic Sea, from the several shores which it washes. But so far even the name both of the British and English Sea was enlarged either by that extraordinary command of the people of Britain at sea or of such as had attained the rights of dominion in Great Britain, which is all one to our purpose. (Ch. 1).[2]

And a little farther he says: "Moreover, seeing both the Northern and Western ocean do stretch to a very great latitude, this to America, that not only to Iceland and the shores of Greenland, but to parts utterly unknown, and so it cannot all be called the British seas; yet because the nation of Great Britain have very large rights and privileges of their own in both those seas, even beyond the bound of the British name, therefore it was thought fit to touch a little upon these particulars".[3] Such is the substance of Selden's doctrine which is the subject of his discussion.

Let us now see in what manner he proceeds to establish such vast pretensions: we shall follow him step by step.

---

[2] *Britannium appellatur, totum illud mare quod per lunatum Gallici littoris recessum seu sinum aquitanicum in Hispaniarum littoral septentrionalia porrigens*; *testis est Mela, quo Pyrenaei promontoria in Oceanum britannicum prcurrere ait, quem tamen sive Gallicum, sive Cantabricum, sive Aquitanicum a littoribus quae alluit, itidem dici nemo nescit. Se dab amplissima sive Britannorum in mari domination, sive eorum qui jura Britannici regni aquisierant* (*quod huic idem est*) *eo usque etiam protensum est maris et Britannici et Anglicani nomen.* L. 2, C. 1.

[3] *Sed vero cum et septentrionalis et occidens Oceanus latissime excurrat* (*hic ad Americam, ille non ad Islandiam slum et Graelandiae littoral, sed ad metas plane incognitas*) *neque totus sic Britannicus dicendus*: *quoniam tamen jura sua amplissima tam in hos quam in illo mari, etiam ltra Britannici nominis metanm, habet serenissimus rex Magna-Britanniae, ideoque neque haec visum est omnino praeterire.* Ibid.

The dominion of the sea is acquired not only by usage, but also and above all by the right of exclusion or admission.[4] This right Great Britain has possessed from the earliest periods.

The times which preceded the invasion of England by Julius Caesar are too fabulous to be confidently referred to, but since the conquest of Great Britain by that illustrious Roman, the Eastern and Southern seas have been considered as being under the British dominion.[5] As to the Northern Sea, it was considered

---

[4] If all these assertions are to be admitted, great difficulties, indeed, would by that means be gotten over, for the question of right would always be decided by matter of fact. But it is easy to be convinced that Selden has been endeavouring to establish a particular system and therefore has been obliged to support it as well as he could without examining to critically into the solidity of his arguments. However, it may be, we think that we have sufficiently demonstrated in the preceding chapters that the mere use of the sea cannot confer a right of exclusive dominion over that element which is common to all mankind; and from thence results this other truth, that a nation cannot acquire of its single authority, that is to say, by the mere effect of its own will and power, a right to exclude other nations from or admit them to a participation of its enjoyment. Such a right requires as a preliminary condition and as its basis a legitimate possession, that is to say, a possession acknowledged by all the interested parties, without this requisite possession is only a matter of fact, the mere result of superior force. We are therefore warranted to say that all the superstructure of Selden's system rests on a foundation which has no solidity and on principle essentially false. To make this evident, it is only necessary to ask this question: is the right of *admission* and *exclusion* a principle or a consequence.

[5] What are the nations by whom such an opinion was entertained? Was it the northern nations? It is well known that the Britons were afraid of the Danes and that they had no relation with those who inhabited the shores of the Baltic. Was it the Germans, a small portion of whom (the Anglo Saxons) effected the conquest of England? Or was it the Gauls and the Franks that came to be accused of this excess of absurdity? And how could the Britons themselves, who were more barbarous and more ignorant than the nations of the continent, think of acquiring the dominion of the sea? How could the idea have been suggested to them? What would have been their object in coveting it, they who had neither ships nor trade, unless, in imitation of Selden, we should give that name to the little boats with which they fished along the coast. Or did the ancient Britons already meditate the conquest of the continent, the very existence of which was

in the most remote ages as incorporated with the English continent.[6]

That maritime sovereignty was maintained until the Romans withdrew their forces from England.[7] At that epoch, the Britons

---

only known to them in consequence of the invasions of their islands by the continental nations of Europe?

It is really surprising to see a grave writer attribute to a barbarous people divided into a number of little sovereignties that national ambition which did not until many centuries afterwards appear among their descendants and a political system, the origin of which is to be traced to very modern times. The Northern Sea has always been considered as tho' it came united to the British continent.

[6] Here we have again a very bold assertion. It is natural to suppose that the ancient Britons had some communications with the neighboring islands; it may be also supposed that they gave their name to the sea which divided them from each other; but it is impossible to conclude from thence that those ignorant men imagine that they were on that account possessed of that sea as their own property to the exclusion of the inhabitants of the islands. We must either believe that the ancient Britons were a civilized, enlightened, subtle, ambitious nation, or reject the view which Selden supposes them to have entertained. But it is sufficient to read the history of those barbarous times to dissipate the illusion on which the author founds his systems and indeed, whoever has attended to the progress of human policy, since the fall of the Roman Empire must be fully convinced that many ages passed before the era began in which ambition conceived and displayed those enlarged views which characterize the modern European policy, which cannot be traced to earlier than the reign of Charles V or the accession of the House of Austria to the Imperial dignity.

[The arguments and authorities on which Selden founded his assertion that Britain possessed or claimed the dominion of the sea in the most remote times are no less curious than the assertion itself. He quotes, for instance, out of treaties, a speech of Galgacus, the Calidonian chief who exhorting his countrymen to fight the Roman invaders, addresses them in these words: "*Nullae ultra terrae, ac nec mare quidem Securium, imminente nobis classe Romana*". No land beyond this, nor even the sea itself, is safe for us, threatened as we are by the British fleet. A strange dominion this, over the sea, when it did not even offer a safe asylum from a pursuing enemy. This forcibly reminds us of the well-known Bull of the Irish Soldier who exclaimed that he had taken a prisoner, but that the prisoner would not let him go – PSD].

[7] No doubt it was not the subjugated Britons who acquired and maintained that maritime dominion; and no doubt also the Romans who called themselves the Lords and Masters of the Universe, did not transmit it to

formed themselves into a Republic and recovered the dominion of the sea which the Romans had before possessed; it was transferred to the heptarchy, until the reign of Egbert; afterwards went to the Saxons, a race of navigators, and then to the Danes. The proofs of the attention given by the British to maritime affairs is to be found in the contribution which they raised under the name of *Danegeld*, the proceeds of which were employed towards the improvement of the navy and maintenance of seafaring men.[8]

The reigns of Edgar and Canute afford positive proofs of maritime dominion. The title of the former was: "*Ego Edgardus, totius Albionis Basilous nec non maritimoram seu insulanorum regum circumhabitantium*". *I, Edgar, King of all Albion and of the maritime or insular kings inhabiting around the same*".[9] And

---

the inhabitants of an island which was, as it were, an imperceptible point in the immensity of their Empire. I do not dwell here on the circumstance that at no period whatever did the Romans pretend to the exclusive dominion of the sea, nor even of the Mediterranean.

Besides, if that dominion, that empire of the sea, was so well protected and secured, how are we to explain the calling of the Saxons, and the invasions of the Danes and Normans? How shall we explain the tribute (Danegeld) which the English paid to the King of Denmark, on the one hand to preserve peace with him, and on the other, to be protected by him against the pirates? This single fact, acknowledged by Selden, destroys, at least down to that period, the ancient maritime dominion of the Britons.

[8] One of the objects to which the Danegeld (Danish money) was applied has been shown in the preceding note; indeed, it is evident from the very denomination of that tribute.

[9] What does this pompous title signify, but that Edgar pretended to be king, emperor, or supreme head over the petty kings of the island in the neighbourhood of England? No mention is made in it of the empire or dominion of the sea. The kings in question were then of Ireland and of the Island of Mona, or Man. The latter soon after recovered her freedom, and her king possessed himself in 1066 of Dublin and the greater part of the county of Leycester [Mr de Rayneval surely means here the Irish province of Leinster, not the English county of Leicester – PSD], while he kept the Scotch under the yoke. Ireland also recovered and preserved her independence until the twelfth century. The title which Edgar assumed could not apply to the northern islands, for at the period that we speak of, they were all under the dominion of Norway. Indeed, history relates, that

it is said of Canute, to prove that the British ocean was under his dominion, that having placed himself on a seat by the seaside as it flowed upon Southampton shore, he thus addressed the rising waters: "Thou, O Sea! and under my dominion and the law upon which I sit also is mine. And there never was any that disobey my command without punishment. Therefore I command thee not to ascend upon my land, nor do thou presume to wet the feet or garments of thy Sovereign". But the tide swelling as at other times did very unmannerly wet, not only the feet, but the legs of his Majesty, and Canute forced to retire, said to his attendants that none was worthy of the name of king but he at whose nod the sea and the land obeyed; and from that moment he refused to wear his crown of gold, converting it to a crucifix. But he did not the less on that occasion profess himself to be the sovereign of the sea.[10]

In this manner our author argues thro' the first twelve chapters of his second book until he reaches the period of the Norman Conquest. Then he seems to enter more fully upon his subject and pursues a closer and more regular course of argument. He devotes seventeen of the twenty remaining chapters to establishing from a variety of sources the exclusive right of Great Britain to the sea which separates England from

---

he maintained a considerable force by land and sea, but it was in order to defend his country from the Danes and by that means he succeeded not in conquering the sea, but preserving peace and tranquility in his own dominions.

[10] Strange that a gasconade should be considered as the evidence of a title to property. How would Canute, a prince distinguished by his wisdom, have proclaimed himself the sovereign of the sea when he himself acknowledged his inferiority and his weakness by flying from it? The anecdote to which Selden alludes is more correctly told by the English historians. Kimber, in his History of England relates it thus: "Walking one day by the seaside, at Southampton, his (Canute's flattering attendants displayed in the most fulsome adulatory strain his great power and the extent of his dominions, nay almost equaled him with the Almighty. To convince them of their folly and impiety, he ordered a chair to e brought and seating himself where the tide was coming and addressed to the sea the speech mentioned by Selden". He was very far at that moment from intending (as Selden would have it) to declare himself the sovereign of the sea.

Germany and France, and in the three last he asserts her claim to the dominion of the Western and Northern seas.

Before entering upon this most elaborate and indeed most interesting part of his work, he thinks proper to lay down the principles which are to govern his discussion and by which he is willing to abide. "Dominion", says he, "is chiefly founded on just possession or occupation and its continuance. Possession is not supposed to be had by the act either of the mind or body, singly and apart, but it is most firmly gotten and retained by the joint concurrence of both; whereupon it is distinguished into civil, that is, where there is a right or title by law; and natural and corporal; and it is requisite that this dominion receive a signal confirmation by a long continued assent, a free and public confession or acknowledgement of such neighbours *whom it most concerns*".[11]

The reader will no doubt recollect that, with the exception of the artful restriction contained in the last sentence, the doctrine[12]

---

[11] *Cum autem dominium omne justa possession sive occupation ejusque continuation imprimis subniti in confesso sit, nec possessionem adipiscomur sive per se animo, sive per se corpore, sed tum corpore tum aniono, et cintroque ea optime recincatur; unde in civilem, seu qua jure est, & naturalem, seu corporatem distribuitur; dominium que illud est indigniter firmatur accesse sit a vicinorum, quorum maxime interest, par multa sacula adstipulatione & liberte atque publica confessione seu recognition.* L. 2. C. 13. –[PSD].

[12] There are three indispensable requisites without which a right of property cannot exist: 1. The thing to which the right is to apply must be susceptible of a permanent occupation; 2. There must be a real, not an ideal, possession of it with the express or implied assent of the parties who have an interest in contesting it. 3. A sufficient period of time must have elapsed to form a legal prescription from which to infer or presume the assent or waiver of the parties concerned. Such are the conditions required by the civil or municipal law, which is obligatory on the member of the same political society, because they have submitted themselves to it. But it is of no force as between different nations, because they are independent of each other. Treaties, indeed, may supply the place of laws, but without such special conventions, how can any right be acquired? Those that are founded on mere force, that is to say, on the violation of the plainest principles of natural law, are not obligatory on anyone and may be controverted at any time by a superior force. I shall again touch upon this

here professed by our author is precisely that for conception, an idea may be formed of the boldness of his argument and, in fact, he attempts no less than to establish on these seemingly liberal principles the pretended right of Great Britain to the dominion of the adjacent seas.

The first ground that he takes is that England and her admirals, from the time of the Norman Conquest, have been styled and have been in fact the *guardians* of those seas. And he endeavours to prove it in the following manner.

After the landing of the Normans, says he, frequent mention is made in our history and public records of the maritime prefects or guardians of the sea. King Henry I gave orders to his *Butsecarli* (people of the sea) to guard the sea and take care than no person from the ports of Normandy should approach the English coasts, by which he meant to secure the sea with a fleet of vessels and not to defend with land forces a maritime province.[13]

---

subject when I come to speak of Selden's assertion that the dominion of the sea may be acquired like the property of a field or meadow.

[13] But it does not follow from thence that Henry I had pretensions to the dominion of the sea. The only rational inference that may be deduced from the orders which he gave is that he considered his dominions to extend to a certain distance beyond the coast; or, in other words, to the waters of his kingdom. The dominion over the jurisdictional waters of a country is not contested by anyone. But at the time we are speaking of, the limits of that dominion were necessarily indeterminate and even arbitrary because cannon and cannon balls were then unknown, and consequently there was no *actio in distans*, and nations extended their range of protection at sea as far as was necessary, or as far as they could, to guard their coasts from the ravages of pirates, whom they were obliged to engage in close combat. Besides, it must be observed that Henry I was at war with William Cliton [William, surnamed Criton, son of Robert, Duke of Normandy, grandson of William the Conqueror, and elder brother to Henry I – PSD] the pretender to Normandy, support by the King of France, Louis VIII, surnamed the Gross. It was therefore natural that Henry should make preparations for the defence and protection of his coast. But these preparations were neither the effect of the pretended dominion or the sea nor a title to acquire it and still less a proof that Henry had it in contemplation. It is important to observe the age in which that prince lived, and for a long time afterwards, the sea was a dreadful scene of robbery and plunder and pirates were then pursued wherever they might

In the succeeding centuries the kings of England used to appoint maritime prefects to guard the British seas, as if it were a continental dominion. Henry the Third appointed Thomas de Moleton captain and guardian of the sea, "*ad custodiam maris et partium maritimarum littoris orientalis*". Other admirals were appointed expressly for the guard of the sea, "*ut custodiam maris habeant*".[14] In the records of Parliament, under the reign

---

be found. There was no criterion by which to fix the line of maritime dominion; it is even probable that none existed, and that all thought themselves free to act everywhere on the ocean, it being considered as the common property of all.

[14] They must not have read the history of Henry III, who understands these words in the sense which Selden ascribes to them. What! That Prince whom the English writers describe as a pattern of weakness and incapacity, whose reign was constantly disturbed by civil wars and who was even made prisoner by his own barons, could have had the ambitious pretension to make himself the master of the sea and at the expense of what nations? Henry had to relations but with St. Louis, who, far from being under the necessity of receiving the law, did repeatedly act the part of an umpire between the King of England and the grandees of his realm.

But after all, what is the real meaning of those words, *custodia, custos*? It is neither more nor less than *guard* and *guardian*. But we may guard a thing that we possess or enjoy in common with others, particularly when by guarding it we promote the safety of something else which is our exclusive property. Of this we have a memorable instance in history. The Hanseatic League had certainly no pretension to the dominion of the sea, they nevertheless exercised a kind of empire over it by means of the superiority of their naval power, they enjoyed, without restriction, the rights of navigation and fishery, and it was in order to protect both, that they waged a war of extermination against the pirates who infested the ocean and particularly the northern seas. Then the Hanse Towns carried on exclusively trade and commerce in those seas; they had even a considerable established at London, with many privileges. But there is no record in existence by which it does appear that they only navigated under the permission or license of the sovereign of England.

We may also adduce the example of the sovereign order of Malta. Everybody knows that it is one of the objects of its institution to fit out ships of war in order to protect the free navigation of the Mediterranean and make war upon the pirates who infest it. Thus, the knights of Malta certainly exercised the functions of guardians of the Mediterranean Sea and yet they never have pretended to any dominion over it.

of Edward the Third, these words are found: "*De treter sur la gard de la pees de la terre, de la marche d'Escoce et de la mier*". To treat for keeping the peace on land in the marshes of Scotland and on the sea. Mention is also in the same records: "*de la saufegard de la terre et do la saufegard de la mier*", Of the safeguard of the land and the safeguard of the sea, and there is a petition of the merchants of London by which they required that the sea that lies between Great Britain and Zealand should be protected as being under the guardianship of the king.[15] Now the

---

We think it proper to add there the following remark. In time of war, squadrons go out to sea, as well to protect the coasts of the country to which they belong, as to watch on the one hand, the motions of the enemy, and on the other, the commerce of neutrals. This may certainly be called a *guard* or *protection*. But will it be inferred from thence that the sovereigns to whom the squadrons belong have the intention of appropriating to themselves the sea in which they are stationed? According to Selden's doctrines, there can be no doubt about it; but common sense and experience demonstrate the contrary. These princes enjoy the sea in common, each guards or protects the interest that he has in it, and that is all. No doubt it was also thus in former time, save the secret views which the sovereigns of England might have entertained or which their writers attribute to them.

However this may be, if the words of Moleton's commission be critically analyzed, it will be found at least redundant; for if Henry III claimed to be the sovereign of the Eastern Sea, and he was so, *a fortiori*, of the shores of his own dominions, and it was unnecessary to mention them. Therefore, the only inference which may be drawn from the commission in question is that Sir Thomas Moleton was authorized, as he well might be, to cruise beyond the limits of the English coast, in order the better to protect it, a precaution which was highly necessary at a time when the sea was infested with a great number of enterprising and dangerous pirates. If Selden's doctrine is correct, it must needs follow that a man who watches at some distance from his house to prevent thieves from approaching it, thereby takes possession of the highway, or of the neighbouring ground on which he is lying in ambush.

[15] What is, according to the law of nations, the force and effect of a petition of the merchants of London? Has ever a similar document been advanced as evidence of property to the prejudice of foreign nations? The petitioners might as well have bestowed on their sovereign the Kingdoms of Norway, Denmark, and Sweden. They might also have made him a present of Embden, that famous nest of pirates.

words *guard* and *guardian* imply the dominion and Empire of the keepers over the thing entrusted to his custody.[16]

Proceeding in this course of argument, Selden lays much stress upon the terms made use of in the diplomas or commissions of the high admirals. "We give and grant to N., the office of our high Admiral of England, Ireland, Wales, and the dominions and islands thereto belonging; of our city of Calais and the marshes thereof, and of Normandy, Gascony, and Aquitain; and we have constituted the said N prefect general of the fleets and seas of our said kingdoms of England and Ireland and of our dominions and islands thereto belonging &c.".

In the reign of Edward the First, the guardians of the sea, called prefects, began to assume the name of admiral. But they were appointed for separate districts. There were three departments or prefectures, the Western, Southern, and Northern, each of which had its prefect. Sometimes there were but two prefects, one for the Western and the other for the Northern seas. The command over those two seas was seldom

---

But after all, what do those merchants say? Nothing, but that the sea which flows between England and Zealand is under the King's protection. But the right of protection belongs to every maritime State in all the known seas; they may have protecting of squadrons in the seas of Africa, in the Arabian Gulf, and in the Indian Ocean; but would they on that account claim to be the sovereigns of all those seas?

[The petition is couched in much stronger language than Mr. Rayneval here makes use of. It does not merely state that what it calls the *Sea of England* is under the King's *protection*, but that another King has been from time immemorial "in possession of the *sovereign dominion* thereof, for the ordaining and establishing of laws, statutes, and prohibitions – with *higher and lower justice* (civil and criminal jurisdiction) to enforce the same on and between all manner of people, *as well the subjects of other dominions as those of England*" – PSD].

[16] This explanation is ingenious, but is it accurate? The sea is common, I have therefore a right to use it to clear my coasts of pirates, and (at the present time) to prevent contraband trade. Surely those precautions do not require that the sea should belong to me; for I can make use of it in the same manner as if I had an exclusive property therein. Therefore a right to make use of the sea is not synonymous with the dominion or ownership thereof.

entrusted to the same person until the title of admiral was inserted in their commissions.

But as the guardian of the sea derived his name from the sea over which he was appointed in the same manner as if it had been a province, so the admiral derived his title either from the fleet by means of which he protected that part of the coast which was entrusted to him, or from the territory to which it belonged, as may be seen in modern commissions. For that reason, from the time of Edward the First to that of Henry the Fourth, that is to say, during a period of one hundred and fifty years, there were admirals of the fleet: "*flotae navium nostrarum versus partes boreales, seu versus partes occidentales seu australes*", or sometimes both of the Southern and Western seas, which were considered as one, beginning at the mouth of the River Thames. The admirals appointed to the command of those seas were styled admirals of England on the sea, before the words above mentioned were inserted in the commissions. The change in the form of the commissions took place under Henry the Fourth in order to establish in an express manner that the admiral of England and Ireland was at the same time admiral of Aquitaine and Picardy. The first admiral thus appointed was Thomas de Beaufort. In the commissions granted afterwards, Picardy was left out, and admirals were commissioned only for England, Ireland, and Aquitaine. That form continued to the beginning of the reign of Henry VIII (about 88 years). In 1513 an alteration was made in the style of these diplomas, and an admiral was appointed under the title of Admiral of England, Wales, Ireland, Normandy, Gascogne, and Aquitaine. A few years afterwards, Calais and the marshes thereof were added, and at the commencement of the reign of Edward the Sixth, Boulogne and the marshes thereof were also included. The commission of the Earl of Warwick runs thus: "Our Admiral of England, Ireland, Wales, and Boulogne, and of the Marshes thereof; also of Normandy, Gascony, and the Aquitaine, and prefect of our fleets and seas",[17] and at the foot thereof "our High Admiral of

[17] *Admirallus noster Angliae, Hiberniae, Walliae, Calesiae, et Boulniae, et marchiarum nostrarum earundem, Normanniae, Gasconiae et Aquitaniae, nec non praefectus generalis classium et marium nostrorum* – [PSD].

England and preface of our fleets and seas".[18] The next high Admiral was commissioned in the very same form of words as above-mentioned, except that Boulogne was omitted, and this last formula was afterwards constantly made use of in the commissions of admirals. Therefore, the admiral is styled prefect general of our fleets and seas. But what are those seas? They are called *the seas of our said kingdom of England and Ireland, our dominions and islands thereto belonging*, that is to say, the *Sea of England, Ireland and Wales*. So in our laws they are styled the Seas of the British Empire and are sometimes denominated by our jurists the four seas of England, being divided with relation to the four quarters of the globe. So that from the form of commissions used under Queen Mary's reign, as well as from the true interpretation of those of former periods, we have certain proofs of the kings of Great Britain's continual possession of their maritime dominion.

It is also in full proof from those documents that the sea, to the guard of which the Admiral is pointed by the King of England in his sovereign capacity, is bounded to the south by the shores of Aquitaine, Normandy and Picardy. Had those provinces always remained under the jurisdiction and in the possession of the English, the admiral might have had there courts of admiralty and exercised his proper jurisdiction, yet by no means could he on that account have been styled commander of the sea itself, as depending of the same provinces, for they are only mentioned as transmarine limits of the British Sea and of the government of the prefect of England and Ireland. In a word, he would have had no other functions, but those exercised at this day by the Admiralty of England over men's persons and goods, a jurisdiction which is undefined, while that of the prefect has fixed and certain limits.

From what has been said, we must conclude that the name of the French provinces inserted in the admiral's commission meant nothing else than the limits of the maritime jurisdiction of Britain and of the British seas entrusted to them to guard and protect, and indeed, from the death of Queen Mary to the present

---

[18] *Magnus admirallus noster Angliae, et praefectur classium et marium nostrorum* – [PSD]

time, that is to say, from the space of seventy-seven years, the names of the opposite shores have been retained in the commissions of the admirals, altho' England has held no territory whatever on the French continent. And it is to be observed that Normandy, which never had been named before in the commissions of the English admirals, was added some centuries after the English had been wholly deprived of that province. Nor let it be said that the names of those dominions were inserted because of the right which the king of England had to the crown of France, for it would then have been sufficient to have mentioned the name of that kingdom in which they would have been comprehended as the lesser in the greater. But France never was named in the commissions of the English admirals.

It is also to be observed that as soon as an alteration was made in the form of the commissions by inserting the names of kingdoms and provinces instead of describing, as formerly, the command of the admirals of England, which was derived from the fleets and coasts over which they were appointed, the name of Aquitaine was added in order that the limits of the places subject to their authority on the one as well as on the other side of the waters might be pointed out by the shores and for the same reason the names of Normandy and Calais, and the marshes thereof, were afterwards added. It is worthy of remark that whilst the kings of England had either Normandy, Aquitaine, or other French provinces in their possession, no other admirals or governor of a maritime province are mentioned, but those to whose care the English Seas were committed, that is to say, the whole sea flowing between Great Britain and the opposite shores, which were all that time in the peculiar and exclusive right of the kingdom of England so subject to them who were placed in command over the English fleets and coasts that there remained neither place nor use for any other commissions of that kind; which may be said likewise of those times in which some of the kings of England stood possessed also of the kingdom of France, as Edward the Third, Henry the Fifth, and Henry the Sixth. Nor is this a bare conjecture, for it is completely proved by the ancient public records concerning the offices constituted by the kings of

England reigning either in France or in those provinces beyond the sea.[19]

---

[19] This long passage which we have thought proper to translate literally deserves to be critically examined, for its object is to establish: 1. That the British maritime dominion or Empire extends along the French coast to the frontier of Spain; 2. That this empire properly belongs to and is inherent in the Crown of Great Britain, and is not derived from her former possession of a great port of the maritime provinces of France.

In order to prove these strange positions, the author adduces the commissions or diplomas of the English admirals and maritime prefects and employs two long chapters in an elaborate analysis of them. We shall endeavour to follow him thro' his reasoning.

According to him, so early as the reign of Edward I, England laid claim to the sovereignty not only of the English coasts, but of all the surrounding seas to an indefinite extent. The evidence on which he relies is the tenor of the commission given to the admirals or maritime prefects. In order to judge of the validity of similar documents, it should be in the first place considered to whom they were intended to be opposed; it could only to the neighbouring nations, for under the reign of the first Edward, and for a long time after, distant countries were but very little known. Indeed, English industry was not as yet in the cradle, and her foreign commerce was as limited in its object as in its extent.

It ought above all to be remarked that in the time of Edward I, Europe exhibited a sense of unrestrained robbery and plunder by sea as well as by land. Let us hear what Hume relates on this subject: "The violence, robberies, and disorder", says he, "to which that age was subject, were not confined to the licencious barons and their retainers at land. The sea was equally infested with piracy. The feeble execution of the laws had given license to all orders of men and a general appetite for rapine and revenge, supported by false point of honor, had also infected the merchants and marines; and it pushed them, on any provocation, to seek redress by immediate retaliation upon the aggressors. A Norman and an English vessel met off the coast of Bayonne; and both of them having occasion for water, they sent their boats to land, and the several crews came at the same time to the same spring. There ensued a quarrel for the preference. A Norman, drawing his dagger, attempted to stab an Englishman, who grappling with him, threw his adversary on the ground; and the Norman, as was pretended, falling on his own dagger, was slain. This scuffle between two seamen about water soon kindled a bloody war between the two nations and involved a great part of Europe in the quarrel. The mariners of the Norman ship carried their complaints to the French King. Philip, without inquiring into the fact, without demanding redress, bade them take revenge, and trouble him no more about the matter. The

Normans, who had been more regular than usual in applying to the Crown, needed but this hint to proceed to immediate violence. They seized an English ship in the channel, and hanging, along with some dogs, several of the crew on the yardarms in the presence of their companions, dismissed the vessel; and bade the mariners to inform their countrymen that vengeance was now taken for the blood of the Norman killed at Bayonne. This injury accompanied with so general and deliberate an insult was resented by the mariners of the Cinque Ports, who, without carrying any complaint to the King, or waiting for redress, retaliated by committing like barbarities on all French vessels without distinction. The French, provoked by their losses, preyed on the ships of all Edward's subjects, whether English or Gascon. The sea became a scene of piracy between the nations. The sovereigns, without either seconding or repressing the violence of their subjects, desired to remain indifferent spectators. The English made private associations with the Irish and Dutch seamen, and the French with the Flemish and Genoese. And the animosities of the people on both sides became every day more violent and barbarous. A fleet of two hundred Norman vessels set sail to the south for wine and other commodities, and in their passage seized all the English ships which they met with; hanged the seamen, and seized the goods. The inhabitants of the English seaports informed of this incident, fitted out a fleet of sixty sails, stronger and better manned than the others, and awaited the enemy on their return. After an obstinate battle, they put them to rout and sunk, destroyed, and took the greater part of them. No quarter was given, and it is pretended that the loss of the French amounted to fifteen thousand men, which is accounted for by the circumstances that the Norman fleet was employed in transporting a considerable body of soldiers from the south".

Mr. Hume proceeds to inform us that this affair was now to become too important to be any longer overlooked by the sovereigns, and they sought, but in vain, for means of reconciliation. War, therefore, broke out between them. Edward was unfortunate. Philip seized Guienne as forfeited, and altho' he had promised by a special Convention to restore that province, he nevertheless retained it. But at last, after many incidents, Pope Boniface VIII interfered as mediator, and the two kings were reconciled on the following conditions: it was agreed that their union should be cemented by a double marriage, that of Edward himself, then a widower, with Margaret, the sister of Philip, and that of the Prince of Wales with Isabella, a daughter of that monarch; on which Philip consented to the restitution of Guienne.

Such is Hume's recital concerning the quarrels between Edward I and France. It is to be remarked (not to lose sight of our subject) that the principal cause of the war had the sea for its object. The French or the Normans had violated (according to Selden's system) the maritime jurisdiction of England as well along the western coast of France as in the Channel; Edward, therefore, had a right to complain of them, and not only to demand an adequate reparation for the injury done, but a solemn recognition of his maritime sovereignty. And yet not a word is said about this pretended maritime dominion; the whole controversy turned upon acts of depredation and cruelty committed on both sides by the mariners of the respective powers and the whole contest was terminated by a double marriage. We must therefore strike off the list of Selden's arguments, all that took place under the reign of Edward I.

As to the diplomas or commissions, those acts of municipal authority which Selden exhibits and analyzes with so much pomp and on which he appears so strongly to rely, they must either be put entirely aside, or returned to the dusty shelves where that author had the good fortune to discover them. But what is worthy of particular remark, is what he says concerning the seas which line the coast of France, from Picardy and Normandy quite to the frontier of Spain. According to this system, the right of exclusive jurisdiction claimed by England over those seas is not as an appendage to the possession of those provinces which she once held, but as a direct prerogative of the English Crown.

We might ask in the first place: where is the written evidence to show that England was ever in possession of that prerogative? Where are the instruments to show that it was ever recognized by the sovereigns of France? Where are the treaties by which it has been sanctioned? And by what title is it that the kings of England pretend to an exclusive jurisdiction over any portion whatever of the seas which surround their kingdom? No doubt it is on the ground of their being the sovereigns of the country, and in order that they may be able to secure the pace and tranquility thereof. But the rights to which they are in this respect entitled, other sovereigns equally possess, and surely the kings of England do not pretend to any supremacy over them. No such diplomacy was thought of under Charlemagne and his immediate successors; altho' they troubled themselves very little about the sea at that time, yet those sovereigns had the same rights over the French Seas, which the kings of England had over those of their own country. That right (as it is by its nature was facultative, that is to say, it might be exercised by those princes whenever they thought proper, no one could deprive them of it against their will, it was inherent and inseparable from their sovereignty. The great vassals of France, and particularly the kings of England, usurped it, as they had already usurped all the rights of supreme dominion. They were in the full possession of those usurped rights when William the Bastard, called the Conqueror, transmitted his Duchy to his successors to the English throne [this is a mistake in point of historical fact. William the Conqueror did not transmit the Duchy of Normandy to William Rufus, to whom he left the throne of England, but to his eldest son, Robert. It was not until after Robert's death that the royal ducal crown was united in the person of Henry I – PSD]. This was the first title to the dominion of the sea which separates Normandy from Great Britain. This dominion extended itself in proportion as the kings of England acquired the western provinces of France, to wit: Aquitaine and Guienne, and thence came the different denominations given to the sea which washes those countries. But I repeat it, the dominion of the sea as far as it respected the jurisdictional waters, was a usurpation over the paramount sovereignty of the throne, and a nonentity, as far as meant to be applied to the high and open sea. That it was the provinces that gave their names to the different seas, as being dependencies of them, is that Armorica or Britanny gave its name to the waters by which it is washed [Selden does not scruple to acknowledge this himself. See the passage of his work, quoted above, Note [a] – PSD]. And that the English, notwithstanding their pretensions on Britanny, as a fief of Normandy, never did claim to its dominion. And why did they never claim the sea which washes the coast of Biscay? It is undoubtedly because they never had the possession of that Spanish province.

But, says Selden, it is so true that the Sea of Guienne, Aquitaine, Normandy, and Picardy did not belong to England as appendages to those provinces, but by virtue of a direct right, that it was not until England had lost all those French territories, that their names were inserted in the commissions of the admirals as the boundaries of the British Sea. Thus, after having lost the principal estate, Great Britain claims to have retained one of its appurtenances! This mode of reasoning is in opposition to the first elements of sound logic. Besides, to acquire a right of property in anything whatever, it is not sufficient to fabricate evidences of title on the mere authority of the claimant; it is necessary to have an exclusive continued possession with the consent of the interested parties. But on the one hand, there can be no such thing as a continual possession of the high sea; and on the other, Selden exhibits no document to prove the consent or acknowledgement of the sovereigns of France, respecting the waters which bound their territory. On the contrary, it is certain that since their expulsion from France, the kings of England never did grant letters patent or passports for the free navigation of those seas to the inhabitants of Guienne, Aquitaine, or Normandy.

We are therefore warranted in rejecting the constructions which Selden endeavours to put upon the commissions of the English admirals and the inferences which he draws from them. The triumphant tone and manner with which he expatiates upon the subject has alone induced us to be so prolix in our extracts and observations. If the reader is curious of seeing at still greater length the logic which Selden employs in treating of

If it should be asked why the coast of Armoria or Britanny is not mentioned, which with those of Picardy, Normandy, and Aquitaine complete the whole tract opposite to the English and Irish seas, the answer is that the King of England was not at any time so possessed of Britanny as to need, or being ousted of it, to be very solicitous about the bounds of the adjacent maritime territory. Besides, the limits of the dominions of the several sovereigns confining on each other were perfectly known and Britanny had its dukes until the reign of Charles VIII of France; however the King of England being disturbed in his possession was bound to take care that past confusion should not be prejudicial to the future distinction of boundaries. Lest therefore it might have been pretended that England, by losing the maritime provinces which she had possessed, had also lost the adjoining seas by want of proper measures for ascertaining the limits of the British Sea, the name of Aquitaine was at first continued in the admiral's commissions and afterwards, that of Normandy was added to it, and since that time both of them, together with Calais and its marshes, which were substituted for the coast of Picardy, have been for the same reason continued to be inserted down to the present day. That reason was not at all applicable to Armoria or Britanny, nor to Flanders and the

---

this part of his subject, we invite him to read the sixteenth and seventeenth chapters of his *Mare Clausum*.

We think proper to conclude this long note with the following remark. England, according to Selden, is the sovereign not only of what is called the British Channel, but also of the seas which wash the northern coast of France. The natural effect of that sovereignty (as our author himself says) is the right of admission or exclusion. Now, Philip the Fair admitted the ships of the Hanseatic League into his ports, and Charles VIII, as well as his father, Louis XI, granted them special privileges. Can it be presumed that either those two princes, or the confederation of Hanse towns, obtained the permission of the English Government to sail thro' the channel and navigate beyond it in the Seas of Picardy, Normandy, and Aquitaine? Not only Selden does not venture on such an assertion, but he does not even say anything that might induce us to suspect it. We may therefore say with perfect confidence that such a permission never was given and, therefore, that the English pretension at least with regard to France remained buried in the diplomas of her admirals or prefects.

eastern shore, all of which, nevertheless, bound the maritime territory of Great Britain.[20]

In corroboration of what has already been said, we must inquire into the nature of the office of admiral in France. The French admirals were not appointed to guard or protect the sea. They had merely the command of the naval forces of that kingdom in whatever sea they might be stationed and a special authority over the person and goods of seafaring men. Charlemagne had a maritime prefect, not to protect the Sea of Armorique or Britanny, but only the coasts thereof;[21] and even that protection was abandoned by the successors of that prince. In the succeeding centuries, France was divided into so many sovereignties that the kings only retained the coasts of Picardy and their naval forces were only employed in expeditions against the Holy Land. Such were nearly in France the functions of the admiral.[22] After the conquest of Normandy, maritime affairs

---

[20] Here Selden acknowledges that England does not claim the Armorique Sea or Sea of Britanny, altho' enclosed with these which she claims to belong to her because she never had peaceable possession of that Duchy. This avowal proves, against the author himself, that it was only as dependencies of her provinces in France that Great Britain occupied the seas which gird their shores. It follows from thence that whatever the author may say that when the kings of England lost those provinces, they also lost the dominion of the circumfluent seas. It is easy to assert the contrary in a diploma, but it is not equally easy to give it effect.

[21] This remark proves that Charlemagne knew and respected the law of nations, or at least that he had an intuitive perception of its principles. That good prince, according to Selden himself, knew that the shores of the sea and nothing beyond them belong to his dominions, and that the open sea was common to all nations. It is singular enough that this respect for the law of nations should be brought forward as the proof of an acknowledgement of the exorbitant pretensions of Great Britain. If the successor of Charlemagne paid less attention than he did to maritime affairs, it was no doubt a great neglect; but can that neglect be a ground on which to establish the maritime dominion of the English Kings?

[22] What has this to do with the dominion of the sea? The sea is an element of which every nation may make use or not as it thinks proper; but a natural right can never be destroyed by *non us*. The sea is free and common to all; no doubt force may interrupt the use of this common right, but it can never destroy it. As to the functions of the admiral, the King of France might regulate them according to his will and pleasure; he might

took a better turn and then the office of admiral was included among the dignities of the Crown, but its duties were restricted to the command of the naval forces. At last, all the maritime coasts of France were successively re-conquered, with the exception of those of the Belgic provinces. Four offices of admiral were created, altho' it often happened that the same person filled more than one. From the reign of Charles V until after that of Henry III, many edicts are to be found concerning the authority of the admirals. They are sometimes styled "our Lieutenant General, throughout the sea, and the shores thereof"; but they never were appointed to command over the sea that flows between France and Great Britain as making a part of the French dominion; and the historians of that nation affirm that the kings of France never had any dominion over the sea,[23] for the possession of the sea coast does not confer the dominion of the sea any more than that of the land adjacent to navigable rivers confers the dominion of these streams; for in France, navigable rivers belong to the king, altho' he is not the owner of the adjoining lands;[24] therefore the functions of the admiral did not

---

attach to that office a jurisdiction over maritime affairs or merely the command of fleets; he might even have no admiral at all and abandon the sea to itself; other nations had no more to do with that than with the style of the commissions of the British admirals.

[23] All this is foreign to the question were we to follow Selden's example we would say that our *Lieutenant général de la mer et grèves* is the lawful guardian of the sea and shores and that consequently the kings of France, as well as those of England, have had pretensions to the dominion of the sea. But we will not make use of so trifling an argument, and we say that where the high sea begins, it is free and not susceptible of possession and consequently of dominion. For why should they have divested their own sovereign of it to transfer it to the sovereign of Great Britain?

[24] If the sovereignty of the continent does not confer upon its possessor the dominion of the sea, the sovereignty of an island does not confer it any more. Then we ask why the kings of England pretend to the dominion of all the confluent seas; if it is not by virtue of their territorial possessions, some other reason must be assigned to support the claim. But where shall we find that reason, and why are the seas called *British* which England claims as her patrimony? Selden tells us himself that it is because they were considered as a province or appendage to the land, forming with it an indivisible whole. It is therefore on the possession of the British Island

extend further than the command of the naval forces. And how could the kings of France think of maritime dominion when their kingdom was torn to pieces by domestic as well as foreign enemies, while England, even in the times of the heptarchy, had always had a supreme acknowledged government for all matters which concerned the general welfare?[25]

On a review of all these facts, we find the following results. From the remotest times, there was only a small strip of sea coast contained within the limits of the French kingdom, and when afterwards that kingdom was enlarged by the conquest of maritime provinces, its kings did not thereby acquire maritime dominion, for we see no trace of it in the monuments of ancient writers.[26] There are, on the contrary, many proofs that the kings of England have continually possessed the whole English shore in its full extent under one consolidated empire, for the space of above one thousand years and that they have during all that time, without interruption, enjoyed the dominion of the sea, as an appendage to the Crown; whence it follows that the sea is considered as a province entrusted to the guardianship of the admirals of England and that the admirals of the opposite shore

---

that the maritime dominion claimed by the sovereign of Great Britain is founded.

As to rivers, the property thereof is regulated by the municipal law of each country and not by the law of nations, and therefore they have nothing to do with the present question. Besides, rivers may be effectually guarded and protected, and therefore are susceptible of exclusive dominion, as well as the shores.

[25] What! Because France was torn by civil wars, because great vessels of the Crown usurped the rights of the sovereign, who being despoiled of his maritime provinces could no longer have a navy for want of sea ports, does it follow that he did not recover with his dominions the rights that were annexed to them and which he could not even have validly renounced? [We cannot go so far as the learned author; if the kings of France had by treaty renounced the navigation of the seas claimed by Great Britain, their subjects would have been bound by the renunciation until either the fortune of war or another treaty had restored them to the exercise of that right which they had thus voluntarily abandoned – PSD].

[26] The reason is that the French were less rapacious than the English. If the shores only are in question, there can be no doubt that France recovered the dominion thereof with that of adjoining territory.

cannot be considered in the same point of view.[27] That is the reason why some centuries ago several neighbouring nations solemnly recognized the right of England by joining with her in a complaint against the encroachments of Rayner Grimbald, admiral of France, because he had tortiously by colour of a commission from the King of France assumed upon himself the office of admiral in the English seas and exercised the same for one year and upwards, &c.

To all the proofs already deduced, Selden adds an inference which he draws from the continued possession of the islands of Jersey and Guernsey. Altho' the kings of England lost Normandy, they still kept the possession of those islands and have preserved it to this day. Whether they are or not to be considered as a dependency of that province, it is not less true that they have remained in the possession of England as a part of her maritime dominion.[28] It is to be remarked that in the time of

---

[27] Such are the pretensions of England, but it cannot be too often repeated, where are the documents in support of them? What is the meaning of shores extending far out at sea? What is a dominion composed of the waves of the ocean? What is a pretended possession which the nature of things itself denies? What is, in short, an empire on a merely ideal possession?

[28] It is very extraordinary, not to say more, to suppose that the islands of Jersey &c. belong to England as a part of her maritime empire or dominion, when it is so well known that they were a dependency of Normandy, and that William the Conqueror and the Kings of England his successors possessed them only as such. But his Duchy was a fief dependent on the crown of France; the islands therefore were likewise subject to the paramount sovereignty of that kingdom. They were therefore no part of the English territory and consequently no part of the maritime dominion of England. After the death of William, Robert, his eldest son, became the sovereign of the islands as part of the Duchy of Normandy to which he succeeded, while the Kingdom of England devolved to his younger brother. After the death of Robert, Normandy and its dependencies passed to William's descendants as a fief of the Crown of France and subject to feudal duties. On the extinction of the Norman race, Normandy should have reverted to the Lord paramount; But without entering into this question, we shall only observe that after remaining sometime longer in the possession of the kings of England, it returned irrevocably under the dominion of the kings of France and no one, undoubtedly, will admit that the dominion of the seas adjacent to that

Philip the Fair and Edward I, several foreign nations acknowledged the dominion of England over that part of the sea, as well as over the islands "by reason of the realm of England, *par rayson de Royalme d'Angleterre*". Nor is it to be omitted that it was only at the time when the British expelled from Normandy retained the above mentioned islands, that France acquired a greater extent of coast, for before that time, those of Aquitaine and Normandy belonged to England and those of Britanny to her Dukes, so that France possessed only a very small strip of land bordering on the sea; and was but little occupied with maritime affairs. Therefore, the English did with greater ease retain the aforesaid possession of the sea and islands.[29]

A further proof of the maritime dominion of the kings of England is derived from the permission which they granted to foreigners to cross or navigate the seas. Henry IV granted leave to Ferrando Certil de Sarachione, a Spaniard, "to sail freely from the port of London, thro' our kingdoms, dominions, and jurisdiction to the town of Rochelle", *per regna, dominia, et*

---

province remained in Great Britain; for no one will believe that the English at the time when they were expelled from that country were in a situation to dictate laws to their conqueror. The islands remained to them together with the shores, and their right to either is not contested. The motives which influenced that arrangement do not belong to our subject.

If, as the author says, several nations acknowledged the dominion of the English court on that part of the sea by reason of the realm of England, this acknowledgement was an act entirely foreign to France, *res inter alios acta*, and stands in no need of refutation.

[29] It is very true that France had a very small extent of coast before she recovered her maritime provinces; but her vassals possessed the remainder for her and in her name; and as fast as those provinces returned to the immediate dominion of our kings, the coasts and shores underwent the same change. If the English, having been expelled from Normandy under Philip Augustus, and afterwards from all France by Charles VII, should still pretend to the exclusive dominion of the seas contiguous to the provinces which they formerly occupied, they must show a contract in due form which secures it to them. But Selden after a careful search among the records of his own country and the heaps of antiquated documents which are preserved in the Tower of London has not been able to discover anything of the kind. We may therefore safely conclude that the dominion of those seas rests on the general principles of the law of nations.

potestatem nostrum usque ad villam de la Rochelle. It is manifest that in their place the words "our dominions and jurisdiction" do relate to the intermediate sea;[30] and when Charles VI, King of France, sent ambassadors to Robert III, King of Scotland, they upon request made to the same Henry obtained a passport for their safe passage: "thro' all our powers, straits, and dominions, as well as by sea as by land" (*par tous noz pourvoirs, destroits et seigneuries, par mer et par terre*).[31] A great number of similar safe conducts were granted by kings Henry IV and Henry VI with the words "as well by sea as by land and rivers" (*tans par mer que par terre et les eaux douces*). Those documents were directed to the admirals or maritime prefects; while those which the kings of France granted to the subjects of England, when they wished to cross over into France, were not directed in the same manner. That which Philip the Long gave to Edward II is inscribed only thus: "Philip, by the grace of God, King of France, To all our Justices and Subjects,

[30] This is quoted by Selden as an additional proof of the maritime dominion of England, but this inference is so unnatural that we might dispense with making any observation upon it. It is, however, proper to remark that Henry was still in possession of the Duchy of Aquitaine; and therefore it was natural enough that he should give a passport to a Spaniard to sail from London to Rochelle, which was within his own dominions; he would have given him one for Russia had England at that time had an intercourse with that Empire. Be that as it may, the words *per regna domina et potestatem nostrum* do not mean the sea that flows between London and Rochelle, they only relate to the point of departure and the place of arrival. If he had meant to designate the intermediate sea, he would and should have said, *per maria nostra*, but it is probable that Henry IV, engaged as he was in domestic feuds, thought very little of the pretensions which our author is pleased to ascribe to him.

[31] Nothing is less conclusive than this passport. It ensured a safe passage to the ambassadors of Charles VI throughout the English dominions by sea and by land, that is to say, wherever the English jurisdiction properly extended, but no farther. Besides, the seas were not safe at that period and it was natural for Charles VI to take all necessary precautions for the safety of his ambassadors. After all, the word sea is one of those generic terms which occasionally receive different acceptions, and it may as well mean the space which is contained within the jurisdictional limits of a country, as the high and open sea.

greetings".[32] Yet, France at that time had an admiral at least in Normandy and Picardy. It is true that afterward the admirals were named in the passports, but the king of England alone, on account of his dominion, did prescribe conditions to those who sailed on the seas. And it was in consequence of that right that the kings of Denmark and Sweden, and the Hanse Towns, requested of Queen Elizabeth that they might have a free passage for the provisions which they intended to carry to Spain during the war in which she was engaged against the Spaniards. We must confess, however, that that permission was denied them, not merely on account of the dominion of the sea, but chiefly to prevent the conveying of provisions to the enemy. And ships belonging to the Hanse Towns and loaded with corn were seized in the very harbor of Lisbon, for having without the Queen's consent (Elizabeth) passed thro' the Scottish and Western seas, on their way to Portugal;[33] which occasioned a lively discussion of this question. How far those who are not enemies may furnish supplies to an enemy? The Hamburghers were then refused the permission to carry arms and warlike stores, but they were allowed that of carrying all other kinds of merchandise.[34] It was at that period that those who a few years before had entreated the Queen to grant them the freedom of the sea began to claim it as a right. About the same time, the king of Denmark sent ambassadors to England to obtain the permission of carrying provisions to Spain, but it was refused, as had been done some time before to the Hanse Towns.[35] Would such a step

---

[32] This difference in the form and style of passports proves nothing, but that each country has its own particular formulas and is not bound to adopt those of other nations.

[33] This was an act of violence, which has nothing to do with the subject that we are treating of.

[34] This has nothing to do with the present question; England, as Selden himself observes, was at war with Spain, and everybody knows that the system of maritime jurisdiction has always varied with respect to neutrals and that the strongest at all times made the laws as best served his interest.

[35] This fact is positively contradicted by Camden, an English writer contemporary with Selden. "The Queen", says he, "most graciously received the ambassadors (of Denmark) and promised on certain conditions to restore the goods, if any had been captured, and not to take any more in future" (*Regina, legatos benignissime complexa, foedera*

have been necessary, had not the dominion of the Queen over the sea been acknowledged? John, King of Sweden, acknowledged it in a letter which he wrote to her in 1587, in which he asked a passport for one of his subjects, saying that he is obliged to pass thro' the Queen's maritime dominions: *Maritimas reginae ditiones pertransire*.[36] If we go a little farther back, we see that Edward I, at war with Philip the Fair, ordered the necessary precautions to be taken to prevent anything from being conveyed by sea to France. The orders of that prince bore this injunction: "Especially to retain and maintain the sovereignty which his ancestors, the kings of England, were wont to have in the said sea so far as concerns the amendment, declaration, and interpretation of the laws by them made to govern all means of nations passing thro' the said sea". King John gave orders to stop and bring into the ports of England all vessels which should be met at sea. And what could such a measure mean, except that the dominion of the sea belonged to England? We also find ordinances from Edward III for the detaining of all vessels in the southern and western sea, of ten tons burthen and upwards to be armed and employed in the king's service. It is to be presumed that this law was equitably carried into execution, that is to say, that a suitable indemnity was allowed to the owners of the vessels so detained.[37]

---

renovanda, bona, si qua fuerint intercepta, restituenda, nec deinceps intercipienda, certis legibus promisit). Those conditions were that all kinds of goods should be free with the only exception of warlike stores.

[36] The application of the King of Sweden for a passport for one of his subjects in time of war between England and Spain is not at all extraordinary. Little respect was paid in those remote times to the law of nations, piratical acts were frequently committed at sea, the maritime usages of England were such as to excite fears for the fate of merchantmen and their cargoes, and the practice of sailing with a convoy of armed vessels had not yet been introduced.

[37] These orders offered no better proof in favor of Selden's position that the commissions of the English admirals or maritime prefects; neither of them can have any binding force on other nations. As to the impressment of foreign vessels to be employed in the king's service, it is an act of violence and not a proof of maritime dominion. In vain does Selden endeavour to palliate it by presuming that it was carried into execution in

After treating of navigation, Selden proceeds to speak of fishing. The records of Parliament prove that in the reign of Richard III a tribute was imposed upon foreigners to whom leave was given to fish in the sea. Henry VI granted that permission to the French and other foreigners "for one year only". It is true that such licences were given to English subjects as well as to aliens, but it was merely to prevent the former from being molested by the latter. It is also true that other princes, such as the King of France, the Duke of Britanny, and the Earl of Flanders, granted licenses or permits of the same description to the English fishermen, but it is evident that the King of England meant as much to assert his maritime dominion as to cultivate amity and friendship with the neighbouring princes while they, on the contrary, had only the latter object in view.[38]

---

a just and equitable manner; it is difficult to connect together the ideas of justice and violence.

[38] By the common law of nations the sea belongs to all mankind, and by a generally established custom the waters near the coast to a certain distance from the shore are considered as a part of the territory and subject to the dominion of the sovereign of the country. There are positive principles from which it is important never to deviate and by which Selden's doctrine concerning fishing and navigation ought to be tested.

Selden mentions the tributes imposed upon foreigners for permission to fish and urges them as proofs of the maritime dominions of Great Britain; but here, as almost everywhere else throughout his dissertation, his favorite mode of arguing is by strained inference to carry the application of his facts beyond the bounds of rational probability, thus verifying the old adage that what proves too much, proves nothing. In arguing from laws, ordinances, and other similar public acts, their literal sense is first to be looked to, and if it is obscure or equivocal, it is to be interpreted by the general principles of law relative to the particular subject. It is always to be presumed that the legislators meant to be governed by those principles. Thus, the acts of private individuals are construed by the rules of municipal law, and those of sovereigns by the principles of the law of nations. Let us now apply these truths to what our author says on the subject of the taxes imposed by England on foreign fishermen in the time of Henry VI.

That prince was engaged in an unfortunate war against France; he was pressed by the most urgent wants, and his subjects were overburthened with taxes. At that particular juncture the parliament laid a tax on foreign fishermen. But where did those men carry on their

In our own times, leave has been granted to Frenchmen to fish for soles, for the table of their King Henry IV, and some of their vessels have been seized for fishing without a license.[39] It has been an ancient custom for the Hollanders and Zealanders to obtain permission to fish on the coast of Scotland.[40] James I issued a proclamation by which foreigners were forbidden to fish in the British or Irish sea, or in the seas belonging to the other islands dependent on the British kingdoms.[41] We do not

---

fisheries? Was it on the coast of England, or on the high sea? Selden does not tell us, but we may very easily supply his omission. Fish is generally caught on the coast, at no great distance from the shore, and therefore within the jurisdictional limits of the territorial sovereign. Of course, foreigners coming to the coasts of England for the purpose of fishing were compelled either to submit to the laws of the country or to withdraw. This is the true and only natural sense of the act of Parliament which Selden relies upon. But he was not satisfied with the plain obvious meaning, because it could not support his system of maritime dominion beyond the coast. He thought it best to argue *a minori ad majus*, contrary to the rules of sound logic. In one word, when the Parliament of England laid a tax on foreign fishermen, those were only means to be the objects of it, who came to fish within the proper maritime jusirdiction of that country. Selden, indeed, asserts the contrary, but does not prove it.

As to the remarks which he makes on the subject of the passports granted by the King of France, the Duke of Britanny, &c., they are so exaggerated that they do not deserve a serious refutation.

[39] Selden does not tell us in what parts the French were allowed thus to fish for soles, nor where the seizures that he speaks of were made. It might be and probably was on the coast and within the jurisdictional limits of England.

[40] The British had clearly a right to grant such permissions if those of Holland and Zealand carried on their fisheries on the coasts of the island of Great Britain.

[41] This proclamation was a mere municipal law. Besides, the denominations of French and British seas are merely descriptions of the situation of a particular sea and have no relation whatever to jurisdictional limits; they are used in the same sense in which we say the seas of Gascony, Biscay, Arabia, America, &c. If France were to say no one shall fish without my leave in the Atlantic Ocean, she would mean no more but that nobody should fish in her jurisdictional waters which are a part of that ocean. And it would never be supposed that by such a prohibition she meant to arrogate to herself the exclusive sovereignty of the Western Atlantic. If the names of seas, bays, and gulfs were *vi termini*, to confer

often meet, it is true, with the forms of those licenses, but the reason is that a general permission to frequent ports and coasts, a right of passage, &c. was often mutually granted between the maritime powers of Europe by conventions or treaties, so that so long as those treaties were in force, the sea was to be enjoyed in common between the subjects of the sovereign with whom the treaty was made and those of the King of England by the former as granting of the mere use, and by the latter as sovereign lords and proprietaries.[42] Sometimes, however, that permission was restricted within certain limits. An agreement was made between our Henry IV and Charles VI, King of France, that the subjects of both might freely fish throughout that part of the sea which is bounded on this side by the ports of Scarborough and Southampton, and on the other by the coast of Flanders and the mouth of the River Seine, and for the safety of the French fishermen, the king ordered passports to be delivered to them. By the assignment of the above limits, the king in virtue of his maritime supremacy excluded the French from the western and northernmost parts of the ocean, while on the part of France, no such claim of maritime dominion can be inferred, for no part of her northern coast is excluded from the limits assigned, and to the westward, she had only the province of Normandy; the remainder was in the possession of the Duke of Britanny and the King of England.[43]

---

the dominion thereof, the Arabian Gulf, for example, would exclusively belong to the Arabians, the Gulf of Mexico to the Spaniards, &c.

[42] There is no foundation whatever for this interpretation, nor is it in the least warranted by the letter or spirit of those treaties of which Selden speaks. The stipulation of the liberty of fishing in favor of both nations was only meant to be applied to the respective coasts; as to the intermediate sea, it was, of course, considered as common, and both were understood to have an equal right to the enjoyment of it. It is absurd to suppose that the one should have had a mere usufructary interest, while the other enjoyed an absolute dominion over it. How can a grave and learned writer decide with so much levity about the most important rights of nations?

[43] The object of this note is only to show that we do not adopt the inferences by which Selden endeavours to support his system, for they stand in no need of a facile refutation. If the King of England was actually in possession of the dominion of the sea, it was not by treaties, but by laws

There is among the records of the privy council a permission granted in 1295 to the inhabitants of Holland, Zealand, and Friesland to fish in the vicinity of Yarmouth. If anyone dared to fish in that sea without a license, he was seized as trespassing on the exclusive right of Great Britain.[44] Another class of proofs is to be found in the laws assigning limits to powers at war with each other, but in amity with England. We have a proclamation of King James I issued in 1604 which is in the following words: "Our pleasure is that within our ports, havens, roads, creeks, or other places of our dominions, or so near to any of our said ports and havens as, au be reasonably construed to be within that title, limit, or precinct, there shall be no force or offense suffered to be done, either from man of war to man of war, or man of war to merchant, or merchant to merchant of either party. But that all of what nation soever, so long as they shall be within those our ports and places of our jurisdiction, or where our officers may prohibit violence, shall be understood to be under our protection, to be ordered by courts of justice and be at peace with each other".[45] After this proclamation, Selden gives a table of the

---

and proclamations that that dominion was to be enforced. He had nothing to do but to give notice of it to the other powers and to take proper measures to cause his rights to be respected.

As to Selden's remark on the subject of the part of Scarborough being designated as the limit to which the right of fishing extended on the English coast, there is absolutely no weight in it, that port is only about thirty leagues distant from the frontier of Scotland, where the King of England had no authority. It was not, therefore, an object to except so small a place from the general grant; it is more probable that Scarborough was only mentioned as the most northern port of any importance on the coast of England and not as a mathematical point of separation or exclusion.

[44] It is evident that this general prohibition as well as the exception made in favor of Hollanders and others extended only to the jurisdictional limits and not to the high and open sea.

[45] This Edict of James I is perfectly plain, correct, and proper. It prohibits all hostilities within the waters of his kingdom because those waters were neutral places. But there is not one word in it from whence it may be inferred, or even supposed, that James had any intention of including within those waters the whole British channel, the Western Sea, and the Atlantic Ocean, quite to the Spanish colonies in America. Such is, however, the opinion of Selden, and of his model, Albericus Gentilis. Had

Selden, instead of indulging himself in fanciful inferences and suppositions, consulted the history of the preceding reign, he would have been convinced that Elizabeth never adopted the thing which he attributes to James I, and yet that princess very well understood the rights which belonged to her crown and knew how to cause them to be respected. The following fact is related by Hume in his History of England:

The celebrated navigator, Francis Drake, having acquired considerable riches by some depredations made on the Spaniards in the Isthmus of Panama and wishing to try new adventures, obtained from Queen Elizabeth four ships and a pinnacle, on board of which 160 sailors. He passed into the South Sea by the Straits of Magellan and, falling on the Spaniards, who expected no enemy in these quarters, he took many rich prizes. He prepared to return with the immense booty which he had acquired. Apprehensive of being intercepted by the enemy, he reached the Pacific Ocean and attempted to find a passage by the North of California, and failing in that enterprise, he set sail for the East Indies and returned by the Cape of Good Hope. After his return, the King of Spain complained of his conduct to Queen Elizabeth. I shall now give the answer of that princess as related by Camden:

The Spaniards have brought those evils upon themselves by their iniquitous conduct towards the British, to whom they have interdicted trade in contempt of the law of nations. Drake shall be brought before a competent tribunal; his riches have been sequestered, for the purpose of making compensation to the Spaniards, if he shall be convicted of having acted against the law, altho' the Queen has spent more money against the rebels whom the King of Spain has incited in Scotland and England than Drake has brought into this country. After all, she could not understand why her subjects, and those of other sovereigns, should be prohibited from resorting to the Indies, that the Spaniards could not persuade themselves that those countries belonged to them by virtue of a donation from the Roman pontiff, who is not acknowledged in such matters to have any authority to bind those princes who owe no obedience to him; a donation by which it would seem that he has invested the Spaniards with the property of that new world, altho' they have no other title to it, but that of having landed there, built huts, and given names to rivers and capes, which is not sufficient to confer a right of property. That that void donation and that imaginary right of property could not prevent other nations from trading with those same regions, from establishing colonies in those places where the Spaniards have made no settlement, prescription being of no avail without actual possession, and from freely navigating that vast ocean, the use of the sea and air being common to all, that no nations, nor private individual, can have an exclusive right to the ocean because it cannot be occupied either by the law of nature or by the usage

limits assigned to foreign vessels and observes that altho' it does not include the whole extent of the sea, which is under the British dominion, yet it must not be inferred that such dominion did not exist. The only object of the King of England in issuing that Edict was the safety of his ports and havens, and if he abandoned that part of the sea which lay without the said limits, to the use of the powers at war with each other, but in amity with him, it was still an act of his supreme authority by which he permitted the use of the open sea under certain restrictions. Besides, James I could not mean by his proclamation to circumscribe the limits of his jurisdiction to any other purpose than that of the war then existing between the Spaniards and Dutch, in every other respect he still remained, as his predecessors had been, the Supreme Lord and moderator of the British Sea forever. Hence the kings of England frequently granted that the islands situated on the coast of Normandy should remain neutral in time of war, which they could do only by virtue of their supreme dominion over the circumfluent seas.[46]

---

of nations". Selden had certainly read this passage in Camden, for he very often quotes that writer in order to refute him. But had he attended to the maxims of Elizabeth, he would have had no occasion to write his *Mare Clausum*, unless he had meant to show that that great princess had betrayed the interests of her Crown. Certain it is that she entirely overthrew the fantastic edifice of maritime dominion which her predecessors are supposed to have created, and consequently, if such dominion now exists we must look for its foundation in the acts of her successors. But we have already seen how insignificant were the acts of possession which Selden attributes to James I.

[46] It is possible that James, when he framed his Edict, may have done it under a mental reservation and confided his secret thoughts to Selden. But even if it were so, it could not avail anything in support of Selden's argument. Nations, as well as individuals, can see nothing in a public act but what is expressed therein. Therefore, the princes contemporary with James knew no more than what appeared on the face of his Edict, nor could they interpret it otherwise than by the known rules and principles of the law of nations. All the maritime powers at this day issue Edicts and proclamations relative to the sea, and it may as well be supposed that they mentally reserve to themselves the dominion thereof, and that such a reservation gives them a legitimate title thereto.

And if as Selden affirmed, the King of England was at that time the sovereign of the sea, he was generous indeed, when he permitted his

A further proof of the maritime dominion of England is to be found in the instructions given to her admirals. Those given in the name of Edward III are deserving of particular notice, as they contain the following words: "Whereas our progenitors the kings of England have before these times been Lord of the English Sea on every side, yea, and defenders thereof against the invasions of enemies; and seeing it would very much grieve us if our kingly honour in this kind of defence should be lost in our time &c". The remainder of this document enjoins to the two admirals to pursue a French fleet intended for the assistance of the Scots and concludes with ordering them not to molest those vessels which do not carry supplies to the enemy.[47] In an address

---

friends to disturb the peace of his territory by their mutual hostilities, which he had in that case clearly a right to forbid.

As to the table showing the limits assigned to foreign vessels, which Selden inserts after the proclamation of King James, the tenor expressly contradicts the inferences which he draws from it, for its object is stated clearly to show the extent of the maritime jurisdiction of England by drawing a straight line from one cape or promontory to another and continuing the same operation along the whole coast. Therefore we must conclude from that very document that James I had consented to circumscribe his maritime jurisdiction with very narrow limits and much narrower than those which Selden lays out for him.

[47] Edward III was undoubtedly a very ambitious prince and might well have aspired to the dominion of the seas since he struggled so long to conquer France and Scotland. He had so much the greater advantage on the seas, that maritime affairs had for a long time been attended to in England while they were absolutely neglected in France. Nevertheless, the commission delivered to his admirals and quoted by Selden only proves the inclination and pretensions of Edward and not at all his rights; for that commission is but a municipal act, it is like those protestations which princes conceal in their archives to be produced at a more favorable time. Besides, Edward does not say that the dominion of the sea belongs to him; but only that his predecessors were masters of the sea; which in figurative style signifies that their power was preponderant on the ocean and so it was with respect to the northern powers and still more so with respect to France. But superiority of strength is not the same thing with the right of sovereignty or ownership, for the legitimate effect of force is power and not right. This was the whole extent of the maritime dominion asserted by Edward in the commissions given to his admirals. He endeavoured to maintain it by preventing the French from carrying supplies to the King of Scotland against whom he was carrying on a desperate war, and he

presented to the same Edward III, it is stated: "That the English in ages past were ever renowned for sea affairs, and they had also so numerous and splendid a navy that the people of all countries esteemed and called the king, 'King of Sovereign of the sea', &c.".[48] And a petition of the Parliament to Henry V is concluded in these terms: "The Commons do pray that seeing our Sovereign Lord the King and his illustrious progenitors have ever been Lords of the Sea, &c.".[49]

It results from those addresses, 1st, that both houses of Lord and Commons did with one consent affirm that the King of England is Lord of the Sea; 2nd, that the sea whereof they speak is the whole of that which flows between France and England: *des côtes d'ambe parties del meer*; 3rd, that the Parliament had a right to impose a tribute upon all foreigners passing thro' that sea, as well as customs in ports. King Henry V acted in this manner in his sole capacity of King of England without respect to his quality of King of France.

Not only the national authorities, but foreigners have solemnly acknowledged the maritime dominion of England. The truth of this assertion appears, 1st, from the lowering of sails by foreign vessels before those of England; 2nd, from an action instituted under the reign of Edward I by several foreign nations against Rayner Grimbald, Admiral of France, in which they acknowledged the maritime dominion of England; and lastly, from the recognition of the said dominion by the Earl of Flanders, under the reign of Edward II in a Memorial presented by his ambassadors about some acts of piracy committed by the

---

entertained no fears of the resentment of Philip de Valois, nor of Jean, his successor.

48 This again is a municipal act, and therefore insufficient. Besides, the words *king of the sea* are here of no more validity than in the admiral's commission; they imply force, but not right. This piece of flattery from the Parliament to the King may be classed with those adulatory expressions which are so frequently used by those who solicit favours from men in power.

49 We refer the reader to the preceding note [48 above] and to the history of the reign of Henry V, when engaged in the conquest of France.

English at sea in the vicinity of Crauden.[50] The Memorial expressly states: *Ipse (Edward) ex dominus dicti maris (anglicani)*, the said Edward is Lord of the English Sea.

Everybody knows that the lowering of the sails at sea is not merely a mark of respect, but an acknowledgement of the sovereignty and dominion of the ocean;[51] at any rate, the French

---

[50] Where is the town of Crauden situated? Selden does not mention it, and it cannot be found on the maps. It is probably some obscure place on the coast of England. Be that as it may, the Flemings had been plundered by Englishmen and their crimes carried into England. They were therefore doubly entitled to apply for redress to Edward II, whether they had been plundered on the high sea or on the coast of England. And he might well have done them justice, tho' he had not the least claim to the sovereignty of the sea, except the jurisdictional waters on the coast. Nothing farther can be inferred from the language of the petition, for the words *dicti maris* are applicable only to the coast near Craudon and not to the sea at large. Besides, how is it possible to reconcile the pretended acknowledgment by the Earl of Flanders of the maritime supremacy of England with the immense trade carried on by the Flemings, particularly with the Hanse Towns, and with that which the Dutch Towns, members of that independent and powerful league, carried on in the northern seas? How can it be supposed that the Hanse Towns should have submitted to receive licenses and safe conducts from England to sail to the ports of Flanders? History informs us that that league was considered as an independent power, that it exercised a real sovereignty at sea, and that it was formidable even to England. And, indeed, it is well known that in the time of Henry IV, the Hanse Towns prohibited all trade with England, captured all the English vessels, landed and committed great depredations in several English provinces, and at last compelled Edward IV to sue in 1474 for the mediation of Charles the Bold, Duke of Burgundy. A treaty was signed at Utrecht, by which it appears that the King of England was far from being in a situation to prescribe laws on the sea and to claim the dominion thereof, for he thought himself very fortunate in securing a free trade in the Baltic. If prior to those events the kings of England were sovereigns of the Northern Sea and of the Sea of Flanders, we must confess that their right of *admission* and *exclusion* (see note [a]), the cornerstone of that sovereignty, was on that occasion shaken to its very foundation (See the History of the Confederacy of the Hanse Towns), but it did not suit Selden to dwell on such melancholy events, neither did it suit his purpose to take notice of the power of the House of Austria, after it had acquired the sovereignty of the Low Countries.

[51] The lowering of the sails is a mark of respect paid to a vessel of war on account of the dignity of its sovereign, and not at all an acknowledgement

of maritime dominion. It is an act of courtesy and not of duty; it was introduced by usage, and usage may abolish it. Besides, it only takes place in the waters of this country to which the vessel of war belongs. In order to be satisfied that the formality of lowering the sails and striking the flag has never been considered as an acknowledgement of the dominion of the sea, it will be sufficient to call to mind the war which Cromwell waged against the Dutch, which ended by the treaty of peace of 1654. It will not be improper to place here a short historical account of that transaction.

The Dutch, considered as partisans of the Stuart family, were so much the more suspected by the long parliament and Cromwell himself that they secretly supplied the Royalists with arms; and as the complaints made on that subject were without effect, orders were given to capture all Dutch vessels on board of which arms and ammunition should be found. That measure insensibly led the two countries to an open rupture. The plan of the British was either to invite the two rising republics under one head, or to destroy that of the United Provinces, the wealth and power of which the British were exceedingly jealous. The scheme of Union having been rejected by the Dutch, the leaders in the long parliament began a negociation with them about the restoration of peace, with a view to draw them into an offensive and defensive alliance. The point principally insisted upon by England was the expulsion from Holland of all the member of the Royal family, as well as their adherents, and namely of William and Mary, Prince and Princess of Orange. That negociation was broken by the English ambassadors on account of the insults they experienced at The Hague; it was immediately after that rupture, in the year 1651, that the celebrated Act of Navigation was made, by which it was enacted that no goods should be imported into the British dominions, either from Asia, Africa, America, or even from the continent of Europe, except on board of British vessels. The States General complained, but in vain, of this rigorous decree, and an unexpected naval engagement in which the English had the advantage broke the negociations which had been resumed and raised the tone of the long parliament. The war, therefore, was continued; but at last the Dutch again sued for peace, and among the conditions proposed by the Parliament was that of acknowledging the dominion of England over the sea. That Article was thus expressed: "The vessels of war and merchantmen of the United Provinces, whether sailing alone or in squadrons, meeting at sea with an English man of war or any ship in the service of England and carrying her national flag, shall strike their colours and lower their top gallant sails until they have passed the British man of war, and they shall submit to be searched, if required, and to gain all other marks of respect due to the said republic of England, to which the dominion and sovereignty over the British Seas of right belong". The Dutch ambassadors, it is said, made no observation about the first point, but exclaimed against the right of search, as it might occasion disorders and confusion, they above all complained that the stipulation was not mutual; but Cromwell persisted in his demands, and it was even the wish of the Parliament that the Dutch should pay a tribute for the liberty of fishing on the British coasts. The public themselves thought that the demands of the Parliament were exorbitant and that endeavoured to justify itself by causing the *Mare clausum, sue de dominis maris* of Selden to be translated into English. That translation was published by express order of Parliament. The translator, in his dedication, extols the great influence of the pen upon public opinion and public events; and he spares no pains to set off the merit of Selden's work, altho' dedicated to Charles I, who a very short time before had lost his head upon a scaffold.

But while the long parliament were contriving the means of carrying on the war and of preparing a glorious peace, it was dissolved by Cromwell, who now assumed the title of *Protector*; and that new sovereign soon concluded a peace with the United Provinces. Altho' he dictated the terms of that peace, and altho' he had before insisted on the article concerning the dominion of the sea, he was contented with stipulating that the freedom of trade and navigation should be restored between the two nations, according to the laws and statutes of the respective republics, who reciprocally bound themselves to defend the ships of each other, in case they should be attacked by some other power; but the honors of the flat was exclusively granted to England, and it was agreed that the Dutch vessels of war should on all occasions strike their colours before those of Great Britain.

Cromwell was blamed for having been satisfied with that stipulation because it left the questions respecting the dominion of the sea undecided and the fisheries still open; and it is said that Munke considered Cromwell's conduct in this instance as little short of treason in thus making a sudden peace and sacrificing all the advantages of the war by means of which he might easily have raised himself to the throne [Comble, *Life of Munke*, p. 74).

We have thought it necessary to enter into these details in order to show the opinion of the English nation the estimation in which the work of Selden was held at that time and probably is to this day; and above all the state in which things were placed by Oliver Cromwell. It is clear from what we have related and from the terms of the treaty of peace that notwithstanding the pretensions of the long Parliament, the Protector, altho' he had it in his power to have dictated the conditions of the peace, was satisfied with vain honors paid to the English fleet in token of its pre-eminence over that of the United Provinces, and that he did not secure even an indirect recognition of the dominion of England over the sea, or at

must understand it so, for they formerly, but in vain, endeavoured to cause themselves, by a similar formality, to be acknowledged for the Sovereigns of the Sea. Their kings Henry II in 1555 and Henry III in 1584 issued Edicts or ordinances to compel foreign vessels sailing on the seas in the vicinity of France to strike their top sails before the ships of the Royal Navy as an acknowledgement of the maritime dominion of the French kings,[52] but the former of those Edicts was not registered by the parliament of Paris, and the second was only sanctioned with modifications referring to ancient usage. And indeed, both those Edicts were contrary to the rights of their neighbours and

---

least of that which is called British. Whatever may have been the cause of this conduct, we are authorized to say, or rather to repeat, that the ceremony of striking the flag is not an acknowledgement of that sovereignty of the seas, which Selden is pleased to attribute to the kings of Great Britain.

I shall conclude this article by citing a note of Barbeyrac upon Puffendorf. The author lays it down (*Droit de la nature et des gens*, Book IV, ch. V, §8) that it is now the established custom for foreign vessels passing by a fortress or a man of war belonging to a prince who claims the sovereignty of that part of the sea thro' which they sail to lower their flag as an acknowledgement of his jurisdiction. On which the commentator makes the following remark: "Mr. Bynkershoek maintains that this is not always an acknowledgment of the sovereignty of that prince (to whom the honor is granted) over that part of the sea where it is paid. As for example, says he, the States General in their treaties of peace made in the years 1654, 1662, 1667, 1674, and 1684 obliged themselves to pay the honors of the flag to the ships of the King of England in all the northern seas as far as Cape Finistère, but that was only because, according to the law of nations, all republics ought to give place to a crowned head and to those that represent him. In short, the custom of saluting in some shape or other the vessels of such nations to whom we own our inferiority is not so new as our author would insinuate.

[52] Whatever may have been the object and the fate of those two Edicts, they do incontestably prove that neither Henry II nor Henry III, two of the weakest kings that ever reigned over France, acknowledged that pretended supremacy of Great Britain. I pass over the conduct attributed by Selden to the parliament of Paris as being foreign to the question; it only proves the ignorance of that body in political affairs and its pretensions to influence the operations of the Government.

of foreign nations in general.[53] But what the French have in vain required as a token of their maritime sovereignty belongs incontestably by a long prescription to England as a proof and a consequence of her supremacy over the ocean.[54] Her right to compel foreign vessels to strike their sails before hers may be traced back to a period of more than four centuries ago, as is proved by the following Edict of King John, addressed in the year 1200 to the commander of the Royal Fleet employed in naval expeditions (which then principally occupied the southern sea): "If any ships or vessels, whether laden or empty, shall refuse to strike their sails at the command of the king's lieutenant or his deputy, but shall make resistance and be taken fighting against the king's fleet; such ships or vessels shall be reputed enemies and shall be confiscated as enemies goods, together with their cargoes, unless the owners or masters thereof shall come in and show that the same ships and goods belong to the friends of our Lord the King, in which case they shall be punished for their rebellion by imprisonment at the discretion of the court". It was considered as high treason to refuse by striking the sails to acknowledge the maritime dominion of Great Britain; penalties were inflicted in the same manner as if the offence had been committed at land within the British territory.[55]

---

[53] This remark is truly curious. How does it happen that the Edicts of the two kings of France were opposed to the rights of all foreign nations, and that the pretensions of England were not so? I am surprised that Selden did not say that those pretensions are advantageous to mankind, and that the interest of the world requires that England should be the absolute mistress of commerce, fishing, and navigation. Similar operations might have been necessary to excite the men who composed the Parliament of England, but we have already shown that they had but little effect upon the mind of Oliver Cromwell, and it is not likely that they will produce much upon that of any man endowed with common sense.

[54] We think that we have sufficiently demonstrated in the first part of this work that no prescription can exist between nations. Therefore, we shall not again undertake to refute what Selden says on that respect. But we ought to observe that that author's edifice being entirely built on that imaginary foundation, it must necessarily crumble with it entirely to pieces.

[55] There is but little to be remarked on the subject of that ordinance, as well as upon the application which Selden makes of it. I shall surely say that he ought to have named those nations which complied with the Edict

As to the action instituted against Rayner de Grimbald, which we have already mentioned, the state of the case is as follows: Philip the Fair, King of France, and Edward I, King of England, being at war with each other, it was mutually agreed that the navigation of merchantmen should not be interrupted. That was called sufferance of war. In 1303 the two kings made together a treaty of alliance by which it was stipulated that they should defend one another against all other whomsoever, except the church of Rome and except also on the part of the King of England, his son-in-law, John, Duke of Brabant, and on the part of the King of France, Albert, King of the Romans and John, Earl of Hainault. And it was moreover stipulated in these words: "Item, it is granted that neither party shall receive, maintain, comfort, or cause any aid or comfort to be given to the enemies of the other, neither shall suffer them to receive comfort, aid, or succor, either of armed men, provisions, or anything else from his dominions or territories, but shall forbid under the penalty of forfeiture of body and goods, and hinder with all his power, honesty and bona fide, any aid or comfort being given to the said enemies within his territory or dominion, and their receiving any kind of comfort, aid or succor in armed men, horses, armour, provisions or any other thing whatever".

It is to be believed that many violations of the maritime truce took place during the war and it being feared that they might be renewed in the course of that which was ready to break out between the king of England on the one side and the king of France and the Earl of Flanders on the other; the two kings appointed joint commissioners to take cognizance of all trespasses, mesprisions, and breaches of truce or sufferances between the said kings of England and France, which might be committed on either side, on the sea coast of England, and others on this side, and also towards Normandy and other sea coasts on the other side" (*es costères de la mer d'Engleterre, et autres par*

---

of Jean Lacksland. It could not be Philip Augustus, who deprived that prince of Normandy and of all the other dominions which he had in France, with the exception of Guienne, and who even summoned him to appear before the Tribunal of the peers of France, who sentenced him to suffer death for the murder of his nephew, Arthur.

cedea, et au sing perdevers Normandie et autres costeres de la mer per de là). War having broken out between Philip, King of France, and Guy, Earl of Flanders, Regnier de Grimbaud or Grimbald had been appointed commander of the French fleet. He was accused of having spoliated the merchants sailing to Flanders, and the attornies or procurators of the prelates and nobility as well as of the Admiral and of the cities and towns of England, together with those of almost all the nations of Europe, exhibited a libel of complaint to the above mentioned commissioners. The introductory part of this document runs thus: "To you the Lord Auditors, deputed by the kings of England and France to redress the wrongs done to the people of their *Realms* and other lands subject to their dominions by land and sea, in time of peace and truce – Show the procurators of the prelates and nobles and of the Admiral of the Sea of England, and of the commonalties of the cities and towns, and of the merchants, marines, messengers, and travelers, and all others of the Kingdom of England and other laws subject to the dominion of the said King of England and of other places, such as of the marine of Genoa, Catalonia, Spain, Germany, Zealand, Holland, Friesland, Denmark, Norway, and of sundry other places of the empire: — That whereas the kings of England by reason of the said kingdom have been from time immemorial in peaceable possession of the Sea of England and islands lying therein &c". And afterwards it proceeds to state that: "Monsieur Reyner Grimbaltz, Master of the Navy of the said King of France, who styles himself Admiral of the said sea, deputed by his Lord aforesaid for his war against the Flemings, after the said alliance made and affirmed, against the form and force of the said alliance and the intention of those who made it, the office of Admiral in the said Sea of England, by commission of the said King of France, tortiously undertook and used for one year and more, taking the people and merchants of the kingdom of England and elsewhere, passing thro' the said sea, with their goods, and the people thus taken delivered to the prison of his said Lord the King of France &c. — Grimbaud in his defence alleged his commission of Admiral, and the indulgence granted by the King of England in consequence of the above mentioned treaty of alliance. He therefore acknowledged the dominion of

Great Britain over the British and adjacent seas; and that dominion was also formally acknowledged by all the nations who were parties to the libel of complaint;[56] and it is important to observe that about the same time, a little before the signing of the treaty of alliance, the King of England did homage to the King of France for the Duchy of Aquitaine, the Earldom of Ponthieu, and other provinces which he held in that Kingdom and was also some time before wholly deprived of them by an *arrêt* of the parliament of Paris, and that about one hundred years before that time, King John was forever dispossessed of Normandy and all his endeavours to regain it, even a little before the making of the treaty of alliance, were fruitless. These facts are highly important in as much as they show that the maritime supremacy of the kings of England is not derived from the possession of those provinces from which the adjoining seas have borrowed their names, but from a right inherent to their crown and kingdom.[57]

That right was also formally acknowledged by Robert, Earl of Flanders, who sent an ambassador to Edward II, to demand redress for some depredations committed in the British Sea near a place called Crauden. It must, however, be confessed that in Flanders and Zealand, besides the mouths of rivers, there are

---

[56] What! All the nations of Europe sent procurators to London to do homage to Edward I, as the sovereign Lord of the Seas? The fact, indeed, would be remarkable if it could be believed. But on close examination of the famous petition, it is easy to be convinced that it is the work of an English lawyer who makes foreigners who probably were unacquainted with the Norman idiom and who cannot be supposed to have been in London at the time, speak the same language with the prelates, nobles, cities, and towns of England. Those foreigners, besides, cared very little how their petition was worded, provided it produced the intended effect; and yet it may be remarked that it was addressed to the joint commissioners appointed by the kings of England and France, who were consequently acknowledged to have both an equal right. However it may be, this petition exhibits on the face of it such a map of absurdity, and the inference which Selden draws from it is so very ridiculous, that we will not trespass on the patience of our readers by dwelling any longer on that strange document and the no less extraordinary arguments to which it has given rise.

[57] We have already refuted this paradox.

many windings and turnings of the sea, whereby the land is so interwoven with it that it would be difficult not to consider it as forming an indivisible whole and consequently as belonging to the continental jurisdiction; that is to say, in the language of ancient records, *deins la jurisdiction et l'estrem de la meer de Flandres*, "within the jurisdiction and stream of the sea of Flanders". But excepting those parts of the sea which must be considered as ports, all the rest, that is to say, the ocean which lies between those transmarine coasts and England, has always been considered as belonging to the jurisdiction of Great Britain.[58]

---

[58] Here is a plain and direct assertion, but where are the proofs in support of it? We are very often under the necessity of asking Selden this question. If in order to obtain redress for some depredations the Earl of Flanders flattered the vanity of Edward II, if he recognized that prince as sovereign of the British Sea, it does not follow that he thereby acknowledged him as sovereign of the Sea of Flanders; and altho' he had made such an improbable acknowledgement, of what consequence would it have been as to other nations? The whole sea, with the exception of that part which washes the shore, is free and common to all. Therefore supposing that the Earl of Flanders had renounced his right in favor of England, it could in no manner prejudice that of others; and notwithstanding his pretended acknowledgement, the Sea of Flanders has remained free to all the other nations of Europe. This is proved, amongst other things, by the free navigation and commerce of the Hanse Confederacy, not only with the cities of Flanders, but also with all the maritime ports of the low countries, quite to the Texel. That intercourse necessarily produced a most active and extensive, as well as profitable, navigation, for the Hanse Towns alone supplied the Flemings with the produce of the northern States, to whom they carried in exchange all the articles of manufacture which were found at that time in abundance and in the greatest perfection in the cities of Flanders. That trade was carried on, as it were, in the view of England. And yet that power did not attempt to prevent it, and she would not have dared to make any opposition to it because the Hanse Towns had the superiority in the northern seas. Besides, what motive had she to be jealous of the trade of those countries? She hardly carried on any external commerce, and she manufactured nothing but a few coarse articles. During several centuries, her whole trade was carried on thro' the Hanse Towns, who purchased the raw materials which the English did not know how to manufacture and gave in exchange the productions of the north. That state of things subsisted even under the reign of Edward III. Flanders was annexed to the Duchy of Burgundy, and the power of the Duke increased in such a manner that it

Such are in substance the arguments by which our author endeavours to prove the pretended dominion of England over what he calls the Eastern Seas, under which denomination he included the German Ocean, the North Sea, the British channel, and the Gulf of Gascony, otherwise called the Bay of Biscay. From thence he passed on to the Sea of Ireland and that which flows to the westward of that kingdom. The islands situated in the Irish Sea, such as *Mona* (now the Isle of Man) and the Hebrides, have experienced great changes, but at last they passed as well as Ireland under the dominion of Great Britain, so that the St. George Channel as an interfluent sea, incontestably belongs to the British realms.[59]

---

rivaled that of the King of France, his paramount sovereign. How is it to be believed that a prince under such circumstances would have consented to acknowledge England as sovereign of the Flemish seas? Certain it is, Selden brings no kind of proof in support of that assertion, so difficult it is to destroy the evidence of known historical facts. We ought to add that the commercial treaties made between the kings of England and the sovereigns of Flanders and of the low countries from 1406 to 1495 offered very favorable opportunities to secure the claims of England to maritime dominion, even by relaxing from it in particular instances; on the contrary, those treaties as well as Selden are silent upon that important point.

[59] Here the question is no more of the dominion of England over the high sea, but merely whether the strait which is called St. George Channel, surrounded with coasts belonging to the King of England and including several islands, is, or is not, a part of the British dominion, and whether foreign vessels are free to navigate therein.

Supposing that all trade were prohibited to foreigners with the ports situated on St. George Channel, including the Orkney Islands, those would, of course, have no cause to induce them to resort to it, and therefore merchant vessels sailing therein would be justly suspected of the intention to carry on a fraudulent trade. Then the British Government would be authorized to search and detain them. The case would be different were that same channel a passage leading to other countries independent from Great Britain, for then, that passage would be free, and the British Government would not prohibit it, without violating the rights of other nations. But St. George Channel only leads to the northern seas which surround the Arctic pole, which is impassable by the ice, and is not even supposed to be inhabited. Therefore, no probable object could authorize the navigation of foreigners thro' St. George Channel, otherwise called the Irish Sea.

As to the Western ocean, it is likewise under the British jurisdiction and extends quite to America. When Sir Humphrey Gilbert did by authority of Queen Elizabeth transport a colony into the new world with a view to recover certain lands in the eastern part of North America, the Queen was by him put into possession for herself and her successors of the port called John in the Island of Baccalaos (Newfoundland), and also of the whole sea as well as land on every side for the space of six hundred miles. There he received his new kingdom of the Queen, as her vassal, by the delivery of a branch and turf, being the usual ceremony in England for transferring the ownership of territorial possessions. Such is the origin of the title of the Queen and her successors to that island; nor was anything more required for transferring the possession of it to her, for as *Paulus* properly says: "it is not necessary that he who intends to take possession of a field should perambulate the whole, but it is sufficient if he enter upon any part thereof, so long as he does it with intent to possess the field in its utmost extent", which may be said of the seas, as well as of unoccupied lands. The observation of *Siculus Flaccus* on certain occupiers of lands is also here perfectly applicable. "They did not", says he, "only occupy so much land as they were able to till, but also all that they received in hopes of being able to cultivate it in future" (*Nec tantum occupaverunt quod colere potuissent, sed quantum in spe colendi reservauere*). It is possible also that the dominion of Great Britain on the immense seas of America does not originate with the possession acquired by Sir Humphrey Gilbert. He rather recovered and enlarged the rights of the Crown, for the Island of Baccalaos (Newfoundland) was added to the British Empire by Sebastian Cabot in the time of Henry VII. Hence it became a custom for some of the commanders of the Royal Navy and for the High Admiral of England (within whose jurisdiction are all the seas subject to the King of England and Ireland as such) to exact a duty from those who came to fish in that sea; which was an unequivocal token of supremacy. The rates of those duties were afterwards settled by a law of Edward VI.[60]

---

[60] England, the sovereign of the Atlantic to the American continent? We have not courage to refute such a nameless pretension. It is strange indeed

The dominion of the King of Great Britain over the Eastern Sea of Scotland is evidenced by the exclusive right of fishing which the English possess in that sea; foreigners are not allowed to fish there without leave first obtained at Edinburgh. There is an old act of the parliament of Scotland which provides: that all those who shall fish for herring on the coast of Scotland, or within the Isles, or out within the friths, shall bring them to free ports &c., where they may be sold to the inhabitants of the same

---

that a man who travels over a country, or wanders thro' the fields, should thereby acquire a right of property to the lands thro' which he has passed. But to be serious, an Englishman named Gilbert sails at random over the ocean in order to discover some distant lands and arrives by chance at the Island of Baccalaos (Newfoundland), takes possession of the port of St. John's, and does homage to the Queen Elizabeth for the whole island. Let us suppose that this mode of acquiring property is lawful (for with this question we have nothing to do), the shores of the island must have made a part of the acquisition, because of them there might be a real, continued possession with intent to keep the same. But to extend that possession and intent to the whole route which Gilbert has sailed over, that is to say, to the entire ocean, is a consequence which I cannot understand, and for that reason I shall not undertake to refute it. I shall, however, observe that the Portuguese were the first who sailed to the East Indies round the Cape of Good Hope. The ocean therefore in that direction exclusively belongs to them. The same might be said of the course which the Spaniards kept when they sailed the first to San-Salvador, one of the Bermuda Islands, and from thence to Hispaniola, and why should not England claim the dominion over seas which Drake sailed, who was the first, prompted by avarice, who undertook to circumnavigate the globe? These inferences are unavoidable, or Selden's proposition is essentially false. We are clearly of the latter opinion.

After all, supposing that the island of Newfoundland had been lawfully acquired, those placed in authority over it might have exacted tribute from foreigners coming for the first time after the acquisition to fish upon its coasts, or in its creeks or havens because those waters belonged to the jurisdiction of the island. But they had no right, except that of the strongest, to exclude those who had been used to fish there before the arrival of the English. Still less could they prohibit them to fish in open sea, and particularly on what are called the Grand and Little Banks. And if we were even to admit that the English had an incontestable right to exact a tribute from foreign fishermen, in the seas and on the banks of Newfoundland, yet that could not be considered as a symbol of dominion over the whole western sea from Iceland to America.

Kingdom; whereby His Majesty's customs be not defrauded and his liege subjects not deprived of the commodity appointed to them by God. Sir William Scott says that a special convention had been made with the Dutch, by which it has been agreed that they should not fish at the distance of less than eighty miles from the coast, but that that regulation gradually fell into disuse, as well in consequence of the negligence of the offices appointed to see it carried into execution, as of the audacity of the Dutch.[61] Thus an end was put to the freedom of fishing which foreigners formerly enjoyed by virtue of treaties.[62] But the more northerly sea which lies opposite to Scotland was in former times under the dominion of the Danes and Norwegians, who owned the islands situated in that part of the ocean; for that reason the inhabitants of the Orkney Islands speak the Gothic tongue even to this day. Four hundred and sixty years ago the

---

[61] The convention or agreement quoted by Selden only proves (and we do not contest it) the exclusive right of the British to fish on the coasts of Scotland, and between and round the islands, that is to say, in their own waters; but it cannot be inferred from thence that England had a right of dominion over the whole of the eastern sea, for it would be then necessary to prove that neither the Danes nor the Norwegians dared to fish for herring in those parts without leave from the King of England. Now it is in proof that the Dutch did not acknowledge that pretended dominion, for England was obliged to come to an agreement with them and to draw a line at the distance of 80 miles (about 26 leagues) from the coast to ensure the tranquility of the respective fishing vessels, and Selden says that even that line was not respected by the Dutch. As to the modern state of things, everyone knows that the nations of Europe carry on the herring fishery without applying to the Court of London for a license.

[62] Treaties and conventions are contracts. The respective nations stipulate their interests therein as they think proper, and as circumstances require. They adopt the rules of the law of nations or deviate from them, as to them seems best. And those who sacrifice their interests to others have nobody to blame but themselves; but their private stipulations cannot invalidate the principles of the universal law of nations, nor affect the rights of other nations. Can it be believed that if the French, Spaniards, oar Russians were to fish for herring in the North Sea, England might lawfully oppose to them the conventions made between her and Holland in the reign of Edward II? Besides, that very convention proves that there was a difference of opinion and that the Dutch did not much respect the pretended dominion of Great Britain.

said islands to the number of thirty-two had a king who paid to that of Norway a tribute of ten marks of gold on his accession to the crown. By a treaty made between Alexander III, King of scots, and Magnus IV, King of Norway, and by another between Robert Bruce, King of Scotland, and Haquin, King of Norway, the above mentioned islands were annexed to the Kingdom of Scotland, and it was natural that the sea should have passed along with them; yet the dominion of that sea was during the greatest part of the time possessed by the Norwegian king. But in the year 1470, Christian I, King of Denmark and Sweden, ceded all his rights as well to the Orkney and Shetland islands, as to all those which lie in the hither part of the Northern Sea. Thus it was that those islands, together with the dominion of the sea, were transferred to the kings of Scotland.[63]

Now we have yet to speak of the vast northern ocean. It washes the islands belonging to the Crowns of Norway and Denmark, and namely Iceland, &c. The right of navigating and fishing in those seas gave rise to several contests between the kings of England and those of Norway. There are treaties existing by which it was agreed that licenses for fishing should be delivered to the English every seven years. Some particular circumstances prevented their being demanded and renewed, and England asserted under the reign of Elizabeth that she had acquired the right of navigating and fishing in that sea by prescription;[64] the point was contested with warmth on both sides, but nothing was finally settled. As to the sea to the northward of Iceland and towards Greenland, it does belong to the King of Great Britain. For that sea, before it was ever used or frequented for the purpose of fishing and particularly for the whole fishery, was first discovered by a company of English merchants trading to Muscovy. Thus, that sea by being first

---

[63] The dominion of Great Britain over the sea which surrounds the Orkney and Shetland islands cannot be decided because that sea is an appendage to the territorial jurisdiction; but it does not follow that Great Britain acquired with those islands the dominion of the Northern Sea. It would be idle to attempt to elucidate by argument so self-evident a proposition.

[64] That plea would not be admitted between individuals in courts of justice and, of course, it cannot avail between nations among whom there is no such thing as prescription.

discovered and occupied became by the taking of corporal possession with intent to keep and preserve the same, the property of the first occupant, in the same manner as all other things not before reduced into natural or legal possession, and therefore, King James was well warranted in writing to Henry Wolton, his ambassador in Holland, and to his other envoys, that he had the sole and exclusive right to the Northern Sea near the coast of Greenland.[65]

---

[65] How many erroneous propositions are contained in this passage! So much so that our readers might suspect that we have not made a faithful extract from the original. We therefore refer them to the text itself of our author. Book II, ch. XXXII.

The author says that the English Company trading to Muscovy, having been the first that discovered and occupied the North Sea, that sea became by the effect of corporal and mental possession, the property of the first occupant. But from what circumstance is to be inferred that mental occupation of a sea over which adventurers are sailing at random? What corporeal possession can they be said to have taken of a fluid in constant motion and which by its nature cannot be confined. What! A vessel tossed about by the winds and waves shall be said to be taking possession of that sea which every moment threatens to bury it in its unfathomable abyss! And thus it is that England pretends to have acquired the dominion of the sea and of the continent of Greenland. Were her merchants commissioned to take possession in her name? Was Greenland an unknown and uninhabited country? Had it never before been frequented by Europeans? Without all these conditions, the English merchants could acquire nothing in the name of their sovereign. Greenland could only be subdued by force of arms and it never was in any manner subdued. Where then is the title of the kings of England? When the Biscayans used to fish for whales in those seas, did they provide themselves with licenses from any power whatever? And now is not that fishery open and free to all nations, altho' very few avail themselves of that liberty?

As to the claim of James I by his ambassadors in Holland, it did not extend to the dominion of the North Sea, but to the rights of fishing on the coast of Greenland. Let us hear what Hume says on this subject (History of England. (London, 1789), VI, p. 183): "Greenland is thought to have been discovered during this reign; and the whale fishery was carried on with great success. But the industry of the Dutch, in spite of all opposition, soon deprived the English of this source of riches". Therefore, notwithstanding the declaration of King James, the English never enjoyed the exclusive or quiet possession of that country, and if her possession, such as it was, could give her the Empire of the northern sea, she must at least have shared it with Holland.

In order completely to elucidate this question, it will not be amiss to give here a short account of the discovery of Greenland.

According to Selden, that country was first discovered by a company of English merchants associated for the purpose of trading to Muscovy. But at what time did that company exist? In the fifteenth century, the whole commerce of Russia, which had not yet any settlement on the Baltic, centered in the free city of Novgorod and was entirely carried on thro' the Hanse Towns. The Czar Ivan Basilowicz subdued that Republic and destroyed their trade in which the British had no share. Under the successor of that prince, England, jealous of the prosperity of the Spaniards and Portuguese who enjoyed the treasures of the Indies, resolved to seek a northern passage to the rich countries of the East. Three ships under the command of Sir Hugh Willoughby sailed from England in May 1553, but were dispersed by a storm, and one only arrived at the place of rendezvous, which was a port of Norway; it appears that the two others were driven to the coast of Greenland, and it was they who in their disrupted state are said to have conquered that country, together with the whole of the Hyperborean Sea. The master of the former vessel, however, resolved with his companions to brave all dangers; they again put to sea, and after a few week's navigation, they anchored in the Bay of St. Nicholas, near Archangel, discovered for the first time by foreigners. The British were indebted to that fortunate circumstance for their direct trade with Muscovy, the privileges they obtained, and the formation of the Company above mentioned.

Let us now compare facts and dates with what the history of Denmark tells us concerning Greenland.

A Norwegian called Eric the Red sailed from Iceland, where he had taken refuge, and landed in Greenland in the year 981; it was he who gave it that name. Leif, his son, gave information of that discovery to Oluf Truggesen, King of Norway, and returned to his father in the year 1000. In 1023 the new colony became tributary of the King of Norway; the Greenlanders who had revolted against King Magnus in 1256 were subdued in 1261. The plague which in 1348 broke out in the North was the cause that Greenland was lost sight of; the last Bishop was appointed in 1406; the Norwegian colony still subsisted in 1540, but it was soon after entirely forgotten. A little while afterwards the kings of Denmark made new attempts to rediscover it, but did not at first succeed. An Englishman named Frobisher landed there in 1576 and gave his name to a place which at this day is impracticable on account of the ice. The King of Denmark sent three vessels in 1605, five in the following year, and Munck who landed in 1616 gave Cape Farewell its name. In 1636 the

Thus we have presented to our readers a faithful analysis of the work of Selden; he concluded with quoting some verses addressed by Grotius to King James I. We shall not insert them

---

Copenhagen Company was created, and vessels were sent from Denmark to Greenland in 1654 and 1670. A short time afterwards Greenland was again forgotten, when at last it was thought of returning thither. The whole of the eastern part was found covered with ice, and it was impossible to effect a landing or to learn the fate of the colonists who had been sent there; they then proceed to the western coast, which was called New Greenland. There it was that the whale fishery was established. The Dutch made themselves master of it and of the trade with the natives. A Norwegian priest named Egède determined in 1718 to go to Greenland; he made his settlement on the western coast in 64 degrees latitude, employed himself in converting the aborigenes, and settled a few colonies of Danes. An association was made under the name of the Greenland Company to whom the King of Denmark gave considerable assistance; but they did not prosper, and the Company having refused to raise a new stock, the King took upon himself that branch of commerce. He established a permanent colony in Greenland and erected a fortress to protect it; but in 1731 he gave orders to all his subjects to leave that country and destroy the colony. New settlers were afterwards sent thither, and that new colony still subsists at this day. The trade of Greenland is carried on by a company of Danes. The Dutch are obliged to keep at the distance of several miles from the coast. I ought to add that besides Frobisher, another Englishman named John Davis discovered in 1585 the strait which bears his name and that another Englishman of the name of Baffin discovered in 1622 the Bay which is named after him.

Those details of which I have given the precise dates do not require a long commentary, for they evidently shew that so early as the tenth century the Norwegians landed in Greenland; that, of course, if we admit the right of the first occupant, it is in favor of Norway and that England could not claim it in consequence of the discovery made by the Muscovy Company, which only could have taken place in the sixteenth century. And even tho' we should make an allowance for the voyages undertaken by Davis, Frobisher, and Baffin, we could not trace them farther than the above mentioned period; and we see that since that time, the Danes have restored and maintained their relations with Greenland and that the Copenhagen Company was formed at the very time that Selden was writing his book. I pass over the settlements made by Egède in the last century and the present state of things, for I must stop at the precise period of time at which it has pleased Selden to award to England the dominion of Greenland, the whale fishery, and the whole Hyperborean Ocean.

here, because Grotius the poet and courtier is not Grotius the Philosopher and historian.

On an attentive examination of the facts and principles on which Selden rests his system, and the inferences which he has drawn from them, it will be easy to be convinced that the pretensions of England to this exclusive dominion of the sea may be traced back, as the writer says, to fabulous times. That she has assumed in that respect the place of the Roman Republic and constantly made the greatest efforts to maintain herself in that station, but at the same time it will clearly appear that those efforts have at no time produced the effects which Selden attributes to them; and that all the inferences which that author draws from facts and precedents are either exaggerated or inaccurate, or in opposition to the plainest rules of logic. In a word, that all his erudition, arguments, and subtleties exhibit only a series of paralogisms and paradoxes. Be that as it may, we think that confining ourselves to the pretensions relative to the British Channel and that part of the Atlantic Ocean which washes the western part of the French Empire, we may peremptorily decide the question by the following dilemma: either the dominion of Great Britain over the above mentioned seas exists, or does not exist. On the first supposition, the northern, southern, and western nations of Europe never could have sailed thro' the channel without the special permission of Great Britain; in the other case, they had no need of such permission, but might sail where they pleased, *jure proprio*. Now if we search into the numerous commercial treaties made by Portugal, Spain, France, and England herself, with the Flemings, the United Provinces of the Netherlands, Denmark, Sweden, Russia, and the Hanse Towns, we find no trace of such permission being granted by the Government of Great Britain, nor any stipulation to that effect. Therefore, all those treaties prove the non-existence of the dominion of England over the British Channel, or over any part whatever of the French coast and Atlantic Ocean.

We shall conclude these observations by stating the following facts out of Hume's history of England. Henry VIII, in order to equip a fleet, was obliged to hire vessels from Hamburgh, Lubeck, Dantzig, Genoa, and Venice. Elizabeth caused a few ships to be built and prevailed upon the merchants to build such as should be sufficiently large to be of service in case of war. In the year 1582, the number of seamen amount to 14,295, and that of vessels to 1,232, among which only 270 were above 80 tons burthen. What a Navy to conquer and preserve the dominion of the seas! I entreat the reader not to forget that I am speaking of the times in which Selden wrote.

A DISCOURSE ON THE CONDUCT OF THE GOVERNMENT OF GREAT BRITAIN IN RESPECT TO NEUTRAL NATIONS

by

Charles Jenkinson, formerly Lord Hawksbury, now Lord Liverpool

---

The following advertisement is prefixed to the Second London Edition, printed in 1794.

> The following discourse was written in 1757 by Charles Jenkinson, Esq., now Lord Hawksbury. Great Britain was at that time engaged in War with France, and the Republic of Holland refused to conform to those treaties of defensive alliance by which she was then bound to assist Great Britain and suffered her subjects not only to trade with France, but to afford protection to the property of the enemy; to supply him with naval and military stores, and to bring to French ports in Europe the produce of the French West India Islands. The British Government ordered all Dutch ships laden with the property of the enemy, or with naval or military stores, or with the produce of the French West India Islands to be seized and to be brought into port for legal adjudication. The merchants of Holland remonstrated against this measure, which deprived them of a most lucrative trade; but the British Government persevered. This Discourse was written in support of the principles on which the British Government at that time acted. It was translated and re-printed in almost every language of Europe; and it is not re-published, from the best edition, at the desire of several noblemen and gentlemen who think that in the present circumstances it may be equally useful.

A Discourse &c.

It is unhappy for the race of mankind that those collective bodies into which it is divided should be subject to the same passions and animosities as the individuals of which they are compared and not have, like them, some visible superior tribunal which might hear and compose their discussions; this might, perhaps, prevent their appeals which are too frequently made to the sword, where the events of war alone, decide the cause, and the sentences, which passeth on the transgressor, brings also to the injured party a large share of misfortune in the execution of it. The welfare of mankind, however, requires that this necessary evil should be confined within the narrowest bounds; and that a grail, where the proceedings are so destructive should be made as short and as equitable as the nature of it will admit. Is the duty therefore of those who are not concerned in the dispute to be extremely attentive to their conduct, that they may not thereby contribute to render their contest unequal; as far as man is concerned, it is force alone on which the decision depends; to add therefore by any means to the power of one party is manifest injustice to the other, and is besides highly injurious to the rest of mankind, since it necessarily tends to spread discord among nations and from a single spark of contention to light up a general flame.

It might be hoped that a duty like this enforced by such powerful nations would be universally observed; and that no private inferior interest would induce any power to transgress it; if some little profits, the object of greedy individuals, should, perhaps, arise from the violation of it, can a nation in general reap a benefit where public justice receives a wound? To act in opposition to this, in hopes of some present advantage, is to establish a dangerous example which may hereafter prove injurious to ourselves; it is to untie the only bond which holdeth nations happily together, and to banish mutual confidence from the various communities of the world.

Such, however, hath been the mistaken conduct of some neutral States during the present War. France consented to the Treaty of Aix-la-Chapelle, that she might the more securely pursue the objects of her ambitions and that under the disguise of peace she might extend and fortify her possession in a part of the world where her arms in time of open war had always, till then, been successful; for this purpose she had artfully contrived that the American rights should not be determined by that treaty, but be left to the consideration of commissaries, to whose decisions she never meant to pay any regard; Canada was her vulnerable part; this therefore she resolved first to strengthen, and then to enter again with more confidence into war; while we were employed in debating our rights, she took more effectual means to end the contest in her favour; she sent frequent supplies to America; she seized and fortified the passes and navigable rivers of that country, drove the English from their possessions, and built forts on the dominions of Great Britain; when the design was thus far advanced, England saw it in all its tenors, and with spirit determined to support her just rights; though forsaken now in her distress by those allies who owe their independence to her protection, she feared not in such a cause to stand alone against all the efforts of France; she sent forth her naval strength, but the enemy soon rendered the attempts of that ineffectual by resolving never to try its force. In what manner was she now to employ it? One only object remained worthy of its attention and that was to destroy the trade of the enemy, and to intercept the succours which she sent to her dominions in America. though this would not crush at once the evil, it would stop at least the sources that fed it; and might in the end contribute to induce the enemy to consent to a reasonable peace.[66]

---

[66] This picture of the causes and events of the war of 1755 is such as might be expected from the professed advocate of the British Government, but the real state of the facts is so well known at this day that the Court of London can never stand acquired of the charge of inordinate ambition, nor its stigma be fixed on the memory of Louis XV in contradiction of the whole tenor of his life. Those facts may be summed up in a few words. The British court was endeavouring to extend the uncertain limits of Acadia or Nova Scotia by encroaching on those of Canada. This occasioned a few skirmishes between some French and English detachments about the possession of certain ports and furnished the Court of London with a pretext to provoke the war which it had before

France endeavoured again to obviate this stroke by her policy; she took off the tax of 50 sous per ton which she always chooses to keep on foreign freightage; she opened even her American ports and admitted other countries into that choice part of her commerce which, by her maritime regulations, she hath at other times so strictly reserved to herself.[67] Neutral nations seized at once on the advantage, and opened to the enemy new channels for the conveyance of those riches by which the wear was to be nursed and protracted; under the banner of friendship they thus served the cause of the adversary whose wealth secured by that protection would have passed safe and unmolested through our fleet; if Britain, again raising her spirit, had not resolved that by this means her naval power should not be rendered useless and seized on the enemy's property, which she found on board neutral ships. It is well-known, however, that her conduct in this respect hath not been universally approved, and that some neutral nations think they have a right to carry in their vessels unmolested the property of our adversaries. As I here differ with them in sentiment, this is the point on which I intend to discourse.

Great and wide governments have always been jealous of national glory; it is an active principle which, properly cultivated, operates in various actions through every member of the State;[68] to preserve this therefore in its purity, is the duty of

---

meditated. While all were yet in Europe in a state of profound peace, she captured the French seamen who were employed in the Newfoundland fishery and several ships of war and merchantmen. Her object was by this sudden aggression to weaken the French Navy, and she succeeded in it. After this, it is easy to appreciate the frightful picture drawn by Mr. Jenkinson of the ambitious views of Louis XV. as well as of the imminent danger to which the existence of Great Britain was thereby exposed. Those high sounding words were necessary to divert the public attention from the conduct of the Court of London and to colour its arbitrary proceedings by the plea of imperious necessity; in short, to justify the authors of the war of 1755.

[67] Has France by this violated the law of nations, the law of war? This point is one of the principal objects of Mr. Jenkinson's discourse. We examine this question in Chapter XXII.

[68] A true principle, but greatly exaggerated. This is especially the case with regard to relations between nations.

everyone who loves his country. Can it then be wondered that the native of a kingdom always celebrated for its public spirit and its upright faith, at a time when these are called in doubt, should interest himself in its defense? No indecent changes shall here be urged against other countries, it is meant to vindicate the honour of our own. It is to be lamented that the necessity of affairs should at such a season have given occasion to this dispute, particularly with that ancient ally of England;[69] who hath so often fought with her under the same banner, in support of the just rights and privileges of mankind; the zeal of any government to encourage the industry of its people is that a British pen can never disapprove: the principle is noble, and merits even our applause; I only mean to show that the present object of it is not just.

I shall therefore examine the rights which neutral powers claim in this respect; first, according to the law of nations, that is, according to those principles of natural law which are relative to the conduct of nations, such as are approved by the ablest writers, and practiced by States the most refined. I shall then consider the alterations which have been made in this right by those treaties which have been superadded to the law of nations, and which communities, for their mutual benefit, have established among themselves.

The right of protection then must have its foundation in some law, and, when considered in relation to any particular cases, it must be founded on that law, by which the interests of the parties concerned are generally determined, and which hath force in that place where the right of protection is claimed. Thus in the present case, if neutral nations have a right to protect the property of thc enemy, it must take its rise from those laws, which are the established rules of conduct between nations, and particularly on that element when this right is supposed to be exerted. No civil or municipal institutions, and much less the privileges existing from them, can here take place; they have no force but under the dominion of those who agreed to their establishment. The question then is: How far, according to the law of nations, doth this right of protection extend? To answer

[69] Holland.

this clearly, we must observe that governments can have succeeded to no other rights, but such as their respective members enjoyed in a state of individuality; and that one nation is now to another, as it were in a state of nature, that is, in the same condition in which man was to man before they entered into society; the right therefore of protection, which individuals would have enjoyed in such a situation is the same which government can claim at present. An individual then in a state of nature would have had an undoubted right to protect his own person and property against any attack; but if I am engaged in contention with another, would he then have had a right to protect him against me? Most certainly not; since he thereby would deprive me of a right which the law of nature, for my own security, would in such case give me, of seizing the property of this my enemy and destroying his person; if he thought my conduct manifestly injurious, so as to call for general resentment; he would, on that account, become my enemy himself, but as long as he calls himself a neuter, to act in this manner against me would be no less absurd than unjust.[70] Such, therefore, and no more, is the right of protection which governments enjoy at present in those places, to which their own dominions do not extend; they have succeeded to the rights only of their respective members, and by consequence these alone can they protect.

But it will be asked – From whence then arises the right, which governments always enjoy, of protecting the property of

---

[70] It is easy to demonstrate the inconclusiveness of this argument. You may pursue the person, and (perhaps) the property of your enemy in his own territory; but your right of pursuit ceases in a third place. You may not therefore pursue him or his property, while both are in a place belonging to me, who am a stranger to your quarrel and independent of our authority, and if when out of my own limits but not within yours, I am in possession of the goods of your enemy, you surely have no right to stop and search me; in short, to make me stand and deliver, for if I do not choose to obey your orders, our controversy must be settled by main force, instead of one enemy you will now have two, and thus you will successively draw upon yourself the enmity of the whole neighborhood, because you will in the person of one have violated the safety of all. See above, C. XXII.

the enemy within the precincts of their own country? It is a consequence of the right of dominion; unless therefore their dominion extends over the ocean, the right of protection cannot there take place; dominion gives a right of enacting laws, of establishing new jurisdiction, and of making all (whether its own subjects or those of other countries) submit to those, who come within the pale of its power. Here then the trials which the law of nations gives, is, as it were, superseded; and any proceedings upon it would of course be unjust; but as soon as you are out of the verge of this particular jurisdiction, the law thereof and the privileges which attend them cease at once and the general laws of nations again have their force; here the property even of an ally hath no other protection than what these laws allow it,[71] being joined therefore to the good of an enemy, it cannot communicate its protection to those since the same law which gives security to the first allows you to seize and destroy the latter. These reasonings are exemplified by a common fact; within the precincts of the dominion of any government, you are not at liberty to search the ships of any country; but is not this liberty universally and immemorially practiced over all on the main sea? And wherefore is this search made; but that, according to the law of nations, all are here answerable for what they may convey?[72]

---

[71] This is undeniably true; but the question still recurs, how far does the law of nations allow a neutral to protect his friend's property on the high seas. The first principle of that universal law from which all others are but corollaries is that nations are mutually independent of each other. It is especially so on the ocean; there you can claim no right or jurisdiction over me, for the sea is not your property any more than it is mine. Wherever we may be placed on that element, we are still independent of one another. Our ship, our cock boat is our castle. You have not a right to search me there, any more than you would on the fast land, if it were our common property.

[72] The responsibility of ships for what they convey supposes some authority, or jurisdiction, on those who are to enforce it, but belligerent States have neither the one nor the other on the high seas. I, who am a neutral, am only responsible to you for my acts done in violation of neutrality because they have an hostile character. Thus, I am responsible if I furnish succours or arms to your enemy, but those facts must be proved, vague suspicions and your own interest cannot supply the place of the

There is something analogous to this in most civil government. Few countries without some places which enjoy a right of protection from the general laws of the State, such as palaces, houses of religion, and the like; and this right generally arises from some pretence to an exclusive jurisdiction; as long, therefore, as any particular property remains within the verge of these; however justly it may be the subject of the law, it is not subject to the power of it, but suppose it conveyed from hence into the public roads beyond the precincts of this particular palace, or convent, the protection it received would vanish at once? And the general laws of the community would fully then have force upon it. Thus, the protection which Governments can give within their dominions extends not to the sea; the ocean is the public road of the universe; the law of which is the law of nations, and all that passes thereon are subject to it without either privilege or exemption.[73]

If this manner of reasoning should not clearly establish my point, I can appeal in support of it to the ablest writers on public law, who will be found to have decided the question in my favour.

---

requisite proof and still less authorize you to seek for it in my own dwelling by searching, that is to say, by ransacking my vessel. This explains the kind of responsibility which the author has established, the right of self-preservation is its only measure and the customs which has introduced the practice of searching ships is founded on the same principle; all beyond it is a wrong, a trespass and a violation of the law of nations.

[73] It is admitted on all hands that the law of nations rules upon the ocean, to the exclusion of all others. The mutual independence of nations is its first fundamental principle; I am therefore upon the high sea as independent of you as you are of me, and you can exercise no other nor greater rights over me than I can over you. In time of peace my ship is my home, and as I am out of your jurisdiction, you have no right to invade it, because the use of the sea belongs to me as well as to you, and I am the natural protector of those who are on board of my floating castle. If as Mr. Jenkinson very justly says the ocean is the highway of mankind, you are guilty of robbery, if you stop, search, and molest me on that highway, precisely in the same manner as if you were to stop a traveler; or a common carrier on an highway on land, out of your own particular jurisdiction?

And first I will produce the testimony of the learned native of Delft, who wrote so nobly on the freedom of navigation to serve his ungrateful country. In one of the passages which are now before me, it is remarkable how much he labours to give the greatest extent to the rights of commerce; and yet with all his laudable bias to this favorite point, he is clearly of opinion that the ship of a nation cannot protect the property of an enemy;[74] he manifestly implies (Grotius, *De jure belli ac pacis*, lib. III, c. 6, sec. 6, in notes) that the vessels even of allies are subject to condemnation on account of the enemies property, with which they are laden; when it appears that this property was put on board them with the consent of the owners of the vessels, but not otherwise. His words are: "*Neque amicorum naves in praedom veniunt ab res hostiles, nisi consensus id factum sit dominorum navis*" (Grotius, *De jure belli ac pacis*, lib. III, c. 6, § 6, in note); but if the enemies property should be found laden on board a neutral vessels without the connivance of the owners, in such cases "that property alone is lawful prize", and speaking again in another place on this point, he says, that if the wrong done me by my enemy is manifestly unjust, and that anyone by affording succours, should encourage him in his enmity against me, "*Jam non tam civiliter tenebitur de damno, sed et criminaliter, ut is judici imminent reum manifestrum eximit*" (Grotius, *De jure belli ac pacis*, lib. III, cap. 1). A fine and animated manner of

[74] If Mr. Jenkinson's reasoning is founded on correct principles, he does not stand in need of the authority of publicists; if on the contrary, it is false, the opinion of those writers cannot make it otherwise. Sound principles and sound logic are all that is required to establish a correct doctrine. As to systems, the law of nations does not admit them, they more properly belong to State policy. Besides I have discussed this question in the XXII Chapter of this work, and I believe that I have there sufficiently demonstrated that on the high seas a belligerent has no right over neutrals, and that the custom which applies to arms and warlike stores is an exception to the general law. After all, I do not hesitate to say that Grotius's opinion is not consistent with his own doctrine on that subject of the freedom of the seas.

expression which shows how clear the opinion of this great author was upon the question.[75]

To the testimony of Grotius I shall add that Bynkershoek, a native also of Holland, and whose sentiments, in point of maritime jurisprudence Barbeyrac often prefers even to those of the former; and what makes even his opinion at this time of great importance, is, that he wrote principally for the use of the Courts and States of the United Provinces and generally confirms what he advanced by their judgments and resolutions. He speaks expressly in favour of my point: "*Ratione consulta*", says he, "*non sum qui videam cur non liceret capere res hostiles, quamois in navi amicua repertas*; *id enim capio quod bostium est, quodque jure belli victori cedit*" (Bynkershoek, *Questionum juris publici*, lib. 1, cap. 14). He then assigns this reason also for his opinion, that as it is lawful to stop on the ocean any vessel, though she carry the colours of a neutral nation, and to examine by her papers to whom she really belongs, and in case she appear to be the property of an enemy, to seize here as a lawful prize;[76] so he can see no cause why this rule should not extend to the effects which any ship may have on board; and if the goods of an enemy should lie there concealed, why they also, by the right of war should not be taken and condemned; he even declares it to be his opinion that the owner of the neutral vessel should, in such a case, lose the price of the freight; a severity which the English Courts of admiralty never practise where some particular circumstance doth not require it.

I shall add to these the opinion of Albericus Gentilis (Albericus Gentilis, *De Advocatione Hispanica*, lib. cap. 28), esteemed the ablest writer on national jurisprudence till Grotius bore the palm from him; and his fame in this respect was so great that Philip III of Spain appointed him perpetual advocate for his subjects in all causes which they might have depending in the Courts of England. This author states a case where the Tuscans had taken the effects of the Turks, at that time their

[75] Grotius speaks here of succours afforded to the enemy and not of the conveyance of innocent goods; the passage quoted, therefore, however eloquent, is not at all applicable in this place.

[76] I have discussed Bynkershoek's opinion above, Chapter XXII.

enemies which they found on board some English ships; and he determines that the Turkish goods are legal prize, but that the captor must pay the freight to the English: "*Transeunt res*", says he, "*cum sua causa, victor succedit in locum victor, tenetur Etruscus pro toto naulo*". The property of the enemy passeth to the captor, but all its consequences attend it; the goods justly belong to him, but he must pay the freighter all which the enemy would have paid, to whose right he hath in every respect succeeded.[77]

To enter particularly into the Sentiments of any more writers on this subject would be equally tedious and unnecessary; it will be sufficient to mention the names alone of such others as are in favour of the question. Among them I find Heineccius (*Heineccius de Navibus ob Vecturam de Netitarum Mercium commissis*), no less famed for his knowledge of Laws, than for his learning in what are the best expositors of laws, the antiquities of governments. Zouch (*Zouch de judicio inter Gentes, pars 2*), who for so many years presided in the Courts of Admiralty of this Kingdom. Voet (*Voet de jure Militari, cap. 5*) and Zuarius (*Zuarius de usu Maris, Consilii*), and Loccenius (*Loccenius de jure Maritimo, lib. Ii, cap. 4*). All of them writers of reputation and whose opinions are universally relied on by all who treat on public jurisprudence.[78]

---

[77] Albericus Gentilis, an English writer, one of Selden's oracles, maintained the right of private dominion over the Sea (See the first part of this work).

[78] This is called *jurare in verba magistri*. There are many requisites to give the weight of authorities to the opinions of a writer, particularly on the Subject of the law of nations. There is but one method by which one may be sure of obtaining the general assent of mankind; it is by laying down no other principles but such as are clearly derived from the nature of things, because they cannot be controverted by any but System mongers. Were we to listen to all the authors cited by Mr. Jenkinson, and a number of their followers, everything would be subordinate to the law of war. It will be so when it is proved that the law of war is the primordial foundation of the law of nations, and that everything is subordinate to it. The remainder then will follow of course, and all further discussion would be superfluous. Until this proof is clearly made out, it is still lawful to think that war is a misfortune, that it is often the effect of the passions of men, and not a constituent principle of human nature, unless we should

I might indeed have wholly omitted the sentiments of these learned individuals. Since we shall find that great communities themselves have confirmed our opinion both by their laws and by their practice. It will not be proper on this occasion to look far back into the early annals of the European States; when the governments of these were yet in infancy, the advantages of commerce were but little understood, and of course the rights of it were not sufficiently regarded; war was then too much the reason of rapine, and they who entered into it meant less to conquer than to plunder. As soon, however, as some better order began to be introduced into these affairs, it then became usual for each party at the commencement of the war to publish a declaration, wherein he specified what kind of trade he would permit[79] neutral nations to carry on with his enemy and the regulations of these were sometimes attended to, and sometimes not, either as the interest of the party neutral inclined him to submit to the restraint, or as the power of the party belligerent enabled him to enforce the execution of it.[80] True it is that the prohibitions which these declarations contain are various, according to the sentiments of the different governments which made them; and on that account they are, perhaps, too unsteady a foundation on which to establish a right; there plainly, however, follows from hence one powerful inference in our favour, that not one can be found amid all this variety which ever permitted neutral nations to protect the property of the enemy; this branch of freightage they all agree unanimously to prohibit.[81]

---

say with Hobbes that God has created man wicked. It is true that thereby everything is explained, except sociability, charity and justice. I pass over in silence this object and advantage of that perfectability of which we are so vain.

[79] This word *permit* is aptly chosen to convey the idea of the dominion of the Sea.

[80] The truth is simply this: the neutral submitted or resisted according to his means, and the belligerent did the same; everything therefore was arbitrary and depended merely on force. See Chapter XV.

[81] Admitting this to be true, it is, after all, but matter of fact, and precedents should never be drawn into principles. Because governments have at times more or less prohibited the carrying of enemy's property.

The free States of Italy cultivated first the interest of commerce: before any vessel had as yet passed the Cape of Good Hope and a shorter passage had been discovered to the East Indies, Venice and Genoa drove the principal trade of the world and dispersed the manufactures of Asia to the different parts of Europe. It naturally followed that these two commercial Republics soonest understood and defined the just rights of navigation;[82] their maritime constitutions still remain collected in the Consolato del Mare; and the reputation of these was so great that as the laws of Rhodes were once to the Romans, and the Laws of Oleron to the western parts of Europe, so these Italian laws became of force universally to all nations which border on the Mediterranean Sea. These have determined the point expressly in our favour. In one of them it is asserted: "*Se la nave o navilio che pigliato sará, fusse di amici, e le mercantile che lui porterá, saranno d'inimici, lo armiraglio della nave o del navilo, che lui piglato haverà, che lui conquella sua nave gli debba portare quello che di suo I inimici sara*". If the ship or vessel which shall be taken belongs to an ally, and the merchandize which she has on board belongs to an enemy, the captain of the armed ship may force or constrain the master of the ship or vessel which he has taken to carry into some port for his account the effects of his enemy which are on board, and it is afterwards added that the master of the vessel must be paid for the freightage of the goods of the enemy (*Il consulato del Mare,*

Mr. Jenkinson would infer from thence that the law of nations prohibits it likewise. Such, alas, is the logic of power; but it is not that of reason and common sense.

[82] Venice and Genoa had no other Code but their exclusive interest, and none of the sovereigns of Italy were able to resist them. It was probably to support their pretensions that the *Consolato del Mare* was written. Neither the author nor the origin of that compilation are known. It was, after all, only a municipal regulation, a mere collection of decisions, and by no means a regular code adopted by all the commercial nations. Therefore, the applications which the author makes of the Rhodian Laws, the Consolato, and the Law of Oleron may be considered as not deserving any attention. All those collections with respect to the age we live in are *res inter alios actae.*

c. 273).[83] And such were not only the constant purpose of their laws, but the practice of their governments was always conformable to it. Their historian (*Nicess. Grogoras, lib. ix*) tells us that in the War between the Venetians and the Genoese, the ships of Grecians, who were neuter, were always searched, and the enemies who lay hid in them were taken out and made prisoners.[84]

It is unnecessary to dwell longer in giving a further detail of the conduct of every nation in this respect; I will therefore confine myself to those who are most concerning in the present dispute; and will shew that as England claims no more at present that what she always enjoyed, so France and Holland have constantly supported the same opinion whenever their interest required it.[85]

It was in the reign of the first Edward, a prince who thoroughly understood the rights of his crown, and had a spirit equal to the support of them, that Philip the Fair of France, being engaged in a war with the Duke of Burgundy, the French admiral took the ships of several neutral nations which were passing through the British channel into the ports of Flanders. Great complaints were made on this subject and Commissioners were appointed to examine into the conduct of the admiral; a libel was there presented against him by almost every trading nation of Europe; the record (see all this more fully treated in the record) of this is still remaining, and if neutral nations had at that time pretended to enjoy the right of protecting the property of the enemy and that the effects which they carried on board their ships could in no case, except in that of contraband, be made lawful prize, we might well expect that this right would here have been claimed and asserted; fear could not in this case have

---

[83] That allowance is in opposition to the alleged principle if the carrying of enemy's goods is prohibited, any violation of the prohibition is a fraud and consequently an offence. Therefore the neutral master ought to be punished at least with the loss of the freight, which is his profit.

[84] This is still practiced at this day by virtue of the indefinite right of search, but a warrior cannot be compared to innocent merchandise.

[85] Their interest? This is the true solution of the problem. This is Mr. Jenkinson's or rather the British Government's law of nations, which they pretend to derive from the principles of universal jurisprudence.

prevented it, for all the world, except France, was on one side of the question; but the record contains no such claim. The injured demand their right on a different principle, because their ships were taken on those seas "where the kings of England (saith the record) have time out of mind been in peaceable possession of the Sovereign Lordship, with the power of appointing laws, of prohibiting the use of arms, of giving protection as occasion should require, and appointing all things necessary for the maintaining peace, justice, and equity among all, as well foreigners as natives, who navigate those seas." Here then the right of protection is placed on that basis on which alone it can properly be founded, the right of dominion; no other pretence is offered; and if I may be allowed to sum up the evidence, as their names are written in the record, "Genue, Cateloigne, Espaigne, Alemaine, Seland, Hoyland, Frise, Denmarck, Norway, and plusours autres lieuse del Empier", all join here in asserting the principles on which I first established my argument.[86]

The annals of Edward III afford still other facts in favour of my opinion: this prince added to his military accomplishments, great sagacity in the science of law, and uncommon attention to the commercial interests of his kingdom; in the second year of his reign he confirmed the Charter of Privileges, which some of his predecessors had before granted to foreign merchants, and particularly to those of the Hanse-towns (*Rymer's Foedera, tom 4, p. 361*), who were at that time the greatest freighters of the western parts of Europe. This instrument may well be

---

[86] This fact is recorded in Selden's celebrated *Mare clausum*. This author relates much in detail the complaints which were made against *Regnier Raimbault*, a French Admiral, and draws from thence one of his principal arguments in favor of the exclusive dominion of Great Britain over all the British Sea or channel to the coasts of Flanders, guarding them. But the complaints demanded the restitution of their ships and goods which had been captured in the waters of Great Britain then at peace; therefore there could be no question about the right to convey enemy's property. Besides, those who prepared the petition would not probably have allowed such a question to be made, for they were English Lawyers. I shall take no further notice of this quotation of Mr. Jenkinson. I shall merely observe that French Commissioners appointed by Philip the Fair were present at the hearing of the controversy and therefore that the *dominium maris* claimed by Great Britain was not acknowledged by France.

considered as a sort of maritime regulation by which England meant to direct her conduct at that time in affairs of this nature; in this, liberty of navigation is fully confirmed; foreign merchants are allowed to carry their goods, whether purchased within the kingdom or without, "*quocumque voluerint*", but with this exception, "*praeterquam ad terras notoriorum et manifestorum hostium regni nostri* (*Rymer's Foedera, tom 4, p. 516*) and some offences being afterwards committed against this charter in the succeeding Wars, it was again renewed in the same manner in the 6th year of this reign; in both these instances the exception is express, that no trade whatsoever should be permitted with the enemy.[87] But this good king, perhaps through a principle of justice and his ardent love of commerce, seems to have practiced this right with more moderation, that is, in much the same manner in which the government of England claims it at present; for in his wars with Scotland, some ships of Great Yarmouth having taken several vessels belonging to the burgesses of the town of Burges, "*Pratendentes bona in iisdem existential fuisse hominum de Scotia*". He directed his precepts to the Sheriff of Norfolk (*Rymer's Foedera, tom IV, p. 328*), and commanding him to set at liberty, and to cause full restitution to be made of the ships, and of such of the goods as belonged to the merchants of Burges, and that he should only retain only that part of the cargo which was the property of the Scotch, his enemies. We find also that when Queen Elizabeth was engaged in war with Spain, she seized several vessels of the Hanse Towns, which were entering into the port of Lisbon; and she urged, among other arguments, the charter above mentioned in defense of her conduct. She was in this respect so satisfied of the justice of her cause that the threats of the German Empire and other neutral powers could not oblige her to relinquish her rights; and though she might perhaps on this occasion give too

[87] This fact is related by Selden as a proof of the maritime dominion of Great Britain and not as a consequence of the prohibition to carry enemy's property. The author says that some vessels from the Hanse Towns laden with grain were seized in the very harbor of Lisbon because they had rashly and without the Queen's permission sailed round Scotland and along the western sea to Portugal.

great extent to this right, yet it is remarkable that Monsieur de Thou, who was himself a great lawyer and had long sat in the Court of Judicature in France, even when he blames the conduct of the Queen in this affairs, passeth his censure upon it not as defective in justice, but only in policy "*in tam alieno tempore*", he says (*Thuanus, lib. 96, vol. 7, p. 511*), "*rerum prudentiores existimabant*[88] *imprudenter factum esse à Regina ab anglis*".

We have as yet mentioned the conduct alone of those English princes who knew how to assert their rights and who ruled their people with glory; but we shall find that even under a weaker government and in a latter period this right of seizing the property of the enemy found on board neutral ships hath been fully claimed and practiced. When Villiers, Duke of Buckingham, presided over the naval affairs of England, and to gratify his own private resentments, had engaged his country in a war against Spain, the British fleet under Pennington took several French vessels, to the number of between thirty and forty which had Spanish effects on board. They were brought into the ports of England, and our Courts of Admiralty condemned the goods of the Spaniards as legal prize, but ordered the vessels of the French to be released, and the freightage to be paid to them. This conduct was avowed by the Court of England and a full representation of it transmitted by the Lord High Admiral to the administration of France about 15 years after this, when the French themselves were at war with Spain; the navy of France took a great many English ships which were laden with the property of Spaniards, and their courts of admiralty condemned not only the enemy's effects, but the English ships which conveyed them.

Thc Earl of Leicester, then ambassador in France, made great complaints on its head; he was answered that the English

---

[88] France very properly retaliated upon England and was at least consistent with the principle that she assumed when she refused to allow freight to the English ships taken in the act of violating her prohibition. After all, this diversity of conduct, the one allowing and the other refusing freight to the neutral master, shews that both France and England acted as they respectively thought proper, and that there was no common rule or usage to bind them. From such arbitrary and versatile proceedings, the jurisprudence of nations cannot certainly be derived.

always acted in this manner; and this answer being transmitted to the Earl of Northumberland, at that time Lord High Admiral, he consulted upon it Sir Henry Martin, the best English civilian of that age, and the most versed in maritime jurisdiction; and by his advice he returned to Lord Leicester the following answer, which at the same time proves the constant opinion and shews the moderation of the British Admiralty on this point: "that", says he (*The Sidney Papers, Algernon Earl of Northumberland to Robert, Earl of Leicester, Nov. 5, 1640*), "which is alleged by the French to be practiced in our courts of admiralty is absolutely denied; and that neither the law nor practice hath ever been to confiscate the goods of friends for having enemies goods among them; we are so far from doing any such act of injustice, as when in time of war we have met with any such prizes, the freight has always been paid by the taker for those enemies goods that he took, and those that belonged unto friends were duly restored to them".

Thus much may suffice to shew the conduct of the people of England. History will also prove to us that Holland hath always exerted the same right. At the beginning almost of that war which the United Provinces sustained in support of their liberties, and even before their Sovereignty was as yet fully established, the people of Zealand scrupled not to carry into their ports all such neutral vessels (*Historia Belgica Stateressi, lib. 5 Camden anno 1575. Zouch de judicio inter Gentes, par. 2*) as were conveying the effects of the enemy, under pretended names from Flanders into Spain, and the court of admiralty of that province adjudged the Spanish property to be legal prize; and though they released the neutral ships, they made them no compensation for their freightage; among these there were some English vessels, and Queen Elizabeth, angry that so young a State and one which had placed itself under her protection, should in any degree interrupt the commerce of her people, at first shewed the effects of her resentment by seizing their ships and imprisoning their merchants; the Zealanders upon this made reprisals; several English vessels were detained and their commanders put under confinement; to endeavor at some settlement of this affair, the Queen sent over to Holland Mr. Robert Beal, her Secretary, and for the same purpose the Prince of Orange dispatched a minister to London; by these means the dispute at least was compromised. The ships and prisoners were on both sides released, but the Queen never obtained restitution of the enemies goods which were taken on board the vessels of her subjects. This fact is worthy of observation, not only as it relates to the conduct of Holland, but as it shews how for a Princess thought herself obliged in equity to yield, whom historians have always described as positive in her temper, and, whenever her right was concerned, of a very tenacious disposition.

Holland, whenever she was engaged in war, almost constantly pursued the same conduct. She sometimes even prohibited the commerce of neutral nations beyond all justice and moderation. In the year 1599 (*Grotii Hist. lib. 8*), when the government of Spain first prohibited the subjects of the United Provinces from trading to the ports of that kingdom, a liberty which had unaccountably been allowed them, from the commencement of their revolt to that period. The States General in revenue published a placart forbidding the people of all nations to carry any kind of merchandize into Spain, the words of Grotius, in the relation which he has given of this affair in his Belgic History, are very full and express: "*Peredictum*", says he, "*retant populo quoscumque cellos commeatus resve alias in Hispatium ferre*; *si qui secus faxint, ut hostibus faventes vice hostirum futuros*". This placart they publicly notified to all kinds and nations, for this reason as the historian expresses it: "*nequis inscitiam excusaret*". The consequences of this notification deserve also our attention. The historian continues: "*Paruit Rex Galliae, ac si quis suorum sex intra menses in Hispaniam navigat, professus est privatum periculum fore*". Henry the Fourth, at that time king of France, though delivered then from all his distress, and arrived at the summit of all his power, scrupled not to submit to this placart, and gave up the interests of all his subjects who should attempt within six months to transgress it. The historian concluded: "*Cateri (reges) silentio transmisere*"; the other powers of Europe made no clamorous complaint against this measure of the State; in silence they passed it over. How unlike was this conduct to that of Holland at present! Charles the Second, in a letter to the States General, of

October 4, 1666, charges them with a remarkable violence of this nature; being at war with some Asiatic Prince in the East Indies, they seized all the ships and goods of the English merchants which were trading to those countries; and the Dutch governors scrupled not only to profess in their declaration: "*qu'ayant depuis peu annoncé la guerre aux princes avec qui ils avaient dessein de trafiquer cette meme guerre devait leur interdire tout commerce avec les dits princes*" (*Charles the Second's letter to the States General, October 4, 1666*).

I omit citing many other instances of their conduct in this particular, but I should appear tedious, especially as one fact still remains which is alone sufficient to evince the opinion of Holland on this point; and the which I rather choose mention, as it happened even after the Dutch had by their negociations endeavoured to establish, as a general maxim among nations, that the goods of an enemy under a neutral banner should pass unmolested. At the commencement of that war which broke out immediately after the revolution, when the first grand alliance was formed against France, Holland entered into a convention (*Convention concluded at London, Aug. 22, 1689*) with England to prohibit totally the commerce of neutral powers with the enemy; in the preamble of this they assign publicly their reasons for it. They say: "that having declared war against the Most Christian King, it behooves them to do as much damage as possible to the common enemy in order to bring him to agree to such conditions as may restore the repose of Christendom; and that for this end it was necessary to interrupt all trade and commerce with the subjects of the said king; and that to effect this, they had ordered their fleets to block up all the ports and havens of France"; and afterwards, in the second and third articles of this Convention, it is agreed "that they would take any vessels whatever king or State it may belong to that shall be found sailing into or out of the ports of France, and condemn both vessel and merchandise as legal prize; and that this resolution should be notified to all neutral States". Such therefore was at this time the avowed opinion of Holland, and England was induced to join with her in this Convention, exceeding thereby those bounds of equity and moderation which she had almost always practiced in this point before, and which she will, I hope, most faithfully observe for the future. These Northern Crowns who were particularly affected by this prohibition contended very vehemently against it; in answer to their objections were urged the circumstances of affairs, the danger of Europe, and the mighty strength of that ambitious power which, if some extraordinary effort was not made, would bring mankind under its subjection.[89] It is remarkable that Puffendorf (*See a letter of Puffendorf in Jno. Gronigii Bibliotheca Universalis Librorum juridicorum, p. 105*), who owed his fortune and employment to one of those Northern Crowns, was of opinion in this case against them and thought that the Convention might be justified. It is not meant here at present either to censure or commend it; circumstances may sometimes make a thing to be lawful which considered by itself would be unjust; but such times are truly unhappy when necessity must be pleaded in support of a right.[90]

It remains that I now inquire into the conduct of France; my proofs (*See the Ordinances of France, Francis I, 1543, c. 4 – 2d Henry III. 1584, c. 69*) on this head will be clear; they are indeed nothing less than the public laws of that kingdom, by some very old French ordinances it is declared not only that the enemies goods shall be adjudged to be lawful prize, but that the neutral vessel which carries them, or the property of any ally which shall be joined with them, shall be joined also in the condemnation. It has always been a maxim of the courts of maritime jurisdiction of France: "*Que la robe d'ami confisque celle d'ennemi*", and so clear were they in this opinion that the laws which established it were repeatedly enacted in the reigns of two of their kings, Francis I and Henry III. Thus the practice of the French marine hath in this particular been conformable to their Laws may be proved by a thousand instances. I shall select one upon the authority of a Minister of Holland which will shew

---

[89] This proves that there was not at that time any settled jurisprudence avowed or recognized by all the nations concerned. The circumstances of the moment were the only rule of conduct.

[90] Necessity is the supreme law; but in general that word is only employed to palliate acts of violence or injustice. What Mr. Jenkinson says on this subject is the touchstone of his whole doctrine.

what their conduct was in that Spanish war which preceded the Pyrenean treaty. In a letter of Monsieur Boréel from Paris to Monsieur de Witt, December 26th 1653: "On tient ici", says he, "pour maxime favorable à leurs interests que leurs ennemis ne doivent recevoir ni défense, ni service du sujets de LL. H. P., en transportant de chez eux quelques marchandises ou commodités, ou d'autres choses qui seraient pour le compte de l'ennemi sous peine, au cas qu'ils les trouvent dans des bâtimens hollandais, d'être déclarées de bonne prise".

But it is not the old laws of France alone that thus determine this point; their more modern regulations confirm it; one of the last and greatest services which Colbert performed to his country was the establishment of a system of naval laws, and wisest and best digested which the spirit of legislation hath ever produced. It is observable that although the ordinance which contained these laws was registered in 1681, several years subsequent to those treaties by which France agreed that neutral vessels should protect the property of the enemy, yet it pays no attention to them, and establishes the contrary doctrine. This proves how little regard France always shewed to that article.[91] The words of

[91] This affords a fresh proof that there was not anywhere any established doctrine on the subject in question. The Treaty of the Pyrenees declares that enemy's goods shall be free under the French and Spanish flags; another treaty between France and England of the 23d of February 1677 contains the same stipulation. The French ordinance of 1681 decides the contrary; the Treaty of the Pyrenees was confirmed by treaties posterior to that ordinance. England herself has established various principles in her several commercial treaties, and those variations are the proof which Mr. Jenkinson offers in support of his prohibitory doctrine.

In order to enable the reader to appreciate what I say, I shall point out some of the treaties in which it is stipulated that free ships shall make free goods: Treaty of Commerce between Louis XIV and the United Provinces, 18 April 1646; between Oliver Cromwell and the King of Portugal, 10 July 1654; between Louis XIV and the Hanse Towns, 10 May 1655; between France and England, 3 November 1655; Treaty of the Pyrenees between France and Spain 17 September 1659; between England and the United Provinces, 15 February 1668 and 1674; between France and England, 24 February 1677; Declaration of War by Holland against France, 9 March 1689; Treaty of Nimeguen, 24 September 1678; between

the ordinance expressly condemn not only the enemies goods, but the neutral ship which carried them: "All ships (saith the law: *Naval Ordinance of 1681, Title IX, Art. 7*) which have goods on board that belong to the enemy shall be good prize".

These laws continue still to be observed in France. At the commencement even of the present war, the French government delivered to Mons. Berkenrode, the Dutch Minister at Paris, a memorial "contenant les precautions" (as the title expresses it) "que doivent prendre les Hollandois conformément à l'ordonnance de la marine et aux reglements de la France, pour éviter que leurs navires soient déclarés de bonne prise". In the preamble of this, the words of the abovementioned law are repeated, and the same rule of condemnation is declared to be still in force. And the seventh article of the memorial lays even a greater restriction on neutral commerce that the ordinance of 1681 seems to have intended; it is there said "*Si les navires Hollandais transportaient des merchandises du cru ou fabriques des ennemis de la France, ces merchandises servient de bonne prise, mais le corps du navire seroit retachés*". By this memorial therefore everything which is either of the growth or manufacture of the enemy's country, when found on board the ships of Holland, though the property does not appear to belong to the enemy, is declared to be good prize. The same restriction evidently extends to all other neutral traders (*see the preamble of the Memorial*). Is not this almost a total prohibition to neutral powers of any commerce with the enemies of France?

Let us now look back on what has been said: the deduction which I have made hath I fear, been tedious; but the importance of the subject by force led me into it. I flatter myself, however, it has appeared that reason, authority, and practice[92] all join to support the cause I defend; by reason I have endeavoured to trace out those principles on which this right of capture is

---

Louis XIV and Queen Anne, Utrecht 1713; between France and Spain, 1742, etc.

[92] As to reason, there is no other but the will of sovereigns directed by their interest; the authorities have been refuted above, the practice has constantly varied. It has never been uniform in any country, even in England. Such are the sources from which the author has drawn his doctrine.

grounded; and to give that weight to my own sentiments which of themselves they would not deserve, I have added the authorities of the ablest writers on this subject; and lastly, I have entered largely into the conduct of nations, that I might not only lay thereby a broader foundation for this right, but that I might the more fully illustrate by the extravagant pretensions of other States[93] in this respect the present moderation of England; no age or country ever gave a greater extent to the commerce of neutral nations, and we have seen that most in the same circumstances have confined it within much narrower bounds.

There remains still, however, one objection to what has been said, and that of so plausible a cast that I cannot leave it without an answer. It has been pretended that the liberty of navigation is destroyed by means of these captures, and a violent restraint hath been put on the lawful industry of mankind. The liberty of navigation, in fair construction, can mean no more than the right of carrying to any mart unmolested the product of one's own country or labour, and bringing back the emoluments of it;[94] but can it be lawful that you should extend this right to my detriment; and when it was meant only for your own advantage, that you should exert it in the cause of my enemy?[95] Each man

[93] This moderation consists in not confiscating the neutral vessel laden with enemy's property, but the goods themselves are seized, and that is the point in controversy.

[94] This definition of the freedom of commerce is truly remarkable and we are curious to know the authority on which it rests. It is painful to us to be obliged to refute similar paradoxes, but when they are asserted by a grave and respectable writer, they ought not to be silently acquiesced in. The rights of navigation are indefinite because it is carried on on a free element; as to commerce, it has not limits but those which the nations engaged in it choose to present. If we were to believe Mr. Jenkinson, a vessel can only sail laden with the productions of its own country and bring back those which it has received in exchange, or the proceeds of her outward cargo in specie. All coasting trade for account of others is prohibited. Therefore the Danes, Dutch, Hamburghers etc. must lay up their ships and the commerce of India and China must no longer be thought of. We will not carry our reflections farther on this extraordinary proposition.

[95] I exercise it for you as well as for your enemy, and for myself likewise. If *detriment* is to be admitted as a lawful ground of prohibition,

hath a right to perform certain actions, but if the destruction of another should follow from them, would not this be a just reason of restraint?[96] The rights of mankind admit of different degrees, and whenever two of these come into competition, the lowest in the scale must always give place to the higher; but you will say, that you had a profit in doing this; if, however, it is otherwise unjust, will that consideration convert it into a right?[97] If you mean that your own commerce ought to be free, that right is not in the least denied you, but if under this disguise you intend to convey freedom to the commerce of the enemy, what policy or what justice can require it?[98] What can neutral nations desire more than to remain amid the ravages of war in the same happy circumstances which the tranquility of peace would have

---

commerce, which is a bond of union and friendship between nations, will fill the world with wars and plunder.

[96] This admits of no doubt, but it is only the weak that suffer themselves to be destroyed; and surely the neutral does not destroy the belligerents by availing himself of some commercial advantages procured to him by the circumstances of the war; otherwise the belligerents would not be satisfied with limiting his commerce; they would prevent it entirely, as England did, notwithstanding her pretended moderation, by the 11th Article of her Treaty with Holland of the 22d of August 1689. That Article declares to be lawful prize all neutral ships and effects found on their way to some port or harbor subject to the dominion of the Most Christian King. This prohibition requires no commentary; it is a remarkable monument of the maritime despotism of Great Britain. Her modern orders flow from the same source.

[97] Where is the injustice? I trade with your enemy and I am also willing to trade with you. The one is my right and the other is my duty. The profit which I derive from this impartial commerce is the result of a favorable chance which the war has thrown in my way and which I have a clear right to avail myself of.

[98] This is contradictory; for in fact, if my commerce is free, I carry it on as I think proper, as I have always done, and as I have a right to do; the advantage which your enemy may derive from it does not concern me at all. At any rate, I offer you the same advantage and therefore you cannot charge me with partiality. The advantages of commerce are reciprocal. I cannot trade with another nation and secure all the profits to myself. No commerce can exist where both parties have not an equal chance. Either say at once that I must not trade at all with your enemy or do not blame me because he comes in sometimes for his share of the advantage.

afforded them? But can any right from hence arise, that you should take occasion from the war itself to constitute a new species of traffic, which in peace you never enjoyed, and which the necessity of one party is obliged to grant you, to the detriment, perhaps destruction, of the other? If this right was admitted, it would become the interest of all commercial States to promote dissension among their neighbours; the quarrels of others would be a harvest to themselves; and from the contentions of others they would gather wealth and power. But, after all, the rights of commerce are not the real cause of this dispute; and liberty of navigation is only a fair pretence which ambition hath thought fit to hold forth, to interest the trading States of the world in its cause, and to draw down their indignation upon England; this is not the first time that a deceit like this has been practiced, when the power of Spain was at its greatest height and Elizabeth wisely contended against the mighty designs of Philip, the capture of some vessels belonging to the Hanse Towns gave occasion to a contest of this nature; but they were the emissaries of Philip that then blew up the flame, and pretending a love to commerce, promoted the ambitious projects of their master. The Queen of England published an apology for her conduct, and this was answered in a virulent and abusive manner, not from any of the Hanse Towns, but from Antwerp, a city under the dominion of Spain, and it seemed to be written (says Thuanus) "*per hominem Philipi partibus addictum, non tam pro libertate navigationis et in Germanorum causa defendenda, quam in Hispanorum gratiam, et ad reginae nomen proscindendum*": the interests of commerce were the pretended cause of his dispute, but the real cause was the interest of Philip; the pretended design was to preserve the liberty of navigation, but the real end was to serve the cause of ambition and to destroy the government of England; this case need not be compared with our own at present; the resemblance is too obvious.[99]

[99] It is a bad argument that proves too much. How could a few cargoes of what carried round about to Lisbon by the northern route operate the destruction of Great Britain? The crime imputed on that occasion to the Hanseatic traders was to have sailed round Scotland without Elizabeth's

Here then we might rest our cause if the law of nations was the only foundation on which this point could be argued, but the bonds of equity have been found too weak to hold the nations of the world to their duty; their interest taught them to renew and confirm these by contracts among themselves and frequently to add thereto certain mutual advantages, greater than what the law of nations singly would have allowed them; let us consider, therefore, what influence these may have in the present case, whatever they are. I mean to give them all the force which reason or justice can require; if our ancestors have betrayed the interest of their country in granting any privileges of his nature, we who have succeeded to their rights are bound to abide by their concessions; it is the happiness of great kingdoms, whose power is equal to the support of their own independency, to be able to act up to those principles which necessity hath often forced little States unhappily to abandon; those scandalous maxims of policy which have brought disgrace both on the name and the profession took their rise from the conduct of the little principalities of Italy, when disrespect by the successive invasions which France and Spain made upon them, they broke or conformed to their leagues, as their own security obliged them; and their refined shifts and evasions formed into systems by able doctors of their councils have composed that science which the world hath called politics; a science of fraud and deceit by which kingdoms are taught to be governed on principles which in individuals would be ashamed to profess; as if there could be no morality among nations, and that mankind being formed into civil societies and collectively considered were set free from all rules of honor and virtue; maxims like these I mean to avoid; to follow them would bring dishonor on my country.

It must then be allowed that there are articles in some of our maritime treaties with other nations which have stipulated that "All which shall be found on board the vessels belonging to the subjects of those countries shall be accounted clear and free,

permission; that Princess thought more of her maritime dominion than of the damage which she might receive from a few shiploads of wheat entering the port of Lisbon. I am indebted to *Selden* for this remark.

although the whole lading or any part hereof shall, by just title of property, belong to the enemies of Great Britain". Such an article is inserted in those maritime treaties which Great Britain hath made with France (*Treaty between Great Britain and France, 24th Feb. 1677*) and Holland (*Treaty between Great Britain and Holland, 2st Dec. 1674.*),[100] it has indeed by some been supposed that the subjects of the crown of Spain have a right to enjoy a privilege of the same nature; certain, however, it is that no such article as that above mentioned can be found in the maritime treaties between that country and Great Britain and particularly in that of Madrid of 1667, which is the principal maritime treaty at present in force between the two kingdoms;[101]

---

[100] This proves that Great Britain has several times relaxed from the severity of her principles in favor of a nation which was able by the extent of her navigation to avail herself of that favor. Thus Mr. Jenkinson's remark does itself overthrow his whole doctrine.

[101] But that is not the only one. There was signed at Utrecht in 1713, which contains the following stipulations (Art. 21): "The Subjects of the respective powers shall with all security and liberty sail to and traffick in all the kingdoms, States, or countries which are or shall be in peace, amity or neutrality with the one or the other". And (Art. 22) "and they shall not be disturbed or disquieted in that liberty by the ships or subjects of the said kings respectively by reason of the hostilities which are or may be hereafter between either of the said kings and the aforesaid kingdoms, countries, or States, or any of them, which shall be in friendship or neutrality with the other". The 22d Article only excepts contraband of war, which alone may be seized and carried away. The 26th Article declares liable to confiscation all goods belonging to the subjects of the respective kings found on board of an enemy's ship.

It does not require a powerful effort of the mind to be convinced after reading the above articles that the contracting parties did not intend to prohibit their subjects from carrying innocent goods, altho' belonging to an enemy. Liberty of trade in the established principle could only be restricted by exceptions, and it is an universal maxim of law, *quod inclusia unius est exclusion alterius.*

But let us return to Mr Jenkinson. He attempts to justify his prohibitory system by maintaining that it has not received any exception, except in favor of the Dutch; but he did not observe that this favor was granted to the very nation which ought to have been excluded from it in preference to all others; for in fact, the Dutch alone carried on more of the coasting trade than all the other commercial countries of Europe, and consequently they did a real prejudice to Great Britain, if the carrying of

but as a mistake in this respect may possibly have arisen from a false interpretation of two articles in the Treaty of Madrid which declare in general (*Treaty of Madrid, 1677*) that "the subjects of the two crowns respectively shall have liberty to traffic throughout all countries cultivating peace, amity, and neutrality with either of them, and that the said liberty shall in no wise be interrupted by any hindrance or disturbance whatsoever, by reason of any hostility which may be between either of the said Crowns and any other kingdoms"; and as the liberty here stipulated may be by some erroneously imagined to extend so far as to grant a right to carry freely the effects of the enemy, it will be proper here to remove this error – and to stop a little to shew the true design and meaning of these articles. This explanation is at present more necessary, as it will tend to illustrate the true sense of other stipulations of precisely the same purport, which may be found in several of our commercial treaties and particularly in the first and second articles of that with Holland of Dec. 11, 1674, a wrong interpretation of which hath already given occasion to great confusion and much false reasoning upon the present question.

It cannot, I think, be doubted that according to those principles of natural equity which constitute the law of nations, the people of every country must always have a right to trade in general to the ports of any State, though it may happen to be engaged in war with another, provided it be with their own merchandise or on their own account; and that under this pretence, they do not attempt to screen from one party the effects of the other; and on condition also that they carry not to either of them any implements of war, or whatever else according to the nature of their respective situations or the circumstances of the case may be necessary to them for their defence. As clear as this point may be, it has sufficiently appeared by the facts deduced above that amid the regularities of

---

enemy's property by neutrals is dangerous to her. We must therefore either say that the English negociators betrayed the interest of their country of that the danger alleged by Mr. Jenkinson is an imaginary one and a mere pretext to subject the navigation of neutrals to arbitrary vexation.

war, the rules of equity in this respect were not always enough regarded; and that many governments in time of war have often most licentiously disturbed and sometimes prohibited totally the commerce of neutral nations with their enemies.[102] About the middle therefore of the last century, when the commercial regulations which at present subsist between the European powers first began to be formed, it became absolutely necessary to call back the attention of governments to those principles of natural right from whence they had strayed and to fix and determine what was the law of nations by the articles of their respective treaties; for this purpose the negociators of that age inserted in their commercial regulations articles (*Treaty of Commerce between France and Holland 1662; Treaty of Commerce between England and Holland, Feb. 17th, 1668; Treaty of Commerce between England and Holland, Dec. 1, 1674; Treaty of Commerce between England and France, Feb. 24, 1677*) to the same purport as above mentioned, asserting in general a right to trade unmolested with the enemies of each other; and these they usually placed among those articles of general import which are commonly first laid down in treaties, as the basis on which the subsequent stipulations are founded. The rule therefore of equity in this case being thus defined, they came afterwards to erect upon it such privileges as that rule alone would not have allowed them;[103] and among the rest, some

[102] This is precisely what England did in 1689. See note 31 above.

[103] This reasoning is evidently false. Mr. Jenkinson acknowledges that the restoration of the principles of natural right and of the freedom of neutral trade was the object of the stipulations to which he alluded. The word *freedom* is easily understood when taken in its plain natural unsophisticated sense, but it is difficult to form an idea of a free trade clogged with so many restrictions as Mr. Jenkinson contends for; it strongly reminds us of the inscription *Libertas*, written on the gate of the prison at Genoa. If the contracting parties intended no more than to restore the law of nations to its pristine vigour, there was no need to superadding to it in favour of neutrals favors and privileges which, as our author himself has labored to prove, threatened the very existence of the Belligerents. Nor is it at all probably that those powers who appear to have been so inimical to the commerce of neutrals with their enemies as to have prohibited it altogether, would of a sudden, not only have returned to the strict principles of neutral rights, but have put their safety in jeopardy

nations, as their interest prompted them, granted mutually to each other, by new and express articles, the right of carrying freely the property of their respective enemies. These last articles therefore must be considered as wholly distinct in their nature from those before mentioned, and in their meaning totally different; the first are an affirmance of an old rule, the last create a new privilege; those only confirm a right which was determined by the law of nations before; these make an exception to that law; if they both imply the same sense, why are both so often inserted in the same treaties (*see the Treaties mentioned above)*? Would the repetition in such a case have been necessary; and to what purpose were new articles added to grant a privilege which was already included in the terms of the preceding?[104] The same exception also of contraband goods is again repeated in the last case as well as in the former; and shews clearly that the property which is the object of the exception in the different articles must likewise in its nature be different; the one relates to the ordinary means of traffic which

---

by granting extraordinary favours and privileges which the law of nations did not call for.

[104] This does not necessarily follow. The *jus gentium* is the law by which all civilized nations are governed in their relations with each other, even tho' there should exist no treaty between them. Nevertheless, most of the treaties between European powers contain stipulations which are merely declaratory of some generally acknowledged rules and principles of that law in order to bind the contracting parties more strongly and strictly to their observance and not only general principles, but particular rules which are in fact but their corollaries, agreed upon in the form of specific articles, in order to avoid, if possible, every future ground of misunderstanding. The reason of this is evident, as there is no common judge between nations and, as general principles, however clear, not infrequently receive different interpretations according to the interest and disposition of the parties, prudence requires that they should guard beforehand against similar misconstructions by such explanations as the nature of the subject will admit of. The particular rules, therefore, which Mr Jenkinson is pleased to call exceptions to the general principle are in fact clear and direct inferences from it, which have been introduced into treaties *ex majore cautela*. Nothing can afford a better proof of the necessity of such express stipulations than the very attempt which is made by Mr Jenkinson to drawn them out of the general rule.

every nation enjoys, its own produce or property; the other to the property of the enemy.[105]

But this point is still more clearly explained by the assistance of other treaties, where articles of the same force as the 21st and 22d of the Treaty of Madrid, are inserted and the intention of them fully made appear from the subsequent parts of the same treaties. In the treaty of commerce between Great Britain and Sweden, of the 21st of October 1661, it is stipulated by the 11th article that "it is by no means to be understood that the subjects of one confederate, who is not a party in a war, shall be restrained in their liberty of trade and navigation with the enemies of the other confederate, who is involved in such war"; and then in the article which immediately follows, the meaning of these words becomes manifestly beyond a doubt; it is there so far from being supposed that they liberty here granted can be so interpreted as to imply a right of conveying the effects of an enemy, but the very attempt to practice it under favour of this liberty is there called "a fraud" (*see the Treaty of Commerce between Great Britain and Sweden, Oct. 21, 1661*); and as a "most heinous crime" is ordered "to be most severely punished" and to prevent any collusion in this respect, the vessels of both parties are required to be furnished with passports "specifying of what nation the proprietors are to whom the effects on board them belong". And in the Treaty of Commerce between Great Britain and Denmark, of the 11th of July 1670, a right of free trade with the enemy is stipulated in the 16th article; and afterwards by the 20th article the extent of this right is made apparent; here the means are set down to prevent the designs of those who under favour of this stipulation should attempt to protect the effects of the enemy, and the illegality of such a

---

[105] Here is another instance of false reasoning. Contraband of war is excepted because it is in its very nature hostile; for that reason it is prohibited in all treaties of navigation and commerce and according to the general opinion of mankind, the prohibition or exception flows from the nature of the things themselves. If maritime jurisprudence were less versatile, less arbitrary, if interest did not so frequently prevail over principle, fewer precautions would be required, everything would be directed by the plain dictates of reason and natural law, and national quarrels would be at an end.

practice being supposed, as not necessary to be expressed, the article then declares, "but lest this liberty of navigation and passage for one ally might during a war which the other may be engaged in, by sea or land, with any other State be of prejudice to such other ally, and the goods belonging to the enemy be fraudulently concealed, under the colourable pretense of their being in amity together, to prevent, therefore, all fraud of that sort, all ships shall be furnished with passports"; the form of which is there set down, and is the same as that mentioned above. From these treaties then it manifestly appears that by a general stipulation in favour of trade with the enemy of another power, negociators never intended to imply a right to carry freely the effects of that enemy; but that to establish such a right, it is necessary to have it expressly mentioned.[106] The 21st and 22d articles therefore of the Treaty of Madrid in which liberty of traffic to the countries of the enemies of Great Britain is thus in general stipulated can be to grant to the subjects of the Crown of Spain no other right but that of carrying on without any injuries, "molestation", or "disturbance", such traffic as would otherwise be legal according to the law of nations, and by this law, in time of war, it never could be legal to protect the effects of an enemy;[107] a privilege, however, like this Great Britain hath consented to grant in her commercial treaties with France and Holland;[108] the first of these is put an end to by the present war; it remains, therefore, that I now discourse on this privilege, as it is stipulated in the British treaties with Holland; and I propose to shew that here also it is extinct. But to give a fuller view of my subject, and to shew the origin and intention of this privilege, it will be necessary to enter a little into the history of it; and to

---

[106] Precisely the reverse. The principle of freedom of trade is first established, but afterwards the contracting parties think proper to limit it. Such is the order observed in the Treaty, and it is conformable to sound logic. "I recognize all your rights, but I require that you will abstain from the use of this particular one". No one certainly will say with Mr. Jenkinson that this restriction does not presuppose liberty of commerce, or that the exception constitutes the general law.

[107] This is a *petitio principii* and an arbitrary restriction of a general clause.

[108] She did the same by a treaty concluded in 1664 between Oliver Cromwell and the King of Portugal.

relate the manner in which the article that grants it was first admitted into treaties.

When the United Provinces had put an end by the Treaty of Munster to that long war which they had so nobly maintained in support of their liberties, and had happily crowned their labours by obtaining a full acknowledgement of their sovereignty, delivered from the cares of war, they wisely turned their thoughts towards the arts of peace; after long contentions among themselves, their commercial provinces had at length obtained the greatest lead in the State; the interest of trade was, of course, the principal object of their council; their enemies were reduced; all who favoured war were not longer in credit; and the views of their ministers terminated chiefly in giving permanence to that extensive traffic which had supported them through all their distress and to the effects of which they principally attributed all their power of freedom.

They were indeed at this time so fully masters of almost all the commerce of the world that they had little else to do but to preserve the possession of it; the public was, on this occasion, amused with a new species of policy, the offspring rather of avarice than ambition, desirous of keeping the rest of mankind in indolence that it might more fully reap the fruits of its own industry; where wealth was at least the first object in view, though in the end it might be accompanied by its usual attendant, power; the arts which they practiced to preserve their fisheries and to secure to themselves alone the trade of the Asiatic spices are well known and not at present to our purpose; they urged loudly the freedom of navigation, till they had made it free indeed for themselves, but they have been charged with practicing a different doctrine on the other side of the line to what the professed on this; and with seeking to establish an exclusive trade on those very seas whose freedom from papal grants and Spanish pretensions the pen of their Grotius had so ably defended.

There was, however, another species of commerce which demanded their attention even more than either of the former; as it was not only a profitable branch of traffic in itself, but as it greatly tended to the security of the rest, by being the principal basis of their naval power; this was the trade of freightage, or the carrying trade, the subject of our present discourse. To understand their views in this respect, we must first take notice of the foundation on which their policy was built; they had succeeded to the Hanseatic traders in becoming the carriers of the world; long possession had, therefore, furnished them with great number of sailors and ships; and to these they added uncommon parsimony and industry, the natural endowments of their people; these made them contented with small profits and enabled them to carry the manufactures of each country even cheaper than the natives of it themselves; with such happy circumstances in their favour, they were sure of making this branch of trade wholly and perpetually their own, if they could, by their negociations and policy, establish two points: the first was that no nation should grant to its own natives any privileges in relation to freightage, which the people of Holland should equally enjoy. And as the consequences of war should otherwise frequently interrupt the course of this traffic, they labored to obtain, as their second point, that whenever any other nation was engaged in war, they might then enjoy, as neuters, the right of protecting the property of its enemies. These points, once obtained, would open a larger field on which their industry might exert itself than what they could otherwise of right pretend to enjoy. They were wise, however, in endeavouring to obtain it; no nation besides themselves had more shipping that what was equal to the carriage of their own manufactures. They alone, therefore, could carry on the freightage of other countries and largely reap, when their neighbours were at war, the advantages proposed.

The regency of Holland labored with great perseverance for the establishment of these two points: their great Minister de Witt (*Lettres de Mons. DeWitt passim*) filled all instructions and dispatches with every argument and motive which his active mind could invent in support of these favourite maxims: they were willing to give up any temporary advantage to gain that which, once acquired, would prove for ages an overflowing spring of wealth. By their negociations they earnestly labored to induce France to comply with their desires in these respects; but here they were a long while unsuccessful. In opposition to the first point of their policy, Fouquet, while he was at the head of the French marine and finances, established the tax of 50 sous per ton on all foreign shipping; and endeavoured thereby to encourage and augment freightage of his own country; and when upon his disgrace Colbert succeeded to his employments, this tax of 50 sous was almost the only part of the former's policy which the latter thought fit to adopt. It is amazing with what zeal and application the Ministers of Holland contended for the abolition of it: France at length relaxed her severity on this head, not so much to favour the trade of the Dutch as in compliance with the interests of her own. Colbert's great scheme to improve the manufactures of his country had in truth better success than his plans for the augmentation of its marine, and the frequent wars in which his ambitious master involved his kingdom gave repeated checks to the freightage of his people. France therefore at least found it necessary to give a larger vent to her manufactures by opening her ports to foreign vessels; and for this purpose she took off the tax of 50 sous by the Treaty of Ryswick, as far as it related to the ships of Holland alone and since that time she has regulated her conduct in this particular as the interest of her trade requires. In time of war, she always remits this tax, as she is then forced to make use of the freightage of neutral nations, her naval power not being equal to the protection of her own; and in time of peace she preserves the tax, or not, as the increase or diminution of her shipping requires, always giving the greatest encouragement to her own marine, which is consistent with the preservation of her manufactures.

France consented sooner to the other point of Dutch policy and granted by treaty to the vessels of Holland, as neuters, the right of protecting the effects of an enemy; the laws of France, indeed, have continued always to determine against this right and in this respect; therefore, their laws and treaties contradict each other; some very ancient ordinance of that kingdom (as we have shewn above) had adjudged as lawful prize in this case, not only the enemies goods, but had joined also in the condemnation the neutral vessel which carried them;[109] the last, however, of these points was remitted as early as 1646 by a temporary treaty

[109] This only proves the uncertainty of maritime jurisprudence.

these made with Holland; the neutral vessel and all the effects of a friend found on board it by this were ordered to be spared; by a subsequent negociation, Holland endeavoured to get this privilege further confirmed and extended; it was one great point of Monsieur Boréel's employment in his long embassy at Paris; at last, however, in the memorable treaty of defensive alliance between Holland and France of the 27th of April, 1662, this favour was obtained in its full extent; by the 35th article (*see the treaties in the letters of D'Estrade, tom 1*) it is reciprocally agreed that all which shall be found on board the vessels of eitherof the contracting parties "*encore que la charge ou partie d'icelle fût aux ennemis sera libre et affranchie*". This article was again renewed by the marine treaty of 1678, and by several subsequent treaties; the marine treaty of December 21, 1739, was the last in which it was inserted; this continued in force during part of the last war; but in the year 1765 the French Government declared this treaty void by an act of council, and it hath never since been renewed. France, from the condition of her marine, could certainly reap no advantage from the insertion of this article in her own treaties; but it was wise in her to endeavor to establish the point as a general maxim of national law among other countries; experience hath proved to her the use of it in time of war.[110]

But Holland most exerted her policy to bring that nation to a compliance with her maxims, whom she most apprehended as her rival in trade: the scandalous ignorance of the English ministers in point of commerce, and the little attention which they paid to their interests of it, gave such advantages for some time to the Dutch, that more vessels of that country were seen in the ports of our colonies than ever of our own; the shipping of England, from the reign of Elizabeth, had been in a constant decline; we should hardly have believed that in the reign of Charles I England could not have furnished more than three merchant vessels of 300 tons, if Sir Josiah Child had not

---

[110] If France consulted in this her own interest, at least it accorded with natural reason and the principles of the law of nations; and her example has been several times followed, even in England. See the XIth article of the Commercial Treaty with Russia of 1734 and the Xth article of that of 1766.

affirmed it; the time at length arrived when we were to be put in this respect on an equality with our neighbours; and to vindicate (as it were) the advantages of our own industry and produce to ourselves; in 1651 the Parliament of England passed into an Ordinance that noble strain of commercial policy, called since the act of navigation; Mr. St. John, returning about this time from his embassy at The Hague, became the happy instrument which Providence made use of to accomplish this great work (*Ludlow's Memoirs, vol. 1, p. 345*); resenting highly the refusal which had there been given to his proposals and the insults which had been offered to his person, he warmly solicited, and at length induced, the Council of State to move the Parliament to pass it; the committee sat five days in forming it; and it was at last published by order of the house with great pomp and ceremony at the Royal Exchange;[111] the Dutch were so sensible of its consequences, that it was the principal cause of the ensuing war; they called it in a manifesto (*The Manifesto of Holland, 1652*), published soon after, "a vile act and order". At the negociations for that peace which put an end to the war, DeWitt labored with his usual industry and acuteness to procure the abolition of it; his efforts were happily in vain; they who made the law attended with vigour the execution of it; the effects of it were immediately apparent. This act of policy alone hath fortunately outweighed all our other follies and extravagancies; though condemned by some of our historians, and unnoticed by others, it hath proved the fertile source of all our naval power; it hath operated insensibly to our preservation and hath been

[111] It was on that occasion that the long parliament ordered Selden's famous *Mare clausum* to be translated into English. His object was to diffuse that writer's doctrine among the English people and to give the sanction of the national suffrage to the negotiations what were then carrying on with Holland in order to oblige that power to acknowledge the maritime dominion of Great Britain, particularly in the channel, which she called her own. Oliver Cromwell, at first the warmest supporter of that pretension, abandoned it as soon as he has expelled his shadow of a parliament and declared himself protector. He made peace with the Dutch and contented himself with obtaining from them the salute at sea, not as an acknowledgement of the pretended dominion of Great Britain, but as a token of deference for his rank and power.

the spring from whence hath flowed the wealth and greatness of England.[112]

Our ancestors, with equal constancy, for some time withstood the other maxim of Dutch policy and would not permit their vessels, as neuters, to protect the effect of the enemy. By a very ancient and remarkable treaty made when the Dukes of Burgundy were sovereigns of the low countries, the contrary opinion had long been established; in that it was determined "Quod subdite Unius Principum Praedictorum (that is, Henry VII, King of England, and Philip, Duke of Burgundy) "non adducent aut adduci facient per mare 'frauduloisê', vel quocumque colore, aliqua bona seu merchandizas inimicorum alterius earundem principum". And it farther stipulated that in case the master of the neutral vessel shall endeavor by a false report to defraud the captor of any of his enemy's effects, he shall be obliged to make good the loss sustained thereby, by the forfeiture of as much of his own. Frequent applications were made before the restoration, both to the parliament and to the protector, to alter the course of proceeding in this respect; but those heads which formed the act of navigation were too wise to consent to this; a particular occasion, however, at last induced England to make the concession; by the Treaty of Commerce made at The Hague 17th of February 1668 this point was fully settled to the satisfaction of Holland, by the 10th articles (*Intercursus Magnus in Rymer's Foedera, vol. XII, p. 585*) of which it was fully stipulated that the shipping of each country should carry freely the goods of the enemies of the enemies of the other. The circumstances of the time and the situation of affairs when this article was framed account for its admission into this treaty, and very strongly apologise for the authors of it; Louis the XIVth had then just commenced the first career of his ambition, and England resolved with spirit to throw herself in

[112] This is not the proper place to analyze this Eulogium of the English Navigation Act because it is but an episode in Mr. Jenkinson's discourse. It is enough to observe that it is foreign to France, because she is not employed in the carrying or coasting trade and far from carrying the productions of other countries, she herself abandons in a great degree the carrying trade in her own productions. A note is not the proper place to enter more fully into the consideration of this state of things.

his way. Holland was then engaged in a strong defensive alliance with France, from whom it was necessary to separate her and to make her join with England to support the independency of Europe. The Dutch ministers seized this fortunate opportunity of obtaining from England the same advantages which they had already acquired by their treaties with France. It hath been the policy of most republics never to enter into any alliance where some benefit doth not accrue to themselves; and Holland could not be expected to deviate from this maxim on the present occasion, in compliment to the King of England, who had always shewn but little affection to the States; the war also with that monarch was but lately ended; and the wound but weakly healed; the French treaty of 1662, besides its defensive stipulations, contained also several commercial regulations, the favorite object of Holland; these had been provisionally referred to a few months before at Breda with a design to prevent any intermediate disputes between England and Holland, until a treaty of commerce, which was then under deliberation, was concluded; but unless these were perpetuated on the present occasion, and formed into a permanent national treaty to which England was averse (*Sir William Temple to Lord Arlington, Feb. 12, 1668*), the States were resolved not to join in the alliance proposed. Mons. De Witt expressly told Sir William Temple "That the treaty of defensive alliance must, for a basis, have at the same time an adjustment of matters of commerce"; and unless this could be obtained, it was the avowed opinion of that great Pensionary not to conclude. Influenced by the sentiments of their minister, the States persisted in the same resolution; they forced at last Sir William Temple to yield the point; apprehensive of the least delay and of the uncertainties which would necessarily follow from it, he ventured to comply with their desires, though he exceeded thereby his instructions; a private promise passed first between him and Mons. De Witt, and in consequence of that, a few weeks after, a treaty of commerce was concluded.[113]

We have before observed that in the 35th article of the Treaty of 1662, the French consented to grant the right to protection to

[113] Ibid., Jan. 24, 1668.

neutral vessels; this, therefore, came of course to be inserted in our commercial treaty of 1668, and the advantages which would arise from thence in favour of the trade of Holland, were the concessions which England then chose to make, that she might obtain the assistance of that republic against France. To what other purpose could England at this time establish a rule of commerce which she had before so often refused, and now so reluctantly granted to the earnest solicitations of the States? Any benefit which the British trade might reap from the mutual stipulation of this article could never be the object which the ministers of this country had in view. The article considered by itself is of the most fatal consequence to the power and trade of Great Britain; when she is at peace and her neighbours are at war, she cannot reap any benefits from it, as for her own shipping is not more than equal to the trade of her people; and when, on the other hand, Great Britain is at war, and her neighbours at peace, it tends to defeat the best part of her power, and to render fruitless the efforts of her naval force; while at the same time, considered as a general maxim of right among other nations, Great Britain neither wants the use of it, as she is equal in time of war to the protection of her own shipping, neither can her merchants enjoy the advantage of it, as the employment of foreign freightage is in most respects directly contrary to her laws. This article was again renewed in the treaty of commerce 1674 in consequence of its having been before stipulated in that of 1668. The treaty of 1674 is the maritime regulation that at present subsists between Great Britain and Holland.

In this manner, therefore, the article having obtained existence in these treaties, we are now to consider whether it is still in force.

Treaties of alliance being nothing more than stipulations of mutual advantages between two communities in favour of each other ought to be considered in the nature of a bargain; the conditions of which are always supposed to be equal, at least in the opinion of those who make it; he, therefore, who breaks his part of the contract destroys the equality of justice of it and forfeits all pretense to those benefits which the other party had stipulated in his favour: "*Si pars una*" (says Grotius) (*Grotius de Jure Belli ac Pacis, lib. ii, cap. Xv, sec. 15*), "*foedus violaverit, poterit altera à faedere discedere, nam capita faederis singular conditionis vim habent*". And Puffendorf (*Puffendorf de jure nat. & Gentium, lib. iii, cap. Viii, sec. 8*), speaking of conventions, says: "nec hos alterum obligant, ubi ab uno legibus conventionis non fuerit satisfactrum".

The next question then is – Hath Holland complied with her part of the treaties or contracts, to which she is mutually bound with England? Hath she performed all that she hath stipulated in our favour? Or hath she been deficient in the execution of some article in which the very life of our alliance is contained? If so material a part should be extinguished, it would be unnatural to suppose that any lesser limb of the treaties should have vigour. Holland, in this case, could have no pretence to require the execution of what may have been conceded in her favour; especially, if the performance of it would operate to the detriment of that ally whose friendship she hath forsaken.

I doubt not but my reader hath already answered in his own mind the question proposed – that the possessions of the Crown of Great Britain in Europe have been attacked by the Armies of France – that in consequence of this on the 2d of August 1756, the British Government made to the States General in proper form the necessary requisition – that in such case Holland is obliged by treaties to grant immediate succours, and after a certain time to join with Great Britain in open war – that she hath not performed these conditions, and hath therefore forfeited all title to any advantages contained in those treaties, and above all, to such as may arise from the nature of the war itself?

I shall state, however, this point of something more particularly. Holland is engaged in three different guaranties or defensive treaties with Great Britain: the first is that ancient original defensive alliance, which hath been the basis of all the subsequent treaties between the two nations; this treaty was designed to have been made immediately after the triple alliance, but the unsteady conduct of the ministers of Charles the Second and the unfortunate attachment of that monarch to the French Court for some years delayed it; it was at least, however, concluded at Westminster the 3d of March 1678. It is (except in two immaterial alterations) an exact copy of the twelve first articles of the French Treaty of 1662; and both were negociated by the same minister, Monsieur Van Beuningen. In the preamble of this Treaty, "the preservation of each other dominions" is set forth as the cause of making it; and the stipulations of it are "a mutual guaranty of all they already enjoyed, or might hereafter acquire by treaties of peace, in Europe only". The farther guaranty, "all treaties which were at that time made or might hereafter conjointly be made with any other power". They promise also "to defend and preserve each other in the possession of all towns or fortresses which did at that time belong, or shall for the future belong, to either of them"; and for this purpose it is determined that "when either nation is attacked or molested, the other shall immediately succor it with a certain number of troops and men of war, and shall be obliged to break with the aggressor in two months, immediately after the party that is already at war shall require it; and that they shall then act conjointly with all their forces, to bring the common enemy to a reasonable accommodation".

That Holland hath not complied with the terms of this guaranty is evident; Minorca, "a possession of the Crown of Great Britain and which she acquired by treaty", had been attacked; this is one case of the guaranty by that attack, "a treaty that was made in common concert"; the Treaty of Utrecht hath been broken; this is a second case of the guaranty; and by these means "England hath been deprived of a possession which of right belonged to her"; this is a third case of the guaranty; and notwithstanding all this, Holland hath not as yet granted the succours stipulated; and many more than two months have passed without her having entered into war conjointly with England, as the treaty requires.

The second species of defensive alliance which subsists between Great Britain and Holland is that which was first agreed to in the treaty of barrier and succession of October the 29th, 1709, and again more particularly stipulated in another treaty to the same purpose of January 29th, 1713; the design of this treaty is the guaranty of the Dutch barrier on one part, and the guaranty of the firmest barrier of British liberty, the Protestant succession, on the other; the stipulations are (*Article XIV of the Treaty of Barrier and Succession of January 29, 1713*) "that in case either should be attacked, the other should furnish at the requisition if the party injured, but at his own expense, certain succours there expressed, and if the danger should be such as to require greater force, that he shall be obliged to augment his succours and ultimately to act with all his power in open war against the aggressor". I pretend not to make any use of this treaty in the present case, and only mention it to give a fuller view of the alliances which subsist between us. Here, however, I will indulge a wish that the case of this guaranty, as far as it relates to the right of the Crown of Great Britain, may never again exist. I always read with sorrow that there ever was a time when the unfortunate dissensions of our people in a point where the whole of their happiness was concerned should have made it necessary to add any other sanction to our own laws than such as our own power can afford them. These days, however, of shame now, I hope, are passed; more than forty years experience of the mildest government must have won the most obdurate heart to confess the present felicity and bless the hand which bestows it. When forgetting ancient errors, we are thus united in defence, the affections of his Majesty's subjects are the happiest guaranty of his right.

I come now to the last species of defensive alliance which subsists between Great Britain and Holland. This was concluded at The Hague the 4th January 1717. To this Treaty France was a party. The intention or view of it was "the preservation of each other reciprocally in the possession of their dominions, as established by the Treaty of Utrecht"; and the stipulations were "to defend all and each of the articles of the said treaty, as far as they relate to the contracting parties respectively, or each of them in particular; and they guaranty all the kingdoms, provinces, States, rights, and advantages, which each of the parties at the signing of that treaty possessed"; and in a Separate Article all this is confined to "Europe only". The succours stipulated in support of this guaranty are much the same as those mentioned above; first "interposition of good offices" – then, "a certain number of forces", and lastly, "declaration of war". This treaty was renewed by the quadruple alliance of 1718, and again by the accession of Holland to the treaty of Hanover of 1726, and last of all by the 3d Article of the Treaty of Aix-la-Chapelle 1748.

Holland hath by no means executed the terms of this guaranty; Minorca, "a possession of the Crown of England in Europe, which she enjoyed at the signing of this treaty", hath been attacked; this is one case of the guaranty. By this attack, "the article of the treaty of Utrecht, by which that possession was ceded to England" hath been broken; this is another case of the guaranty. I need not again observe that Holland, in consequence of this, hath neither granted the succours nor declared war, as this treaty also requires.

It will, however, perhaps be objected "that Great Britain was the aggressor in the present War, and unless she had been first attacked, the case of the guaranties doth not exist". True it is, that the treaties which contain these guaranties are called defensive treaties only; but the words of them, and particularly of that of 1678, which is the basis of all the rest by no means express the point clearly in the sense of the objection; they guaranty in general "all the rights and possessions" of both parties against "all kinds, princes, republic, and States"; so that if either "shall be attacked" or "molested", whether it be "by hostile act or open war" or "in any other manner whatsoever, disturbed in the possession of his estates, territories, rights, immunities, and freedom of commerce"; it then declares what shall be done in defence of these objects of guaranty by the ally who is not at war; but it is nowhere mentioned, as necessary, that the attack of these should be the first injury or attack. Nor doth this loose manner of expression appear to have been an omission of inaccuracy. They who have framed these guaranties, certainly chose to leave this question without any farther explanation, to that good faith which must ultimately decide upon the execution of all contracts made between sovereign States. It is not presumed they hereby meant that either party should be obliged to support every act of violence of injustice which his ally might be prompted to commit through views of interest or ambition. But, on the other hand, they were cautious of affording too frequent opportunities to pretend, that the case of the guarantie did not exist and of eluding thereby the principal intention of the alliance; both these inconveniencies were equally to be avoided; and they wisely thought fit to guard against the latter of these, no less than the former. They knew that in every war between civilized nations each party always endeavours to throw upon the other the odium and guilt of the first act of provocation and aggression, and that the worst of cases was never without its excuse. They foresaw that this alone would unavoidably give sufficient occasion to endless cavils and disputes, whenever the infidelity of an ally inclined him to avail himself of them. To have confined therefore the case of the guaranty by a more minute description of it, and under closer restrictions of form, would have subjected to still greater uncertainty a point which, from the nature of the thing itself, was already too liable to doubt; they were sensible that the cases would be infinitely various, that the motives to self-defense, though evidently just, might not always be universally apparent, that an artful enemy might disguise the most alarming preparations, and that an injured nation might be necessitated to commit even a preventive hostility before the danger which caused it would be publicly known. Upon such considerations these negociators wisely thought proper to give the greatest latitude to this question, and to leave it open to a fair and liberal construction; such as might be expected from friends, whose interest these treaties were supposed to have forever united and such on the present occasion Great Britain hath a right to demand.

If, however, we should, for the present, waive this interpretation and allow the treaties to have all the meaning which they who make this objection require, the evidence of facts will sufficiently prove that France was the aggressor in the present war. If we look to America, the present war there is little more than a continuation of the last; repeated usurpations of the possessions of Great Britain have been there the constant employment of France, almost from the hour in which the treaty of Aix was signed; and these were at last followed by an avowed military attack upon a fort belonging to the Crown of Great Britain by regular troops acting under a commission from the Court of France. If we consider America as having no concern in the present question, the same ambitious power will also be found to have been the aggressor in the European War; France early manifested her hostile intentions in Europe in 1753 in direct opposition to the express stipulations (*Ninth Article of the*

Treaty of Utrecht; fourth article of the Treaty of The Hague, 1717, and Seventeenth Article of the Treaty of Aix-la-Chapelle) of three solemn treaties. She began to restore the port of Dunkirk and Holland then considered this action in such a light as induced her in conjunction with the British Government to present a memorial against it. France also gave another proof of her hostile intentions by her design to invade Great Britain, avowed by her ministers in every court in Europe and sufficiently manifested by the preparations which she publicly made for it. And these were likewise followed by an open attack upon a European island belonging to Great Britain, an attack upon the island of Minorca. It seems indeed allowed by the opinion of the parties concerned that by the attack of Minorca, the European war was first completely opened, notwithstanding all which had passed elsewhere, proposals for an accommodation of the American disputes were never discontinued, nor the war considered as universal, till that island was absolutely invaded. As for the captures at sea, the avowed cause upon which these were taken sufficiently evinces that they undoubtedly belong to the American War; they were made in consequence of the hostilities first commenced in America, and were seized as reprisals for the injuries there committed upon the property of the people of England; as facts they were always declared to be taken up by the ministers of that kingdom, and the virtue of them to be on that account obtained (*See the British Declaration of War*); and upon application made to parliament soon after the seizure of them, the legislature expressly refused to distribute them among the captors, as they have done in respect to all other prizes which have been made since the war of Europe began. But even if this distinction which puts the question out of all doubt had not been made by the ministers of England, these captures surely can never be looked upon but as a part of the American war; it will not certainly be denied that such a war may extend itself to the Ocean, without having changed either its nature of denomination; what but captures at sea have been the great constituent part of every American war before the present; as a war upon the American continent must always be supported by succours sent from Europe, it is absurd to suppose that either party in this case would not endeavour, as far as he was able, to take or destroy entirely the shipping of his enemy, by which alone the succours could be conveyed. Countries which have very little internal force within themselves cannot be defended but by such troops as are thrown into them; to defeat therefore the only means by which this relief can be effective must be esteemed as material a part of such a war as the means to invest a fortress are a material part of a siege. But after all, these captures were subsequent to the restoration of the port of Dunkirk, or the (*Undoubted intelligence was received of this before the 27th August 1755, when general orders were given to bring in French vessels; the Syson and the Alcide were taken on the coast of America, and are therefore in every light a part of that war*) preparations to invade Great Britain; and these can never be considered but as undoubted facts of aggression; it is not the first military action alone, but hostile preparations where the design is apparent (*Quanquam et aliquando favor defensionis ab illius partibus Stat, qui prior arma alteri infert; puta si quis ... hostem invasionis jam certum, per celeritatem oppresserit, dum ille adhuc in adparando bello est occupatus". Puffendorf de jure Nat. & G. Lib. 8, cap. 6, sec. 3*), and the usurpation of another's rights, or the denial of justice; which in the opinion of the ablest writers denominate the aggressor. The object of the defensive treaties are "rights, immunities, and liberties" no less than "towns or territories", and "the disturbance" or "molestation" of the former, as well as "the attack" of the latter, are expressly declared to be cases within the guarantees.

A more subtle objection will still perhaps be in order to what has been said. It will be urged "that though France was the aggressor in Europe, yet that it was only in consequence of the hostilities commenced before in America; with which it is determined by treaties that Holland is to have no concern, and that the rights contested at present are not contained in the guaranties". If the reasoning on which this objection is founded was admitted, it would alone be sufficient to destroy the effects of every guaranty and to extinguish that confidence which nations mutually place in each other on the faith of defensive alliances; it points out to the enemy a certain method of avoiding the inconvenience of such an alliance; it shews him where he ought to begin his attack; let only the first effort be made upon some place not included in the guaranty, and after that he may pursue his view against the very object without any apprehensions of the consequence; let France first attack some little spot belonging to Holland in America, and her barrier would be no longer guaranteed; To argue in this manner would be to trifle with the most solemn engagements. The proper object of guarantees is the preservation of some particular country in the possession of some particular power. The treaties above-mentioned promise the defence of the dominions of each party in Europe simply and absolutely, wherever they are "attacked' or "molested". If in the present war the first attack was made out of Europe, it is manifest that long ago an attack hath also been made in Europe; and that it is beyond a doubt the case of these guarantees.

Let us try, however, if we cannot discover what hath once been the opinion of Holland on a point of this nature. It hath already been observed that the defensive alliance between England and Holland of 1678 is but a copy of the twelve first articles of the French treaty of 1662. Soon after Holland had concluded this last alliance with France, she became engaged in a war with England; the attack then first began, as in the present case, out of Europe, on the coast of Guinea; and the cause of the war was also the same, a disputed right to certain possessions out of the bounds of Europe, some in Africa and other in the East Indies; Hostilities having continued for some time in those parts, they afterwards commenced in Europe; immediately upon this Holland declared that the case of that guaranty did exist, and demanded the succours which were stipulated. I need not produce the memorials of their ministers to prove this; history sufficiently informs us that France acknowledged the claim, granted the succours, and entered even into open war in the defence of her ally. Here then we have the sentiments of Holland on the same article in a case minutely parallel: France also pleads in favour of the same opinion, though her concession in this respect checked at the time her youthful monarch in the first essay of his ambitions delayed for several months his entrance into the Spanish provinces, and brought on him the enmity of England.

If any doubt can yet remain about the meaning and interest of this article, it may farther be proved from the opinion of the minister who made it. Immediately after Holland was engaged in the war above mentioned, she sent to the Court of France Monsieur Van Beuningen to press the execution of that guaranty, which he had himself concluded. It is remarkable that in his conversations on this subject with Monsieur de Lionne that the same objection was debated against which I now content. Van Beuningen treated it with great contempt, he asked Monsieur de Lionne (*Lettre de M. Van Beuningen à M. De Witt. December 26, 1664*) of the pretence of the European war being only a continuation of that of Africa was what the English alone alleged to deprive them of the succour of France, or whether the French Minister laid any stress upon it as an argument at all to be supported. De Lionne at first gave him to understand that he thought it of the same weight: "*à quoi je répondis*", says Van Beuningen, "*que je ne croyais pas que cette objection fut sérieuse, puisqu'il dit alors, que celui qui a commencé de guerre en Europe, n'a ne pouvait passer pour troubler la paix et le commerce en Europe, parce qu'il l'avait troublé ailleurs auparavant*", and then he adds: "*ce que j'ajoutai à ce raisonnement, pour réfuter cette objection, resta sans réplique*". This was the same Monsieur Van Beuningen who negociated our defensive treaty of 1678; he made the terms of both these guaranties precisely alike; and we before shewed that our common case at present is exactly the same as this on which his opinion hath been produced.

If, however, the words of these treaties had been against the interpretation which hath been given them, I might justly have appealed to the spirit of them, as alone a sufficient foundation on which to build my opinion. The whole design of all these our alliances with Holland is to form a barrier against the power of those mighty kingdoms whose ambition might otherwise induce them to destroy the independency of Europe. They are, in fact, a regular continuation of that policy which gave birth to the Triple Alliance, where the dangerous spirit of the French councils first began to appear. To answer this great end, they guaranty the possessions of those two maritime countries who, from their wealth, their internal strength, and their incapacity of having any ambitious views themselves, are the best security against the designs of others. But as the obligations of these guaranties are too considerable to be made use of on trifling occasions, for this purpose the contracting parties have made one exception: the rights of the European kingdoms in the distant parts of the world, and particularly in America, are very uncertain and the cause of frequent dissensions, and it is well known that wars have there subsisted for many years between the trading subjects and commercial companies of the several nations, while the mother countries have lived, if not in friendship, at least in peace; this then is the case particularly except from the guaranty; but this exception must always be so interpreted as to be made consistent with the principal intention of the alliance. If some great country out of Europe should become of so much importance that for the interest of Europe it ought to remain in the hands of the present possessors; if the same great disturber of mankind, after many fruitless attempts in his own neighbourhood, should now turn his thoughts another way and should endeavour, by distant diversions, to enfeeble that power on whose consideration the safety of the public very much depends, and to deprive her of the sources of her wealth, which she hath always so largely expended in support of the common cause, would a generous friend, who attends to the spirit of his engagements, say that the case of the guaranty did not then exist? And, when the reason of the exception is vanished, would he urge the pretence of it as an excuse for giving up the principal point on which the alliance was constructed? But if to this distant attempt the enemy should add an open and avowed war in Europe, should threaten the mother country with invasion, attack her fortresses and take occasion from thence to spread his armies over the continent, shall this pretended exception still be urged when the literal case of guaranty is now become apparent? On this weak foundation shall a wise people, under such obligations, not only refuse to grant assistance, but not permit their forsaken ally to make a full use of his power? Holding back in this manner his arm, when they will not stretch forth their own, and claiming from the very contracts they have broken that privilege which they turn to the destruction of her ally. The absurdity is shocking; such, however, is the present case of

England. Unhappy in her friendships! She hath neither that assistance from allies which they are bound by treaty to give her, neither is she allowed to exert even her own force, though abandoned to her own defence.

In this manner the point might be determined on a general view of these treaties; and this alone would be sufficient; but it may be farther proved that the article on which Holland founds her right of protecting the property of the enemy, as far as it relates to the present case, hath been particularly repealed long ago. The treaty in which this article was inserted was concluded the 1st of December 1674. Four years after this, in 1678, was made that defensive alliance in which it was stipulated between Holland and England, "that if either party should be attacked in Europe, the other should declare war against the aggressor two months after he is required". By this treaty, therefore, two months after England is attacked by France in Europe, Holland must become the enemy of the latter as well as England; and to be the enemy of another means certainly to distress his trade and seize his property, not to preserve the former and protect the latter. If this therefore is the right interpretation of the word enemy, this article directly and positively declares that two months after France has attacked the European possessions of England, the ships of Holland shall not have a right to protect the effects of the French. This therefore is derogatory to the 8th article of the maritime treaty of 1678, and as being posterior to it, absolutely repeals it. In all laws (and such are treaties in respect to nations) the last enacted always set aside the former, so far as they disagree. Cicero (*Cicero de Inventione*) says it ought to be considered: "*utra lex posterius sit lata, nam postrema quaeque gravissima*".

But the maxim is not necessary on the present occasion since the same article is again repealed by two subsequent treaties in words as positive as can be used; for in that treaty (*Treaty of Friendship and Alliance between England and Holland, August 1689*) by which they were again renewed upon the accession of the present family to the throne, the treaties of 1674 and 1678 are expressly mentioned and made of both a part; and it is there declared that "they shall have the same force and effect as if they had been inserted in these treaties verbatim; that is to say, so far as they not differ, or are contrary to one another, yet as whatever hath been established by any later treaty shall be understood and performed in the sense therein expressed, without any regard had to any former treaty". Can it then be doubted that the articles above-mentioned are "contrary to one another", as much as peace and war, as much as friendship and enmity? Is not the defensive alliance of 1678 "a later treaty" than the marine regulation of 1674? And ought not therefore, according to the words of the renewal, "the article of the latter to be performed in the sense therein expressed, without any regard being had to the former". Since then, the year 1689, this article as far as it relates to the present case, hath been twice repealed. This much, therefore, may suffice to shew, that the right of Holland in this respect is extinct.[114]

---

[114] Mr. Jenkinson has entered into much detail to prove, 1st, that France was the aggressor in the war of 1755; 2d, that a particular quarrel in American, if the hostilities should extend to Europe, calls for the execution of a guarantee limited to Europe only; 3d, that the Dutch were obliged in the latter case to fulfill the stipulations contained in their Treaties of Alliance with Great Britain; 4th, that for want of a due execution of their treaties of alliance, the Treaty of Commerce separately made was to be considered as null and void; 5th, that that Treaty being thus put aside, the Dutch flag could no longer enjoy the privilege of covering enemy's property.

We shall not discuss the question who was the aggressor in the war of 1755; it has long been decided and put at rest. Neither shall we examine whether the *casus foederis* existed with regard to Holland, or whether for want of having executed the guarantee stipulated in her treaties of alliance of 1678 & seq. their commercial treaty was *ipso facto* annulled. We shall only make two observations: 1st, that a treaty is not annulled when there is no obligation to carry it into execution, and that it is not in any case annulled *ipso facto*; but there must be a formal complaint and notice given by the party who claims its creation. 2d, that a treaty which neither is the basis nor the consequence of another continues to subsist, altho' the other has become caducory. 3d, that so little has England considered the Treaties of 1674 and 1678 as annulled, that in 1778 at the commencement of the American War, she only required the former to be modified with respect to naval forces. This last fact destroys the whole of Mr. Jenkinson's system. We shall only add that the Court of London experienced a refusal on both points, and that it was from that time that all political ties between Great Britain and the United Provinces were broken,

There remains one more claim to be considered; a claim which, if report had not averred, would by no means deserve an answer. The northern crowns, whose commercial treaties with Great Britain contain not any article which gives them expressly a right to carry the property of the enemy, have endeavoured to deduce this right from a general stipulation which is to be found in some of their treaties, declaring that "they shall be treated in the same manner as the most favoured nation". If Great Britain therefore hath granted by treaty to any other nation the right in time of war of becoming the carrier of her enemies, they think they are justly entitled to be admitted to the same favour. Under this pretence they claim this privilege, as stipulated in the Dutch treaty of 1674; but it has been proved also that the treaty of 1674, as far as it relates to the present case, is no longer in force; if the inference therefore was otherwise just, the foundation being thus destroyed, whatever is built upon it must necessarily fall with it. But this stipulation of equal favour, from the very nature of it, can relate to nothing else but such advantages as may be granted to foreign traders by the municipal laws or ordinances of each country; such as equality of customs, exception from the rigour of ancient laws, which would affect them as aliens, and the privileges of judges-conservators and consuls; these are the proper objects of favour, and because the whole detail of these could not easily be specified in a treaty for this reason they are thus comprehended in a general article. If the rights conceded by treaties were the objects of this stipulation, to what purpose were any other articles added. Since this would contain them all and would alone include every privilege which past or future treaties could afford them? And can it be supposed that any nation mentioned in this manner to preclude itself from the power of exchanging by treaty, with some particular country, any great right should, in such case, be universally forfeited to the people of every other nation who would thus reap the benefit without having been parties to the bargain? But this point is made clear beyond a

---

and that Holland became the ally of France until the epoch of the late revolution which changed the government of that country.

doubt from the words of the treaties themselves, where this general equality is stipulated.

In the treaty of commerce between Great Britain and Sweden, of the 24th of October 1661 (the principal one at present in force between the two countries) the fourth article, which contains this stipulation, plainly makes it refer to such favours only, as may be enjoyed in matters of traffic within their respective dominions. The treatment which the contracting parties shall there give to the subjects of each other is the principal purpose of the article; it specifies many particulars, and among the rest it stipulates, that the people of both countries shall have "Liberty to import and export their goods at discretion, the due customs being always paid, and the laws and ordinances of both kingdoms universally observed"; and then, manifestly connecting this with what follows, it adds, "which things being presupposed, they shall hold such ample privileges, exemptions, liberties, and immunities, as any foreigner whatsoever doth or shall enjoy"; they general equality therefore here stipulates plainly relates to those places alone where the customs of these kingdoms are to be duly paid, and the laws and ordinances of them are in force, and that is only within their respective dominions. The privileges here conceded cannot possibly have any larger extent and to confirm the sense of the article still more strongly to the explanation which hath now been given of it, the words "in the dominions and kingdoms of each other" are twice repeated, to determine clearly where that trade must be carried on, to which this favour is meant only to be granted; if, however, any doubt could yet remain in respect to this interpretation, they who made the treaty have given the strongest proof, that under this article they never intended to imply a right of carrying the property of an enemy, since, by the 12th article of this same treaty, an attempt of that nature is pronounced to be "a heinous crime" and the strongest provisions are made to prevent it. In the treaty of commerce between Great Britain and Russia, of the 2d of December 1734, this stipulation of equal favour is inserted in several articles, but it appears in every one of them to relate to nothing else but the particular privileges which the subjects of each were to enjoy while they were trading with the dominions of the other. In the second article this equality is expressly said to be granted throughout the "dominions of the contracting parties in Europe". In the third it relates only "to the favourable reception of the subjects of each other in the ports of their respective countries". In the 14th it grants only an equal freedom to import "such merchandise into each other's dominions as is allowed to the subjects of any other country", and in the 28th it refers only to the "respect and treatment which is to be given to the subjects of one party who come into the dominions of the other". In the treaty of commerce between Great Britain and Denmark of the 11th of July 1670, the latest at present in force between the two countries, the stipulation of equal favour is inserted in the 40th article; it is there said "If the Hollanders, or any other nation, hath, or shall obtain from his Majesty of Great Britain, any better articles, agreements, exemptions, or privileges, than what are contained in this treaty, the same and like privileges shall be granted to the king of Denmark and his subjects also, in most full and effectual a manner". That these privileges relate only customs and other advantages of the same kind, might be proved from the whole tenor of this treaty; but it will be sufficient to shew that the right of carrying the property of the enemy cannot possibly be intended by it. Holland had obtained this right in 1668, two years before the Danish treaty was concluded; if therefore the stipulation of equal favour contained in the 40th article could extend to an advantage of that nature, the merchants of Denmark would have been immediately entitled to it from the hour the treaty was signed, the ministers of that kingdom could not be ignorant of this; and yet in the 20th article they have positively forbid the exertion of any such right. They have even expressed the greatest apprehension, lest any liberty conceded by this treaty should be interpreted to that purpose; "lest such freedom of navigation", says the article, "or passage of the one ally, and his subjects, and people during the war, which the other may have by sea or land with any other country, may be to the prejudice of the other ally, and that goods and merchandise belonging to the enemy may be fraudulently concealed under the colour of being in amity; for preventing fraud and taking away all suspicion, it is thought fit the ships, goods, and men belonging to the other ally, in their passage and voyage be furnished with letters of passport", and in the passport the king of Denmark hath bound himself to declare that the ship and goods with which it is laden "belong to his subjects, or to others having an interest therein, who are the subjects of neutral powers; and that "they do not appertain to either of the parties now engaged in war". Nothing more, I hope, need be said to refute this weakest pretence to a right of carrying freely the property of the enemies of Great Britain.[115]

As there is no article, therefore, which grants a right of this nature at present in force in any of these commercial treaties, it is unnecessary to shew that most of the captures which England hath made of the vessels of neutral nations ought not properly to be referred to it, but may be justified by another part of the said treaties, where it is declared (*Art. IXI, Treaty of 1674 between Great Britain and Holland; the same article is found in every other commercial treaty*) "that all goods are contraband which are carried to places blockaded or invested".

The debate here would turn on the real existence of the blockade. To evince this I might shew what opinion the Dutch had of a naval blockade in 1630 (*Placart of June 26, 1630*), when they pretended to have blocked up all the coast of Flanders, and openly avowed that they would take and condemn

---

[115] Mr. Jenkinson's interpretation is perfectly just, and he might have added that those general stipulations by which favors are granted in general terms relate only to the commerce of the subjects of the contracting powers with each other, and therefore ought not to be extended in their application beyond the limits of their respective dominions; whereas those which are expressly made to regulate the commerce that may be carried on in time of war involve the interests of the belligerent governments. If, therefore, a sovereign engaged in war maintains the commercial relations which he has stipulated in a treaty with a neutral power, he fully complies with his engagement. But as to what respects navigation in time of war, he is only bound by special treaties or by the general rules of the law of nations. Every power has a right to insist upon the observance of those rules, independent of all treaties not entered into by themselves; for conventions between nations are not of a different nature from that of contracts between individuals; they are only obligatory when voluntarily entered into, and where there is no special engagement, the rules of the common law are to govern, and the common law of nations is the *jus gentium*.

all neutral ships which had the most distant appearance of being bound to the ports of that country. I might also shew their opinion of the same in 1689, when they declared (*Convention between England and Holland 1689*) publicly to the neutral nations that they designed to block up all the ports of France. I might observe that as the possession of the principal avenues to a town constitutes a blockade by land; and that it is not necessary for this purpose to have made a complete line of circumvallation; so by keeping a great squadron of ships of war cruising constantly before the ports of an enemy, by destroying in this manner totally his trade, and preventing his fleets of war from ever venturing out, except now and then a ship or two by stealth, a blockade ought certainly to be considered as completely established by sea, I might further prove the cause from its effects, and shew that the American islands at last have experienced all the consequences of such a situation; where want of communication with the mother country, distress and famine fully declare that they have been invested. But as this topic may not perhaps relate to the case of every capture and depends on the particular state of a variety of facts, I shall not dwell any longer upon it at present. The question hath here, I hope, sufficiently been argued on principles which are plain and comprehensive, on those equitable regulations which nature hath established among nations, and on those particular contracts with which communities have bound themselves. And as I before endeavoured to prove that neutral nations had no right by the former of these obligations to protect the property of the enemy; so now it hath been shewn by what policy the Dutch first obtained this privilege; by what treaties it hath since been taken from them; and by what conduct they have lately forfeited whatever might remain of this right. It hath also, I flatter myself, appeared with how little reason other neutral powers under colour of any articles in their treaties of commerce, have claimed the enjoyment of such a right. Upon the whole, therefore, I will now beg by permission to conclude that the naval power of England hath been conducted during the present war with no less justice than spirit; that the faith of our sovereign is as spotless as his courage; and that the honor of the county is unblemished.

The basis of just complaint being thus removed, those idle clamours which have been founded upon it by no means merit our attention; to charge England with ambition must appear so absurd to all who understand the nature of her government, that at the bar of reason it ought to be treated rather as calumny than accusation. Possessed of every blessing which civil government can produce, she is open to no temptation with which ambition might seduce her; pursuits of that kind might possibly operate to the destruction of her constitution, and her system of happiness might be subverted by the augmentation of her power. It must always be the interest of England to protect the just rights of commerce and to support those principles which promote the labours of mankind, since she herself can only be great from the virtuous industry of her people. To obtain the largest extent from the exertion of this, is the point to which all her policy should tend; and if forsaking these maxims, she should seek to enlarge her power by any act of ambitious injustice, may she then, for the welfare of the human race,[116] cease to be any longer great and powerful! Her courts of maritime jurisdiction are more wisely calculated to preserve the freedom of navigation than those of any other country; as they are not subject to the control of her executive power, the passions of her princes or ministers can never influence the decisions of them; and foreign traders have in favour of their property all the security which the nature of the thing will admit, the consciences of wise men determining upon matters of right, whom the threats of power cannot affect, and so are set free, as far as possible, from all bias and partiality; and to the honor of the learned persons who at present preside in those courts, one impartial testimony shall here be produced in their favour. Though treaties have expressly pointed out to all who may there think themselves injured, a regular method of

[116] These sentiments do honor to the principles and patriotism of Mr. Jenkinson, but the peace of 1763 has proved that they did not in the least influence the determination of the British Cabinet. This reminds me of what the celebrated Lord Bacon once told the Duke of Buckingham respecting the danger which Great Britain would run by extending the sphere of her dominion abroad. England had reason to remember that wholesome but useless advice when she was obliged in 1783 to abandon her American colonies.

redress before a superior tribunal, the merchants and freighters of Holland have never ventured as yet to bring to a hearing, or even to put into a way of trial, any one of the appeals which they have made from the determination of these judges, giving thereby cause to presume that they made them with no other intention but to delay the execution of the sentences; and conscious of the invalidity of their rights, they have in this manner plainly confessed the real equity of those decisions which have been passed upon them. That amid the confusions of war, some irregularities may be committed, is a misfortune too true to be denied, but the circumstances of the case under impossible to be wholly prevented. They are the consequences of all wars, not alone of the present. To destroy the trade of the enemy, it is necessary to employ privateers which cannot always be kept under those strict rules to which a more regular force is subject; these maritime hussars may sometimes exceed their commissions, and be guilty of disorders, the authors of which cannot always be punished; because the nature of the fact renders the discovery of them difficult. But can the crimes of these be imputed to ministers, whose ears are always open to complaints, and who labour, as much as possible to redress them? The privateers of England are already made subject to every restraint, which naval policy hath as yet invented to force them to conform to their duty. If, however, these are found insufficient, and if any more successful means can be discovered to prevent every unjust depredation by which the evils of war may be diminished, confident I am that Great Britain will be the first to adopt them; let them be consistent only with the use of her naval power, and conformable to justice, the British legislature will enact such into a law and the British ministry will attend most steadily to the execution of them.

But after all, the wisest regulations on occasions like this cannot be expected to answer fully the end proposed; the system of humanity is nowhere perfect, but in respect to nations its weakness is most apparent; the softer ties of natural affection among these have little effect, and no coercive bonds of power exist to regulate and control their passions; it is the virtue of government alone, on which the general prosperity depends, and treaties have no better sanction than what that virtue can give them. These were the principles on which I first commenced my discourse; by these the rules of communities are instructed to amend, as far as possible, by their prudence, what nature hath left imperfect. Ambition or avarice will augment the evil; moderation may prevent it. Every little inconvenience must be patiently suffered where a superior right makes it necessary. The love of our country should never induce us to act contrary to that love which we ought to bear to mankind, since the interests of both, if they are rightly pursued, will always be found consistent with each other.[117]

[117] The reader will himself apply these wise and virtuous reflections to the conduct of Great Britain in the present war.

A Memorial Delivered by Sir Joseph Yorke to the Deputies of the States General on the 2 November 1778

Their High Mightinesses will have received by the answer from Lord Suffolk, one of his Majesty's Principal Secretaries of State, to the Count Welderen, dated the 19th of October, the most convincing proofs of his Majesty's friendship towards them.

After an explicit detail of the hostile and unprecedented of his most Christian Majesty, which conduct occasioned the seeming irregularity of the Court of Great Britain in seizing the ships appertaining to neutral powers bound to the ports of France, the measure hath been fully explained on the principles of necessity and self-defence, against an enemy who hath ever acted covertly and by surprise. The moderation and equity of the King my master would not permit him to disregard the complaint of the subjects of their High Mightinesses from the moment there appeared a possibility to renew them. It is for this reason that his Majesty has declared his intention to release the Dutch vessels under conditions of the most amicable and the least disadvantageous, as far as circumstances will admit. The war, however, still continues, and the active endeavours of the enemy to push matters to extremity obliges his Majesty to guard against the danger. He wishes, nonetheless, to involve his good neighbours and allies as little as possible; and although France has even threatened to invade his Majesty's dominions and territories, having, for that purpose, assembled numerous armies on their coasts, the King, my master, still forbears to claim such succor from their High Mightinesses as they are bound to grant, by the most explicit and solemn treaties, whenever such succours may be on his part required, namely, the treaty of 1678, and the Separate Article of 1716; his Majesty confines himself for the present solely to lay before their High Mightinesses the state of affairs, the motive of his conduct, and the necessity he finds himself under to take measures for his own defence, and the preservation of his dominions.

It is only with this view that I am ordered by his Britannic Majesty to propose to their High Mightinesses a conference to consider of the most proper means towards an amicable regulation of such a mode of proceeding in future, respecting such articles as his Majesty, without yielding to his enemies, cannot possibly suffer them to be supplied with. It cannot have escaped the attention of their High Mightinesses that Lord Suffolk in explaining his Majesty's sentiments to Count Walderen, fully demonstrated the King's sincere desire to pay the strictest regard to the faith of treaties, as far as they do not directly tend to expose him to imminent danger. It is by no means his intention, nor is it his wish, to cause the least interruption to he commerce of Holland, usually carried on with France, excepting warlike and naval stores, and even this restriction shall be enjoyed with equity, and I am confident, with every possible degree of generosity.

I therefore, in obedience to my instructions, have taken the liberty to request an audience to know whether, in consequence of the answer delivered to Count Welderen, their High Mightinesses are resolved to open a conference with me? On my part, I entreat you to assure their High Mightinesses that as well from my being authorized by his Majesty as from my being personally disposed after a residence in this country of 27 years; their High Mightinesses will find me in every readiness to attend to their complaints and regard for their welfare; and I flatter myself that in the course of the conference I shall convince them that whatever forced and affected turn may have been given to the conduct of my Court, it has been founded on the justice, moderation and necessity of our situation. In expectation of the decision of their High Mightinesses on what I have laid before them, I trust that their known equity and friendship towards his Majesty agreeable to their recent assurances by their Envoy will prove sufficient not to authorize their subjects to carry naval stores, under convoy, to France, as being the most dangerous object to the security of Great Britain.

The affectionate language of his document, the moderation which it displays, the reluctance with which the British Court appears to have ordered the seizure of a considerable number of Dutch vessels and its apparent anxiety to redress the injury will appear very strange when compared with the real views of Sir Joseph Yorke. His object was to draw Holland into a war in which she was not at all bound to interfere and to prevail upon her to annul a treaty which had subsisted for more than a century, so that she would have been made the instrument to check the prosperity of her own commerce by the abandonment of her neutral rights and would immediately have been placed in a state of hostility with respect to France. Such incontestably were the views of the Cabinet of St. James, and Sir Joseph Yorke in this Memorial does not take pains to conceal them. Holland, however, did not fall into the snare and she endeavoured to secure her neutrality by joining the coalition of the three northern powers in 1780.

England did not consider that coalition as an act of hostility on the part of the northern crowns. Her whole resentment fell upon the United Provinces. This fact deserves to be particularly noted.

The following document filled the measure of British intrigue, and its style is very different from that of the one which immediately preceded it.

MEMORIAL PRESENTED BY SIR JOSEPH YORKE, AMBASSADOR EXTRAORDINARY AND PLENIPOTENTIARY OF THE KING OF GREAT BRITAIN TO THEIR HIGH MIGHTINESSES, THE STATES GENERAL OF THE UNITED PROVINCES OF THE LOW COUNTRIES ON THE 22D OF JULY 1779

High and Mighty Lords,

Since France, by the declaration made at London on the 13th of March last year, fully discovered the vast and dangerous designs which the Family Compact had before announced to Europe, this part of the world must bear witness to the wisdom and moderation of the King of Great Britain, who endeavoured to ward off the calamities of war, avoiding as much as possible, engaging his neighbours and allies.

A conduct like this, founded in the most pointed moderation, seemed so much to embolden the court of Versailles, that after perfidiously encouraging of rebel subjects under the mask of liberty, commerce, and independence, to plunge a poignard into the heart of their mother country; France, not contented with so hostile a proceeding, has, without any national quarrel, drawn Spain into its views and, without any plausible reasons to colour the design, is making every preparation that an imperious disposition can dictate to invade the British islands.

On the news of these extraordinary and great preparations, our High Mightinesses cannot but justify the pressing and reiterated instances which the King of Great Britain could not but make to you, relative to the naval armament; and the notorious danger of England will no doubt convince all the subjects of these Provinces, who have hitherto spoke against it of the necessity of this request of my court.

But those motives, which were only palliatives to prevent an evil, are now out of season; the danger is become imminent, and the remedy must be speedy. The stipulations of a treaty founded on the interests of trade only, must give way to those founded on the dearest interests of the two nations.

The moment is come to decide whether Great Britain, who has spilt so much blood, and expended so much treasure to succor others, and to maintain liberty and religion, is to have no other resources against the malice and envy of her enemies, than her own courage, and her own internal strength; whether she is to be abandoned by her most ancient friends and allies, to the most ambitious views of the House of Bourbon, which would crush all, to reign over all; and whether Europe in general, and your High Mightinesses in particular, will with indifference see a system established which will evidently destroy that equilibrium which is the only guarantee of your commerce, liberty, and even existence itself.

The King, High and Mighty Lords, has too high an opinion of the understanding, the good faith, and the wisdom of the Republic to doubt a moment of the sentiments of your High Mightinesses on this occasion. A nation whose history contains scarce anything but the detail of the dangers which the ambition of France successively created, whose best days began with their union with England; in short, a nation accustomed to exact the literal execution of a hard treaty, has too much generosity not to fulfill those which have united the interests of the two nations upwards of a century.

It is in this persuasion, joined to all that is held most sacred amongst men, that the underwritten Ambassador Extraordinary and Plenipotentiary from the King of Great Britain, has, by express order, the honour to notify to your High Mightinesses, that the danger which threatens his kingdoms, necessitates his Majesty to reclaim, without loss of time, the succours stipulated in the treaties of 1678, and others, and of which the *casus foederis* is so fully explained in the Separate Article of 1716. His Majesty expects the same with confidence from a neighbor who has never failed in his engagements, and for the rest confides in the divine benediction on the justness of his cause, and on the fidelity and valour of his subjects.

The underwritten waits with the greatest impatience for a just, speedy, and favourable answer, and is ready to confer with the deputies of your High Mightinesses on what steps are further necessary to be taken.

[signed]
Joseph Yorke

Hague, July 22, 1779

Declaration of War against the Hollanders

Manifesto

George R.

(L.S.) Through the whole course of our reign, our conduct towards the States-General of the United Provinces has been that of a sincere friend and faithful ally. Had they adhered to those wise principles which used to govern the Republic they must have shewn themselves equally solicitous to maintain the friendship which has so long subsisted between the two nations, and which is essential to the interests of both; from the prevalence of a faction devoted to France, and following the dictates of that court, a very different policy has prevailed. The return made to our friendship, for some time past, has been an open contempt of the most solemn engagements and a repeated violation of public faith.

On the commencement of the defensive war, in which we found ourselves engaged by the aggression of France, we shewed a tender regard for the interests of the States-General, and a desire of securing to their subjects every advantage of trade, consistent with the great and just principle of our own defence. Our ambassador was instructed to offer a friendly negociation, to obviate everything that might lead to a disagreeable discussion; and to this offer, solemnly made by him to the States General, the 2d of November 1778, no attention was paid.

After the number of our enemies increased by the aggression of Spain, equally unprovoked with that of France, we found it necessary to call upon the States General for the performance of their engagements. The fifth article of the perpetual defensive alliance between our Crown and the States General, concluded at Westminster the 3d of March 1678, besides the general engagements for succours, expressly stipulates "That that party of the two allies that is not attacked, shall be obliged to break with the aggressor in two months after the party attacked shall require it". Yet two years have passed without a single assistance given to us, without a single syllable in answer to our repeated demands.

So totally regardless have the States been of their treaty with us that they readily promised our enemies to observe a neutrality, in direct contradiction to those engagements; and whilst they have withheld from us the succours they were bound to furnish, every secret assistance has been given the enemy and inland duties have been taken off for the sole purpose of facilitating the carriage of naval stores to France.

In direct and open violation of treaty, they suffered an American Pirate to remain several weeks in one of their ports; and even permitted a part of his crew to mount guard in a fort in the Texel.

In the East Indies, the subjects of the States General, in concert with France, have endeavoured to raise up enemies against us.

In the West Indies, particularly at St. Eustache, every protection and assistance has been given to our rebellious subjects. Their privateers are openly received into the Dutch harbours, allowed to refit there, supplied with arms and ammunition, their crews recruited, their prizes brought in and sold, and all this in direct violation of as clear and solemn stipulations as can be made.

This conduct, so inconsistent with all good faith, so repugnant to the sense of the wisest part of the Dutch nation, is chiefly to be ascribed to the prevalence of the leading magistrates of Amsterdam, whose secret correspondence with our rebellious subjects was suspected long before it was made known by the fortunate discovery of a treaty, the first article of which is:

"There shall be a firm, inviolate, and universal peace, and sincere friendship, between their High Mightinesses the Estates of the Seven United Provinces of Holland and the United States of North America, and the subjects and people of the said parties; and between the countries, islands, cities, and towns, situate under the jurisdiction of the said United States of Holland and the said United States of America, and the people and inhabitants thereof, of every degree, without exception of persons or places".

This treaty was signed in September 1778 by the express order of the Pensionary of Amsterdam and other principal magistrates of the city. They now not only avow the whole transaction, but glory in it; and expressly say, even to the States General, that what they did "was what their indispensable duty required".

In the meantime, the States General declined to give any answer to the Memorial presented by our ambassador; and this refusal was aggravated by their proceedings upon other business, nay upon the consideration of this very subject to internal purposes; and while they found it impossible to approve the conduct of their subjects, they still industriously avoided to give us the satisfaction so manifestly due.

We had every right to expect that such a discovery would have roused them to a just indignation at the insult offered to us, and to themselves, and that they would have been eager to give us full and ample satisfaction for the offence, and to inflict the severest punishment upon the offenders. The urgency of the business made an instant answer essential to the honour and safety of the country. The demand was accordingly pressed by our ambassador in repeated conferences with the ministers, and in a second Memorial it was pressed with all the earnestness which could proceed from our ancient friendship, and the sense of recent injuries; and the answer now given to a Memorial on such a subject, delivered about five weeks ago, is, That the States have taken it *ad referendum*. Such an answer, upon such an occasion, could only be dictated by the fixed purpose of hostility meditated, and already resolved, by the States, induced by the offensive councils of Amsterdam thus to countenance the hostile aggression which the magistrates of the city have made in the name of the Republic.

There is an end of the faith of all treaties with them, if Amsterdam may usurp the sovereign power, may violate those treaties with impunity, by pledging the States to engagements directly contrary and leaguing the Republic with the rebels of a sovereign to whom she is bound by the closest ties. An infraction of the law of nations, by the meanest member of any country, gives the injured State a right to demand satisfaction and punishment. How much more so when the injury complained of is a flagrant violation of public faith committed by leading and predominant members in the State? Since then, the satisfaction we have demanded is not given, we must, though most reluctantly, do ourselves that justice which we cannot otherwise obtain; we must consider the States General as parties in the injury which they will not repair, as sharers in the aggression which they refuse to punish, and must act accordingly. We have therefore ordered our ambassador to withdraw from The Hague and shall immediately pursue such vigorous measures as the occasion fully justifies, and our dignity and the essential interests of our people require.

From a regard to the Dutch nation at large, we wish it were possible to direct those measures wholly against Amsterdam; but this cannot be, unless the States General will immediately declare, that Amsterdam shall, upon this occasion, receive no assistance from them, but be left to abide the consequences of its aggression.

Whilst Amsterdam is suffered to prevail in the general councils and is backed by the strength of the State, it is impossible to resist the aggression of so considerable a part without contending with the whole. But we are too sensible of the common interests of both countries not to remember, in the midst of such a contest, that the only point to e aimed at by us, is to raise a disposition in the councils of the Republic to return to our ancient union, by giving us that satisfaction for the past, and security for the future, which we shall be as ready to receive as they can be to offer, and to the attainment of which we shall direct all our operations. We mean only to provide for our own security by defeating the dangerous designs that have been formed against us. We shall ever be disposed to return to friendship with the States General, when they sincerely revert to that system which the wisdom of their ancestors formed, and which has now been subverted by a powerful faction conspiring with France against the true interests of the Republic, no less than against those of Great Britain.

G. R.

St. James
December 20, 1780

At the Court of St. James, the 20th of December 1780.

Present

The King's Most Excellent Majesty in Council.

His Majesty, having taken into consideration the many injurious proceedings of the States General of the United Provinces, and their subjects, as set forth in his Royal Manifesto of this date, and being determined to take such measures as are necessary for vindicating the honour of his Crown, and for procuring reparation and satisfaction, is pleased by and with the advice of his Privy Council, to order, and it is hereby ordered that general reprisals be granted against the ships, goods, and subjects of the States General of the United Provinces, so that as well His Majesty's fleet and ships, as also all other ships and vessels that shall be commissioned by letters of marque or general reprisals, or otherwise, by His Majesty's commissioners for executing the office of Lord High Admiral of Great Britain, shall and may lawfully seize all ships, vessels and goods belonging to the States General of the United Provinces, or their subjects, or others inhabiting within any territories of the aforesaid States General, and bring the same to judgment in any of the Courts of Admiralty within his Majesty's Dominions; and to that end his Majesty's advocate General, with the advocate of the Admiralty, are forthwith to prepare the draught of a commission and present the same to his Majesty at this board, authorizing the Commissioners for executing the Office of Lord High Admiral or any person or persons by them empowered and appointed, to issue forth and grant letters of marque and reprisal to any of his Majesty's subjects, or other whom the said Commissioners shall deem fitly qualified in that behalf, for the apprehending, seizing, and taking the ships, vessels, and goods belonging to the States General of the United Provinces and their vassals and subjects, or any inhabiting within the countries, territories, or dominions of the aforesaid States General; and that such powers and clauses be inserted in the said Commission as have been usual, and are according to former precedents; and his Majesty's said Advocate-General, with the Advocate of the Admiralty, are also forthwith to prepare the draught of a Commission and present the same to his Majesty at this Board, authorizing the said Commissioners for executing the office of Lord High Admiral to will and require the High Court of Admiralty of Great Britain, and the Lieutenant and judge of the said court, his surrogate or surrogates, as also the several courts of admiralty within his Majesty's dominions, to take cognizance of and judicial proceed upon all and all manner of captures, seizures, prizes, and reprisals of all ships and goods that are, or shall be taken, and to hear and determine the same; and according to the course of Admiralty and the Law of nations, to adjudge and condemn all such ships, vessels, and goods, as shall belong to the States General of the United Provinces, or their vassals and subjects, or to any others inhabiting within any of the countries, territories, and dominions of the aforesaid States General; and that such powers and clauses be inserted in the said commission as have been usual, and are according to former precedents; and they are likewise to prepare, and lay down before his Majesty at this board, a draught of such instructions as may be proper to be sent to the courts of admiralty in his Majesty's foreign governments and plantations for their guidance herein; as also another draught of instructions for such ships as shall be commissioned for the purposes aforementioned.

Answer of the States-General to the Manifesto of the King of Great Britain

If ever the annals of the world have furnished an instance of a free and independent State being attacked by an enemy in the most unjustifiable manner, and without the least appearance of right or equity, by a neighbouring power allied for a long time, and bound by ties founded on the basis of common interest, it is without doubt the Republic of the United States of the Netherlands which finds itself in that case with his Majesty the King of Great Britain, and his ministers. From the beginning of the disputes which had arisen between that kingdom and its American colonies, their High Mightinesses, no wise obliged to interfere, had taken the firm and determined resolution to adopt and strictly to adhere to the most exact neutrality; and when the said disputes had kindled the flames of a war which hath embroiled more powers than one; and spread in several parts of the world, their High Mightinesses have constantly observed and maintained the same line of conduct; whilst in the meantime they have taken care to give on many occasions and in some instances of a very essential nature, the most convincing proofs of their sincere inclination to conform to the wishes of his majesty; so far as they could do it without going against the rules of impartiality or bringing in question their rights of sovereignty.

It was with this view, and for this purpose, that their High Mightinesses from the beginning and at the requisition of his Britannic Majesty caused most express inhibitions to be published against the exportation of all warlike stores to the colonies of his Britannic Majesty in America; and against all fraudulent trade with the said colonies; and in order that the said prohibitions should be more effectually carried into execution, their High Mightinesses made no difficult to take such farther steps as greatly circumscribed their own navigation and trade of their subjects with the Dutch colonies in the West Indies.

It was to further the above purposes that their High Mightinesses sent the most exact orders to all commanders and governors of their colonies, and settlements, as well as to the commanders of their ships of war, carefully to abstain from doing in regard to the American flag anything from which could be justly inferred or deduced an acknowledgement of the independency of the said colonies; and it is also, especially to the above interest that their High Mightinesses having received a memorial presented to them by the English ambassador, full of the heaviest complaints against the governor of St. Eustache, condescended to deliberate on the said memorial; though couched in terms little consonant with the regard which sovereign powers owe to each other, the consequence of the said deliberation was the immediate recall of the said governor whom their High Mightinesses called to an account for his conduct, and who was not permitted to return to his residence till he had cleared himself of all the charges brought against him, before a court of justice; a copy of whose proceedings was soon after transmitted to the minister of his Britannic Majesty.

By such measures as these their High Mightinesses, who always earnestly wished to avoid giving the smallest cause of discontent to his Britannic Majesty, have constantly endeavoured to promote and cultivate perfect harmony; but his Britannic Majesty's conduct towards the Republic has been diametrically opposite.

The differences between the courts of London and Versailles had scarcely broke out when they beheld the ports of England filled with Dutch vessels which were unjustly seized and detained; these vessels navigated upon the faith of the treaties and were not laden with any other merchandise than what the express tenor of the treaties had declared free and legal. They beheld those free cargoes forced to submit to an arbitrary and despotic authority. The Cabinet of St. James's knowing no other rules than an assumed right of temporary convenience, thought proper to appropriate those cargoes to the use of the crown by a forcible purchase, and to employ them in the service of the king's navy. The most earnest and serious representations on the part of their High Mightinesses against these proceedings were ineffectual, and it was in vain that they urged in the strongest manner possible the treaty subsisting between England and the Republic. By this treaty, the rights and liberties of the neutral flag are decisively and clearly stated. The subjects of Great

Britain had fully enjoyed the advantages of this treaty, in the first and only case, wherein it pleased the court of London to remain neuter, while the Republic was engaged in a war. Certainly there in a reciprocal case that court could not, without the greatest injustice, refuse the enjoyment of the same advantage to the Republic; and as little right as his Britannic Majesty had to withhold the advantageous effects of this treaty from their High Mightinesses, he had as little foundation for attempting to make them quit the neutrality they had embraced, and to force them to plunge into a war, the cause of which related immediately to their rights and possessions of his Britannic Majesty lying beyond the limits of defensive treaties. And notwithstanding the treaty, his majesty, from the commencement of the difference with the crown of France, has made no scruple of infringing and violating it. The trespasses and infractions made on this treaty on the part of Great Britain and the arbitrary decision of the courts of justice in that kingdom, directly contrary to the express sanction of the same treaty, multiplied daily. The merchant vessels became the innocent victims of these actions and accumulated violences of the English men of war and privateers. They did not, however, rest there. The very flag of the States was not spared, but openly and outrageously insulted by a hostile attack upon the convoy under the care of the rear-admiral Comte de Byland. The strongest representation from the States to his Britannic Majesty were disregarded, the ships taken from the convoy were declared good prizes, and this insult on the flat of the Republic was very soon followed by an open violation of their neutral territory, as well in Europe as America. They will content themselves, however, with reciting two examples.

At the island of St. Martin his Britannic Majesty attacked and carried away by force several vessels that lay at anchor under the cannon of the fort, where according to the inviolable rights of mankind the vessels ought to have found secure asylum. The insults committed by an armed English vessel on the coast of the Republic, near the island of Goedereede, furnished a second example of these violations. These insults were carried so far that many of the inhabitants of the island who dwelt on the shore, where they ought to have supposed themselves secure from any disturbances, were exposed by the violence of the fire from the ships to such imminent danger that they were forced to retire to the interior part of the island. Yet, for these unheard of proceedings, the Republic notwithstanding the strongest and best founded representations, has not obtained the smallest satisfaction.

Affairs being thus situated, so that their High Mightinesses had no other alternative left them but to see the navigation and commerce of their subjects on which the ruin or prosperity of their republic alone depends, totally annihilated, or else to adopt measures hostile to their old friend and ally; at this period the Empress of Russia urged by a generous magnanimity of disposition thought proper to interfere, and with as much affection as humanity invited the Republic to take the just measures and such too as were entirely consistent with the treaty subsisting between the States and other powers, for the defending and maintaining in conjunction with her Imperial Majesty, and the other northern powers, those privileges and immunities which the rights of nations and the most solemn treaties allowed to neutral flags.

This invitation could not but be infinitely agreeable to their High Mightiniesses since they considered it as a means of securing the undisturbed commerce of their subjects upon the most solid basis and on holding out a method of protecting their independence against every infraction at the same time that it proposed nothing at all derogatory to the alliance contracted between them and his Britannic Majesty or the other belligerent powers. But this was a measure of which the court of London endeavoured to deprive the Republic by proceeding with precipitation to the most desperate extremities by recalling their ambassador, by the publication of a Manifesto containing a list of fictitious grievances, and by granting letters of marque and pretended reprisal against the States, their subjects and their property, by which violence indeed this court did nothing more than clearly carry into proof and practice the designs which they have for a long time fostered of disregarding the true and essential interests which connect the two nations, and of destroying the bonds of their ancient amity by an attack so replete with injustice.

It will not be at all necessary to enter into an elaborate refutation of the reasons and pretended griefs which were alleged in the Manifesto, to convince every impartial man of their entire want of solidity. It will be sufficient to observe in few words with respect to the offer which was made by his Britannic Majesty for opening an amicable conference; that the sole object of these conferences cold only be this, to take into consideration the naval treaty spoken of above; that the construction of this treaty, conceived as it is, in terms the most clear and express, could not be a subject of any doubt or equivocation; that it gives the neutral powers a free right of conveying to the belligerent powers all kinds of naval stores; that the Republic neither proposing anything else to themselves, nor desiring anything more of his Britannic Majesty than the quiet, undisturbed enjoyment of rights stipulated in this treaty, a point so manifest and incontrovertibly equitable, could not perceive any reason or motive for a negociation or any other new convention, which must have been derogatory to the treaty in question, particularly as their High Mightinesses could not prevail upon themselves, nor experience the least disposition to renounce, voluntarily, rights justly acquired, nor to desist from their rights by a regard for the court of England; a renunciation which though advantageous to one of the belligerent powers, would be totally incompatible with the principles of neutrality and by which their High Mightinesses would, from another quarter, have subjected the State to dangers which they think it is their duty most solemnly to avert. A renunciation also would have carried with it a most inseparable injury to their commerce and navigation, which is the principal support of the Republic, and the source of all their prosperity; for the different branches of their commerce are severally so intimately connected with each other, so as to form one whole, that it is impossible to separate one part of so principal a nature as was expected by the court of London; without the entire ruin and destruction of the general body; not to mention that all this time, when their High Mightinesses made a reasonable difficulty of acceding to the proposed conference, they yet qualified and tempered this effectual exercise of their rights by a provisional resolution.

As for the succours required their High Mightinesses cannot dissemble that they never could conceive how his Britannic Majesty thought himself justified to insist, under the most distant appearance of right or equity, for the assistance stipulated by the treaties at the time when he had already foregone the obligation which they imposed on him towards the Republic. Their High Mightinesses were not less surprised to see that, whilst the disturbances in America and their direct consequences could not affect the Republic by virtue of any treaty, and that the assistance had not been required before the declaration of the court of Spain had increased the number of belligerent powers; his Britannic Majesty had nevertheless taken occasion from this event to insist on his demand with so much ardour and earnestness as if his Majesty had a right to pretend and maintain that a war being once kindled between him and some other power was alone sufficient to compel the States to grant directly and without any previous examination, the said stipulated assistance.

The Republic, it is true, had bound itself by treaties to aid and assist the kingdom of Great Britain whenever that power should be attacked or threatened with an unjust war; the Republic was moreover to declare war in such a case against the aggressor; but their High Mightinesses never intended to give up that right which is the nature of a defensive alliance and which cannot be disputed to the allied powers to examine first and before they grant the required assistance or take part in the war the principle of the dissensions which have prevailed; the nature of the differences from which they sprang; as also to investigate and maturely weigh the reasons and motives which may inform the *casus foederis*, and which are to form the basis of the equity and lawfulness of the war, on the part of that confederate State claiming the aforesaid assistance. There is not a treaty extant by which their High Mightinesses have foregone the independence of the States or sacrificed their interest to those of Great Britain, so far as to deprive themselves of the right of so necessary and indispensable an examination; by taking such steps as might insinuate that they should be looked upon as compelled to submit to the pleasure of Great Britain, by granting the required assistance, even when the above court, being at variance with another power, thinks proper to prefer a war to an amiable accommodation on well supported complaints.

It is not therefore through spirit of party or the scheme of a predominant cabal, but after a mature deliberation and by a desire of supporting the dearest interests of the Republic, that all the provincial States respectively have with one voice testified they were of opinion that the assistance required should be politely refused; and their High Mightinesses would not have failed to communicate to his Britannic Majesty, in consequence of those resolutions, an answer to the repeated requests for assistance had they not been prevented from doing by the violent and unprecedented insult offered to the Dutch flag under the command of rear admiral Byland; by their being refused redress on so serious a matter, and by his majesty's declaration, no less strange than unjust, in regard to the suspension of the treaties which subsisted between him and the Republic. There were so many events, which, as they required deliberations of a different kind, put an end to those which were held in consequence of the aforesaid requisitions. It is in vain, and in opposition to all truth, that endeavours have been used to multiply the number of grievances by alleging the suppression of duties on exports, as a measure calculated to facilitate the carrying of naval stores over to France; for, besides, that the said suppression is an object which respects the interior regulation of commerce, to which all sovereigns have an uncontroverted right and for which they are accountable to no one, the matter has been put in deliberation, but never finally resolved upon; so that those duties are still on the former footing; and what is set forth respecting this matter in the Manifesto is totally groundless, though it cannot be denied that the conduct of his Britannic Majesty towards the Republic furnished their High Mightinesses with but too many motives to justify such a measure on their part.

The displeasure of his Britannick Majesty in regard to what has been done for Paul Jones is equally groundless. Their High Mightinesses had for many years before given general and positive orders for the admission into their ports of all privateers and armed ships, with their prizes; orders which have been observed and executed without the least exception; in this case their High Mightinesses could not desist from such orders, in regard to an armed ship which provided with a commission from the American Congress, was in the Texel, together with the frigate of a sovereign power, without assuming the part of judges and giving a decision in a matter which their High Mightinesses were not obliged to take any cognizance of, and in which it seemed to them contrary to the interest of the Republic to interfere. Their High Mightinesses therefore thought it best not to swerve from the rules established for so long a time, but resolved to lay the strongest injunctions, lest the said privateers and armed ships should take in any warlike stores, and desired them to quit the road as soon as possible, without being permitted to sojourn, but as long as would prove absolute necessary to repair the damage suffered at sea; declaring formally at the same time, that in the case of a longer delay their departure should be positively insisted upon. To this purpose the commanding officer in the said road took care to make every requisite disposition, the effects of which the privateer of Paul Jones had hardly time to prevent. In regard to what has happened in other parts of the world, the information transmitted to their High Mightinesses from time to time, from the East Indies, are in direct opposition to those which seem to have been laid before his Britannic Majesty. The frequent complaints of the East India directors, addressed to them, and which the love of peace had obliged the latter to smother, as it were, in their breasts are so many incontrovertible proofs of the assertion. The measures taken in regard to the West Indies before mentioned will serve at all times for an unquestionable proof of the sincerity of the seal and of the attention with which their High Mightinesses have assiduously endeavoured to observe in these countries the most exact and strict neutrality; nor could their High Mightinesses find out the least legal proof of any infraction of their orders in this respect.

As for what concern the project of an eventual treaty of commerce with North America, framed by a member of the government of the province of Holland, without the sanction of any public authority; and the Memorial presented on this matter by the chevalier Yorke, the matter happened as follows.

As soon as this ambassador had presented a Memorial dated Nov. 10, 1780, their High Mightinesses, without notice the expressions, rather unbecoming between sovereigns, with which this Memorial abounded, did not delay entering into the most serious deliberation on that matter; and by their resolution of the 27th of the same month; they did not hesitate to disclaim and disapprove publicly whatever had been done in this affair.

After this they had every reason to expect that his Britannic Majesty would have acceded to this declaration since he could not be ignorant that their High Mightinesses have no jurisdiction over the respective provinces and that it was to the States of Holland to whom, as being invested as the States of the other provinces with a sovereign and exclusive authority over their subjects, was to be submitted, an affair which their High Mightinesses had no reason to doubt but the other States of the said provinces would regulate according to the exigency of the cases and conformably to the laws of the State and the principles of equity. The eagerness with which the chevalier Yorke by his second Memorial insisted on the punishment, could not, of course, but appear very strange to their High Mightinesses, that if he did not receive the very same day an answer to his Memorial in every respect satisfactory, he should find himself obliged to acquaint his court thereof by an extraordinary courier. Their High Mightinesses, informed of this declaration, soon perceived its importance as a manifestation of the measures already determined on in the king's council; and although according to the established custom, such verbal declarations from foreign ministers admit of no deliberation, they nevertheless thought proper to set it aside on this occasion and to desire their recorder to wait on the chevalier, and inform him that his Memorial had been taken *ad referendum* by the deputies of the respective provinces, according to the received custom and constitution of government; adding at the same time what seemed designedly omitted in the Manifesto, that they would endeavour to frame an answer to his Memorial as soon as possible, as the constitution of government would permit. In consequence thereof, a few days after, the deputies of the province of Holland gave notice to the assembly of their High Mightinesses that the States of their province had *una voce* resolved to require the advice of their court of justice in regard to the requisition of punishment, requesting the said court to give their opinion as soon as possible, foregoing all other affairs. Their High Mightinesses did not fail to acquaint the chevalier Yorke with the above resolve; but what was their surprise and astonishment when they understood that the said ambassador, after having read his instructions, had sent a note to the recorded, wherein he called the above said resolve illusive and flatly refused to transmit it to his court! This obliged their High Mightinesses to send it to the Count Welderen, their Minister in London, with orders to lay it immediately before the minster of his Britannic Majesty; but the refusal of the latter created an obstacle to the execution of those orders.

All the circumstances of this affair being thus exposed, the impartial public will be enabled to appreciate the principal motive or rather pretence to which his Britannic Majesty has had recourse, in order to give scope to his designs against the Republic. To this we may reduce the whole matter: his Majesty was informed of a negociation which would have taken place between a member of the government of one of the provinces, and a representative of the American Congress; which negociation intended to lay the plan of a treaty of commerce to be concluded between the Republic and the said colonies, *casu quo*, that is to say, that in case the independency of those colonies should be acknowledged by the crown of England; this negociation although conditional, and holding by a clause which depended on the anterior act of his Majesty, this negociation, which without the said act, or anterior declaration could not have the least effect, was so misconstrued by his Majesty, and excited his displeasure to such a degree, that he thought proper to require from the States a public disavowal and disapprobation, as well as a complete punishment and satisfaction. It was in consequence, and without the least delay, that their High Mightinesses acceded to the first part of his requisition; but the punishment insisted upon was not within their power, and they could not assent to it without striking at the root of the fundamental constitution of the State. The States of the province of Holland were the only ones to which it pertained lawfully to take cognizance of it, and to provide thereto by the ordinary means and the authority of the Laws. This sovereign State adhering to the maxims which oblige them to respect the authority of the Laws, and fully convinced that the maintaining that department in all the integrity and impartiality which are inseparable from it, is the firmest basis of the supreme power; that sovereign State obliged by what is held most sacred, to defend and protect the rights and privileges of its subjects, could not forget itself so far as to submit to the will of his Britannic Majesty, by attempting to overturn those rights and privileges, and exceeding the limits prescribed by the fundamental laws of its government; these Laws required the intervention of the judicial department and those were the means which the above States resolved to use, by requiring on this object the advice of the court of justice established in their province.

By an adherence to this method it was that before the eyes of his Britannic Majesty the English nation, and all Europe, were displayed the unalterable principles of that justice and equity which from the leading feature of the Dutch Constitution, and which in so important a part of public administration, we mean that which concerns the exercise of the judiciary power, will forever serve as a bulwark against whatever cold militate with the security and independence of a free nation. It was also by these means and by following this road that, far from precluding justice, or evading the punishment required, a free course, on the contrary, has been laid open to a regular process conformably to the constitutional principles of the Republic; and by the sound reason, in short, depriving the court of London of any pretence to complain of a denial of justice, care has been taken to anticipate the least shadow or appearance of reason, which might have authorized that court to make reprisals; to which, nevertheless, it has had recourse without scruple, in a manner equally odious and unjust.

To these ends, and since, after the repeated outrages and heavy losses which the subjects of this Republic must have experienced from his Britannic Majesty, their High Mightinesses find themselves furthermore provoked, and assailed by his aforesaid Majesty, and compelled to use those means which they have in hand, in order to defend the precious rights of their liberty and independence; they entertain the firmest hope that the Lord of Hosts, the God of their fathers, who by the palpable direction of Providence, supported and carried this Republic through the greatest dangers, will bless the means which they have determined to employ, by crowning the justice of their arms with the ever triumphant assistance of his own omnipotent protection; whilst their High Mightinesses will ardently sigh after the instant, when they shall see their neighbor and old ally, but now their enemy, recalled to sentiments more moderate and equitable. And it is at that period, where their High Mightinesses will improve all the opportunities which, consonant with the honor and independence of a free State, may tend to a reconciliation between them and their old friend and ally.

This given and settled in the assembly of their High Mightinesses, our Lords the States General of the United Provinces, at The Hague, the 10th day of March 1781.

– Signed, Cocq van Haeften, vt. plus bas. By command, H. Fagel.

INDEX OF NAMES

Roman numerals below in lower case refer to the pagination of the introductory materials. Upper case Roman numerals (**I**, **II**) refer to volumes I or II above. Arabic numerals refer to pagination within volumes I and II following the introductory materials.

www.ingramcontent.com/pod-product-compliance
Lightning Source LLC
LaVergne TN
LVHW090002031026
849161LV00028B/3076/J
* 9 7 8 1 6 1 6 1 9 4 0 4 8 *